Under
the
Influence

ALCOHOL AND HUMAN BEHAVIOR

John Jung

California State University, Long Beach

Brooks/Cole Publishing Company
Pacific Grove, California

Brooks/Cole Publishing Company
A Division of Wadsworth, Inc.

Printed in the United States of America

10 9 8 7 6 5 4 3 2 1

Library of Congress Cataloging-in-Publication Data
Jung, John.
    Under the influence : alcohol and human behavior / John Jung.
      p.   cm.
    Includes bibliographical references and index.
    ISBN 0-534-20448-1
    1. Alcoholism.   2. Alcoholism—United States.   I. Title.
  RC565.J86   1993
  616.86'1—dc20   92-43587
                                                           CIP

Sponsoring Editor: *Claire Verduin*
Marketing Representative: *JoAnn Ludovici*
Editorial Associate: *Gay C. Bond*
Production Editor: *Linda Loba, Nancy L. Shammas*
Manuscript Editor: *Lorraine Anderson*
Permissions Editor: *Carline Haga*
Interior Design: *E. Kelly Shoemaker*
Cover Design: *Laurie Albrecht*
Art Coordinator: *Lisa Torri*
Typesetting: *Kachina Typesetting, Inc.*
Printing and Binding: *Malloy Lithographing Inc.*

To Tomy:
Think when you drink
so you won't stink

CONTENTS

— S E V E N —

Alcohol Use Disorders:
Definition and Prevalence   106

— E I G H T —

Alcoholism: The Role of Heredity
and Environment   124

— N I N E —

Family Dynamics and Alcoholism   144

— SIXTEEN —

Ethnic Differences in Drinking Patterns and Consequences 271

— SEVENTEEN —

Prevention of Alcoholism and Alcohol-Related Problems 294

PREFACE

Alcoholic beverages are widely available and consumed in contemporary society. Alcohol has an impact not only on the physical and psychological functioning of drinkers but also on the well-being of those around them. People drink to relieve stress, have fun, and celebrate special occasions. Unfortunately, there is also a darker side of alcohol: abuse and dependency, and the associated misery and suffering. At times, it is difficult to realize that the same substance, alcohol, is involved in such divergent consequences.

In the public mind, only alcoholic drinkers constitute the "alcohol problem." The much larger population of "social" drinkers is regarded as not needing study, except perhaps by marketing consultants for the alcohol industry. This inability to see or look for the interrelationship between acceptable and unacceptable drinking levels impedes our willingness to study and confront the problems related to alcohol.

The majority of social drinkers start with mostly positive benefits from drinking but some of them eventually become alcoholics or develop alcohol dependence and the ignominious consequences. Even social drinkers are capable of becoming intoxicated occasionally and then experiencing negative outcomes ranging from cognitive, motor, and emotional impairment to accidents and physical harm.

It is important for everyone involved in the study of human behavior, ranging from psychologists to social workers to educators, nurses, and counselors to acquire a basic understanding of the causes and effects of alcohol consumption, not only by alcoholics but also by social drinkers. While popular books on alcoholism are abundant, ranging from confessionals to therapeutic guides to moral condemnations of the dangers of drinking, scientifically based books for students without an advanced background in research methodology and technical knowledge are few.

This book addresses the need for an integrated overview of the major theories and research findings on the psychology of alcohol use and abuse. I first provide an overview of the history of American alcohol attitudes and use, then a survey of the extent and nature of current drinking practices in the United States, followed by an examination of the physiological and psychological effects of alcohol consumption. The major psychological theories about why drinking occurs are presented.

Achieving consensus on definitions of *alcoholism* or *alcohol dependency* is a problem facing the field. I devote considerable attention to major approaches such as the disease concept held by Alcoholics Anonymous and the scientifically derived *Diagnostic and Statistical Manual* (DSM-III-R) criteria and alcohol dependence syndrome formulations. Much of the confusion in the field is due to this lack of definitional agreement, as seen in the heated discussion of the 1970s about whether "alcoholics" could (not should) drink in moderation. The answer depends in part on which definition of *alcoholic* you use or accept.

A fascinating question that always arises about alcoholism is that of the influence of heredity and environment. Often this issue is presented in either/or terms. I present the increasing evidence that shows the joint influence of genetic and environmental events on drinking patterns. Inherited temperamental differences that represent risk factors for alcohol dependency combine with the level of environmental stressors experienced to determine the likelihood of alcohol dependency.

One environmental factor of great concern is family interaction. Excessive drinking often disrupts family processes and may have a major impact on the psychological development of children, possibly contributing to future drinking problems for them. Next, personality differences are examined, both as factors that may predispose individuals to have drinking problems and as possible consequences of being alcohol-dependent.

I present the major approaches to psychological treatment of alcoholism and the problems associated with evaluation of treatment effectiveness. I describe the rival approaches, Alcoholics Anonymous, and learning-theory-based models. Then I examine the problems of relapse, a common process associated with many substance addictions, and approaches for preventing it.

Discussions of drinking problems are often presented in terms of a hypothetical "typical alcoholic," ignoring the fact that alcoholics differ on important variables, such as gender, age, and ethnicity. Several chapters discuss theories and findings about the nature of these differences that may prove important in designing more effective individualized treatment and prevention programs for subpopulations. Finally, I consider the variety of methods used for prevention of alcohol problems and examine their effectiveness. It is now recognized that we cannot avoid or solve the alcohol problems as individuals, because our society encourages, glamorizes, and even pushes alcohol. (Try to dine in a nice restaurant without first ordering an alcoholic beverage or two.) Social and legal policies regarding alcohol availability can do much to improve the environmental context and minimize excessive alcohol consumption. Unlike the lament of Samuel Taylor Coleridge's Ancient Mariner, "Water, water everywhere, nor any drop to drink," our complaint might be "Booze, booze everywhere, and too much to drink."

Alcohol research properly involves the contributions of numerous disciplines, including anthropology, sociology, neurophysiology, and of course, psychology. As a psychologist, I focus not surprisingly on individual behavior, but I have tried to reflect the interdisciplinary nature of the field of alcohol studies by including material from other disciplines to show the value of biological, psychosocial, and cultural factors. This book provides a basic scientific background for courses in many disciplines in which there is interest in the impact of alcohol on human behavior, including psychology, counseling, nursing, medicine, social work, and interdisciplinary programs dealing with substance abuse.

I have been fortunate to have had the assistance of several colleagues who read portions of the manuscript. Their suggestions have helped improve the presentation immensely and I want to acknowledge the help of Alan Berger, Mary Benjamin, and Douglas Parker. Several of my "Psychology of Alcohol" classes offered helpful suggestions and encouragement on early drafts.

My thanks also go to the reviewers of this text. Their thoughtful comments and suggestions helped make this a better book. They were: Dorothy Bianco, Rhode Island College; Robert Chapman, La Salle University; Floyd Grant; John C. Lewton, University of Toledo; Linda Lee Marshall, Mankato State University; James Royce, Seattle University; and Joan Welker, University of Nevada at Reno.

The editorial expertise at Brooks/Cole has helped immeasurably to improve the overall quality of the final product. Finally, thanks to Jeff Jung, who majored in English, for laboring through earlier drafts of the entire manuscript and for providing invaluable editorial services that improved the readability of the book. My investment in his college tuition has proven to be a good one.

John Jung

Overview

No one can say with certainty how or when alcoholic beverages were discovered, but they have been known to exist in most civilizations throughout recorded history. Alcoholic beverages like beer or wine are derived from the fermentation of grains and grapes, respectively. They have been used in rituals and ceremonies as well as for healing purposes since ancient times. In the earliest known book, the *Ebers Papyrus,* written around 1500 B.C., there is a medical prescription calling for eating castor berries and drinking beer. The ancient Egyptians honored the god Osiris, who cultivated the vine and created wine and beer. Hippocrates, the Greek father of medicine, is known to have recommended wine for its therapeutic properties. The Greeks paid homage to wine through Dionysus, the god of wine (known to the Romans as Bacchus), with celebrations and festivities. Fermented rice wines were known in the Far East as well in ancient China and India.

Later, in the tenth century, the Arabians invented distillation, a process by which the alcohol from fermented beverages is extracted by boiling it until it vaporizes. Then, the alcohol is recaptured after condensation to create more potent beverages with higher concentrations of alcohol. Distilled spirits became part of the array of alcoholic beverages.

In our society today, alcoholic beverages are readily available in many homes as well as in stores, bars, and restaurants. Drinking is permissible in many public facilities such as parks, theaters, and stadiums. Distillers, wineries, and breweries spend vast sums of money to advertise in newspapers and magazines and on television with messages implying that life without alcoholic beverages is incomplete. Good times, glamorous friends, and personal success are depicted as part of what people experience with alcoholic beverages.

Alcohol has had an influence, for better as well as for worse, on many aspects of human behavior. On the positive side, alcohol plays a role in promoting social cohesion and harmonious interaction. It is important as a symbol of life representing water, milk, and blood. Drinking alcoholic beverages is widely used to celebrate friendship, rites of passage, and religious occasions. However, there is also the negative aspect of alcohol when its use is associated with destructive and harmful personal and social consequences. In view of the widespread and significant impact of alcohol on human behavior, the study of the causes of alcohol consumption and of its psychological effects is an important endeavor.

We begin our study by posing some central questions that will guide our inquiry. We then briefly examine the two faces of alcohol before turning to a survey of historical attitudes toward alcohol in the United States.

Some Central Questions

Following is a preview of some of the broad issues and questions about the psychology of alcohol that will be raised in this book. Details and documentation of research evidence will be deferred to subsequent chapters.

Why Do People Drink Alcohol?

A psychology of alcohol use must account for the wide variety of occasions and conditions for drinking. People drink alcohol when they feel sad, depressed, or lonely, but they also drink when they feel happy, elated, and sociable. They drink in groups but they also drink alone. They drink at certain social functions—dinners and parties—but not at others. Social pressure to conform to drinking norms may lead some individuals to drink to avoid appearing unsociable. Social conventions and norms call for ceremonial drinking on many festive occasions and at celebrations. Finally, norms and values about drinking, which differ across cultures, provide a broad contextual setting in which the other factors operate.

How Does Alcohol Affect the Drinker?

Next, what are the major effects of drinking alcohol, especially on behavior and experience? How are basic psychological processes such as learning, memory, cognition, judgment, emotion, motivation, mood, and social interaction affected by alcohol? These effects can also be viewed as determinants of subsequent drinking, acting to either sustain, increase, or reduce it. The effects of alcohol are varied and complex, depending on the drinker and even varying for the same drinker in different settings or at different times. Alcohol can reduce tension in many instances through its physiological actions as a central nervous system depressant. Yet, in some situations such as at a party, consumption of alcohol typically seems to increase arousal and energy. Thus, the social context, as well as physiological processes, determines a person's reaction to drinking.

Personality differences may also play a role in determining the effects of alcohol. After drinking, some people become aggressive and hostile, others show avoidance and uninvolvement, and still others seem more relaxed and friendly. Social factors such as the reactions and behaviors of others may also influence the impact of alcohol on the drinker. These reactions will depend on the situation. Drinking at a party is generally acceptable and even encouraged, but not at work, so our reactions to the drinker will generally be more favorable in the former than in the latter context. In short, there seems to be no universal effect of alcohol on the drinker, because the expectations of the drinker combine with the social context to produce the eventual outcome of drinking alcohol.

Why Do Some Drinkers Develop Problems?

Another major question is why some drinkers eventually develop problems associated with their drinking while others do not. Although most adult members of many societies enjoy alcohol without apparent problems, an unfortunately sizable minority encounter major difficulties from their drinking, with the extreme case being that of skid-row derelicts who are without hope, without jobs, and without respect for themselves or for others. These distressing facts are sometimes easily overlooked because so many of us seem to be able to drink alcoholic beverages with no apparent adverse consequences. Yet the undeniable reality is that excessive consumption of alcohol devastates the lives of countless drinkers as well as their families and friends. Even though most of them may never hit skid row, they do pay the toll of physical, mental, and economic ruin brought on by the repeated heavy use of alcohol. Homicides, suicides, major accidental injuries, aggression, and depression are just a few of the costs of alcohol abuse. Even the occasional excessive use that may not render one an alcoholic may still create intoxication levels sufficient to cause accidents, violence, and other mayhem with life-shattering impact.

Eventually, drinking leads to problems for some drinkers. Can we draw a line that distinguishes "alcoholics" from nonalcoholic or social drinkers? What determines who will become an alcoholic or alcohol abuser? To what extent does heredity and to what extent does environment determine this outcome?

How Can Alcoholism Be Treated and Prevented?

Alcoholism is without doubt a major health threat, creating serious physical and mental health problems. What approaches, based on psychological theory and research, exist to help alcoholics recover? How effective are different treatments? Why do relapses occur in many cases? Can the relative effectiveness of alternative treatments be adequately evaluated, since the controlled observations required for scientific rigor are usually absent in clinical settings?

An ounce of prevention is the proverbial cost-effective alternative to treatment. What effective psychological approaches to the primary prevention of alcohol abuse and alcoholism have been developed and applied? Can programs aimed at shaping positive attitudes toward alcohol and safe use patterns in children and adolescents be successful if the larger social and cultural environment entices and beguiles youth with visions of chemical solutions to psychological problems?

Each of these broad questions has been answered with numerous definitions, theories, and explanations involving physiological, psychological, and sociological factors. In all likelihood, multiple factors act concurrently, sometimes with counteracting influences, to produce the observed differences in drinking behavior, consequences of drinking, and degree of success in recovery from alcoholism. Therefore, theories that focus on single causes will probably not prove as successful as explanations that consider the interplay of multiple determinants of drinking, ranging from the physiological to the sociological.

Two Faces of Alcohol

Alcohol, then, is a double-edged sword. On the one hand, it can be a positive social force, acting to promote conviviality and social cohesion. It is a prominent ingredient of festive occasions such as parties, weddings, and celebrations. It helps people overcome anxiety, boredom, and inhibitions. On the other hand, alcohol when used excessively can cause misery and suffering of the greatest magnitude for the abusers and their loved ones.

A small but significant percentage of drinkers will eventually succumb to the tragic outcome known as alcoholism. Once addicted to alcohol, these drinkers find it extremely difficult to regain control over their lives, and indeed, many never do. Alcohol abuse and alcoholism affect the whole person, not just the physical but also the psychological and spiritual aspects. Careers and reputations are destroyed, economic resources are lost, marriages and families are broken up, and self-respect disappears. The alcoholic's damage is not limited to himself or herself but also threatens the psychological and economic well-being of spouses, children, parents, and other relatives and close friends.

This dilemma for society created by alcohol has no easy solution. People start out drinking with little awareness of the personal likelihood of alcoholism. The vast majority of drinkers never imagine that they might someday become members of the lost legion of alcoholics, as a sizable minority of them will. Fortunately, most of them manage to drink and function adequately so that by no stretch of the imagination would they be classified as "alcoholics." Nonetheless, many of these drinkers may suffer physical and psychological problems directly attributable to drinking. Estimates from the *Seventh Special Report to the U.S. Congress on Alcohol and Health* published by the Department of Health and Human Services (1990) indicate that 10.5 million American adults show signs of alcoholism or alcohol dependence, with another 7.2 million persons classified as alcohol abusers.

One cannot place an accurate price tag on the cost of alcohol's damage. Most estimates focus on costs of lost productivity and expenditures for treatment since it is more difficult to place a price on psychological damage. Rice, Kelman, Miller, and Dunmeyer (1990) arrived at an estimate of $70.3 billion for 1985, and by adjusting for inflation and population growth, estimated a cost of $85.9 billion in 1988. Caution is advised in interpreting cost estimates since different researchers use different methods and assumptions. Thus, a different source reached an estimate of over $89.5 billion for the year 1980, almost a decade earlier (U.S. Department of Health and Human Services, 1987). For 1990, the total cost is estimated by this source at over $136 billion (U.S. Department of Health and Human Services, 1990).

Social History of Attitudes toward Alcohol in the United States

To understand alcohol's role in our society, it is important to examine the history of attitudes toward and practices involving alcohol in American history. These attitudes and practices have varied greatly at different times. Estimates of national alcohol consumption since 1850 based on alcohol tax records have shown that aside from the Prohibition years from 1919 to 1932, per capita consumption generally increased until the 1980s. Figure 1-1 shows that the level went from 2 gallons of *absolute alcohol* (the rough equivalent of 4 gallons of whiskey) per capita in the post–World War II era, to about 2.7 gallons by 1981. Such averages can be misleading since about half of the total alcohol consumed is imbibed by only 10 percent of the drinkers (U.S. Department of Health and Human Services, 1990). The figure for absolute alcohol, rather than the actual volume of alcoholic beverages consumed, is used because it adjusts for the fact that different types of beverages contain different percentages of alcohol: 5 percent for beer, 13 percent

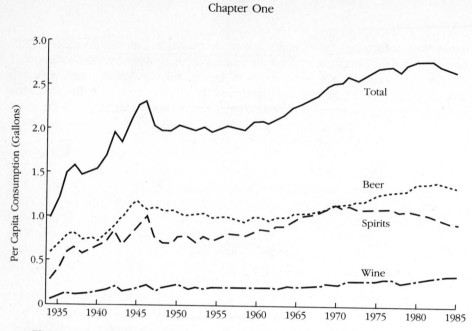

Figure 1-1 Apparent U.S. per capita consumption of alcoholic beverages in gallons of pure alcohol from the end of Prohibition to 1984.
Source: from *Fifth Special Report to the U.S. Congress on Alcohol,* 1984, Washington, DC: U.S. Government Printing Office.

for wine, and 41 percent for distilled spirits (U.S. Department of Health and Human Services, 1990).

Consumption trends and levels differ with the specific type of alcoholic beverage, whether wine, beer, or distilled spirits. Distilled spirits consumption has declined steadily after peaking in the 1970s, while beer and wine consumption remained stable during most of the 1980s. Between 1987 and 1989, apparent consumption of all three types of beverages showed declines (Williams, Stinson, Brooks, Clem, & Noble, 1991).

Colonial Views

In colonial America, alcohol drinking was a widespread, generally tolerated and accepted activity. Alcohol was not only widely available as a beverage but also served as a home remedy for many physical ailments. Historians such as Gusfield (1963) recognize that drunkenness was commonplace, but it was not considered a social problem in the society of that era. However, from the early 1700s to the mid-1800s the drunkenness and alcohol abuse increased, generating greater societal awareness and disruption as the nation changed from an agrarian economy to an urban industrial one.

The Temperance Movement

The widespread social problems such as poverty, crime, and disorderly public conduct created by excessive use of alcohol led to the development of reformist movements influenced by religious groups such as the Quakers and many Protestant denominations. Organized efforts against alcohol were formed such as the American Temperance Society in 1833. As the campaign gathered strength, by the late 1800s calls for temperance gave way to efforts to eliminate alcohol as organizations such as the Women's Christian Temperance Union (WCTU) and the Anti-Saloon League led the fight against the evils of alcohol.

Prohibition

These pressures for social reform eventually led to the legal abolition of alcohol consumption in 1919 with the passage of the Volstead Act. This solution ultimately proved unworkable for a variety of reasons, not the least of which was the fact that illegally manufactured alcohol was still available for consumption. In 1932 the act was repealed, and less extreme measures were sought to preserve the right to drink while preventing the havoc created by excessive alcohol use.

The Moral Model

During the Temperance and Prohibition eras, the prevalent view of alcoholism involved the moral judgment that excessive drinking was sinful behavior and reflected a lack of willpower. Blame was placed primarily on the alcoholic, who was held to be responsible for his or her own situation. Little sympathy was given to the drunkard, who was ridiculed as a "skid-row bum," ignoring the possibility that alcohol was also being abused by many otherwise respectable citizens who were gainfully employed.

Alcoholics Anonymous

In the mid- to late 1930s two strange bedfellows fostered the movement that led to a major shift in the societal stance toward alcoholism away from the moral model. One party consisted of perhaps the most influential grassroots mental health development in the United States, Alcoholics Anonymous (AA). In addition to its impact on alcoholism, it has also served as a model for innumerable other self-help groups formed to deal with other psychological and social problems.

The inauspicious founding of this organization in Akron, Ohio, involved informal meetings between two alcoholics, a stockbroker named Bill Wilson and a physician, Dr. Bob Smith, who discovered they were able to help each other achieve sobriety. After first acknowledging their powerlessness over alcohol, they were able to begin on the road to recovery. Many of the ideas and the philosophy underlying AA had been used by earlier temperance groups, including the Washingtonians in the 1840s and an evangelical religious movement known as the Oxford Group in the early part of this century. However, it was not until AA emerged that the underlying philosophy of these approaches achieved its highest success. Bill W. and Dr. Bob, as they called themselves to protect their anonymity for fear of being stigmatized, discovered that recovery occurred from meeting with other alcoholics to share personal stories and to read and discuss inspirational materials. Through this program for recovery, alcoholics achieved a spiritual reawakening and regained control of their lives with the support of one another.

From this humble beginning was born the self-help program of AA in 1935. Bill Wilson began to disseminate this ideology and these techniques to any alcoholics who wanted to stop drinking. The original publication of *Alcoholics Anonymous* in 1935 (Alcoholics Anonymous World Services, 1935), now in its third revision, was a major factor in spreading AA. This book, affectionately termed the "Big Book" by AA members, contains the story of Bill Wilson's alcoholism as well as personal stories of the recovery of alcoholic men and women that provide inspiration for many alcoholics. Today AA is recognized throughout the world as one of the most remarkable therapeutic programs ever developed, not only for alcoholism but for other forms of addiction as well. Specific details and evaluation of AA as a treatment method will be presented in Chapter 11.

Scientific Models

The other party opposing the moral model of alcoholism, scientific researchers, had more empirical and less personal motives for their interest in alcoholism. They wanted to apply the methods of rigorous science to study alcoholism and alcohol abuse just as scientists study any other type of phenomenon. The approach espoused by scientific investigators emphasized reliance on objective evidence, quantifiable variables, controlled experiments, and theories with testable hypotheses. This approach encompassed three different models.

The Medical Model. In the influential formulation of a noted scientist, E. M. Jellinek, alcoholism is a disease (Jellinek, 1960), one that can be and should be amenable to treatment and cure, in much the same manner as many physical diseases. The idea that alcoholism is a disease was not original with Jellinek, but dates back as early as 1785 with the views of Benjamin Rush, an eminent American physician. However, during the 1800s the moral view prevailed and drunkenness was regarded as sinfulness. If alcoholism were recognized as a disease rather than a character defect, a number of significant implications followed. The medical profession, due to its commitment to the treatment of diseases, could no longer justify ignoring the plight of alcoholics. Society would not be able to continue to blame alcoholics for their problem since diseases are medical problems and uncontrollable by those afflicted. This view of alcoholism as a disease fit AA's views on the physical origins of alcoholism and was wholeheartedly promoted in their philosophy.

In his original formulation, Jellinek (1952) distinguished between addictive and nonaddictive alcoholic drinkers, maintaining that the disease model applied only to the addictive drinker, who is susceptible to eventual loss of control after years of excessive drinking. As to the causes of the differences between addictive and nonaddictive alcoholics, Jellinek speculated that a so-called Factor X existed, possibly a predisposing metabolic or physiological difference, although he did not rule out differences in lifestyle as a determinant either. But Jellinek (1960) later modified his definition of alcoholism by broadening its scope to cover "any use of alcoholic beverage that causes any damage to the individual or to society," hoping to draw more awareness to alcohol problems.

Robinson (1972) pointed out the confusion created by the inconsistency in Jellinek's two formulations. Robinson also suggested that even if alcoholism is accepted as a disease, diseases vary along such dimensions as the extent to which they are infectious or the degree to which they are inheritable. The type of disease used as one's model of alcoholism may hold different implications for understanding and treatment. Thus, problems may occur in treatment if the physician and the drinker disagree in their assessment as to whether that individual is an alcoholic or about the nature of alcoholism as a disease.

The medical model or disease conception of alcoholism has proved influential in altering negative social attitudes toward alcoholics, leading to a more humane concern with their plight. Treatment and rehabilitation, not condemnation and ostracism, have become accepted as the appropriate response.

In addition, during this era when the medical model was being formulated, other important strides toward greater scientific study of the biomedical and psychological aspects of alcoholism were made. Jellinek and other researchers developed a Center for Alcohol Studies at Yale University, now situated at Rutgers University, which was at the forefront in encouraging others to undertake research on alcohol problems as a legitimate goal of scientific investigation. The establishment of a major scientific periodical, the *Quarterly Journal of Studies on Alcohol* (now the *Journal of Studies on Alcohol*), provided an influential outlet for researchers to disseminate their findings.

A National Committee for Education on Alcoholism (later to be renamed the National Council on Alcoholism and Drug Dependency) was formed at Yale University in 1944. This influential coalition of voluntary organizations in communities all over the nation has promoted alcohol education and treatment.

As it became increasingly clear that alcoholism affected people from all walks of life in devastating ways, large private philanthropic foundations came forth to provide funding for many research, treatment, and prevention activities.

The Behavioral Model. In the 1960s, the study of alcohol use assumed a different emphasis in the work of behaviorally oriented researchers. They focused more on the *drinking behavior* of alcoholics and viewed it as a learned response that, like any other form of acquired behavior, could be reinforced or controlled by its consequences. They avoided speculation about intrapsychic states such as denial, craving, and loss of control that were major aspects of lay beliefs as well as of influential organizations such as Alcoholics Anonymous.

Behaviorists question the validity of the disease conception of alcoholism. Though they would not deny that alcoholics have physical diseases stemming from their excessive drinking, they reject the view that alcoholism per se is a physical disease. They argue that medical diseases have an identifiable set of symptoms that develop in a certain sequence, whereas alcoholism does not. Defenders of the disease conception counter that the behaviorists hold too narrow a definition of disease and that many physical diseases involve substantial variations in symptomatology.

These researchers study alcoholics in clinical and experimental settings as well as laboratory animals under better controlled but artificial conditions. They emphasize objective observation of quantifiable aspects of behavior under the influence of alcohol, in comparison to behavior in a sober state. The goal is to find methods of modifying drinking behavior to bring it to acceptable levels.

The controversy between AA and behaviorists over the question of whether alcoholism is a disease is complicated by the common use of the term *disease* as a metaphor. *Disease* is often used to denote any pathological condition. Thus, for example, dishonesty consists of behaviors such as lying and cheating. Metaphorically speaking, we condemn dishonesty as a "cancer" or disease because as it spreads, it destroys the quality of our social relationships.

The metaphorical use of the term *disease* should be distinguished from the view that alcoholism is a medical disease. Thus, one would not call upon a surgeon to "treat" dishonest persons for this "disease" with a scalpel. Instead, one might try to modify these behaviors through a variety of psychological techniques including counseling, punishment, guilt, and social modeling. The dishonest person would be expected to assume responsibility for changing these behaviors. In the same respect, critics of the disease concept of alcoholism such as Peele (1989) view excessive drinking behavior, or dependence on alcohol, as an unacceptable and harmful form of behavior, not as a disease in the medical sense.

The Epidemiological Approach. An important approach to the study of alcoholism involves the field of epidemiology, which measures the extent of drinking in the general population and identifies the major correlates of its occurrence. National surveys such as those started by Cahalan and his associates in the mid- to late 1960s (Cahalan, Cisin, & Crossley, 1969) have been periodically repeated to provide evidence of temporal patterns. Such surveys of drinking practices are invaluable for determining how often and in what quantity alcohol is consumed by what types of individuals with respect to major demographic variables such as age, gender, and social class.

The Role of the Federal Government

Thus we have seen that improvements in social attitudes toward the plight of alcoholics were brought about largely by the rise of AA and the funding of research by private sources. These developments were influential in generating momentum to press for federal programs. The leadership of recovering alcoholics such as Marty Mann, a woman who worked to found the National Council on Alcoholism in 1944, helped call national attention to the need for more programs. It was still another 25 years before the federal government recognized the problem by funding national programs. Senator Harold Hughes of Iowa was a leader in prompting the federal government to acknowledge the scope of alcohol problems as a major health issue, with the passage of the Comprehensive Alcohol Abuse and Alcohol Prevention, Treatment, and Rehabilitation Act of 1970. As a result, the National Institute on Alcohol Abuse and Alcoholism (NIAAA) was funded in 1971 by the federal government to provide leadership in alcohol research, treatment, prevention, and public education. Although political pressures have caused the distribution of funds for various goals to fluctuate over the years, the NIAAA has been a major factor in fostering important research programs on vital topics in the field of alcoholism research. From a research budget of about $10 million when the NIAAA was created in 1971, the level of funding has expanded so that 20 years later the 1992 budget was over $169 million. In addition to these funds for basic research, NIAAA is budgeted for prevention, training, and treatment programs.

Focus and Goals of This Book

This book is concerned exclusively with the psychology of alcohol. The coverage does not include the frequent use of alcohol in combination with other drugs of all types—over-the-counter, prescription, and illicit. Several valid reasons can be offered for this decision to limit the scope of coverage. Alcohol is the beverage and drug of choice for most American adults, consumed by more people than any other drug. Our society approves of, and even glamorizes, its use in a variety of situations, as can be seen in advertising for alcoholic beverages and in portrayals on television and in the movies.

There is no dispute about the seriousness of abuse of other drugs, especially those that are illegal, but the very illegal nature of those drugs makes their use and their consequences very different from those related to alcohol, which, although subject to some restrictions, is legally available to adults. Many who drink alcohol without any reservations would never think of experimenting with illegal drugs.

Still, many drinkers do use alcohol with other drugs, and it is important to determine the nature of interactive effects. Therefore one caution is that some conclusions from the large body of alcohol research to be presented in this book may be limited in generalizability to polydrug abusers. Despite this problem, the choice was made to restrict the coverage to evidence from studies of alcohol use and abuse. To attempt to cover a number of drugs in this volume would prevent the depth of coverage needed to adequately present the issues and findings pertaining to alcohol.

Conclusions

Many major changes have occurred in the past 50 years in attitudes about alcohol and the level of alcohol consumption in American society. At the same time, views of the causes of alcoholism and how society should react toward alcoholics have changed. The major social movement created by Alcoholics Anonymous in the 1930s transformed the plight of alcoholics from a hopeless one fraught with moral condemnation into a situation that offered hope and understanding. The treatment void produced through the neglect of professionals was replaced by the self-help movement created by fellow alcoholics. The concurrent move to conduct scientific research on the causes and nature of alcoholism had fewer immediate con-sequences and less public visibility but was also an important development with significant long-range potential for improving our understanding, treatment, and prevention of alcohol problems.

Unfortunately, these complementary movements have clashed over their con-ception of the nature of alcoholism. The disease conception of alcoholism, central to AA ideology and the formulation of a leading researcher, E. M. Jellinek, has been called into question periodically since the 1960s by some researchers. The con-troversy is partially based on the question of whether alcoholism should be viewed primarily as stemming from physiological or from psychological factors. Whereas physiological factors are less variant across individuals and less readily changed, psychological and behavioral factors are generally viewed to be modifiable.

Instead of viewing alcoholism as either physiological *or* psychological, we might consider the possibility that there are both types, or even several other types, of alcoholism. All individuals who have been diagnosed or classified as "alcoholics" may appear similar in that they drink excessively and have adverse consequences associated with such behavior, but the underlying causes, and by implication, the effective treatments, for different subgroups may be quite disparate.

Despite the substantial gains of the medical model since the 1930s, in the mind of the public, many aspects of the moral model still exist. Some physicians are reluctant to treat alcoholic individuals due to the heavy stigma they bear in our society. The moral view often seems more influential than the medical model in affecting social attitudes and policies related to alcoholism. Ames (1985), while noting the apparent incompatibility of these two rival conceptions, also recognized that the two approaches do overlap.

Physical health impairments associated with alcoholism, according to the moral perspective, are secondary to the moral weakness that was originally responsible for the alcoholic drinking. This philosophy holds that a complete cure must include a spiritual or moral transformation and that treating the drinking behavior alone is insufficient. Alcoholics Anonymous is a prime example of this approach to dealing with alcoholism. Its reputation of success assures that it will continue to be a strong influence on the public perception of alcoholism.

The 1980s saw the beginning of some important social movements and attitude changes related to alcohol that are continuing to grow in their impact on the role of alcohol in the society of the 1990s. A neo-Temperance movement exists today as social concerns with health have led to a moderation of drinking and a change in drinking style. More compassion for the victims of alcohol abuse such as those injured and killed by intoxicated motorists was mobilized by Mothers Against Drunk Driving. Stricter laws and stronger enforcement have resulted so that more drinkers are more cautious before mixing their drinking with their driving. Some states have lowered the legal minimum blood alcohol content that can be used as evidence of alcohol impairment for drivers. Research findings about the risks to fetuses posed by mothers' drinking during pregnancy increased awareness and concerns about dangers to unborn children. Public establishments that serve alcohol must display warnings about such risks in many states. Warning labels of risks to health are required on alcoholic beverage containers. More evidence about the adverse impact of parental alcoholism on children who as adults experience alcoholism themselves or other forms of maladjustment, has increased the participation in mutual-support organizations such as Adult Children of Alcoholics. These are striking examples of the kind of changes that have been brought about by social action to restrict the use of alcohol to safer conditions than in the past.

However, more large-scale changes in society will be needed to further reduce the havoc created by alcoholism and alcohol-related problems. As a society, we are in conflict over the proper use of alcohol. People want their freedoms, including the right to drink as they choose, but society must impose sanctions—legal, economic, and moral—to regulate alcohol consumption to minimize, if not prevent, psychological and physical harm to drinkers and those around them. Exactly how to achieve both goals is a real dilemma and our society has shown ambivalence in its approach, as captured in a speech by a Mississippi senator to the state legislature in 1958 about his position on alcohol:

> If, when you say whisky, you mean the devil's brew, the poison scourge, the bloody monster that defiles innocence . . . the evil drink that topples the Christian man and woman from the pinnacles of righteous, gracious living into the bottomless pit of degradation and despair, . . . then certainly I am against it with all of my power. But, if you when you say whisky, you mean the oil of conversation, the philosophic wine, the stuff that is consumed when good fellows get together . . . if you mean that drink, the sale of which pours into our treasuries untold millions of dollars, which are used to provide tender care for our little crippled children, our blind, our deaf, our dumb, our pitiful aged and infirm, to build highways, hospitals and schools, then certainly I am in favor of it. This is my stand. I will not retreat from it; I will not compromise.

References

Alcoholics Anonymous World Services (1935). *Alcoholics Anonymous*. New York: Author.

Ames, G. (1985). American beliefs about alcoholism. In L. Bennett & G. M. Ames (Eds.) *The American experience with alcohol: Contrasting cultural perspectives*. New York: Plenum Press.

Cahalan, D., Cisin, I. H., & Crossley, H. M. (1969). *American drinking practices: A national study of drinking behavior*. New Brunswick, NJ. Rutgers Center for Alcohol Studies.

Gusfield, J. R. (1963). *Symbolic crusade: Status politics and the American temperance movement*. Urbana, IL: University of Illinois Press.

Jellinek, E. M. (1952). Phases of alcohol addiction. *Quarterly Journal of Studies on Alcohol, 13,* 673–684.

Jellinek, E. M. (1960). *The disease conception of alcoholism*. New Brunswick, NJ: Hillhouse Press.

Peele, S. (1989). *Diseasing of America: Addiction treatment out of control*. Lexington, MA: Lexington Books.

Rice, D. P., Kelman, S., Miller, L. S., & Dunmeyer, S. (1990). The economic costs of alcohol and drug abuse and mental illness: 1985. Rockville, MD: National Institute of Drug Abuse.

Robinson, D. (1972). The alcohologist's addiction: Some implications of having lost control over the disease concept of alcoholism. *Quarterly Journal of Studies on Alcohol, 33,* 1028–1042.

U.S. Department of Health and Human Services. (1987). *Sixth Special Report to the U.S. Congress on Alcohol and Health.* Rockville, MD: U.S. Government Printing Office.

U.S. Department of Health and Human Services. (1990). *Seventh Special Report to the U.S. Congress on Alcohol and Health.* Washington, DC: U.S. Government Printing Office.

Williams, G. D., Stinson, F. S., Brooks, S. D., Clem, D., & Noble, J. (1991). *Surveillance Report #20: Apparent per capita alcohol consumption: National, state, and regional trends, 1977–1989.* Rockville, MD: National Institute of Alcohol Abuse and Alcoholism.

The Extent of Drinking, Alcoholism, and Alcohol-Related Problems

People drink alcohol in a variety of contexts, with the amount consumed varying on different occasions. In addition, wide variations in drinking patterns exist among different individuals. Studies that measure the circumstances and extent of drinking in the general population yield valuable information. These surveys provide a picture of the overall impact of alcohol on society by showing the extent to which alcohol consumption occurs with, as well as without, negative consequences to drinkers. Identification of the differences in alcohol use and abuse among sub-groups of society along lines of age, sex, ethnicity, social class, religion, and geographical region, to name a few of the most important dimensions, offers important clues to help explain why people drink alcohol. This chapter first describes the basic methods of such survey studies and then presents the major findings about drinking patterns in the United States.

The Epidemiological Approach

Epidemiology is the subfield of public health that deals with the measurement of the number of new cases or *incidence* and the number of existing cases or *prevalence* of some disease, disorder, or impairment. These rates of occurrence are determined for specific points in time or over an extended period such as the past year or during an individual's lifetime.

The epidemiological method obtains data about the demographic correlates of alcohol use and abuse. These data are invaluable in testing hypotheses and theories about the factors responsible for alcoholism and alcohol problems (Helzer, 1987). For example, sex is a variable that has been almost universally found to be related to alcoholism, with males usually at greater risk or having a greater likelihood of developing alcohol use disorders. Sex is a predictor of risk for alcoholism; hence, it is referred to as a *risk factor*. The identification of sex as a risk factor for alcoholism does not reveal the basis for this association. The process could be based in biological differences or it could reflect differences in social attitudes toward male and female drinking. Nevertheless, this information could influence prevention and treatment approaches so that programs could be developed to deal more appropriately with that portion of the population at greater risk.

Rather than basing conclusions on a self-selected sample of those who seek or receive treatment, scientific suveys use samples chosen at random to ensure that the respondents represent a cross-section of the general population. Such surveys are expensive and time-consuming but can provide important information not otherwise available. Researchers can ask respondents about aspects of their drinking experience such as reasons or motives for drinking, effects of drinking, and the role of drinking contexts.

Epidemiologists look for patterns of drinking behavior for purposes of comparison. The next section describes how such patterns are measured.

Measures of Drinking Patterns

Drinking patterns vary among drinkers in many ways. Drinkers differ in the *frequency* of their drinking (how often they used alcohol in a given period of time such as the past month or year) and the *quantity* of their drinking (the number of drinks consumed on a single drinking occasion). Drinkers may also differ in the consistency or regularity of their consumption patterns over different drinking occasions. In addition, there may be differences in the rates of drinking (time to consume a drink), the maximum number of drinks consumed on a single drinking occasion, and the extent to which drinking occurs together with eating.

Epidemiologists have developed several different ways to measure drinking patterns. These include the quantity-frequency index, the proportion of drinking at different quantities index, and measures of the frequency of intoxication.

The Quantity-Frequency (QF) Index

Although the specific items on surveys that assess drinking behavior differ slightly from survey to survey, typically surveys assess the *quantity* (number of drinks) consumed on the usual (or recent) drinking occasion and the *frequency* of drinking occasions in a given interval. With regard to quantity, different alcoholic beverages vary in their concentration so that the volume of alcohol contained in each type of drink must be factored into the assessment. The amount of *absolute alcohol* is equal to only half of the proof of the beverage, so that someone who drinks 6 ounces of 100-proof bourbon, for example, has consumed only 3 ounces of absolute alcohol. In making comparisons of the quantity of alcohol consumed when different types of alcoholic beverages are consumed, researchers define a *drink* as a 12-ounce beer, a mixed or straight drink containing 1½ ounces of distilled spirits or liquor, or a 5-ounce glass of wine.

This equation is justifiable since these volumes of the major beverage types contain approximately the same amount of absolute alcohol and therefore are likely to produce the same effect on the drinker. However, the validity of the assumption behind this equation may not be entirely accurate since drinkers who typically refer to each type of alcoholic beverage may also differ in age, sex, social class, body weight, or personality, as well as with regard to the conditions under which they typically drink. Klatsky, Armstrong, and Kipp (1990) examined surveys from more than 53,000 white members of a California prepaid health plan. Of the 51 percent indicating a preferred alcoholic beverage, those who preferred wine were generally women, nonsmokers, more highly educated, or younger to middle-aged members with low health risks. Liquor was favored by men, heavier drinkers, and middle-aged or older members with less education and with risk factors for major illnesses. Finally, beer was the preferred beverage among younger members, a group that scored at intermediate levels between the wine and liquor preferrers for most traits.

Survey items assessing frequency of drinking typically ask how often the individual has consumed different amounts of alcohol in the past month: several times a day, daily, several times a week, more than once a month but not weekly, and so on. Based on answers to items regarding quantity and frequency for each of the three main types of alcoholic beverages—beer, wine, and liquor or distilled spirits—a quantity-frequency (QF) index is calculated for each beverage by multiplying the quantity by the frequency. Then these QF scores for the three beverages are summed to produce an aggregate measure of the total volume of absolute alcohol consumed. The type of alcoholic beverage consumed is not viewed to be as important as the total *volume* of alcohol contained in the drinks consumed in a given time period.

The QF measure has limitations but is still a frequently used index. One problem is that the same total volume can be consumed by someone drinking heavily on a few occasions and someone drinking lightly on many occasions, but the effect produced by these two patterns will undoubtedly differ. The QF index ignores the likelihood that for a given drinking episode, heavier drinking should produce more serious risks of physical damage and adverse behavioral effects than lighter drinking.

A related problem is that the QF index does not acknowledge variability in drinking over time for an individual, because the wording of items asks for the typical or usual amount consumed. As a result, it cannot differentiate between drinkers who reach the same total volume while drinking a similar amount each time and those who drink variable amounts on each occasion. Cahalan, Cisin, and Crossley (1969) addressed this problem by including a variability index (QF-V) that combined the *maximum* amount consumed on any single occasion with an item assessing the *typical* amount consumed.

The Proportion of Drinking at Different Quantities Index

An alternative index to the QF measure is the proportion of drinking occasions involving various quantities, particularly heavier ones. This measure can distinguish light drinkers who never drink excessively from those who are usually light drinkers but once in a while consume large amounts, an important distinction that would not be detected by the QF index.

The proportion of drinking index is also not without limitations, for it does not consider the frequency of drinking. Two drinkers could have the same proportion of drinking at different quantities but still differ in how often drinking occurs. Thus, both a drinker who drank daily and one who drank only five times a year could be indexed as a drinker who drinks five or more drinks on 20 percent of drinking occasions. The total amount of alcohol consumed, and the adverse consequences, would be high for the first drinker while they would be negligible for the second drinker.

Frequency of Intoxication

One problem with most survey indexes based on the average total amount of drinking such as the QF index is that they do not focus on the most disruptive aspects of drinking. Knupner (1984) has argued in favor of greater reliance on an index of the frequency of *intoxication*—that is, how often dangerous levels of alcohol are consumed. It may be more useful to know how often someone is incapacitated by heavy consumption than to identify how often an individual has a single drink, because that small amount involves less risk of harming self or others than amounts that create intoxication.

Findings of Two Major Epidemiological Surveys

In this section we will examine the findings of two major epidemiological surveys describing drinking patterns in the general population. Drinking patterns and their relationship to problem behavior will be noted.

Alcohol Research Group Surveys

The first large-scale general population surveys of American drinking practices were initiated in the late 1950s at George Washington University and continued into the 1960s by the Social Research Group and its successor, the Alcohol Research Group, at the University of California at Berkeley (Cahalan, 1970; Cahalan et al., 1969; Cahalan & Room, 1974). These national surveys were landmark studies and represented a considerable improvement in methodology over prior surveys that were based mainly on special populations such as clinical cases and prison inmates. In these, as in most surveys, alcohol consumption items involve retrospective self-reports that are not readily corroborated.

In the first survey, Cahalan et al. (1969) found that about two-thirds of the men and half of the women drank alcohol at least once a year, but half of them never drank more than three drinks per occasion. Men were more likely than women, 21 versus 5 percent, to be classified as heavy drinkers (five or more drinks per occasion). Younger drinkers in their 20s were the most likely to consume five or more drinks on a drinking occasion, a behavior that abated more with each successive older age group. Over the age of 50, many respondents were abstainers, especially among women. Later national surveys by the Alcohol Research Group in 1979 (Clark & Midanik, 1982) and in 1984 (Hilton, 1988b; Hilton & Clark, 1987) generally upheld these findings.

In addition to assessing the quantity and frequency of drinking, these surveys also examined the problems created by alcohol such as physical impairment, social difficulties, legal troubles, and financial problems. Using a list of 11 such "problems," Cahalan (1970) used an arbitrary criterion of 7 or more of these problems to classify respondents as problem drinkers. On this basis about 9 percent (15 percent for males, 4 percent for females) of the 21-years-and-over population could be considered problem drinkers. In addition, "moderate" levels of alcohol-related problems occurred for many males (43 percent) and a sizable minority of the females (21 percent).

In addition to this descriptive evidence, which was valuable in uncovering the extent of alcohol problems, the surveys led to the conception of "problem drinking" (Cahalan, 1970), an alternative to Jellinek's (1960) disease concept of alcoholism, which was endorsed by AA. The value of this distinction can be seen in that some drinkers who did not show signs of physical or psychological dependence on alcohol nonetheless had numerous alcohol-related problems of the variety listed earlier; conversely, some drinkers who exhibited alcohol dependence or alcoholism had few of these alcohol-related problems.

Thus, specific symptoms of the disease such as binge drinking, psychological dependence, and loss of control that appeared in a sample of problem drinkers the first time they were surveyed were not present for many of the problem drinkers when they were followed up on only five years later. The fact that many of these adverse effects of drinking at Time 1—such as problems with relatives or friends, police, finances, and job—underwent remission or disappeared between the two assessment times for many drinkers did not agree with Jellinek's disease conception of alcoholism as a progressive and irreversible syndrome in which a more or less invariant order of successive symptoms should appear at predictable times in the sequence. Instead, the findings suggested that problem drinkers tend to pass in and out between problem drinking and problem-free periods.

NIAAA Harris Polls

The National Institute on Alcohol Abuse and Alcoholism (NIAAA) commissioned a series of Harris Poll surveys (for example, Harris, 1971) on alcohol attitudes and practices in the general population during the 1970s. The overall findings were similar to those of the Alcohol Research Group. Because some of the survey items were identical to those used in federally funded alcoholism treatment centers, it was also possible to make direct comparisons between the drinking of the general population and institutionalized alcoholics.

This comparison suggested that alcoholics in treatment were substantially more impaired than the heavy drinkers among the general population classified as problem drinkers. Prior to treatment, the alcoholics had been consuming a daily amount of alcohol that was about three times as high as that reported by the heavy drinkers in the general population.

The prevalence of various drinking levels in these and several similar national surveys conducted over the decade of the 1970s were summarized by Wilsnack, Wilsnack, and Klassen (1986). They consistently found that a higher percentage of men than women drank heavily, while the reverse was true for abstention. Heavy drinking was defined as a QF drinking score over the past 30 days that exceeded an average of 1 oz. of absolute alcohol per day; moderate drinking was defined as an average of .22 to .99 oz./day; and light drinking as less than an average of .22 oz./day.

Findings of Studies Relating to Temporal Trends

Using data from the 1984 National Alcohol Survey based on probability samples of persons over 18 years of age, Hilton and Clark (1987) compared previous results from the American Drinking Practices study (Cahalan et al., 1969) and found little change from 1967 to 1984 in the prevalence of heavy drinking, defined in their survey as drinking five or more drinks on one occasion and being drunk at least once a month. In their comparison, they used only those items that were identical across the two surveys, limited to questions about the quantity and frequency aspects of drinking.

Such stability was somewhat surprising given that the per capita consumption level increased in that period. One might expect that this increased consumption pattern would be accompanied by an increase in heavy drinking as well as drinking problems. However, in Hilton and Clark's comparison they used only two time points widely separated in time. If heavy drinking had first increased and then reversed during that interval, the researchers could have easily missed detecting the change.

In an extended comparison shown in Table 2-1, Hilton (1988c) compared results of 1964 and 1984 national probability surveys as well as responses from surveys conducted between 1971 and 1981. Although strict comparability across surveys was not possible because some items were not identical, stability in most

Table 2-1 Selected measures of alcohol consumption in 1964, 1979, and 1984 by percentage.

	1964	1979	1984
1. *Abstainers*			
Men	15	17	17
Women	30	23	27
2. *Frequency of drinking*			
Men			
Daily[a]	7	17*	10
Weekly[b]	44	46	47
Monthly[c]	28*	15	18
Yearly[d]	7	5	7
Abstainer	15	17	17
Women			
Daily	3	3	3
Weekly	21	34*	26
Monthly	24	18*	26
Yearly	22	22	18
Abstainer	30	23	27
3. *Monthly volume consumed*			
Men			
More than 60 drinks	15*	19	23
30.1–60 drinks	17	17	19
15.1–30 drinks	16	19*	12
0–15 drinks	38*	29	28
Abstainer	15	17	17
Women			
More than 60 drinks	4*	5	7
30.1–60 drinks	6	12	9
15.1–30 drinks	9	11	11
0–15 drinks	51	49	46
Abstainer	30	23	27
4. *Frequency of drinking five or more drinks on an occasion*			
Men			
Weekly	19*	24	31
Monthly	16	20	18
Less than once per month or never	50*	39	34
Abstainer	15	17	17

(*continued*)

Table 2-1 Selected measures of alcohol consumption in 1964, 1979, and 1984 (by percentage) (*continued*)

	1964	1979	1984
Women			
Weekly	3*	4*	8
Monthly	6*	12	12
Less than once per month or never	61*	61*	54
Abstainer	30	23	27
5. *Frequency of getting high*			
Men			
Weekly	—	14	11
Monthly	—	18	23
Less than once per month or never	—	52	49
Abstainer	—	17	17
Women			
Weekly	—	5	5
Monthly	—	10	14
Less than once per month or never	—	62*	55
Abstainer	—	23	27
6. *Frequency of getting drunk*			
Men			
Weekly	—	3*	6
Monthly	—	9	10
Less than once per month or never	—	72	86
Abstainer	—	17	17
Women			
Weekly	—	1	2
Monthly	—	4	3
Less than once per month or never	—	73	68
Abstainer	—	23	27
N (unweighted)			
Men	(321)	(235)	(787)
Women	(410)	(336)	(1159)

*Significantly different from 1984 figure by difference of proportions test at 0.05 level.
[a]Once per day or more often.
[b]At least once per week but less often than once per day.
[c]At least once per month but less often than once per week.
[d]At least once per year but less than once per month.
Source: from "Trends in U.S. drinking patterns: Further evidence from the past 20 years," by M. E. Hilton in the *British Journal of Addiction (1988c)*, *83*, 269–278. Copyright © 1988 by the Society for the Study of Addiction to Alcohol and Other Drugs. Reprinted by permission.

indexes of drinking such as abstention, frequency, quantity, and frequency of getting drunk or high was found for both men and women.

Although the studies show stability of overall drinking over the period of 20 years from the late 1960s to late 1980s, a more detailed analysis (Hilton, 1988c) found that there have been increases in heavy drinking (five or more drinks on an occasion or eight or more drinks/day) especially among young males between ages 21 and 34, changes that were missed by earlier surveys that used lower consumption criteria for defining heavy drinking.

A study by Hasin, Grant, Harford, Hilton, and Endicott (1990) involving comparisons across four national surveys conducted between 1967 and 1984 also supports the view that there has been a rise in the prevalence of alcohol use disorders. They constructed a scale consisting of 11 items that measured alcohol-related problems that appeared on all four surveys. Using an arbitrary criterion score of 3 or more to define their index of multiple problems, Hasin et al. found a 50 percent increase for men, from 11.4 to 17.4 percent, and a 200 percent increase for women, from 2.3 to 5.2 percent, over this 20-year period in the lifetime prevalence of multiple alcohol-related problems among current drinkers between ages 22 and 59. Current prevalence (within the past year) of multiple problems showed even larger increases in this period, doubling for men and tripling for women.

Findings of Studies
Relating to Demographic Factors

In this section, we present major findings about the relationship between a number of demographic variables—such as sex, age, and geographical region—and differences in drinking patterns. Since the early surveys either did not examine ethnic differences or had very small or unrepresentative convenience samples that were overrepresented by heavy drinkers, we will not examine ethnic differences here. Ethnic differences in drinking will be discussed in detail in Chapter 16.

Sex Differences

Hilton (1988c), in agreement with other surveys, found that men drank more frequently and in larger amounts than did women, as indicated in Table 2–1. For example, 12 percent of the men were daily drinkers while only 4 percent of the women were. Not surprisingly, then, men also were five times more likely to get drunk during a week than women were. Heavy drinkers, defined in terms of 60+ drinks per month, represented 21 percent of men but only 4 to 5 percent of women. Conversely, a higher percentage of women, 36 percent, versus 24 percent of men were abstainers. These sex differences were similar across 20 years in three different surveys done between 1964 and 1984, suggesting that sex differences in drinking patterns have been stable.

Harford, Parker, Grant, and Dawson (1992) obtained data from more than 49,000 respondents in the 1988 National Health Interview Survey. Using data from more than 26,000 men and women who were employed during the two weeks prior to the survey, they found similar differences in the percentage of each sex who currently used alcohol, with 68 percent of males and 49 percent of females reporting 12 or more drinks in the preceding year. More detailed analysis of women's drinking appears in Chapter 14.

Occupational Differences

In the study just cited by Harford et al., a higher percentage of white-collar than blue-collar workers were current drinkers, defined as having consumed 12 or more drinks in the past year. This difference held for both men and women. However, the opposite pattern existed for the quantity of alcohol consumed, with a higher average daily consumption by blue-collar workers. Alcohol dependence, a measure of problems with drinking (defined in detail in Chapter 7), was also more prevalent among blue-collar workers.

Parker and Farmer (1990), based on results of household surveys with 1,367 employed men and women in Detroit, proposed that alcohol abuse could be a form of coping with stress. For white-collar workers, stress often stems from time pressure and competition leading to burnout. Stress for blue-collar workers more often is due to the lack of challenge from dull and repetitive tasks. These researchers suggested that higher risks for alcoholism may exist at either level of work if there is a lack of fit between the employee's needs and the job's demands.

Age Differences

The extent of alcohol use varies with age. Higher consumption levels occur with the younger groups, with groups over 50 being lower on several measures of drinking. The notable exception is daily drinking, a variable that is stable over age (Hilton, 1988c). The 1984 National Alcohol Survey found that the percentage of men aged 18 and over who drank ranged from 82 percent for those in the 18–29 age group to 58 percent for those 60 years and older. Women showed a similar range from 74 percent for 18–29 years of age to 49 percent of those over age 60. Measures that reflect heavy drinking, alcohol dependence, and adverse consequences also showed lower rates for older age groups. Chapter 15 examines in more detail drinking patterns and determinants for adolescents and for the elderly.

Regional Differences

Alcohol use and its consequent problems are not equivalent in all regions of the country, particularly with regard to abstinence. As shown in Figure 2-1, there were large variations in the amount of alcohol consumed per capita in different states in 1981. A history of temperance and prohibition has characterized regions such as the southern states, where fundamentalist religious attitudes have been strong and associated with higher levels of abstinence. Attitudes toward drinking and drunkenness are more negative in these regions and there are stronger legal restrictions on the availability and drinking of alcohol.

Over the decade from 1977 to 1986, substantial increases and decreases in apparent per capita consumption occurred in many states, as shown in Figure 2-2, but the relative rankings were maintained (Steffens, Stinson, Freel, & Clem, 1988).

Room (1983) observed that when alcohol consumption statistics are viewed on a per drinker basis instead of a per capita basis, there is actually higher consumption in the drier than wetter regions. That is, given that the *total* drinking amount is comparable across regions, the drier regions with their *fewer* drinkers must also have more *heavy* drinkers, in order to achieve that comparable total level of drinking. As a consequence, in dry regions there might paradoxically also be more alcohol-related problems stemming from these more numerous heavy drinkers.

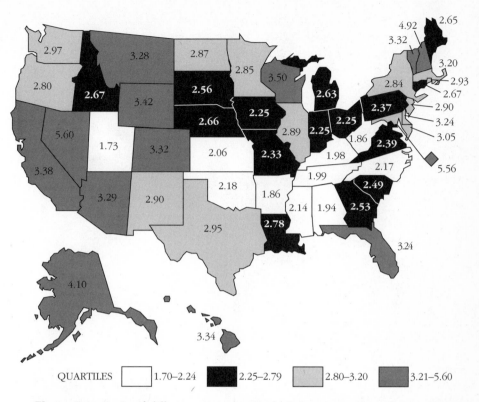

Figure 2-1 Regional differences in apparent alcohol consumption per capita, age 14 and older, 1981.

Source: from *Fifth Special Report to the U.S. Congress on Alcohol,* 1984, Washington, DC: U.S. Government Printing Office.

Hilton (1988a) attempted to replicate Room's findings to see if the regional trends in abstention persisted. Previous studies have shown stable levels of per capita apparent consumption from 1964 to 1979, but per drinker apparent consumption was higher in drier regions, as were the tangible consequences of drinking when measured on a per drinker basis. Heavy drinking in drier regions may be more explosive, leading to more aggression and belligerence.

Hilton analyzed regional differences in a 1984 national random survey with interviews of about 5,000 adults over age 18. Problematic drinking was defined in terms of drinking behaviors and immediate correlates thought to be indicative of alcohol dependence such as unsuccessful attempts to lessen drinking, memory loss, and morning drinking. Abstention was defined as drinking less than once in the last year or not at all.

As shown in Table 2-2, regional differences were found showing more problems in drier regions, as found in the prior study, in apparent consumption and in abstention rates when a per-drinker index (based on drinkers only, shown in the bottom half of the table) rather than the typical per-capita index (based on all respondents, shown in the top half of the table) was used. These differences were

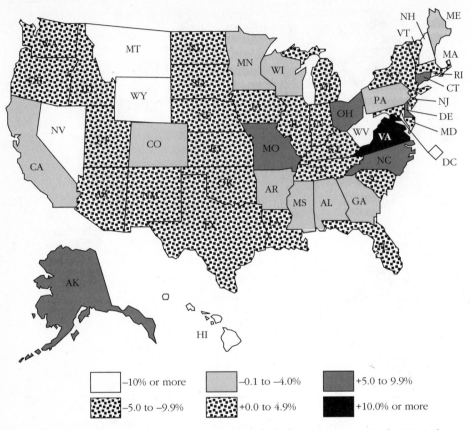

Figure 2-2 Percent change in per capita alcohol consumption in the United States, 1977–1986.

Source: from *Seventh Special Report to the U.S. Congress on Alcohol,* 1990, Washington, DC: U.S. Government Printing Office.

more pronounced for problems with tangible consequences such as health, finances, and interpersonal conflicts than they were for the problematic drinking itself.

In an abstinence subculture, it might be expected that attitudes toward alcohol would generally be more negative even if drinkers in that region consume more heavily and with more problems than in drinking regions. In Hilton's study, however, no major regional differences in attitudes about alcohol were found. Hilton concluded that the high per-drinker consumption rate and the conservative drinking attitudes in drier regions generate unresolved tensions.

Regional differences in alcohol problems were found for men but not for women. In drier regions, drinking males had more consequences related to aggression such as belligerence, accidents, problems with spouses and friends, and trouble with the police.

Unlike males, females showed regional differences in attitudes toward drinking and drunkenness. In the South, although females drank as much and had as

Table 2-2 Regional distribution of drinking problems (by percentage).

		Men		Women	
		Wetter Regions	Drier Regions	Wetter Regions	Drier Regions
(a)	*All respondents*				
	Loss of control	3.6	3.4	1.9	1.2
	Symptomatic behavior	3.5	4.1	1.3	0.5
	Binge drinking	0.7	2.2	0.6	0.4
	Problematic drinking	6.7	6.8	3.5	1.6*
	Belligerence	3.0	4.8	2.0	0.8
	Problems with spouse	8.2	12.3*	3.5	2.7
	Problems with relatives	0.7	0.2	0.1	0.1
	Problems with friends	4.4	7.4	2.8	1.7
	Job problems	2.3	3.0	1.1	0.5
	Problems with police	1.5	3.0	0.1	0.0
	Health problems	1.5	1.6	0.6	0.6
	Accidents	0.5	2.9*	0.2	0.5
	Financial problems	3.0	2.7	1.4	1.5
	Tangible consequences	8.5	13.7*	4.5	3.0
	N	1087	1006	1601	1527
(b)	*Drinkers only*				
	Loss of control	4.4	5.2	2.7	2.3
	Symptomatic behavior	4.2	6.3	1.9	0.9
	Binge drinking	0.9	3.3	0.8	0.8
	Problematic drinking	8.1	10.5	4.9	3.1
	Belligerence	3.7	7.3*	2.8	1.5
	Problems with spouse	9.9	18.8*	5.0	5.2
	Problems with relatives	0.9	0.3	0.1	0.1
	Problems with friends	5.3	11.3*	3.9	3.2
	Job problems	2.8	4.6	1.6	1.0
	Problems with police	1.8	4.6*	0.2	0.0
	Health problems	1.8	2.4	0.8	1.2
	Accidents	0.6	4.5*	0.3	0.9
	Financial problems	3.6	4.2	2.0	2.9
	Tangible consequences	10.3	21.0*	6.3	5.7
	N	849	682	969	712

*Proportions for wetter and drier regions significantly different at $p < 0.05$.
Source: from "Regional diversity in United States drinking practices," by M. E. Hilton in the *British Journal of Addiction (1988a), 83*, 519–532. Copyright © 1988 by the Society for the Study of Addiction to Alcohol and Other Drugs. Reprinted by permission.

many problems as those in other regions, they were less likely to hold favorable attitudes toward drinking and drunkenness than females in other regions.

Findings: Abstention

Abstainers have received less study than alcoholics have, perhaps because they do not appear to represent problems for society. Different studies have found from 14 to 34 percent of those surveyed were abstainers, but these studies lump all current abstainers together, thus failing to recognize the heterogeneity of this category. Goldman and Najman (1984), in a four-year population survey of 5,320 Boston adults, identified several subtypes of abstainers: lifetime abstainers (58 percent), current abstainers without a prior drinking problem (34 percent), and current abstainers with a prior drinking problem (9 percent). One would expect these subgroups to differ in many ways. Thus, the subgroup of abstainers with a prior drinking problem consisted mostly of males with higher occupational skills and with moderate to frequent prior consumption. Their ideology about abstinence was similar to that of AA.

Hilton (1986) compared abstention rates in 1964 and 1979 based on general population probability surveys. Abstainers (defined in the survey as those who never drink or drink less than once a year) consistently disapproved of drinking in a variety of contexts. Hilton identified four sets of reasons for abstention: moral objection, dislike of drinking consequences, "inconsequential" reasons, and abstinent family background. Militant views against drinking were stronger for lifelong abstainers who had moral reasons for their behavior. Abstainers also tended to have more disapproving attitudes about sexual issues such as premarital and extramarital sex than drinkers. Both drinkers and abstainers held negative attitudes on issues related to alcohol problems such as drinking and driving or belligerence.

Hilton (1986) found that little or no change in abstention rates occurred over the 15 years between 1964 and 1979. There was no convergence over time for either sex or age differences in level of abstention. Regional and religious affiliation differences in abstention did not weaken either. The possibility that the older generation is more abstemious and is being replaced by a wetter younger generation was not supported.

Conclusions

Epidemiological studies tell us how demographic factors such as age, sex, and geographic region are related to the frequency and quantity of alcohol consumption. Most surveys agree in showing that men drink more frequently and in larger amounts than women do. Young adults drink larger amounts, with successively older groups drinking less. Drinking patterns also differ by geographic region, with traditionally dry areas such as the South showing more abstainers but also more alcohol-related problems by those who do drink. Temporal trends can also be identified, with indications that patterns of drinking between the 1960s and 1980s have shown little overall change in many aspects for either men or women. Closer scrutiny, however, suggests that heavy drinking has increased for 21- to 34-year-old males.

Such descriptive evidence is essential for identifying the scope of the problem of alcoholism, testing theories of causation, and developing appropriate prevention and intervention programs. However, caution must be exercised in drawing conclusions since many alcohol use patterns can be explained in more than one way. Thus, the decline in total drinking over the decade of the eighties could reflect the impact of prevention campaigns, greater general concern with a healthier lifestyle, or other societal changes such as changes in economic conditions.

Whereas the epidemiological surveys have used probability samples selected at random from the general population, studies of alcoholics have relied on clinical populations such as hospitalized patients and members of AA. These two populations are quite different, so that failure of findings from one group to agree completely with those obtained from the other should not be surprising.

A number of findings from general population surveys seemingly contradict tenets of the influential disease conception of alcoholism. General population surveys (for example, Clark & Cahalan, 1976) have not supported the idea that all alcoholics show the same set of symptoms such as loss of control and psychological dependence. Little relationship has been found between level of drinking and loss of control. Problem drinkers have not been found to show progressive or irreversible patterns of symptoms, as many symptoms disappear later while others appear that were absent earlier. However, it is conceivable that the problem drinkers studied in general population surveys have not been as severely impaired as the "alcoholics" studied by Jellinek. It would be useful if the same measuring instrument could be used with both populations to allow better comparisons.

References

Cahalan, D. (1970). *Problem drinkers: A national survey.* San Francisco: Jossey-Bass.

Cahalan, D., Cisin, I. H., & Crossley, H. M. (1969). *American drinking practices: National study of drinking behavior.* New Brunswick, NJ: Rutgers Center for Alcohol Studies.

Cahalan, D., & Room, R. (1974). *Problem drinking among American men.* New Brunswick, NJ: Rutgers Center for Alcohol Studies.

Clark, W. B., & Cahalan, D. (1976). Changes in problem drinking over a four-year span. *Addictive Behaviors, 1,* 251–259.

Clark, W. B., & Midanik, L. (1982). Alcohol use and alcohol problems among U.S. adults: Results of the 1979 national survey. In National Institute on Alcohol Abuse and Alcoholism (Ed.), *Alcohol consumption and related problems* (Monograph No. 1, pp. 3–52). Washington, DC: U.S. Government Printing Office.

Goldman, E., & Najman, J. M. (1984). Lifetime abstainers, current abstainers and imbibers: A methodological note. *British Journal of Addiction, 79,* 309–314.

Harford, T. C., Parker, D. A., Grant, B. F., & Dawson, D. A. (1992). Alcohol use and dependence among employed men and women in the United States in 1988. *Alcoholism: Clinical and Experimental Research, 16,* 146–148.

Harris, L. (1971). *American attitudes toward alcohol and alcoholics. Prepared for the National Institute of Alcohol Abuse and Alcoholism.* New York: Lou Harris & Associates.

Hasin, D., Grant, B., Harford, T., Hilton, M., & Endicott, J. (1990). Multiple alcohol-related problems in the United States: On the rise? *Journal of Studies on Alcohol, 51,* 485–493.

Helzer, J. E. (1987). Epidemiology of alcoholism. *Journal of Consulting and Clinical Psychology, 55,* 284–292.

Hilton, M. E. (1986). Abstention in the general population of the U.S.A. *British Journal of Addiction, 81,* 95–112.

Hilton, M. E. (1988a). Regional diversity in United States drinking practices. *British Journal of Addiction, 83,* 519–532.

Hilton, M. E. (1988b). Trends in drinking problems and attitudes in the United States: 1979–1984. *British Journal of Addiction, 83,* 1421–1427.

Hilton, M. E. (1988c). Trends in U.S. drinking patterns: Further evidence from the past 20 years. *British Journal of Addiction, 83,* 269–278.

Hilton, M. E., & Clark, W. B. (1987). Changes in American drinking patterns and problems 1967–1984. *Journal of Studies on Alcohol, 48,* 512–522.

Klatsky, A. L., Armstrong, M. A., & Kipp, H. (1990). Correlates of alcoholic beverage preference: Traits of persons who choose wine, liquor or beer. *British Journal of Addiction, 85,* 1279–1289.

Knupner, G. (1984). The risks of drunkenness (or, Ebrietas Resurrecta): A comparison of frequent intoxication indices and population sub-groups as to problem risks. *British Journal of Addiction, 79,* 185–196.

Parker, D. A., & Farmer, G. C. (1990). Employed adults at risk for diminished self-control over alcohol use: The alienated, the burned out, and the unchallenged. In P. Roman (Ed.), *Alcohol problem intervention in the workplace* (pp. 27–43). New York: Quorum.

Room, R. (1983). Region and urbanization as factors in drinking practices and problems. In B. Kissin & H. Begleiter (Ed.), *The biology of alcoholism: The pathogenesis of alcoholism: Psychosocial factors* (pp. 555–604). New York: Plenum Press.

Steffens, R. A., Stinson, F. S., Freel, C. G., & Clem, D. (1988). *Apparent per capita alcohol consumption: National, state, and regional trends, 1977–1986* (Surveillance Report No. 10). Rockville, MD: National Institute of Alcohol Abuse and Alcoholism.

Wilsnack, S. C., Wilsnack, R. W., & Klassen, A. D. (1986). Epidemiological research on women's drinking, 1978–1984. In National Institute on Alcohol Abuse and Alcoholism (Ed.), *Women and alcohol: Health-related issues* (Research Monograph No. 16, DHHS Pub. No. ADM86-1139, pp. 1–68. Washington, DC: U.S. Government Printing Office.

THREE

The Physical Effects of Alcohol

Alcoholic beverages come in many different forms and types such as wine, beer, and distilled spirits or hard liquor. It is a popular belief that different types of alcoholic beverages produce different effects. Klein and Pittman (1990) surveyed a national sample of more than 2,000 people to identify their perceptions of the relationship of wine, beer, and distilled spirits to various alcohol problems. Distilled spirits and beer were blamed to a much greater extent than wine for problems such as fighting, rowdiness, and drunken driving.

All alcoholic drinks, however, contain the same active ingredient, called *ethyl alcohol* or *ethanol*. Depending on the type of beverage, ethanol's percentage of the total volume ranges from low levels of around 3 to 4 percent for beer and around 12 to 14 percent for wine, to higher levels such as 45 to 50 percent for distilled spirits such as liquor. But regardless of whether the beverage is beer, wine, or liquor, or any of the myriad variants of these three basic types, if the amount of ethanol consumed is equivalent, the same type of physiological and behavioral effects should occur.

Alcohol is a depressant of the central nervous system, although the expectation and typical reaction of drinkers in many situations is exactly the opposite, that of disinhibition or excitation. Thus, Lukas and Mendelson (1988) found that after consuming a moderate amount of alcohol, nonalcoholic volunteers reported feelings of improved well-being for a short period following drinking.

To better understand the actions of alcohol on the body, we will examine what happens after alcohol is consumed. Evidence concerning the short-term or acute effects on the nervous system will be followed by findings about the long-term effects on major systems of the body.

What Happens to a Drink?

Since alcohol is a beverage, it must first enter the drinker's mouth and then go down the esophagus and enter the stomach. Alcohol is an irritant—as anyone who has taken a shot of straight hard liquor can attest—to the mucous membrane linings of the gastrointestinal tract. Most people prefer to mix their distilled spirits in decorative but diluted concoctions to avoid this irritant. Although a small loss of alcohol occurs through perspiration or urination, more than 95 percent of it is absorbed directly and quickly through the linings of the stomach and small intestine into the bloodstream for distribution to the rest of the body. If the drink has been diluted or the person has recently eaten food, the absorption may be slowed down.

Alcohol or ethanol is primarily metabolized by the liver, where the enzyme alcohol dehydrogenase (ADH) breaks ethanol down into acetaldehyde (ACH). This toxic ingredient is then broken down further by another enzyme called aldehyde dehydrogenase (ALDH) into acetate, and then to water and carbon dioxide, products that are nontoxic and will be eliminated from the body. If the rate of alcohol ingestion exceeds the capacity of the liver to detoxify ethanol, the result is an accumulation of alcohol with an attendant intoxicating effect on the drinker, as evidenced by slurred speech, staggering, and impaired perceptual motor coordination. Upon recovery of sobriety, the drinker may encounter the unpleasant experience of a "hangover" as the price for the previous evening's excessive use of alcohol. As Samuel Butler, a 17th-century English poet, astutely observed long ago, "If the headache would only precede the intoxication, alcoholism would be a virtue."

Blood Alcohol Concentration (BAC)

The amount of alcohol consumed is one obvious important factor in determining its effects on the drinker. One index commonly used to identify the level of consumption is the blood alcohol level (BAL) or concentration (BAC).

Breath analyzers are instruments such as gas chromatographs that appraise ethanol concentrations based on breath samples. This measure is indirect but is more convenient than the use of actual blood or urine samples. However, because ethanol concentrations are not equal throughout all parts of the body, indirect measures are not without flaws. Such measures underestimate the BAL in the most important area, the brain, which has the most impact on behavior. Despite this shortcoming, breath samples are reasonably reliable indexes of blood alcohol level.

A commonly used index of blood alcohol concentration is the weight in grams or milligrams of alcohol in 100 milliliters of blood, expressed as a percentage, mg %. The relationship between BAC and the number of drinks consumed within the past hour for persons of varying weight is depicted in Figure 3-1. A "drink" here refers to a mixed drink containing 1¼ ounces of liquor or 4 ounces of wine or a

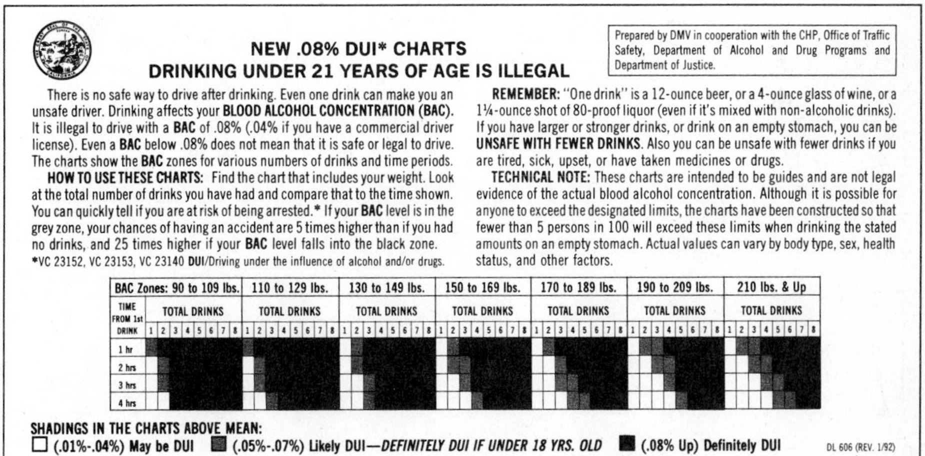

Figure 3-1 BAC as a function of number of drinks, time since drinking, and weight.

Source: from California Office of Traffic Safety, California Department of Alcohol and Drug Programs and California Department of Justice. Reprinted by permission.

12-ounce can of beer, each containing a comparable amount of alcohol. As a rough guide, each drink consumed within an hour increases the BAC by about .03 mg. %.

The value used to define unacceptable levels for driving an automobile legally varies, but a reading of .10 is common. A generation ago, levels of .15 were commonly acceptable (Thompson, 1956), but some states have lowered the limit to .08. A BAC of .10 indicates that one-tenth of 1 percent of the blood contains alcohol. Using a "typical" 150 lb. male for illustrative purposes, this level might be obtained by drinking three to four drinks within the past hour. A female of equivalent body weight, however, will have a higher concentration due to the higher percentage of body fat in females. But many factors—such as past drinking experience, time since last meal, or use of drugs—moderate the effect of a given amount of alcohol. There will also be individual differences depending on the age, size, and health of the drinker.

Temporal Aspects of BAC

As alcohol is absorbed into the blood and circulated throughout the body, the BAC rises to a peak. If the BAC over time is represented as a curve, the *ascending* limb of the BAC curve refers to the portion between the end of drinking until a peak level is obtained, as shown in Figure 3-2. As alcohol is metabolized and eliminated from the body, the BAC level declines from the peak level. The *descending* limb of the BAC curve is the section following the peak until the ethanol level is reduced to

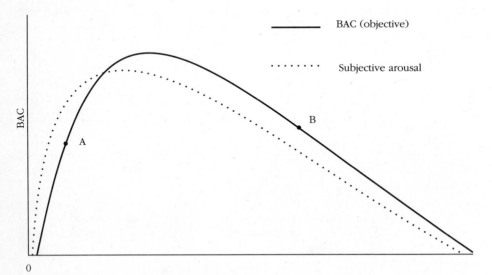

Figure 3-2 Changes in BAC (objective) and subjective arousal over time after drinking. At points A and B the BAC level is equal, but on the ascending limb subjective arousal at point A is higher than objective BAC, whereas on the descending limb at point B, subjective arousal is lower than objective BAC.

zero. For any BAC level less than the peak, there are two points where that level occurs, one on the ascending and one on the descending limb.

The *subjective* effect of a specific BAC level differs, depending on whether that given value is on the ascending (see point A in Figure 3-2) or on the descending limb of the curve (see point B in Figure 3-2). Due to the process of adaptation by which we tend to notice less and less as time goes by, we tend to feel less intoxicated at point B on the descending limb than at point A on the ascending limb of the curve for the same BAC level. Nonetheless, the actual impairment of sensory motor functions may be the same for a given level regardless of which limb we are dealing with. But since the subjective experience is one of less intoxication on the descending limb, the drinker may be willing to undertake risks such as driving a car even though the BAC level is still dangerously high. Thus, a drinker may stop drinking well before trying to drive home from a party. The BAC has already peaked and is now on the descending limb, and although it may still be high, the drinker subjectively feels more sober than is warranted and therefore feels ready to get behind the wheel and drive.

Tolerance

The transition between being a beginning or light drinker and a problem drinker or alcoholic is usually gradual. The old Chinese saying "First a man takes a drink, then the drink takes a drink, and then the drink takes the man" illustrates the insidious nature of alcoholism. As one drinks regularly over time, *tolerance* for alcohol is developed. The same amount of alcohol that previously produced a given effect is no longer adequate. A higher amount is now required to produce the same effect. What is commonly referred to as holding one's liquor seems to reflect this typical adaptation process. With more tolerance the drinker underestimates the true BAC, often leading the drinker to take greater risks.

The gap between anticipated and subjective (actual) reactions to alcohol may differ with the drinker's experience with alcohol. Gabrieli, Nagoshi, Rhea, and Wilson (1991) compared expected and experienced effects of alcohol in 387 male and female drinkers against observer ratings. Based on their drinking history, subjects were classified into three levels of consumption: high, moderate, and low. Subjects consumed alcohol in the laboratory to produce a BAL that was the equivalent of two drinks an hour over two hours. They then took a battery of tests measuring sensory-motor performance, performance on cognitive and perceptual tasks, and autonomic responses. Assessments of their euphoria and feelings of intoxication were made by subjects as well as by trained observers.

Anticipated sensitivity was measured by drinker ratings of the extent to which they expected to experience intoxication, negative emotions, and euphoric emotions after four drinks. Subjective perceptions of mood after drinking were assessed with a mood inventory. In addition, observers rated the drinkers for intoxication, negative emotions, and euphoric emotions. The results showed that heavy drinkers tended to underestimate alcohol effects (objective ratings higher than subjective ratings) whereas the inexperienced, light drinkers tended to overestimate (objective ratings lower than subjective ratings) alcohol effects.

Based on the fact that the observer ratings showed more impairment for the heavy than for the lighter drinkers, Gabrieli et al. concluded that heavy drinkers may underestimate alcohol effects due to tolerance. Observer ratings of the effects of alcohol were generally greater than either the anticipated or the subjective ratings of effects made by the drinkers. Gabrieli et al. suggested that heavy drinkers may be likely to develop further problems because they don't expect that actual effects of alcohol will be as high as they are.

Withdrawal

Since alcohol is a central nervous system depressant, there is a tendency for a rebound effect of hyperexcitability when its effects wear off after a drinking episode ends (Linnoila, 1989). This acute withdrawal involves highly variable symptoms ranging from sweating, tremors, and anxiety to seizures, hallucinations, and delirium. With higher degrees of drinking, as with alcoholics and chronic heavy drinkers, the magnitude of this withdrawal reaction is more pronounced. The irritability and discomfort experienced during the lack of alcohol is precisely what triggers the addicted drinker to redose with more alcohol. Hence, a vicious and escalating cycle is generated.

Clinical observations of the magnitude and prevalence of withdrawal may sometimes underestimate the intensity of the adverse reactions since many alcoholics are admitted into hospitals following only a brief period of intoxication or have usually been given a sedative, which tends to diminish withdrawal reactions.

A more dramatic picture of withdrawal reactions was reported in a classic laboratory study (Isbell, Fraser, Wikler, Belleville, & Eisenman, 1955) in which alcohol was made freely available to ten hospital patients who were healthy morphine addicts who had not used narcotics for three months. Most of the patients drank for 48 to 87 days before alcohol was suddenly withheld from them. Within 8 to 16 hours after detoxification, an acute withdrawal syndrome occurred that included a number of symptoms such as perspiration, weakness, tremor, nausea, irritability, sleep disturbance, diarrhea, and elevated blood pressure. In some cases, grand mal seizures occurred within 48 to 96 hours after alcohol was withheld. In two cases, delirium tremens, involving extreme tremors and hallucinations, occurred.

Withdrawal symptoms can last up to several days, but with medical care, the detoxification involves less severe reactions than reported by Isbell et al. The typical medical treatment involves use of benzodiazepines (such as Librium, Valium) and vitamins to sedate the hyperexcitability of the nervous system. Barbiturates have also been used but involve the risk of cross-tolerance so that the patient may adapt quickly and fail to benefit. Newer drugs such as clonidine and beta adrenergic blockers have been employed successfully (Liskow & Goodwin, 1987). As the symptoms abate, the medical treatment is gradually reduced.

Sleep Disturbance

Chronic alcohol use has been found to disrupt sleep. Sleep involves several distinguishable stages, identified by electroencephalogram (EEG) brain wave recordings (Dement, 1976). These phases, stages 1–4 and rapid eye movement (REM) sleep, repeat themselves over five cycles of about 90 minutes duration each during the course of a night's sleep. REM sleep, the last stage in each cycle, is the time when dreams appear to be most prevalent.

The acute effects of alcohol appear to be sedative. Rundell, Lester, Griffiths, and Williams (1972) examined sleep patterns of young nonalcoholic males after they received a single dose of alcohol and found quicker sleep onset, reduced latency of slow wave sleep in stages 3 and 4, and abbreviated REM. In the second half of the night, levels of REM sleep rebounded, as if compensating for earlier losses. In repeated dose studies, the effects found on the first night disappeared. In contrast, chronic alcohol use seems to increase arousal, possibly through the destruction of, or release of, biogenic amines such as serotin and norepinephrine (Lester, Rundell, Cowden, & Williams, 1973).

Among alcoholics, drinking acts to suppress the REM stage of sleep and disrupt dreaming (Williams & Salamy, 1972). In addition, chronic alcoholics undergo fragmented sleep with frequent interruptions of wakefulness (Johnson, Burdick, & Smith, 1970). As a result, they often drink more in an attempt to induce sleep, but unfortunately this behavior is self-defeating and further accentuates the disruption.

Acute Effects of Alcohol

Acute effects of alcohol consist of its immediate or short-term influence during an episode of drinking, whereas chronic effects involve the long-term consequences of alcohol use over a long period of repeated use. We will consider acute effects before turning to a more detailed examination of chronic effects.

In determining acute effects, it should be noted that they may differ for populations varying in drinking history. Specifically, acute effects should differ for light drinkers or nondrinkers and alcoholics since the latter develop tolerance with repeated exposure to alcohol. Laboratory studies of acute effects typically, but not always, use nonalcoholics who receive small doses (one to two drinks) of alcohol. Ethical issues would arise if large doses were administered to either nonalcoholics or alcoholics (National Advisory Council on Alcohol Abuse and Alcoholism, 1989), so such procedures are rare.

When differences are observed between alcoholics and nonalcoholics following alcohol consumption, it is tempting to conclude that any observed deficits in the alcoholics are due to their chronic use of alcohol. But comparisons of the acute effects of alcohol on alcoholics and nonalcoholics may be confounded by other factors correlated with alcohol use. Alcoholics may differ from nonalcoholics in ways other than the amount of alcohol consumed, such as personality traits or physical health. Some of these factors may be responsible for, or at least contribute to, any differences observed between alcoholics and nonalcoholics in reactions to alcohol.

One problem is that without a longitudinal comparison in which at least two different measurement times are involved it is not possible to rule out the chance that some initial differences existed among the two populations prior to the development of alcoholism in one group. These initial differences—for example, in metabolism of alcohol—could be responsible for the differences observed later between alcoholic and nonalcoholic groups. However, in this example, we could not conclude that these differences were the *result* of alcoholism. These differences might instead represent the continuing influence of factors that contributed to the development of alcoholism in the first place.

Types of Evidence

A variety of methods have been used to determine the effects of alcohol on the nervous system, including anatomical evidence available from autopsies, neurological correlates, and behavioral evidence. The three types of evidence are not always in agreement. Anatomical differences observed between alcoholics and nonalcoholics or in before/after comparisons of individual alcoholics may reflect causes, effects, or simply correlates of alcoholism. These differences may or may not also be accompanied by detectable neurological and behavioral differences. Similarly, neuropsychological differences may not involve functional consequences for behavior.

The rapid development of more advanced computer techniques has offered impressive new technology for study of the relationship of brain structure, functioning, and alcohol use. A review by Pfefferbaum and Rosenbloom (1990) described research with tools that examine anatomical structure with three-dimensional images such as scans by computerized tomography (CT) and magnetic resonance imaging (MRI) to improve our visualization of the physical structure of the brain. Research with CT has shown brain tissue shrinkage and more cerebrospinal fluid in the resulting larger ventricles in alcoholics. However, this shrinkage appears to reverse somewhat under abstinence. Use of MRI, which unlike CT can distinguish between white and gray matter (two different types of brain tissue), has revealed that alcoholics have greater decreases in both gray and white matter than do age-matched controls.

However, as noted earlier, structural differences do not necessarily imply functional differences. Use of techniques such as positron emission tomography (PET) and cerebral blood flow (CBF) enables measurement of the brain processes, as opposed to structures, by the examination of changes over time in the distribution and accumulation of oxygen and other chemicals in the brain with and without the presence of alcohol. These measures are highly indirect indexes of actual physiological processes, obtained through the tracing of radioactive materials introduced into the body, and are still open to interpretation. PET studies (Chao & Foudin, 1986) as well as research with CBF (Risberg & Berglund, 1987) have suggested there may be reduced blood flow and cerebral glucose utilization in alcoholics, again with evidence that these processes can be reversed with abstinence.

Central Nervous System

Alcohol affects the central nervous system through a complex process. The basic unit of the nervous system is the neuron. These approximately 1 trillion cells (Charness, 1990) send and receive neurochemical information to and from each

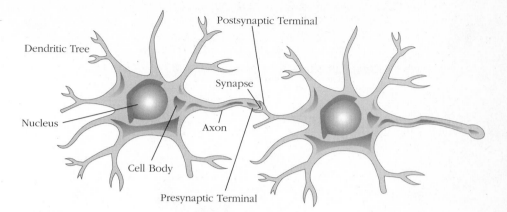

Figure 3-3 Components of neuronal structure.
Source: from "Alcohol and the brain," by M.E. Charness, in *Alcohol Health and Research World, 1990, 14(2),* 85–89.

other. Each neuron has a network of dendrites or fiber endings that extend into the spaces between cells known as *synapses* to receive information. Then the cells send the information forward to the dendrites of as many as 1,000 adjacent neurons through their single axons, fibers that extend beyond the cell body. Figure 3-3 shows two adjacent neurons, with the sending neuron referred to as the *presynaptic cell* and the receiving neuron termed the *postsynaptic cell.*

Neuron Membrane Processes. Ion channels, which are proteins on the neuron membrane, regulate the action potential or flow of electrically charged chemicals called ions through pores in the cell membrane. Ions, in turn, effect neural transmission through the cell. The G proteins in the cell, as shown in Figure 3-4, are activated in this process to admit important chemicals known as neurotransmitters across the synapse from one neuron into adjacent or postsynaptic neurons. Neurotransmitters, described in more detail later, regulate the flow of information among the neurons throughout the nervous system.

Consumption of alcohol, unlike other addictive drugs, does not affect specific brain receptors but appears to influence the nervous system at the level of the neuronal membrane (Harris & Buck, 1990). Alcohol disrupts the typical balance of the half protein and half lipid composition of the membrane, altering the passage of other chemicals in and out of the neuronal cells. As shown in the box "Summary of Major Effects of Alcohol on Neurons," alcohol increases the chloride ion entry through the actions of GABA, an inhibitory neurotransmitter, so that there is reduced neuronal excitability. Alcohol also inhibits the amino acid glutamate, the major excitatory neurotransmitter responsible for allowing higher levels of calcium ions into cells, primarily through the N-methyl-D-aspartate (NMDA) receptor, with the net effect of creating a sedative influence.

Processes within Each Neuron. Important regulatory functions and metabolism within each neuron involve enzymes called *secondary messengers,* so named

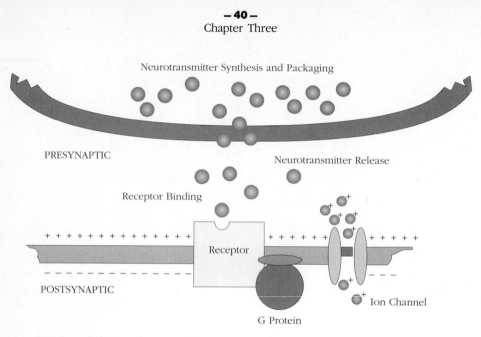

Figure 3-4 Synaptic transmission.
Source: from "Alcohol and the brain," by M.E. Charness, in *Alcohol Health and Research World, 1990, 14(2),* 85–89.

because they pass information from receptors on the membrane to the inner part of the neuron. One especially important messenger is cyclic guanine monophosphate (cGMP), which is generated by the NMDA receptor. Another secondary messenger, cyclic adenosine monophosphate (cAMP), is valuable for its role in molecular synthesis of RNA. Both of these secondary messenger systems appear to be disrupted by the actions of ethanol (Tabakoff & Hoffman, 1987) and could be the basis for the observed acute effects of alcohol on behavior.

Neurotransmitters. Neural messages move from individual neurons to other neurons throughout the nervous system. Chemicals known as *neurotransmitters* such as dopamine, serotonin, and norepinephrine are released to serve this communicative function among neurons (Charness, 1990). Each neuron has different receptor sites that appear to recognize or accept the different types of incoming neurotransmitters across the synaptic junction, the gap separating each neuron from nearby neurons. When a specific type of neurotransmitter is received at the membrane of the postsynaptic neuron, it "binds" to or fits the receptor site in much the same way a key opens a lock. This process modifies the permeability of the receptor so that it increases or decreases the excitability of that cell, depending on the specific neurotransmitter. According to Tabakoff, Hoffman, and Petersen (1990), the levels of these important neurotransmitters appear to be altered by the consumption of alcohol. These changes may be an important factor in determining the influence that alcohol has on behavior and experience.

Serotonin (5-hydroxytryptamine or 5-HT) is an important regulator of mood and consummatory behavior such as eating that is diminished by heavy alcohol use or may be naturally lower for alcoholics. Violent and impulsive behaviors have also been associated with lowered serotonin levels, according to Lidberg, Tuck, Asberg, Scalia-Tomba, and Bertilsson (1985). Tabakoff et al. (1990) speculated that alcoholics may be self-medicating with alcohol in a futile attempt to increase their serotonin levels. One of the new developments for countering the assumed consequences of low serotonin levels such as depression typically observed among alcoholics is the use of serotonin uptake inhibitors (SUI) such as fluoxetine or Prozac to block the depletion of this neurotransmitter.

Dopamine (DA) is a neurotransmitter that may underlie rewarding and pleasurable experiences. It appears to first increase with alcohol use but eventually shows a decline wth continued drinking. This pattern parallels the subjective effects of alcohol for many drinkers. Norepinephrine (NE) is often higher with increasing arousal such as stressful situations. Alcohol seems to be associated with higher levels of NE, even after withdrawal develops.

Another category of neurotransmitters, called neuropeptides, includes the tetrahydroisoquinolines (THIQs) that are created in the brain from the combination of dopamine with the acetaldehyde resulting from alcohol metabolism.

Davis and Walsh (1970), using laboratory animals, found that alcohol may increase the levels of THIQs produced by the brain. THIQs seem to induce preference for alcohol, possibly through actions at opiate receptors in the brain. As with other endogenous opiates such as endorphins, THIQs are capable of reducing pain. Like other opiates, they are addictive and the individual may experience craving following withdrawal.

There may be a genetic factor determining the levels of THIQs, as some studies (Schuckit, 1984) found that sons of alcoholics produce higher levels of THIQs than sons of nonalcoholics. This view fits with the findings that acetaldehyde levels following alcohol consumption were higher among individuals from families with a positive history of alcoholism (Schuckit & Rayses, 1979). One interpretation is that THIQs may mediate the intoxication and even the withdrawal reactions to drinking alcohol. Thus, the addictive basis of alcoholism may involve the inherited tendency among some drinkers to generate higher levels of THIQs from their alcohol intake than other drinkers who do not tend to develop alcohol problems.

Peripheral Nervous System

The peripheral nervous system is also affected by alcohol. Traditionally, the portion known as the autonomic nervous system has been conceived of as an autonomous system that is beyond voluntary control. It is involved with maintaining homeostasis or balance between bodily processes and environmental demands. When individuals are faced with stressful and emotional situations, their cardiovascular responsiveness may be reduced by alcohol (Sher, 1987).

Alcohol also affects the somatic nervous system, which is involved with motor coordination and static ataxia (body sway). The inability of most drinkers to walk a straight line when intoxicated vividly illustrates this point. However, individuals considered to have high risk for alcoholism show less motor impairment following alcohol consumption (Schuckit, 1987) than those at lower risk.

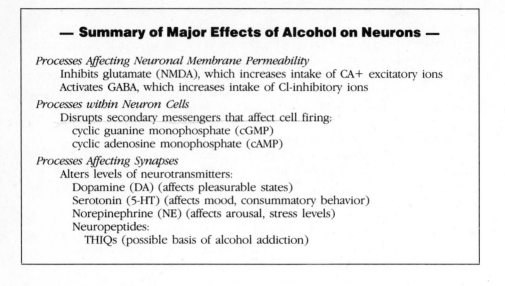

— Summary of Major Effects of Alcohol on Neurons —

Processes Affecting Neuronal Membrane Permeability
 Inhibits glutamate (NMDA), which increases intake of CA+ excitatory ions
 Activates GABA, which increases intake of Cl-inhibitory ions

Processes within Neuron Cells
 Disrupts secondary messengers that affect cell firing:
  cyclic guanine monophosphate (cGMP)
  cyclic adenosine monophosphate (cAMP)

Processes Affecting Synapses
 Alters levels of neurotransmitters:
  Dopamine (DA) (affects pleasurable states)
  Serotonin (5-HT) (affects mood, consummatory behavior)
  Norepinephrine (NE) (affects arousal, stress levels)
  Neuropeptides:
   THIQs (possible basis of alcohol addiction)

Chronic Effects of Alcohol

We now turn to a description of the effects of long-term alcohol use on the body. Specifically, we will examine its effects on the brain, the liver, the gastrointestinal tract, the muscles, the cardiovascular system, the immune system, and the reproductive system. We will also look at alcohol's role in cancers and fetal alcohol syndrome.

Brain

Comparison of alcoholics and nonalcoholics shows that wider sulci (the gaps between the convolutions of the outer layer of the cerebral cortex) and larger cerebral ventricles (cavities) exist among alcoholics that parallel changes typically found with aging. Measures of the electrical activity in areas of the brain with noninvasive techniques such as the EEG and event-related potentials (ERP) have shown differences between alcoholics and nonalcoholics (Begleiter, Porjesz, Bihari, & Kissin, 1984). For example, a widely used ERP measure is the P300 wave, so called because it occurs 300 milliseconds after a stimulus is presented. It is regarded as a measure of cognitive processing of sensory stimulation and attention to incoming stimuli. Lower amplitudes of the P300 wave have been found in response to sensory tests (Begleiter et al., 1984) among sober alcoholics, suggesting that they may have impaired cognitive or attentional ability.

Such differences have also been found in sons of alcoholics even prior to the development of alcoholism in the offspring (Patterson, Williams, McLean, Smith, & Schaffer, 1987). Furthermore, this impairment has been found to persist after treatment for alcoholism.

Liver

The liver serves as the main detoxifier (Lieber, 1984; 1988) for the metabolic breakdown of alcohol. As pointed out earlier, the enzymes alcohol dehydrogenase (ADH) and aldehyde dehydrogenase (ALDH) work to eliminate alcohol from the body. In addition, an alternative mechanism for eliminating alcohol has been identified, the microsomal ethanol-oxidizing system that seems to allow heavy drinkers to metabolize alcohol more rapidly (Lieber & DiCarli, 1970). As long as the rate of intake does not exceed the elimination rate, the liver should function adequately. But when drinking rates increase, it cannot keep up and may eventually sustain damage. The average adult can oxidize one drink in approximately one hour.

Chronic heavy alcohol use can also cause a buildup of triglycerides or fatty tissues in the liver, impairing its capacity to metabolize alcohol (Rubin & Lieber, 1968). In addition, hepatitis or inflammation of liver tissue may occur from excessive alcohol intake. For many, but not all, hepatitis leads to cirrhosis of the liver, which involves the formation of scarring tissue so that it can no longer effectively eliminate the ethanol from the body. The extent to which the liver is damaged by alcohol abuse has been found (Frezza et al., 1990) to be greater for women because they have a smaller capacity for metabolizing alcohol during the first pass through the liver.

Ironically, after heavy chronic drinking damages the liver of alcoholics, a *reverse* tolerance effect occurs in which less alcohol is needed to produce a given effect. Due to liver disease caused either by alcohol or other factors, there is a reduced capacity for metabolizing the alcohol consumed so that the drinker will become intoxicated at lower levels of consumption.

Normal functions of the liver include the production of bile for digestion of fats; albumin, which helps regulate fluid balance in cells of the whole body; globulin, which helps fight infections; and prothrombin, which helps clot blood in order to stop wounds from bleeding. Chronic alcohol abuse can impair all of these vital functions of the liver.

Gastrointestinal Tract

From the mouth, alcohol must traverse the esophagus, stomach, and duodenum to reach the small intestines, where the majority of it is released into the bloodstream. Although low doses of alcohol may stimulate secretion of digestive juices, larger doses act to inhibit them as well as irritate mucous membranes (Gottfried, Korsten, & Lieber, 1976) and produce adverse effects throughout the gastrointestinal tract. Acute intake of alcohol activates gastric oversecretion, which can lead to gastric hemorrhages, while chronic use of alcohol impairs gastric acid secretion (Cook, 1981). The tendency of alcoholics to use aspirin to reduce their discomfort is another factor affecting bleeding. These processes can produce lesions in the small intestine, where nutrients are absorbed into the blood system. The consequence is a reduction in the uptake of important amino acids, glucose, vitamins, and electrolytes.

Other parts of the gastrointestinal tract such as the pancreas are also adversely affected by chronic alcohol use (Fenster, 1982; Van Thiel et al., 1981). Digestive enzymes ordinarily produced by the pancreas are blocked by alcohol-induced swelling of cells, leading to malnutrition. Eventually the enzymes break out of the pancreatic linings creating acute hemorrhagic pancreatitis, which causes severe abdominal pain, nausea, and vomiting. Another function of the pancreas is the production of insulin, which helps convert blood sugars into stored energy. Damage to the pancreas impairs insulin production, resulting in a secondary form of diabetes.

Muscle Systems

Skeletal or striated muscle that is under voluntary control can be damaged by alcohol abuse (Rubin, 1979). Myopathy, a disorder involving muscle weakness, cramps, and pain occurs with excess chronic alcohol consumption. Smooth or involuntary muscle has recently been found to be adversely impacted by alcohol abuse as well. Thus, alcohol reduces sphincter pressure in the lower esophagus (Hogan, Viegas De Andrade, & Winship, 1972).

Cardiovascular System

The cardiovascular system includes the heart and the circulatory system of arteries and veins that extend throughout the body. The heart, which is actually a muscle, although a very vital and special type, pumps blood through this network to carry oxygen and nutrients throughout the body as well as remove waste materials.

Cardiomyopathy is damage to the heart that impairs its ability to contract and reduces its effectiveness in pumping blood (Rubin, 1979), leading to shortness of breath, fatigue, palpitations, and eventually in many cases, congestive heart disorders (Regan, 1990). Although heart disease gradually develops from years of drinking, there is evidence it can be reversed with abstinence.

There is some controversy, however, about the effects of drinking on the heart. Epidemiological studies (for example, Klatsky, Friedman, & Siegelaub, 1979) of male drinkers found that those who drank a moderate (one to two drinks per day) amount of beer were actually less likely than nondrinkers to suffer coronary arterial diseases such as myocardial infarction (heart attack). The conclusion was drawn that moderate drinking might bestow some protective chemical, possibly high-density lipoprotein cholesterol (Criqui, 1990), associated with more alcohol intake, that reduces the risk of heart attack. Alternatively, alcohol may thin the blood, reducing risks of embolism (blood clots).

However, other interpretations are also possible dealing with lifestyle factors such as diet, exercise, or coping skills. Perhaps nondrinkers are too tense and rigid in comparison with moderate drinkers, who have a more relaxed attitude. Thus, it might be this generally lower reaction to stress rather than consumption of alcohol per se that is responsible for the presumed benefits and lower rate of heart attacks for moderate drinkers. However, it should be noted that among drinkers, those who consume the most are at the highest risk of heart attacks, possibly due to the acetaldehyde produced by drinking. This toxic metabolic byproduct of alcohol may cause enlargement of the mitochondria, impairing their function of providing energy for heart contractions (Lange & Kinnunen, 1987).

Shaper (1990) questioned conclusions from studies of more than 7,700 middle-aged men in the United Kingdom showing that drinking one to two drinks per day was associated with lower mortality than for nondrinkers. He argued that many of the nondrinkers may have been heavy ex-drinkers who had had to reduce their consumption for health reasons. Therefore, the long-term harm of such earlier abuse, rather than their current lack of drinking, may have contributed to the higher mortality rate found among these now nondrinkers. However, this view is challenged by later research (Klatsky, Armstrong, & Friedman, 1986) that found no differences between ex-drinkers, infrequent drinkers, and lifelong abstainers in risk for hospitalization for myocardial infarction. Also, mortality rates did not differ for ex-drinkers and lifelong abstainers (Klatsky, Armstrong, & Friedman, 1990).

Whether one or two drinks a day help in reducing coronary arterial disease, abundant evidence exists that such benefits of drinking are offset by the higher risk of other types of cardiovascular disease—such as strokes, arrythmia, and hypertension—attributed to chronic alcohol abuse (MacMahon, 1987).

Cancers

Cancers of the oral cavity, pharynx, and larynx appear to occur more often in heavy drinkers (Elwood, Pearson, Skippen, & Jackson, 1984). However, since many heavy drinkers also tend to be heavy smokers, any link between drinking and cancer could partly be due to the role of smoking. Most sections of the gastrointestinal tract have also shown higher risk for cancer due to heavy drinking (Lieber, Seitz, Garro, & Worner, 1979).

A number of possible mechanisms by which ethanol might cause cancer have been proposed (Lieber, Garro, Leo, & Worner, 1986), including contact-related localized effects, nutritional and vitamin deficiencies, disruptions of DNA metabolism, induction of microsomal enzymes that activate carcinogens, and disruption of immune system responsiveness. Driver and Swann (1987) noted that ethanol may not directly produce cancers but may instead act through disruption of the enzymes that control carcinogens.

Among women, one of the leading causes of cancer deaths is breast cancer (Podolsky, 1986). Williams and Horm (1977) examined the relationship between alcohol use and breast cancer in more than 7,500 cases and concluded that drinkers were from 1.2 to 1.6 times more likely to have breast cancer than nondrinkers. However, other studies (for example, Webster, Wingo, Layde, & Ory, 1983) have not confirmed these findings. Feinstein (1988) argued that some of the inconclusiveness is due to methodological problems in some of the epidemiological studies on this topic.

Immune System

Closely related to the adverse role of alcohol in the incidence of cancer is the evidence that alcohol abuse may disrupt the body's abilities to combat certain infectious diseases due to decreased white blood cells such as lymphocytes, macrophages, and neutrophils, which kill bacterial invasions (Lieber et al., 1979). However, many other independent factors such as malnutrition, infection, and liver diseases unrelated to alcoholism may also undermine the immune system.

Thus far, there is no evidence of a direct effect of alcohol on the acquired immune deficiency syndrome (AIDS), according to Kaslow et al. (1989). Alcohol may indirectly affect AIDS if it serves to increase other behaviors known to contribute to AIDS such as unsafe sex practices or sharing of needles among drug users. In addition, alcohol might indirectly worsen conditions for those already infected by disrupting their already impaired immune systems.

Reproductive System

Among males, ethanol may lower the male sex hormone testosterone, at least temporarily (Cicero, 1982). With alcoholics, sexual impotence and impaired performance may also result (Van Thiel, 1983). Even if they are able to consummate sexual activity, fertility may be impaired because alcohol reduces the seminal fluids that enable the ejaculated sperm to travel rapidly in order to fertilize ova.

Alcohol does not spare females from sexual dysfunction either (Hugues et al., 1980; Mello, 1988), as alcohol abuse may be related to impaired menstruation, ovarian atrophy, spontaneous abortion, and infertility. It is unclear whether these outcomes are due to direct toxic effects of alcohol on the hypothalamus, pituitary gland, or ovaries, or due to alcohol-induced fluctuations in hormones such as estrogen and progesterone that fluctuate over the menstrual cycle (Lex, 1991). The precise mechanisms for these disruptions are complex and may not entail direct effects of alcohol. For example, other alcohol-related diseases such as liver dysfunction or malnutrition stemming from alcohol abuse could disrupt sex hormones, menstruation, or ovulation.

Fetal Alcohol Syndrome (FAS)

For centuries, there has been a suspicion that alcohol consumption is undesirable for pregnant women. Children of alcoholic mothers were observed to be impaired in physical and psychological development. In ancient Carthage, a ritual against drinking alcohol by newlyweds on the wedding night was observed as a precaution against alcohol-induced birth defects (Smith, 1982).

However, it was not until the 1970s (Jones, Smith, Ulleland, & Streissguth, 1973; Streissguth, Herman, & Smith, 1978) that scientific research produced evidence for a fetal alcohol syndrome (FAS). It is estimated that there are from 1 to 3 cases of FAS per 1,000 births (U.S. Department of Health and Human Services, 1983), although the rates are much higher among some lower socioeconomic groups, especially Native Americans and African Americans. Estimates also depend on the methodology. Prospective data based on observations at the time of birth tend to produce lower estimates because some symptoms do not appear until a few years later, whereas retrospective studies that link mental retardation to recall of the mothers' earlier drinking, during pregnancy tend to yield much higher rates. Abel and Sokol (1987), in a survey of studies conducted worldwide, found rates of FAS as high as

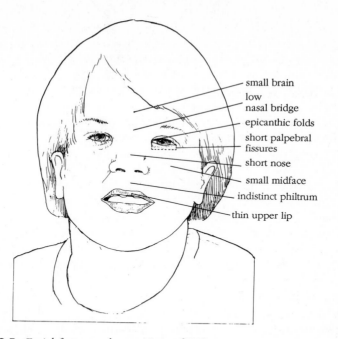

small brain

low
nasal bridge

epicanthic folds

short palpebral
fissures

short nose

small midface

indistinct philtrum

thin upper lip

Figure 3-5 Facial features characteristic of FAS.

Source: from "Teratogenic effects of alcohol in humans and laboratory animals," by A. P. Streissguth, S. Landesman-Dwyer, J. C. Martin, & D. W. Smith in *Science (1980), 209,* 353–361. Copyright © 1980 by the American Association for the Advancement of Science. Reprinted by permission.

2.9 per 1,000 in retrospective studies, compared to 1.1 per 1,000 in prospective studies.

The FAS baby has a low birth weight and a retarded pattern of physical growth. As shown in Figure 3-5, it is characterized by a pattern of facial malformations including small head circumference, misshapen eyes, flattened midface, sunken nasal bridge, and elongated philtrum (the vertical groove between the nose and mouth). Other malformations may occur in major internal organs as well. The central nervous system shows abnormal functioning and there is evidence of neurobehavioral impairment. Behaviorally, the FAS baby may exhibit abnormal neonatal development, sleep problems, childhood hyperactivity, and mental retardation.

A ten-year follow-up on 8 of the 11 young children (2 had died) in the original study of FAS was reported by Streissguth, Clarren, and Jones (1985). These in-dividuals' deficits were still pronounced, in both the physical and the psychological dimensions. They were below average in height and weight and also had de-veloped new problems such as hearing and vision problems. Four were severely mentally retarded and the other 4 were borderline retarded.

Whereas a drink or two might produce a BAC level that might be considered safe for an adult woman (for example, .05 mg. %), it represents a much stronger concentration for the much smaller fetus that shares the same blood content with the mother. The toxic levels may be particularly hazardous during the first trimester of pregnancy (Clarren, Alvord, Sumi, Streissguth, & Smith, 1978), when developmental changes are greater, a period when the drinking woman is unfortunately less likely to know she is pregnant.

Only a small percentage of the children of alcoholic mothers suffer FAS, suggesting that a number of factors may combine with the alcohol abuse to exert these damaging irreversible effects. But it seems clear that there is considerable risk to unborn children of heavily drinking expectant mothers.

Less extreme, but still worrisome, problems may occur for pregnant women who drink at much lower levels than alcoholics or problem drinkers. The Seattle Pregnancy and Health Study (Streissguth, Martin, Martin, & Barr, 1981) has examined about 500 children born to white middle-class married women. Subtle neurological and behavioral deficits were found in proportion to the amount of alcohol consumed during pregnancy (Streissguth et al., 1984). The extent to which the mother drank during pregnancy was correlated with the degree to which newborn infants were slower to habituate to or tune out a repeated stimulus and slower to begin sucking to an appropriate stimulus.

Deficits on these indexes of attention persist throughout childhood. At age 4, children whose mothers drank more during pregnancy scored more poorly on vigilance and reaction time tasks, suggesting that the alcohol may have impaired neonatal neurological development. These less severe effects, referred to as fetal alcohol effects (FAE), as opposed to the more severe fetal alcohol syndrome (FAS) found with children of alcoholic mothers, occurred even for women with modest levels of drinking.

The percentage of alcoholic women, let alone social drinkers, whose babies develop these problems is actually small in absolute terms. Of course, if your baby is the one with the abnormality, it is no consolation to know that others drank similar or even greater amounts without damaging their child. The dilemma for expectant mothers is deciding whether the risk of an FAE or FAS child due to drinking is worth taking. In many states public establishments that serve alcohol now are required to post warning signs about the dangers of alcohol for pregnant women, but it is unclear how effective they are.

Conclusions

Alcohol is rapidly absorbed into the bloodstream and affects the central nervous system. By altering the membranes of neurons, alcohol affects the normal balance of neurotransmitters. These changes produce a depressant effect on the central nervous sytem. Low or moderate amounts of alcohol can be detoxified or eliminated from the body by the liver efficiently so that the toxic byproducts of alcohol metabolism such as acetaldehyde are prevented from accumulating. Tolerance for alcohol develops with continued use so that the same dose produces a diminished effect, which leads many drinkers to increase the amount consumed.

When used excessively over a long period of time, alcohol can produce a number of serious physical and medical problems in most major systems of the body. While some of the effects may be direct, as in the case of fatty liver, other effects may be indirect, such as malnutrition or bodily injury due to accidents and falls. Chronic effects may occur even for those for whom the acute effects may have been minimal. Thus, an alcohol abuser may function well on a daily basis for years as the nervous system develops tolerance for alcohol. However, when alcohol is not available, the alcoholic will experience highly unpleasant withdrawal reactions involving physical discomfort, agitation, and irritability.

Long-term excessive alcohol consumption impairs the functioning of all major organs so that eventually most alcoholics will be confronted with a physical toll of damage stemming from the cumulative effects of alcohol. In particular, damage to the liver disrupts the ability to detoxify alcohol as efficiently as in the past so that reversal in tolerance occurs, with less alcohol producing the same effect that formerly required more alcohol. Due to the long delay between drinking and these types of adverse effects, it is not surprising that the physical consequences of chronic excessive drinking are very difficult to detect and prevent.

Considerable publicity has been given to epidemiological studies that suggest coronary arterial disease is lower for men who drink moderately, implying that drinking is beneficial for the cardiovascular system. However, other interpretations of these results have not been ruled out. Furthermore, even if coronary arterial disease is alleviated by moderate use of alcohol, there may be a trade-off since other types of cardiovascular disease such as cardiomyopathy, strokes, and hypertension appear to be more likely to occur with chronic alcohol use.

Alcohol consumption by pregnant women may have profoundly damaging, irreversible effects on the physical and mental condition of the developing fetus. Pregnant women who drink, then, carry a double burden of potential harm to the fetus as well as to themselves. A moving personal and factual account (Dorris, 1989) of the nature of FAS and the impact it has on the family can be found in a book, *The Broken Cord,* written by M. Dorris, the father of an FAS child.

References

Abel, E. L., & Sokol, R. J. (1987). Incidence of fetal alcohol syndrome and economic impact of FAS-related anomalies. *Drug and Alcohol Dependence, 19,* 51–70.

Begleiter, H., Porjesz, B., Bihari, B., & Kissin, B. (1984). Event-related potentials in boys at risk for alcoholism. *Science, 225,* 1493–1496.

Chao, H. M., & Foudin, L. (1986). Symposium on imaging research in alcoholism. *Alcoholism (NY), 10,* 223–225.

Charness, M. E. (1990). Alcohol and the brain. *Alcohol Health and Research World, 14,* 85–89.

Cicero, T. (1982). Alcohol-induced deficits in the hypothalamic-pituitary-luteining hormone axis in the male. *Alcoholism (NY), 6,* 207–215.

Clarren, S. K., Alvord, E. C., Jr., Sumi, S. M., Streissguth, A. P., & Smith, D. W. (1978). Brain malformations related to prenatal exposure to ethanol. *Journal of Pediatrics, 92,* 64–67.

Cook, P. J. (1981). The effects of liquor taxes on drinking, cirrhosis and auto accidents. In M. H. Moore & D. R. Gerstein (Eds.), *Alcohol and alcohol policy: Beyond the shadow of prohibition* (pp. 255–285). Washington, DC: National Academy Press.

Criqui, M. (1990). Comments on Shaper's "Alcohol and mortality: A review of prospective studies": The reduction of coronary heart disease with light to moderate alcohol consumption: Effect or artifact? *British Journal of Addiction, 85,* 854–857.

Davis, V. E., & Walsh, M. J. (1970). Alcohol, amines, and alkaloids: A possible biochemical basis for alcohol addiction. *Science, 167,* 1005–1107.

Dement, W. C. (1976). *Some must watch while some must sleep.* San Francisco: San Francisco Book.

Dorris, M. (1989). *The broken cord.* New York: Harper & Row.

Driver, H. E., & Swann, P. F. (1987). Alcohol and human cancer (review). *Anticancer Research, 7,* 309–320.

Elwood, J. M., Pearson, J.C.G., Skippen, D. H., & Jackson, S. M. (1984). Alcohol, smoking, social and occupational factors in the aetiology of cancer of the oral cavity, pharynx, and larynx. *International Journal of Cancer, 34,* 603–612.

Feinstein, A. R. (1988). Scientific standards in epidemiologic studies of the menace of daily life. *Science, 242,* 1257–1263.

Fenster, L. F. (1982). Alcohol and disorders of the gastrointestinal system. In N. J. Estes & M. E. Heinemann (Eds.), *Alcoholism: Development, consequences, and interventions* (pp. 136–143). St. Louis: C. V. Mosby.

Frezza, M., DiPadova, C., Pozzato, G., Terpin, M., Baraona, E., & Lieber, C. S. (1990). High blood alcohol levels in women: The role of decreased gastric alcohol dehydrogenase. *New England Journal of Medicine, 322,* 95–99.

Gabrieli, W. F., Jr., Nagoshi, C. T., Rhea, S. A., & Wilson, J. R. (1991). Anticipated and subjective sensitivities to alcohol. *Journal of Studies on Alcohol, 52,* 205–214.

Gottfried, E. B., Korsten, M. A., & Lieber, C. S. (1976). Gastritis and duodentitis induced by alcohol: An endoscopic and histologic assessment (abstract). *Gastroenterology, 70,* A-32, 890.

Harris, R. A., & Buck, K. J. (1990). The processes of alcohol tolerance and dependence. *Alcohol Health and Research World, 14,* 105–110.

Hogan, W. J., Viegas De Andrade, S. R., & Winship, D. H. (1972). Ethanol induced acute esophageal motor dysfunction. *Journal of Applied Physiology, 32,* 755–760.

Hugues, J. N., Cofte, T., Perret, G., Jayle, M. S., Sebaoun, J., & Modigliani, E. (1980). Hypothalamo-pituitary ovarian function in 31 women with chronic alcoholism. *Clinical Endocrinology, 12,* 543–551.

Isbell, H., Fraser, H. F., Wikler, A., Belleville, R. E., & Eisenman, A. J. (1955). An experimental study of the etiology of "rum fits" and delirium tremens. *Quarterly Journal of Studies on Alcohol, 16,* 1–33.

Johnson, L. C., Burdick, H. A., & Smith, J. (1970). Sleep during alcohol intake and withdrawal in the chronic alcoholic. *Archives of General Psychiatry, 22,* 406–418.

Jones, K. L., Smith, D. W., Ulleland, C. N., & Streissguth, A. P. (1973). Pattern of malfunction in offspring of chronic alcoholic mothers. *Lancet, 1,* 1267–1271.

Kaslow, R. A., Blackwelder, W. C., Ostrow, D. C., Yerg, D., Palenicek, J., Coulson, A. H., & Valdiserri, R. O. (1989). No evidence for a role of alcohol or other psychoactive drugs in accelerating immunodeficiency in HIV-1 positive individuals. *Journal of American Medical Association, 261,* 3424–3429.

Klatsky, A. L., Armstrong, M. A., & Friedman, G. D. (1986). Relations of hospitalization. *American Journal of Cardiology, 58,* 710–714.

Klatsky, A. L., Armstrong, M. A., & Friedman, G. D. (1990). Risk of cardiovascular mortality in alcohol drinkers, ex-drinkers and nondrinkers. *American Journal of Cardiology, 66,* 1237–1242.

Klatsky, A. L., Friedman, G. D., & Siegelaub, A. B. (1979). Alcohol use, myocardial infarction, sudden cardiac death, and hypertension. *Alcoholism: Experimental and Clinical Research, 3,* 33–39.

Klein, H., & Pittman, D. J. (1990). Perceived consequences associated with the use of beer, wine, distilled spirits, and wine cooler. *International Journal of the Addictions, 25,* 471–493.

Lange, L. G., & Kinnunen, P. M. (1987). Cardiovascular effects of alcohol. *Advances in Alcohol and Substance Abuse, 6,* 47–52.

Lester, B. K., Rundell, O. H., Cowden, L. C., & Williams, H. L. (1973). Chronic alcoholism, alcohol, and sleep. In M. M. Gross (Ed.), *Alcohol intoxication and withdrawal: Experimental studies* (pp. 261–279). New York: Plenum Press.

Lex, B. W. (1991). Some gender differences in alcohol and polysubstance users. *Health Psychology, 10,* 121–132.

Lidberg, L., Tuck, J. R., Asberg, M., Scalia-Tomba, G. P., & Bertilsson, L. (1985). Homicide, suicide and CSF 5-HIAAA. *Acta Psychiatrica Scandinavica, 71,* 230–236.

Lieber, C. S. (1984). Alcohol and the liver: 1984 update. *Hepatology, 4,* 1243–1260.

Lieber, C. S. (1988). Metabolic effects of ethanol and its interaction with other drugs, hepatotoxic agents, vitamins, and carcinogens: A 1988 update. *Seminars on Liver Disease, 8,* 47–68.

Lieber, C. S., & DiCarli, L. M. (1970). Hepatic microsomal ethanol-oxidizing system: In vitro characteristics and adaptive properties in vivo. *Journal of Biological Chemistry, 245,* 2505–2512.

Lieber, C. S., Garro, A. J., Leo, M. A., & Worner, T. M. (1986). Mechanisms for the interrelationship between alcohol and cancer. *Alcohol and Research World, 10,* 10–17.

Lieber, C. S., Seitz, H. K., Garro, A. J., & Worner, T. M. (1979). Alcohol-related diseases and carcinogenesis. *Cancer Research, 39,* 2863–2886.

Linnoila, M. (1989). Alcohol withdrawal syndrome and sympathetic nervous system function. *Alcohol Health and Research World, 13,* 355–357.

Liskow, B. I., & Goodwin, D. W. (1987). Pharmacological treatment of alcohol intoxication, withdrawal and dependence: A critical review. *Journal of Studies on Alcohol, 48,* 356–370.

Lukas, S., & Mendelson, J. (1988). Behavioral concomitants of ethanol and drug reinforcement. In L. S. Harris (Ed.), *Problems of drug dependence, 1987* (Research Monograph No. 81, DHHS Pub. No. ADM88–1564, pp. 422–427). Rockville, MD: National Institute on Drug Abuse, 1988.

MacMahon, S. (1987). Alcohol consumption and hypertension. *Hypertension, 9,* 111–121.

Mello, N. K. (1988). Effects of alcohol abuse on reproductive function in women. In M. Galanter (Ed.), *Recent developments in alcoholism* (pp. 253–276). New York: Plenum Press.

National Advisory Council on Alcohol Abuse and Alcoholism. (1989). *Recommended council guidelines for ethyl alcohol administration in human experimentation.* Rockville, MD: National Institute on Alcohol Abuse and Alcoholism.

Patterson, B. W., Williams, H. L., McLean, G. A., Smith, L. T., & Schaffer, K. W. (1987). Alcoholism and family history of alcoholism: Effects on visual and auditory event-related potentials. *Alcohol, 4,* 265–269.

Pfefferbaum, A., & Rosenbloom, M. J. (1990). Brain-imaging tools for the study of alcoholism. *Alcohol Health and Research World, 14,* 219–231.

Podolsky, D. M. (1986). Alcohol consumption and the risk of breast cancer. *Alcohol Health and Research World, 10,* 40–43.

Regan, T. J. (1990). Alcohol and the cardiovascular system. *Journal of the American Medical Association, 264,* 377–381.

Risberg, J., & Berglund, M. (1987). Cerebral blood flow and metabolism in alcoholics. In O. A. Parsons, N. Butters, & P. E. Nathan (Eds.), *Neuropsychology of alcoholism: Implications for diagnosis and treatment.* New York: Guilford Press.

Rubin, E. (1979). Alcoholic myopathy in heart and skeletal muscle. *New England Journal of Medicine, 301,* 28–33.

Rubin, E., & Lieber, C. S. (1968). Alcohol-induced hepatic injury in nonalcoholic volunteers. *New England Journal of Medicine, 278,* 869–876.

Rundell, O. H., Lester, B. K., Griffiths, W. J., & Williams, H. L. (1972). Alcohol and sleep in young adults. *Psychopharmacologia, 26,* 201–218.

Schuckit, M. (1984). Prospective markers for alcoholism. In D. W. Goodwin, K.T.V. Dusen, &

S. A. Mednick (Eds.), *Longitudinal research in alcoholism* (pp. 147–169). Boston: Kluwer-Nijhoff.

Schuckit, M. (1987). Biological vulnerability to alcoholism. *Journal of Consulting and Clinical Psychology, 55,* 301–309.

Schuckit, M. A., & Rayses, V. (1979). Ethanol ingestion: Differences in blood acetaldehyde concentrations in relatives of alcoholics and controls. *Science, 203,* 54–57.

Shaper, A. G. (1990). Alcohol and mortality: A review of prospective studies. *British Journal of Addiction, 85,* 837–847.

Sher, K. J. (1987). Stress response dampening. In H. T. Blane & K. E. Leonard (Eds.), *Psychological theories of drinking and alcoholism* (pp. 227–271). New York: Plenum Press.

Smith, D. W. (1982). Fetal alcohol syndrome: A tragic and preventable disorder. In N. J. Estes & M. E. Heinemann (Eds.), *Alcoholism: Development, consequences, and interventions* (2nd ed., pp. 187–192). St. Louis: C. V. Mosby.

Streissguth, A. P., Clarren, S. K., & Jones, K. L. (1985). Natural history of the fetal alcohol syndrome: A 10-year follow-up of eleven patients. *Lancet, II,* 85–91.

Streissguth, A. P., Herman, C.S., & Smith, D. W. (1978). Intelligence, behavior, and dysmorphogenesis in the fetal alcohol syndrome: A report on 20 patients. *Journal of Pediatrics, 92,* 363–367.

Streissguth, A. P., Landesman-Dwyer, S., Martin, J. C., & Smith, D. W. (1980). Teratogenic effects of alcohol in humans and laboratory animals. *Science, 209,* 353–361.

Streissguth, A. P., Martin, D. C., Barr, H. M., Sandman, B. M., Kirchner, G. L., & Darby, B. L. (1984). Intrauterine alcohol and nicotine exposure: Attention and reaction time in four-year-old children. *Deveopmental Psychology, 20,* 533–541.

Streissguth, A. P., Martin, D. C., Martin, J. C., & Barr, H. M. (1981). The Seattle longitudinal prospective study on alcohol and pregnancy. *Neurobehavioral Toxicology and Teratology, 3,* 223–233.

Tabakoff, B., & Hoffman, P. L. (1987). Biochemical pharmacology of alcohol. In H. Y. Meltzer (Ed.), *Psychopharmacology of alcohol: The third generation of progress* (pp. 1521–1526). New York: Raven Press.

Tabakoff, B., Hoffman, P. L., & Petersen, R. C. (1990). Advances in neurochemistry: A leading edge of alcohol research. *Alcohol Research and Health World, 14,* 138–143.

Thompson, G. N. (1956). *Alcoholism.* Springfield, IL: Charles C Thomas.

U.S. Department of Health and Human Services. (1983). *Fifth Special Report to the Congress on Alcohol and Health.* Washington, DC: U.S. Government Printing Office.

Van Thiel, D. H. (1983). Ethanol: Its adverse effects on the hypothalamic-pituitary-gonadal axis. *Journal of Laboratory Clinical Medicine, 101,* 21–33.

Van Thiel, D. H. & Lester, R. (1979). The effect of chronic alcohol abuse on sexual function. *Clinics in endocrinology and Metabolism, 8,* 499–510.

Van Thiel, D. H., Lipsitz, H. D., Poreter, L. E., Schade, R. R., Gottlieb, G. P., & Graham, T. O. (1981). Gastrointestinal and hepatic manifestations of chronic alcoholism. *Gastroenterology, 81,* 594–615.

Webster, L. A., Wingo, P. A., Layde, P. M., & Ory, H. W. (1983). Alcohol consumption and risk of breast cancer. *Lancet, 2,* 724–726.

Williams, H. L., & Salamy, A. (1972). Alcohol and sleep. In B. Kissin & H. Begleiter (Eds.), *The biology of alcoholism. Vol. 2. Physiology and behavior* (pp. 435–483). New York: Plenum Press.

Williams, R. R., & Horm, J. W. (1977). Association of cancer sites with tobacco and alcohol consumption and socioeconomic status of patients: Interview study from the Third National Cancer Survey. *Journal of the National Cancer Institute, 48,* 527–547.

FOUR

The Psychological Effects of Alcohol: Nonsocial Behaviors

What is the effect of drinking alcohol on major aspects of behavior and experience? In this chapter we will examine findings about the relationship between alcohol consumption and several important psychological processes. Identifying the underlying mechanisms by which alcohol produces its effects is a central goal of this research. *Pharmacological* explanations attribute these effects to the chemical influence of the alcohol. However, *psychological* factors may also be partly or entirely responsible. Many effects of alcohol that are attributed to pharmacological factors are partly due to the social context of the drinking and to the expectations of the drinker. For example, at a party people expect to have a good time. Alcohol may be consumed and people may later regard the alcohol to have been a major factor behind the pleasant experience. However, the alcohol may not have been the primary cause of the happy experiences because most of the people present would have had a positive experience anyway. Nonetheless the belief that alcohol is a social lubricant may have led to the attribution that it was alcohol that produced or at least enhanced the positive experiences. Alcohol, because it also may relieve anxiety or tension, can facilitate the occurrence of pleasurable experiences by "allowing" the drinker to forget conscious controls and inhibitions. In other contexts, drinking can lead to quite different effects. For instance, when an angry and frustrated crowd drinks heavily, aggressive and hostile feelings and violent behavior may be unleashed.

Expectancies about the effects of alcohol, which will be discussed further in Chapter 5, may also be determined by the individual's background, knowledge, and past experiences with alcohol. Whatever the source, these factors are psychological rather than pharmacological in nature. To understand how alcohol affects behavior, it is necessary to analyze the contributions of both types of factors. In this chapter, we will do so while focusing on nonsocial behavior: cognition, mood and emotion, and sensory-motor activity. We begin by considering the methodology used by researchers studying alcohol's effects on behavior.

Methodology

Controlled versus Uncontrolled Observation

Two major research methods have been used to examine how alcohol affects behavior and experience. *Naturalistic* or *uncontrolled observation* examines correlations between alcohol use and behavioral outcomes. Often, several alternative interpretations of an observed relationship are possible. For example, it might be observed that those who consume more alcohol during lunch work less efficiently after lunch. One interpretation of this evidence is that the alcohol has a negative effect on work performance.

However, an alternative explanation is that workers who drink more at lunch are different from those who drink less in some other important aspect related to work performance. It is possible, for instance, that workers who are less motivated or under more stress might be more likely to drink more at lunch. Even without the influence of alcohol, then, their work would be inferior compared to the performance of those who drink less. *Self-selection* may be operating here, with those who drink more being psychologically different from those who drink less. Consequently, we cannot safely attribute the differences in work performance entirely to the differences in alcohol consumption in this case.

The second major method for obtaining evidence is the *experiment* or *controlled observation*. To study the question just described using an experiment, two groups of workers would be formed *randomly,* and one group would arbitrarily be assigned the task of drinking heavily during lunch. The other group would be instructed to drink only a small amount. Under this method, self-selection on the basis of drinking history would be prevented from creating any differences in work observed between the two groups.

Since the only systematic difference between the two groups would be the amount of alcohol consumed during lunch, it would be more likely that differences in work performance after lunch could be explained in terms of the effects of alcohol. The problem with experimental evidence is that it may not be highly generalizable to behavior under natural conditions, where the level of drinking, for example, is not an "assigned" activity but is one that involves a voluntary or self-determined decision.

In this chapter we will discuss research using both types of methods. It is important when evaluating and interpreting the findings of each study to note the strengths and weaknesses of the method used. Uncontrolled observations are often useful in generating ideas or hypotheses that can then be evaluated more carefully through controlled observations to rule out alternative explanations. Thus, combining evidence obtained from both methods is often most effective.

Expectancy Controls and the Balanced Placebo Design

Earlier laboratory experiments on the effects of alcohol on behavior included a test condition to control for the expectancy of receiving alcohol by administering a placebo (nonalcoholic beverage) to subjects who were told that it contained alcohol. In this traditional design, any differences in behavior between these subjects and those in another group who expected *and* received alcohol were attributed to the effect of alcohol. But this procedure failed to assess any influence that expectancy of receiving alcohol per se may have contributed, since both groups expected alcohol. Because this type of expectancy was equal across the two conditions, investigators could not detect any impact that mere expectancy of consuming alcohol might have exerted on psychological experiences and behavior.

An elaborate research design known as the *balanced placebo design* was developed by Marlatt, Demming, and Reid (1973) to address this issue. As shown in Figure 4-1, this design isolates pharmacological and psychological effects by using four different test conditions. Half the subjects receive an alcoholic beverage such as vodka mixed with tonic in a 1:5 proportion and half receive a nonalcoholic beverage such as tonic water, disguised to resemble a cocktail. To increase credibility, a small amount of alcohol may be rubbed around the top of the glass to provide

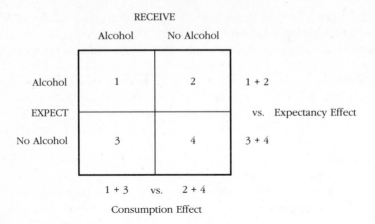

Figure 4-1 The balanced placebo design.

the odor of alcohol. In addition, half of each of these two groups is told that they have an alcoholic drink while the other half is told that they have a nonalcoholic beverage.

This complex design allows the evaluation of a *consumption effect* by comparison of the combined two groups that receive alcohol (groups 1 and 3) with those combined two groups that do not (groups 2 and 4), regardless of whether they expect alcoholic beverages. In addition, it allows the assessment of an *expectancy effect* by comparison of the combined two groups that expect alcohol (groups 1 and 2) with those combined two groups that do not expect alcohol (groups 3 and 4), regardless of what they actually receive. Interaction effects also can be examined with this design to see if the effect of alcohol varies, depending on the type of expectancy. Thus, alcohol consumption might produce a difference in some behavior if the drinkers believe they are drinking (expect to receive) an alcoholic beverage, but might not have an effect if they believe they are consuming a nonalcoholic drink.

To minimize confusion, it is important to keep in mind that two different types of expectancy will be discussed in this chapter, expectancies about the *effect* of alcohol and expectancies about the *type of beverage* that will be received, alcoholic or nonalcoholic. In natural settings, we receive the type of beverage that we expect to have; hence, we cannot isolate the pharmacological effect of alcohol from the effect of expecting to receive an alcoholic beverage. In contrast, a balanced placebo design used in the laboratory is able to separate these effects. Some drinkers receive the type of beverage they expect, while others do not receive the type of beverage expected. When the term *expectancy* is used in connection with experiments, most of the time it refers to this expectation about the type of beverage that will be consumed and not to the expected effects of alcohol.

Marlatt and Rohsenow (1980) found that the expectancy of having received even a small dose of alcohol such as one drink has a stronger effect on cognitive processes than whether alcohol was in fact consumed, at least for light-to-moderate drinkers. Thus, expectancy per se may play a major role in affecting behavior, producing effects that would have been attributed entirely to pharmacological factors in studies that did not use the balanced placebo design.

One limitation of the balanced placebo design is that not everyone may have identical beliefs or expectancies about alcohol's effects. And in the few experiments where different expectations about alcohol's effects are provided to different groups, these expectations may not be equally credible. All the balanced placebo design can do is control who believes they had alcohol and who does not; it does not determine if the subjects have different expectancies about the effects of alcohol. Another limitation is that it can only be used with low doses of alcohol, below a BAC of .04 mg. % (Martin, Earleywine, Finn, & Young, 1990), because problems of credibility (or ethics) arise if large doses of alcohol are given to subjects who are misinformed that they are receiving nonalcoholic beverages.

Cognition

Alcohol use has been found to have an effect on cognitive functions such as memory, verbal skills, and visual-spatial-motor coordination. We will examine these effects and the explanations proposed for them.

Acute Effects on Memory

Early models of human memory implied that similar processes were involved across a variety of memory tasks, but a wide variety of memory processes and models have been proposed subsequently (Klatsky, 1980). Memory can involve short-term recall of either recent information and events or long-term memory of information acquired long ago. Distinctions exist (Tulving, 1983) between memory involving knowledge about general versus specific information (semantic versus episodic memory). Different cognitive processes may occur in different aspects of memory such as encoding, storage, and retrieval of information. Hastroudi and Parker (1986) suggested that the acute effects of alcohol are selective, impairing some, but not all, aspects of memory.

Parker and Noble (1977) administered several cognitive tasks to middle-aged male professionals, of whom 36 percent were classified as heavy drinkers, 55 percent moderate drinkers, and 9 percent light or nondrinkers. Except for the heavy drinkers whose performance was impaired by alcohol, they found no effect of drinking on memory on a free recall task where a list of words was presented and was to be recalled in any order. They also found no correlation between the *frequency* of drinking and cognitive performance when age was controlled to adjust for the fact that age is correlated with drinking level and possibly, memory. However, *abstract* conceptual performance was inversely related to the amount consumed per occasion, suggesting that even among social drinkers alcohol can be a factor that is disruptive to cognitive functioning.

Craik (1977) distinguished between the effects of alcohol on different depths of cognitive processing. He found parallels between the types of cognitive deficits associated with aging and those due to intoxication, with both showing greater deficits when the tasks required deeper processing and attention. If the task required reflection or conscious integration of information, intoxication was harmful to performance, but on tasks that activated preexisting semantic structures, there was no noticeable impairment of performance. Thus, sorting words into different categories based on their meaning or comprehending prose passages was unaffected by intoxication.

Hartley, Birnbaum, and Parker (1978) presented intoxicated and sober subjects with a sentence frame task in which they had to decide whether a particular word fit the blank space in a sentence frame. Three levels of sentence complexity were used. This type of task is more complex than simple recall because elaborative processing of the material is involved. Subjects then received an unannounced memory test of the words they had judged. Recall was poorer for the intoxicated subjects. Even providing the sentence frames later as a retrieval cue failed to reduce the deficit in comparison to the sober subjects.

Studies with the balanced placebo design have generally shown expectancy, but not consumption, effects on memory (Marlatt & Rohsenow, 1980). Poorer memory occurred if subjects thought they had consumed alcohol. In other words, what they believed they would drink, alcohol or placebo, was more important than what they actually received. Some studies, however, have produced conflicting findings. MacVane, Butters, Montgomery, and Farber (1982), for example, found that male social drinkers were not adversely affected by expectancies of drinking alcohol on a concept learning task.

Peterson, Rothfleisch, Zelazo, and Pihl (1990) found consumption, but not expectancy, effects, perhaps because they used a higher alcohol dose. They gave a test battery assessing delayed memory, planning and foresight, word fluency, vocabulary, abstract thinking, reaction time, and pursuit-rotor tracking to college male social drinkers following one of three dose levels. The highest alcohol dose, which produced BALs of approximately .10 mg. %, impaired delayed memory functions, paralleling deficits in clinical patients known to have temporal lobe lesions.

Cognitive functions such as verbal fluency and planning, known to be related to injury to the prefrontal area of the cerebrum, were also disrupted by high doses of alcohol. The pursuit-rotor task, which involves more complex motor coordination, also believed to be controlled by the frontal lobe, was impaired by alcohol, but speed of motor control as measured by reaction time was not. In contrast, measures of general intelligence such as vocabulary and recall of general information were not affected by alcohol.

But other plausible explanations for the relationship between alcohol consumption and poorer cognitive functioning can be offered. Grant (1987) suggested the possibility that less intelligent persons may drink more excessively, or that other factors such as anxiety could produce both poorer cognitive performance and higher drinking levels. Either of these hypothesized factors, lower intelligence or higher anxiety, could lead to the observed relationship between drinking levels and cognitive performance. Parsons (1986) also pointed out that most studies of alcohol effects on cognition in nonalcoholic drinkers have used volunteers rather than random samples, a factor that might restrict generalizability.

Parsons (1986), as well as Grant (1987), concluded after reviews of many studies that the evidence about the effect of alcohol on cognition is inconsistent. Some disagreement may be due to the types of tasks and the drinking histories of the subjects used in different studies. For example, Hastroudi and Parker (1986) proposed that alcohol produces a subtle impairment not noticed even by the drinker on some, but not all, types of memory tasks. Parsons (1986) also suggested that the type of task is important, with those involving nonverbal abstraction, new learning, memory, and perceptual-motor performance being more sensitive to alcohol effects.

Chronic Effects on Memory

A comparison (Williams & Skinner, 1990) of heavy with moderate to infrequent drinkers who were matched in terms of age, sex, socioeconomic level, and education showed much poorer performance by the heavy drinkers on a battery of cognitive, verbal, and logical reasoning tasks. These deficits were even greater among those with lower education.

One possible physical basis for cognitive deficits stemming from chronic heavy alcohol use is the Wernicke-Korsakoff syndrome (Martin, Adinoff, Weingarter, Mukherjee, & Eckhardt, 1986), a set of disorders attributed to organic brain damage. Wernicke's disease, a disorder involving confusion, ataxia (body sway), and ocular disturbances such as diplopia (double vision), is assumed to be due to thiamine deficiency and other vitamin deficits associated with prolonged alcohol use. Korsakoff's psychosis involves a short-term memory impairment (alcoholic amnestic disorder) that occurs despite the ability to engage in other intellectual activities (Berman, 1990). With this disorder, also known as anterograde amnesia, the alcoholic has difficulty remembering recent events and learning new information. In addition, alcoholism may result in a dementia, or global deficit of intellectual function, so that abstraction and judgment are impaired.

A different interpretation (Berman, 1990) of these impairments views the memory deficits as part of a syndrome of interrelated disruptions due to alcohol that also involve emotion and motivation. Thus, poorer attention, lower motivation, and diminished affect due to alcohol consumption might all contribute to poorer performance on memory tasks. Memory, this interpretation reminds us, is not a function that operates independently of other processes.

Events experienced while intoxicated may not be recalled when the subject is later tested under sober conditions, a phenomenon commonly referred to as a *blackout*. This consequence of chronic heavy drinking is not to be confused with passing out or fainting, because the drinker is conscious during blackouts. There is evidence (Goldman, 1983; Ryan & Butters, 1983) that some of these cognitive deficits are partially or completely reversible by a period of abstinence.

Blackouts are similar to a laboratory phenomenon involving alcohol and memory known as *state-dependent learning* (Weingartner & Faillace, 1971). Information learned while under the influence of alcohol may be better recalled later if the test is administered when the individual has been drinking and not, as might be assumed, when sober. This finding suggests that memory is better if the cues associated with the event to be remembered are similar to those present at the time the event was originally experienced. However, there is no evidence that memories of events that occurred during blackouts are recalled better when the drinker consumes alcohol again.

Neuropsychological Impairment and Its Explanations

Impaired neuropsychological functioning due to damage or atrophy of cerebral hemispheres as well as inner regions of the brain such as the limbic system and diencephalon may result from chronic drinking (Berman, 1990). Performance of sober alcoholics on the Halstead-Reitan test—a battery of items consisting of tasks based on functions such as speech, finger tapping, or pursuit-rotor tracking, which involve a variety of brain areas—is impaired in comparison to age-matched controls, but not to the extent found among patients with traumatic head injury who presumably suffer from brain damage.

Parsons and Leber (1981) proposed three hypotheses for the neuropsychological basis of cognitive deficits among alcoholics: the diffuse/generalized effects hypothesis, the frontal lobe hypothesis, and the right hemisphere hypothesis. In addition, Jones and Parsons (1971) pointed out the similarity between alcohol effects and aging effects, leading to a premature aging hypothesis of the effects of alcohol.

The Diffuse/Generalized Effects Hypothesis. This hypothesis holds that alcohol impairs both hemispheres of the brain more or less equally, so that all functions are disrupted by alcohol to the same extent. In contrast, the next two hypotheses assume that deficits are specific to certain areas of the brain.

The Frontal Lobe Hypothesis. Evidence for localized brain damage in the frontal lobes was sought by Parsons and Leber (1981), who compared performance of older chronic alcoholics and brain-damaged patients on visual-spatial tasks involving a series of problems. Alcoholics did as well as controls on initial problems, but with successive problems they performed more poorly than controls. Both alcoholics and brain-damaged patients were found to be equally impaired in comparison to control patients. Parsons and Leber concluded that the deficit is not perceptual or verbal per se but involves errors due to perseverative tendencies of responses from earlier problems creating errors on later problems. Because impairment of attention is associated with the frontal lobe and limbic system, these researchers inferred that alcohol might produce frontal lobe damage.

The Right Hemisphere Hypothesis. Verbal skills were less impaired than the visual-spatial-motor coordination of alcoholics in studies by Tarter (1975) and by Jenkins and Parsons (1981). The lateralization of brain function has been well documented, with evidence showing that the verbal functions are served by the left hemisphere while the visual-spatial-motor skills are controlled by the right hemisphere. Therefore, the pattern of impairment found with alcoholism led to the hypothesis that the right hemisphere might be an area where damage is likely.

Early studies (for example, Jones & Parsons, 1971) found that relative to controls, alcoholics showed little impairment on tasks controlled by the left side of the brain (verbal), whereas performance on tasks involving the right side of the brain (nonverbal or spatial) was disrupted. Researchers concluded that chronic alcohol use may impair the functioning of the right hemisphere.

A study by Goodglass and Peck (1972) employed a dichotic listening task in which auditory cues were presented to either ear. The task was to press the key on either the left-hand or the right-hand side, depending on whether the auditory cue had been presented to the left or right ear, respectively. Alcoholics, in comparison to controls, had longer reaction times when the cue was presented to the left ear, suggesting that the right hemisphere (which governs left-side functions) had suffered more damage from alcohol use.

Some disagreement exists about the validity of the right hemisphere hypothesis as an explanation for these findings of performance deficits. Several reservations were offered by Ellis and Oscar-Berman (1989). For one thing, visual and verbal tasks are heterogenous categories. All tasks of either category may not be controlled by the brain in the same manner. In contrast to studies supporting the right hemisphere hypothesis, studies by Ryan (1980), Ryan and Butters (1986), and Bolter and Hannon (1986) involving tasks with greater attentional demands have shown that alcoholics can show impairment on verbal tasks as well as on nonverbal tasks.

It is possible that when less impairment occurs on verbal than on visual tasks, factors other than differential damage to brain hemispheres may be operating. Ellis and Oscar-Berman (1989) argued that the two tasks (verbal and nonverbal) were confounded with task difficulty, with the nonverbal being more difficult. Consequently, the complexity of strategies used by subjects would differ for the two types of tasks. Thus, alcoholics may do less well whenever the task involves elaboration of strategies, as would be the case for many verbal tasks. But if a verbal task does not require such elaboration, they should not be as impaired.

Studies (for example, Oscar-Berman, 1988) using perceptual asymmetry tasks such as dichotic listening tasks in which different stimuli are directed toward each ear yielded results that also called the right hemisphere hypothesis into question. Alcoholics showed no differences from age-matched controls on these tasks in producing ear advantages of the same type.

The Premature Aging Hypothesis. Jones and Parsons (1971) noted the similarity between right hemisphere function deficits found in alcoholics and impairments that are thought to be a function of organic deterioration in aging. The parallel has led to the suggestion that chronic alcoholics suffer premature aging of the central nervous system.

An alternative explanation for the same pattern is the age sensitivity hypothesis, a view that older brains are more vulnerable to alcohol impairment than younger brains. This version (see Chapter 15) argues that the results reflect a differential vulnerability, where young alcoholics show no difference from nonalcoholics, but older alcoholics show impairment relative to controls. In general, the impairments due to age differences exceed those found between alcoholics and age-matched controls, implying that the effects of alcoholism on cognition are not the same as those of aging.

In addition, it appears that some deficits in cognitive functioning found in alcoholics may be recovered following a period of abstinence. Goldman (1983) noted that some impairments on cognitive tasks found during the first week of abstinence disappear two to four weeks later. Ryan and Butters (1986) found that the abnormal EEG brain wave pattern in alcoholics showed some degree of recovery of function after three to six weeks of abstinence. Since recovery of cognitive deficits from aging does not generally occur, this finding challenges the premature aging hypothesis.

Mood and Emotion

Drinking is often motivated by the belief that alcohol can decrease negative affective or mood states such as anxiety and tension and increase positive or pleasurable moods. Researchers have attempted to measure these effects in the laboratory, with mixed findings. We will examine some of these findings, and factors that may account for the discrepancies.

Changes Over the BAC Curve

One factor that may be responsible for conflicting findings is that different studies may have assessed mood at different points of the BAC curve without recognizing that the effect of alcohol changes over the course of the BAC curve. Sutker, Tabakoff, Goist, and Randall (1983) assessed BAC at several points after nonproblem drinkers received a small dose of alcohol. They found that when the BAC was rising, drinkers felt elated and stimulated, but when the BAC had peaked and was descending, they felt depressed and tired. This biphasic effect of alcohol may reflect both physical and psychological factors. At the physical level, the central nervous system is depressed by alcohol, allowing disinhibition of restraints and the experience of pleasurable feelings. Then, after drinking stops and the BAC starts to decline, there is an opposite rebound of negative feeling states. At the psychological level, there may be anticipation of tension relief during the early part of a drinking episode, followed by fatigue and regret after drinking ends and the BAC declines.

The Effect of Dose Level

A different but related aspect of alcohol consumption that affects mood is dose level. Unfortunately, many studies that examine the effect of alcohol on mood with college subjects have used only one dose, usually a small amount consisting of one to two drinks, and the results may not be generalizable to large amounts. Tucker, Vuchinich, and Sobell (1982) recommended that studies compare mood for several dose levels administered to the same subjects to provide a more valid test. In addition, because BAC is a joint function of dose and time since drinking, they suggested that mood be assessed at several time points, at baseline before drinking starts and during the ascending as well as the descending limbs of the BAC curve.

The Expectancy Effect

The failure to separate expectancy from pharmacological factors is another weakness of most studies prior to the use of the balanced placebo design in the mid-1970s. The balanced placebo design allows a comparison of the extent to which expectancies alone influence the affective reactions to alcohol, separate from the effect of alcohol.

Unfortunately, the evidence with this design is not consistent. Mood enhancement occurred with greater alcohol consumption in some studies when expectancy was controlled (Polivy, Schueneman, & Carlson, 1976), but other research (Tucker, Vuchinich, & Sobell, 1981) found an expectancy effect, suggesting that mood changes may be due primarily to the expectation of receiving alcohol.

McCollam, Burnish, Maisto, and Sobell (1980) examined the effects of several factors on the relationship of alcohol consumption to mood: the setting, quantity of alcohol consumed, and mood prior to drinking. They conducted a laboratory study with male undergraduates to see if moderate alcohol consumption (BAC = .06 mg. %) would increase self-reports of positive affect. The experiment was designed to compare the effects of alcohol consumption, expectancy, and phase of the BAC curve.

The results indicated that higher alcohol *consumption* led to self-reports of higher positive affect and less depression. Higher ratings of bodily sensations occurred with rising BAC, although physiological measures showed inconsistent changes. Variations in alcohol *expectancy* made little difference, contrary to other studies with the balanced placebo design for other types of processes. McCollam et al. argued that expectancy had minimal effect in their study because their task required subjects to pay high attention to body affective states, whereas the tasks used in other studies minimized attention to bodily sensations.

The Effect of Setting

Drinking in the laboratory experiment setting can be an anxiety-producing experience because the subject is aware of being evaluated. There is no assessment of the subject's existing mood at the start of the experiment, a factor that can influence mood levels during the experiment.

In contrast to the laboratory situation, drinkers ordinarily consume alcohol in a wide variety of moods, both positive and negative. Alcohol may magnify these existing moods when drinking is initiated. The angry or depressed individual may decide to drink to forget problems, while the happy individual may engage in drinking to celebrate a positive event with loved ones. These different types of motives must be considered in determining how alcohol will affect subsequent moods. In addition, an individual may drink for different reasons in different contexts and these factors must be examined in predicting the effects of alcohol.

Sex Differences

Sex must also be considered as a determinant of how alcohol affects mood. Sutker, Allain, Brantley, and Randall (1982) examined the effect of alcohol in reducing negative affect in male and female social drinkers faced with the possibility of receiving electric shock if they made errors on a learning task. Male subjects had the lowest anxiety if they both expected and received alcohol. In contrast, this condition produced the greatest anxiety among female subjects. Among females, the least anxiety occurred when unexpected alcohol was received. This pattern suggests that alcohol relieves anxiety pharmacologically, but that when women know they are receiving alcohol, at least in a research study, this awareness counteracts such relief and creates tension.

The study of alcohol effects on mood with women is complicated further by the existence of biological factors such as menstruation that may interact with the effects of alcohol. Sutker, Libet, Allain, and Randall (1983) compared three groups: women with normal menstrual cycles, women using oral contraceptives, and men. The women with normal menstrual cycles reported more frequent drinking to relieve negative moods, particularly during the menstruation phases. Comparable cyclical patterns in mood or drinking to relieve mood were not found in the other two groups.

Nonproblem Drinkers versus Alcoholics

The effects of a given amount of alcohol on mood should be different for nonproblem drinkers and alcoholics. Since alcoholics will have developed greater tolerance to alcohol than nonproblem drinkers, a small dose that might increase mood for lighter drinkers may have little effect on the mood of alcoholics. On the other hand, the size of the dose needed by an alcoholic to produce an effect may be much greater than the light drinker can consume.

It has already been noted that nonproblem drinkers experience positive affect shortly after drinking begins, followed by a decline to a neutral or slightly negative mood (McCollam et al., 1980; Sutker, Tabakoff, Goist, & Randall, 1983). A different pattern is typically observed with alcoholics. Nathan and O'Brien (1971) allowed chronic alcoholics access to alcohol under supervised conditions. During the first 12 to 24 hours of drinking, they reported some relief from negative moods, but with more time there was a shift toward increased negative affective states such as depression. Similar patterns have been found in other studies (for example, Mello & Mendelson, 1971).

The Effect of Attentional Demands

Steele and Josephs (1988) believed that an important additional factor that must be considered in studies of alcohol's effect on mood and emotion is the extent to which the drinker has other tasks to perform. On the premise that alcohol serves to reduce our capacity to deal with demands on our attention processing, they predicted that if someone is busy with a demanding task that might ordinarily generate tension, consumption of alcohol will serve to reduce tension by interfering with the capacity for attention to it. In contrast, if the drinker is doing little else when drinking, alcohol may *increase* tension since the drinker may focus on worrisome problems without the demands on attention of other activities.

In one experiment, Josephs and Steele (1990) told intoxicated and sober subjects they would have to make a speech in 15 minutes about aspects of their body and appearance that worried them. Half were kept busy with another task while waiting and half were not. As predicted, Josephs and Steele found that anxiety was reduced in the group that was both busy and intoxicated while it increased for the groups that were not busy, not intoxicated, or neither busy nor intoxicated.

There is also a positive side: alcohol may also ironically facilitate more pro-social behavior. In one study, subjects performed a boring task under sober or intoxicated conditions. Then the experimenter made a request for further assistance on the boring task. Intoxicated subjects were more likely than sober ones to continue helping, presumably because the alcohol had impaired their memory of the boringness of the task, according to Josephs and Steele.

The extent to which alcohol might alter stress may also depend on the temporal sequence in which the alcohol and stressor are experienced (Sayette & Wilson, 1991). Most laboratory studies of the effects of alcohol on stress expose the subjects to stress after they have consumed the alcohol. Many real-life drinking situations do involve this temporal order, but in other instances stress is encountered before drinking takes place.

Sayette and Wilson (1991) hypothesized that the relationship of alcohol to stress would vary depending on which of these two types of situations is involved. Since alcohol reduces attention, it was predicted that receiving alcohol first would involve less stress because the subject would not attend to the stressor as closely. In contrast, exposure to a stressor prior to receiving alcohol would produce more stress because more attention would be focused on the stressor.

Male moderate-to-heavy social drinkers, given either an alcoholic or a placebo beverage, were required to give a speech for three minutes about what they disliked about their body and appearance. During the waiting period, measures of heart rate were recorded before and after the drink. As predicted, a stress-dampening effect of alcohol on heart rate occurred only if the drink preceded the stressful speech.

Sensory-Motor Activity

Attention and Reaction Time

Alcohol has not been found to affect simple reaction time where a person has to detect or react to a single stimulus (Moskowitz & DePry, 1968), but these results may not be highly relevant to tasks outside the laboratory. Divided attention tasks where several stimuli are present simultaneously are more commonly encountered in naturalistic situations such as driving an automobile or operating equipment in the workplace.

Moskowitz and Burns (1971) conducted controlled studies that demonstrated reaction time's disruption by alcohol at low doses equivalent to one or two drinks taken within the past hour on tasks requiring divided attention. Subjects attended to a primary auditory or visual target and pressed a key when other distractor stimuli occurred at random peripheral background locations. Divided attention tasks are approximations to the kinds of demands placed on automobile drivers such as noticing other vehicles in the periphery, reading street signs while steering through heavy traffic, or talking on a car phone while merging onto a crowded freeway. Studies of divided attention have implicated alcohol use, even at low-to-moderate levels below the level of .10 mg. % that is legal in many states, as a factor that may contribute to a high percentage of accidents (Moskowitz, Burns, & Williams, 1985). This effect of alcohol may be indirect, working through its influence on information processing of the central nervous system and brain rather than directly through toxic effects on motor coordination or gross muscle movement.

Drinking and Driving

One area of great social concern where alcohol might create impairment of sensory-motor processes with serious consequences is automobile driving. This common activity involves coordination of many processes including sensory attention, motor coordination, perceptual judgment, and reaction time.

A leading cause of death in the United States is traffic accidents; in addition, tens of thousands sustain serious injuries. Moreover, statistics from the Fatal Accident Reporting System compiled by the National Highway Safety Administration clearly show that alcohol is involved in a high percentage (over 75% of drivers who die) of traffic fatalities occurring within 30 days of the accident (Fell, 1990).

Undoubtedly, there are many more drivers who drink and drive and live to repeat it without being involved in an automobile accident than there are drivers who drink and drive and have accidents. A survey of 34,395 respondents in 26 states in 1986 (Smith & Remington, 1989) revealed that 7.2 percent of drinkers admitted to driving after having "perhaps too much to drink" during the month preceding the telephone interview.

The accurate measurement of the role of alcohol in traffic accidents, fatal as well as nonfatal, cannot be based only on those who are involved in crashes but also requires the determination of the percentage of intoxicated drivers in similar driving conditions who are *not* involved in collisions. One study (Borkenstein, Crawther, Shumate, Ziel, & Zylman, 1964) in Grand Rapids, Michigan, conducted in conjunction with police authorities, involved administering roadside breathalyzer tests of blood alcohol levels to about 6,000 motorists involved in accidents. A control group of more than 7,500 drivers not involved in accidents were stopped at the same time of day and given similar BAL tests at the sites where accidents occurred.

In general, a greater percentage of those drivers involved in automobile accidents than of nonaccident drivers in the control group had alcohol in their blood, especially for levels above .08. This was true even after other differences between the accident and accident-free drivers such as age, sex, race, and education level were controlled for. One interesting exception was that the percentage of drivers with accidents showing a low BAC (up to about .05 mg. %, the equivalent of less than two drinks in the past hour) was actually *lower* than the percentage of drivers not involved in an accident. This unexpected dip in the curve relating blood alcohol level and accidents, dubbed the Grand Rapids Dip, does not necessarily mean that having a drink helps you drive better in any physiological sense. Rather, it is also possible that most of those who had consumed one or two drinks, as opposed to none, were mindful of the fact and consequently a bit more cautious in their driving to avoid driving violations or accidents.

Perrine, Waller, and Harris (1971) conducted a similar roadside study in a rural setting to compare the similarities and differences among four groups of drivers who: had fatal collisions (deceased drivers), had no collisions (roadside drivers), had clear driving records for the past 5 years (clear record drivers), or had a previous arrest for driving under the influence (DUI drivers). Drivers (or next of kin in cases of fatally injured drivers) reported their drinking frequency and quantity. As shown in Figure 4-2, the self-reports of DUI offenders marked this category as having the highest percentage of heavier drinkers, whereas the other categories generally consisted primarily of lighter drinkers.

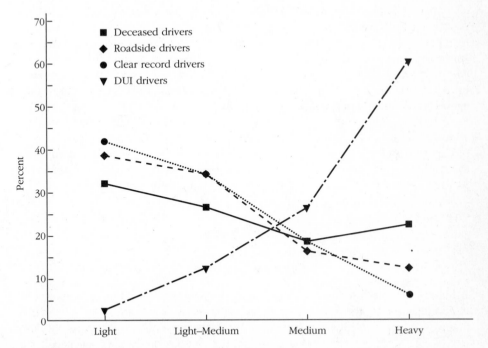

Figure 4-2 Proportion of deceased, roadside, clear record, and DUI drivers with light, light-medium, medium, or heavy Quantity-Frequency Index for preferred beverage.

Source: from "Who are the drinking drivers?" by M. W. Perrine in *Alcohol Health and Research World, 1990, 14(1),* 26–35.

These findings suggest that DUIs are not an "unlucky" subsample of the overall population of drivers who had been drinking and who just happened to be arrested on an isolated occasion of driving after having had "a few too many." Perrine (1990) argued that the DUI group probably represents a heavier drinking group that has repeatedly engaged in drinking and driving, unlike the other groups of drivers. Although 14 percent of the roadside drivers (the group with no collision or arrest) showed measurable blood alcohol levels, of which 2 percent were above .10, these drivers appear to have been able to "get away" with their drinking and driving, thus far. Most drinking drivers are not problem drinkers or alcoholics (Vingilis, 1983), but there is a subset of drinking drivers who may be reckless, impulsive, and irresponsible, and hence more likely to be involved in collisions. This high-risk subgroup of drinking drivers may be more likely to be alcoholics than the group as a whole.

These findings do not mean that alcohol does not impair important processes necessary for safe driving but indicate that other factors such as personality differences must also be considered. A temperament that leads an individual to drive after excessive drinking, especially repeatedly, is also a determinant of the likelihood of being involved in a collision or being arrested for DUI (Donovan & Marlatt, 1982).

There is a greater representation of young drivers than any other age group in all types of fatal crashes. To what extent does alcohol have a direct role in producing this effect? Studies of fatal automobile accidents show a much higher incidence rate among young drivers (age 16 to 19) irrespective of alcohol use, suggesting that inexperienced drivers are more likely to have accidents. Coupled with the use of alcohol, which they also have less experience with, young drivers have a double risk. In traffic fatalities involving youth in 1987, 31 percent of those aged 16 to 20 and 45 percent of those aged 20 to 24 had been drinking alcohol (Fell & Nash, 1989). The Grand Rapids study found that when no alcohol is involved, the accident rate is appreciably higher for the very young male and the over-70-year-old driver than for any other age group. As the dose of alcohol used by the driver in the accident increases, drivers of all ages have a greater chance of having an accident, but the increase is greater at either end of the age spectrum.

Issues related to the prevention of drinking and driving will be discussed in Chapter 17.

Conclusions

A determination of the effects of alcohol on behavior and psychological experience is complicated by the existence of both pharmacological and psychological influences. When alcohol is consumed, drinkers usually hold expectations about the effects that alcohol will produce. In some situations, at least for nonalcoholics, merely expecting to receive alcohol may be sufficient to produce the expected influence.

The balanced placebo design is one method aimed at examining the combined as well as separate influences of the expectancy of consuming alcohol and the pharmacological factor. Studies using this paradigm have shown that for light-to-moderate drinkers, many behaviors are altered by the belief or expectancy that they have consumed alcohol. However, the method is limited to the study of acute effects of small doses of alcohol due to ethical problems as well as to issues of credibility. Outside the laboratory and its controlled experiments, expectancy and pharmacological effects are inseparable and may even reinforce each other.

Thy psychological and behavioral effects of alcohol depend on numerous factors including amount of alcohol, time since consumption, and expectancies. The same person may drink for different reasons in different contexts, while different persons may drink in a given situation for various reasons. For example, the effect on aggressive tendencies for someone drinking due to depression may be different from the effect for someone drinking to relieve tension or because of boredom. These personality and situational factors must be examined in addition to identifying expectancies when predicting the effects of alcohol.

The reactions to alcohol consumption may differ for light and heavy drinkers, even before drinking problems develop. Thus, the psychological effects of alcohol cannot be fully understood without including consideration of other differences among individuals who differ in their voluntary levels of alcohol consumption.

The psychological effects of a given amount of alcohol for chronic abusers and alcoholics differ from those for light-to-moderate drinkers. First, as noted in Chapter 3, depending on the extent of alcohol abuse, chronic use may have produced tolerance, organic damage, and nutritional deficits. Second, the psychosocial deterioration associated with alcoholism may alter the expectancies and motives for drinking. Such differences should lead to different behavioral and experiential consequences of alcohol consumption for those who are versus are not alcohol-dependent.

References

Berman, M. O. (1990). Severe brain dysfunction. *Alcohol Health and Research World, 14,* 120–129.

Bolter, J. F., & Hannon, R. (1986). Lateralized cerebral dysfunction in early and late stage alcoholics. *Journal of Studies on Alcohol, 47,* 213–218.

Borkenstein, R. F., Crawther, R. W., Shumate, R. P., Ziel, W. B., & Zylman, R. (1964). *The role of the drinking driver in traffic accidents.* Bloomington, IN: Indiana University Department of Police Administration.

Craik, F.I.M. (1977). Similarities between the effects of aging and alcoholic intoxication on memory performance construed within a "levels of processing" framework. In I. M. Birnbaum & E. S. Parker (Eds.), *Alcohol and human memory* (pp. 9–21). Hillsdale, NJ: Lawrence Erlbaum.

Donovan, D. M., & Marlatt, G. A. (1982). Reasons for drinking among DUI arrestees. *Addictive Behaviors, 7,* 423–426.

Ellis, R. J., & Oscar-Berman, M. (1989). Alcoholism, aging, and functional cerebral asymmetries. *Psychological Bulletin, 106,* 128–147.

Fell, J. C. (1990). Drinking and driving in America: Disturbing facts, encouraging reductions. *Alcohol Health and Research World, 14,* 18–25.

Fell, J. C., & Nash, C. E. (1989). The nature of the alcohol problem in U.S. fatal crashes.

[Special issue: Drinking, driving, and health promotion.] *Health Education Quarterly, 16,* 335–343.

Goldman, M. S. (1983). Cognitive impairment in chronic alcoholics: Some cause for optimism. *American Psychologist, 38,* 1045–1054.

Goodglass, H., & Peck, E. A. (1972). Dichotic ear order in Korsakoff and normal subjects. *Neuropsychologia, 15,* 397–407.

Grant, I, (1987). Alcohol and the brain: Neuropsychological correlates. *Journal of Consulting and Clinical Psychology, 55,* 310–324.

Hartley, J. T., Birnbaum, I. M., & Parker, E. S. (1978). Alcohol and storage deficits: Kind of processing? *Journal of Verbal Learning and Verbal Behavior, 17,* 635–647.

Hastroudi, S., & Parker, E. S. (1986). Acute alcohol amnesia. In H. D. Cappell, F. B. Glaser, Y. Isreal, H. Kalant, W. Schmidt, E. Seller, & R. C. Smart (Eds.), *Research advances in alcohol and drug problems* (pp. 179–209). New York: Plenum Press.

Jenkins, R. L., & Parsons, O. A. (1981). Neuropsychological effect of chronic alcoholism on tactual-spatial performance and memory in males. *Alcoholism: Clinical and Experimental Research, 5,* 26–33.

Jones, B. M., & Parsons, O. A. (1971). Impaired abstracting ability in chronic alcoholics. *Archives of General Psychiatry, 24,* 71–75.

Josephs, R. A., & Steele, C. M. (1990). The two faces of alcohol myopia: Attentional mediation of psychological stress. *Journal of Abnormal Psychology, 99,* 115–126.

Klatsky, R. L. (1980). *Human memory: Structures and processes.* San Francisco: W. H. Freeman.

MacVane, J., Butters, N., Montgomery, K., & Farber, J. (1982). Cognitive functioning in men social drinkers: A replication study. *Journal of Studies on Alcohol, 43,* 81–95.

Marlatt, G. A., Demming, B., & Reid, J. (1973). Loss of control drinking in alcoholics: An experimental analogue. *Journal of Abnormal Psychology, 81,* 233–241.

Marlatt, G. A., & Rohsenow, D. J. (1980). Cognitive processes in alcohol use: Expectancy and the balanced placebo design. In N. K. Mello (Ed.), *Advances in substance abuse: Behavioral and biological research* (pp. 159–199). Greenwich, CT: JAI Press.

Martin, C. S., Earleywine, M., Finn, P., & Young, R. D. (1990). Some boundary conditions for effective use of alcohol placebos. *Journal of Studies on Alcohol, 51,* 500–505.

Martin, P. R., Adinoff, B., Weingarter, H., Mukherjee, A. B., & Eckhardt, M. J. (1986). Alcoholic organic brain disease: Nosology and pathophysiologic mechanisms. *Progress in Neuropsychopharmacological Biological Psychiatry, 10,* 147–164.

McCollam, J. B., Burnish, T. G., Maisto, S. A., & Sobell, M. B. (1980). Alcohol's effects on physiological arousal and self-reported affect and sensations. *Journal of Abnormal Psychology, 89,* 224–233.

Mello, N. K., & Mendelson, J. H. (1971). A quantitative analysis of drinking in alcoholics. *Archives of General Psychiatry, 25,* 527–539.

Moskowitz, H., & Burns, M. (1971). The effect of alcohol upon the psychological refractory period. *Quarterly Journal of Studies on Alcohol, 32,* 782–790.

Moskowitz, H., Burns, M. M., & Williams, A. F. (1985). Skills performance at low blood alcohol levels. *Journal of Studies on Alcohol, 46,* 482–485.

Moskowitz, H., & DePry, D. (1968). The effect of alcohol on auditory vigilance and divided-attention tasks. *Quarterly Journal of Studies on Alcohol, 29,* 54–63.

Nathan, P. E., & O'Brien, J. S. (1971). An experimental analysis of the behavior of alcoholics and nonalcoholics during prolonged problem drinking. *Behavior Therapy, 2,* 455–476.

Oscar-Berman, M. (1988). Normal functional asymmetries in alcoholism? *Aphasiology, 2,* 369–374.

Parker, E. S., & Noble, E. (1977). Alcohol consumption and cognitive functioning in social drinkers. *Journal of Studies on Alcohol, 38,* 1224–1232.

Parsons, O. A. (1986). Cognitive functioning in sober social drinkers: A review and critique. *Journal of Studies on Alcohol, 47,* 101–114.

Parsons, O. A., & Leber, W. R. (1981). The relationship between cognitive dysfunction and brain damage in alcoholics. *Alcoholism, 5,* 326–343.

Perrine, M. W. (1990). Who are the drinking drivers? The spectrum of drinking drivers revisited. *Alcohol Health and Research World, 14,* 26–35.

Perrine, M. W., Waller, J. A., & Harris, L. S. (1971). *Alcohol and highway safety: Behavioral and medical aspects* (Technical Report DOT HS 800 600). Washington, DC: National Highway Traffic Safety Administration.

Peterson, J. B., Rothfleisch, J., Zelazo, P. D., & Pihl, R. O. (1990). Acute alcohol intoxication and cognitive functioning. *Journal of Studies on Alcohol, 51,* 114–122.

Polivy, J., Schueneman, A. L., & Carlson, K. (1976). Alcohol and tension reduction: Cognitive and physiological effects. *Journal of Abnormal Psychology, 85,* 595–600.

Ryan, C. (1980). Learning and memory deficits in alcoholics. *Journal of Studies on Alcohol, 41,* 437–447.

Ryan, C., & Butters, N. (1983). Cognitive deficits in alcoholics. In B. Kissin & H. Begleiter (Eds.), *The pathogenesis of alcoholism* (pp. 485–538). New York: Plenum Press.

Ryan, C., & Butters, N. (1986). Neuropsychology of alcoholism. In D. Wedding, A. M. Norton, & J. S. Webster (Eds.), *The neuropsychology handbook* (pp. 376–409). New York: Springer.

Sayette, M. A., & Wilson, G. T. (1991). Intoxication and exposure to stress: Effects of temporal patterning. *Journal of Abnormal Psychology, 100,* 56–62.

Smith, P. F., & Remington, P. L. (1989). The epidemiology of drinking and driving: Results from the behavioral risk factor surveillance system, 1986. *Health Education Quarterly, 16,* 345–358.

Southwick, L., Steele, C., Marlatt, A., & Lindell, M. (1981). Alcohol-related expectancies: Defined by phase of intoxication and drinking experience. *Journal of Consulting and Clinical Psychology, 49,* 713–721.

Steele, C. M., & Josephs, R. A. (1988). Drinking your troubles away II. An attention-allocation model of alcohol's effect on psychological stress. *Journal of Abnormal Psychology, 97,* 196–205.

Sutker, P. B., Allain, A. N., Brantley, P. J., & Randall, C. L. (1982). Acute alcohol intoxication, negative affect, and autonomic arousal in women and men. *Addictive Behaviors, 7,* 17–25.

Sutker, P. B., Libet, J. M., Allain, A. N., & Randall, C. L. (1983). Alcohol use, negative mood states, and menstrual phases. *Alcoholism: Clinical and Experimental Research, 7,* 327–331.

Sutker, P. B., Tabakoff, B., Goist, K. C., Jr., & Randall, C. L. (1983). Acute alcohol intoxication, mood states, and alcohol metabolism in women and men. *Pharmacology Biochemistry and Behavior, 18,* 349–354.

Tarter, R. E. (1975). Psychological deficit in chronic alcoholics. *The International Journal of the Addictions, 10,* 327–368.

Tucker, J. A., Vuchinich, R. E., & Sobell, M. B. (1981). Alcohol consumption as a self-handicapping strategy. *Journal of Abnormal Psychology, 90,* 220–230.

Tucker, J. A., Vuchinich, R. E., & Sobell, M. B. (1982). Alcohol's effects on human emotions: A review of the stimulation/depression hypothesis. *International Journal of the Addictions, 17,* 155–180.

Tulving, E. (1983). *Elements of episodic memory.* New York: Oxford University Press.

Vingilis, E. (1983). Drinking drivers and alcoholics: Are they from the same population? In R. G. Smart, F. B. Glaser, Y. Isreal, H. Kalant, R. E. Popham, & W. Schmidt (Eds.), *Recent advances in alcohol and drug problems* (pp. 299–342). New York: Plenum Press.

Weingartner, H., & Faillace, L. A. (1971). Alcohol state-dependent learning in man. *Journal of Nervous and Mental Disease, 153,* 395–406.

Williams, C. M., & Skinner, A. E. (1990). The cognitive effects of alcohol abuse: A controlled study. *British Journal of Addiction, 85,* 911–917.

FIVE

The Psychological Effects of Alcohol: Social Behaviors

The preceding chapter discussed the disruptive impact of alcohol on physiological, cognitive, and affective processes. Such influences also affect interpersonal behavior because cognitive and affective factors modify the appraisal and meaning of social situations. The pharmacological effects of alcohol restrict attention and alter mood, both of which may influence social behavior. In addition, beliefs and expectations about the effects of alcohol may affect social interactions. For example, a facetious comment may be misinterpreted by someone who has been drinking as a hostile comment, leading to conflict. In contrast, someone who is lighthearted from drinking might not interpret criticism as threatening. In this chapter we will examine research on the relationship of drinking to two major aspects of social behavior: aggression and sexual activity.

Aggression and Violence

What is the relationship between the heavy use of alcohol and the occurrence of aggression? Since alcohol is commonly believed to be a disinhibitor, aggressive tendencies may increase with drinking due to either pharmacological or expectancy factors. Intoxication may lead some drinkers to perceive certain situations as more threatening and therefore to resort to aggression.

An alternative, or at least supplementary, explanation for a correlation between alcohol consumption and aggression is that excessive use of alcohol makes the drinker appear obnoxious to others. Intoxicated drinkers may be likely to provoke altercations with others, with aggression occurring in the form of arguments and eventually physical violence.

Naturalistic Evidence

Ample evidence exists to suggest that alcohol use precedes or accompanies violent behavior. In more than half to two thirds of homicides and assaults, the offender and/or the victim had been drinking (Mayfield, 1976; Welte & Abel, 1989). A high incidence of alcohol use has been reported in rape cases (Amir, 1967) and in date or acquaintance rape (Abbey, 1991). About 60 percent of 913 women interviewed (Klassen & Wilsnack, 1986) reported experiencing some form of sexual aggression from men who had been drinking. A review of studies on assault by Gerson (1978) showed that in the majority of cases, both offender and victim had been drinking. In many of the other instances, alcohol was involved, but only the offender or the victim had been drinking. Victims of violent drinkers tend to be similar to the aggressors, being young, never married, and frequenters of bars (Fillmore, 1985). The victims typically are acquaintances of the aggressors.

Studies of incarcerated violent offenders reviewed by Collins (1986) showed a greater prevalence of alcohol problems for these inmates as compared to the general population. Collins and Schlenger (1988) examined data on more than 1,300 male felons and controlled for background variables such as age, race, educational level, marital status, and number of prior arrests. This comparison revealed that violent offenders were more likely to have reported drinking prior to their arrest than nonviolent inmates. However, a similar comparison showed that whether the inmate met the criteria for being classified as alcohol-dependent was unrelated to the type of offense. In other words, it is likely that the acute effect of alcohol, rather than its chronic use, is more likely to be the factor contributing to violence. As suggested by Pernanen (1976, 1981), intoxication may impair cognitive processes and judgments, leading to the misinterpretation of cues and in turn to violent interactions.

One limitation to the evidence, however, is that it is based on self-report. Drunkenness may be resorted to as an "excuse," as proposed by MacAndrew and Edgerton (1969), if offenders think they may obtain a lighter sentence when their misdeeds are perceived as due to the influence of alcohol.

Domestic Violence

Studies of family violence show that a high percentage of these incidents involves drinking by one or both parties (Straus & Gelles, 1986). Leonard, Bromet, Parkinson, Day, & Ryan (1985) found that among blue-collar working men, those with more serious drinking problems were more likely to be involved in marital physical violence. However, it has been argued (Gerson, 1978) that for many families the violence might occur even without the alcohol. A baseline measure of the level of violence that occurs without the use of alcohol is needed to interpret the influence of alcohol.

Aggression by Men toward Women. Orford et al. (1975) found that close to half of the wives of men at an alcoholism clinic reported violence and physical harm from their husbands. Without data on rates of domestic violence from a comparison group of nonalcoholics, however, it is not easy to interpret this type of finding. Frieze and Knoble (1980) compared self-identified battered married women with matched control women from the same neighborhoods. Although even the control group contained some battered wives, the severity of violence was higher for women with heavier drinking husbands.

The manner in which alcohol is related to domestic violence may not be the same in all marriages. Based on structured interviews, Frieze and Knoble found that for some couples, both drank excessively and drinking was often causally related to the violence. For other couples, drinking was not excessive, nor were the couples especially violent unless drinking occurred. Yet a third group was found that had high levels of violence but few problems with excessive drinking, so that the drinking may not have been a contributing factor to their domestic violence.

In cases of wife battering, Gelles (1972) found that offenders often use alcohol as an excuse for their actions, acting as if the violent behavior would not have occurred without the influence of the alcohol. Wives who were alcoholic were more likely than nonalcoholic wives to be a victim of spousal violence (Miller, Downs, & Gondoli, 1989), possibly because they were perceived as not deserving better treatment because of their alcoholism.

Van Hasselt, Morrison, Bellack (1985) compared couples who were either abusive, maritally discordant but nonabusive, or happily married. The level of drinking by wives was not a predictor of the spouse abuse received, whereas the level of the husbands' drinking was directly related to greater spousal abuse.

Aggression by Women toward Men. More varied effects of alcohol occur among women, partly due to multiple factors affecting the process such as hormonal and menstrual cycles. Thus, Jones and Jones (1976) found that intoxication from a given dose of alcohol is higher before the onset, and lower with the onset, of menstrual periods. In general, a given amount of alcohol seems to have a more adverse effect on females than on males, possibly because it is more concentrated due to lower body weight, more fat tissues, and less body water.

Beckman (1978a) noted that differences between male and female alcoholics were similar to those found between nonalcoholic males and females. Women in both cases are less aggressive than men because they drink as a means of achieving "femininity" (Wilsnack, 1973), a motive that might interfere with aggressive tendencies. But Beckman (1978b) also found evidence that not all women alcoholics are similar in these tendencies, with some experiencing more sex-role conflict than others.

Frieze and Schafer (1983) suggested that the physical size disadvantage is another reason why females would not aggress toward males. However, this argument overlooks the use of weapons, which can readily negate this disadvantage. Perhaps a more compelling inhibitor for most women has been the socialization to avoid physical aggression in favor of conflict resolution through psychological methods or even to "turn the other cheek" to avoid disharmony.

Another question is whether there is a sex-role bias. Thus, in cases where both parties are violent, who is reported as the instigator, the male or the female? And if both had been drinking, is the violence attributed more often to the male than the female? Again, the cultural norm and expectancy is that females are, or should be, less aggressive, and this belief could bias perceptions against the male as the primary aggressor in these types of situations.

Controlled Studies

Due to the difficulty of interpreting and controlling incidents of natural aggression, experiments have been conducted to help understand the role of alcohol in aggression. Laboratory studies of aggression are mostly limited to the use of electric shock for instigating aggression. This artificial method allows objective and standard measurement of the intensity and duration of the stimuli. In experiments, for ethical reasons, the goal is not to provoke realistic, and possibly uncontrollable, aggression but to make the subject think that someone has aggressed against her or him. Then, an opportunity to retaliate against the aggressor is provided to the victim.

To achieve these goals in the laboratory, a face-to-face confrontation between the aggressor and the victim is undesirable and unnecessary. In these experiments, the subjects are typically paired with strangers who are potential targets for aggression either because they provoke the subject or because they are convenient targets for displacement of aggression. For instance, a confederate of the experimenter pretending to be a subject insults the real subject by making negative evaluations of the latter's task performance. Then the situation is reversed and the subject is instructed to administer electric shocks to the confederate subject for any errors made in a learning task. The two subjects are placed in separate rooms to increase the likelihood that aggression will occur. These studies are artificial and often have *demand characteristics,* cues that may suggest to subjects what their behavior should be.

Taylor and Leonard (1983), as well as Bushman and Cooper (1990), concluded that results of traditional design studies using an experimental and a placebo control group show that alcohol leads to more aggression. However, Hull and Bond (1986) found in their review of balanced placebo design studies, which control for expectancy, that effects of both consumption and expectancy on aggression were inconsistent across different studies. They hypothesized that the heterogeneous results about expectancy effects on aggression may be due to individual differences in subjects' need for expressing aggression. For example, among individuals expecting alcohol, only those who have experienced recent frustration may display aggression.

The effects of alcohol consumption on aggression also may vary depending on the situation and the extent to which conflict about expressing aggression may exist. Thus, Steele and Southwick (1985) found alcohol consumption effects only when the aggressive behavior in the situation involved high conflict. Even when people are angry with another person, they often have some conflict or reluctance to engage in aggression because of potential adverse social consequences, especially when sober. However, when people have consumed large amounts of alcohol, they are more prone to act on these aggressive urges.

Josephs and Steele (1990) viewed this tendency of alcohol to release our inhibitions against aggression as a form of "alcohol myopia" in which our short-sighted impulses are dominant over our long-range interests. They argued that this effect is due to the disruptive effects of even a few drinks on our attention. When we are sober, we can weigh the pros and cons of engaging in a specific behavior, but when we are intoxicated, attention allocation is diminished so that such considerations are obstructed.

Sexual Activity

Popular belief and folklore holds that alcohol use enhances sexual arousal and desire, as aptly phrased by Ogden Nash: "Candy is dandy but liquor is quicker." Sexual encounters frequently involve the use of alcohol, as it is assumed to enhance sexual arousal, lower inhibitions, and facilitate seduction, weakening the resistance of the less willing partner as well as intensifying the courage and amour of the initiating partner. However, though alcohol may increase sexual interest and arousal, it may actually impair sexual performance, so that as Shakespeare's gatekeeper observed in *Macbeth,* Act II, Scene 3, " . . . much drink may be said to be an equivocator of lechery."

Developmental Evidence

As adolescents mature, they become involved in activities such as sexual intimacy and alcohol consumption that were previously forbidden to them and are generally restricted to adults. Since alcohol is popularly viewed as a disinhibitor, it would hardly be surprising that drinking alcohol and having sex often occur together. Robertson and Plant (1988) reported that about half of the adolescents in their study reported drinking alcohol at the time of their first sexual intercourse. Sexually active adolescents were found to be more likely to use alcohol than those who have not engaged in sexual intercourse (Coles & Stokes, 1985).

With the major health threat of AIDS, the question of whether alcohol use affects the likelihood of use of condoms during sexual intercourse is particularly relevant. Sexual intercourse increases the risk of AIDS and other sexually transmitted diseases, if "unsafe" sex such as intercourse without the use of condoms is practiced. The likelihood of unsafe sex practices by drinking adolescents might be greater because alcohol may impair judgment. Indeed, it has been found that young women who are heavy drinkers are less likely to use contraception (Zucker, Battistich, & Langer, 1981) and that heavy drinker adolescents are less likely than nondrinker peers to use condoms (Hingson, Strunin, Berlin, & Heeren, 1990).

However, these correlational studies do not prove that alcohol causes adolescents to take greater risks such as unprotected sexual intimacy. Surveys dealing with behaviors during *specific* sexual incidents provide stronger evidence about the role of alcohol use in sexual behavior because the temporal relationship between them can be determined. Robertson and Plant (1988) found that nonuse of contraception at first intercourse was much more likely for those who had been drinking than for those who had not at the time. Flanagan, McLean, Hall, and Propp (1990) found that about 65 percent of the women surveyed at a family planning agency had used alcohol when engaging in sexual intercourse in the past month, and 43 percent had done so during their first experience with sexual intercourse. Overall, then, the evidence suggests that alcohol use may contribute to riskier sexual practices such as unprotected intercourse among sexually active adolescents.

The relationship between alcohol use and protected sex among adolescents is much stronger than for adults (Leigh, 1990). Leigh and Morrison (1991) suggested that these differences may reflect the fact that drinking and sexual activities are new experiences during adolescence, both of which usually involve breaking strong inhibitions. Alcohol may therefore serve as a more powerful disinhibitor for adolescents than for adults, for whom these activities are generally more acceptable.

Clinical Evidence

Clinical studies deal with a more restricted population. Thus, the population studied by Masters and Johnson (1966) consisted only of individuals who were seeking treatment for sexual dysfunction, not for alcoholism, although alcohol was found to be a possible contributing factor in many instances of sexual dysfunction. Impaired sexual performance among this population may have been due to the acute effects of alcohol in some cases, but to the chronic effects in other instances. Also, alcohol abuse could be viewed as a result of sexual dysfunction, one that might produce further sexual problems eventually.

Lemere and Smith (1973) noted that among chronic alcoholics, impaired sexual performance may be a possible consequence of alcoholism. They found impotence in only 8 percent of males, due primarily to the inability to have erections rather than to loss of desire. They found little loss of libido among women alcoholics, although Kinsey, Pomeroy, Martin, and Gebhard (1953) found high incidence of "frigidity" and sexual conflict in this population.

Beckman (1979) compared alcoholics with a control group of "normals" as well as a control group of psychiatric patients. She found that alcoholic women, as contrasted with the control groups, reported strongest desire for sexual intercourse when drinking, engaged in it most often when drinking, and enjoyed it most often when drinking. However, the fact that their reported levels of sexual satisfaction were lower than for women in the control groups suggested that they may have been using alcohol to "treat" their sexual problems.

In identifying the causes of sexual dysfunction, most views have placed the blame on some aspect of the impaired individual. However, because dysfunction also may be a function of the partner, this may be an oversimplification. Thus, alcoholic wives are often married to alcoholic husbands. If the wives are sexually uninterested or unsatisfied, to what extent are these conditions created or influenced by the alcoholism of their husbands? If the husbands themselves are physiologically impaired by alcohol or are less attractive psychologically due to their intoxicated condition, they may contribute to the wives' lack of sexual responsiveness as well.

Conversely, sexually inhibited wives may turn to alcohol or be encouraged by their husbands to drink to overcome inhibitions. Reliance on alcohol over many years in order to engage in sex may lead to the wife's eventually becoming alcoholic, and in turn, becoming less attractive to her husband. This creates a vicious circle, with further impairment of sexual interest and performance.

The stigma traditionally associated with homosexuality in our society may contribute to greater alcohol problems among this population. Rates of alcohol problems have been reported to be around 30 percent for homosexual men (Lohrenz, Connelly, Coyne, & Spare, 1978), much higher than the 10 to 15 percent estimates usually found for men in general population surveys. Beckman (1979) found that 20 percent of her sample of alcoholic women reported homosexual experiences, with 6 percent of them considering themselves homosexuals. These levels were higher than those for a nonpsychiatric control group or those found by Kinsey, Pomeroy, Martin, and Gebhard (1953) in their classic studies of human sexuality.

These estimates, based on clinical samples, may not reflect an accurate picture for the whole population of homosexuals. The other convenient source of evidence has been gay bars, because they have been a major social gathering place for homosexuals. However, drinking might be expected to be higher among bar patrons than for the homosexual population as a whole. Paul, Stall, and Bloomfield

(1992) questioned previous estimates as artificially high, although they believe alcohol problem rates are higher for homosexuals than for the general population.

McKirnan and Peterson (1989) recruited a sample of 3,400 respondents from readers of a gay newspaper. They found alcohol problems existed to a greater degree among homosexuals than among the general population, but not to the extent that earlier studies with less representative samples had shown. Their results showed that only 14 percent of gay men and lesbians in their Chicago sample abstained from alcohol use, as compared to 29 percent in national general population surveys. In addition, alcohol problems were higher in the gay sample (23 versus 12 percent); however, the rate of heavy drinking of 15 percent was comparable to the 14 percent found in the general population. Lower rates but similar patterns of drinking and drinking problems were found among lesbians in comparison to heterosexual women.

If drinking problems of homosexuals are in part a response to the stigmatization of homosexuality, one would predict a decline in such problems as societal attitudes toward homosexuals become more accepting, as they have in the past generation.

Naturalistic Evidence

Some studies of alcohol's influence on sexual activity involve retrospective analysis of special populations. One example is a study of sex offenders such as rapists and pedophiles by Gebhard, Gagnon, Pomeroy, and Christianson (1965). These researchers attempted to determine whether drinking had been involved in these offenses. About two thirds of the offenders reported being intoxicated at the time of the offense, but this type of evidence is suspect due to its self-serving nature. It does not explain how the alcohol contributed to the offense. Many more drinkers exist who do not commit such crimes even though they have the "opportunity." A more complete picture of the role of alcohol in these crimes also requires data about the effects of alcohol use on sex offenses by a "control" group of sex offenders who did not get caught.

Experimental Evidence

Finally, laboratory experiments can be used to study actual physical aspects of human sexual response, although this method raises issues of ethics as well as generalizability due to the artificial nature of the laboratory setting. In one early study that did not use the balanced placebo design, Farkas and Rosen (1976) gave drinks that produced BACs of either 0, .025, .050, or .075 mg. % to male college students while they watched an erotic film. A device called a plethysmograph was attached around the penis to measure the degree of penile tumescence or erection continuously during the film viewing. They found that low doses of alcohol slightly enhanced sexual arousal, but higher doses actually weakened sexual response for males.

Wilson and Lawson (1976a) conducted a similar study with college women who viewed an erotic film after four different doses of alcohol received on separate occasions while wearing a vaginal plethysmograph consisting of a photocell inside a Plexiglas tube to assess changes in vaginal blood pressure as an index of sexual arousal. The immediate BALs measured after drinking were 0, .026, .049, and .079 mg. % for the four different doses. Thus, the highest level was near the amount considered to be illegal for driving an automobile in many states. Increased alcohol dose *reduced* sexual arousal at the physiological level, as measured by vaginal pressure-pulse scores, although the women reported an enhanced subjective arousal.

Use of the balanced placebo design allows a separation of pharmacological and psychological influences on sexual arousal. Wilson and Lawson (1976b) varied expectancies about the type of beverage male college subjects would receive, alcoholic or nonalcoholic, as well as the type of beverage consumed. Subjects viewed erotic films depicting both heterosexual and homosexual content. An expectancy effect occurred, with more physical and subjective arousal in the group expecting to receive alcohol than in the group that did not expect to receive alcohol. There was no alcohol consumption effect, but the researchers used only one dose (.04 mg. %) in this study and it was low.

Wilson and Lawson (1978) replicated this study with women as subjects. They found that expectancy did not increase physiological arousal even though it did lead to increased subjective arousal. Alcohol consumption, however, impaired physical arousal.

It should be recognized that studies in laboratory settings are highly artificial and involve relatively low doses of alcohol for ethical reasons. Low doses are especially dictated to maintain credibility when the balanced placebo is used. These studies rely on samples of college students, who are hardly representative of the general population. Even among college students, the subjects can be viewed as a biased sample since those who have volunteered for sex research were found by Wolchik, Braver, and Jensen (1985) to have had greater sexual experience and more liberal sexual attitudes as well as more sexual problems.

The general implication of these findings, summarized in Figure 5-1, is that, contrary to popular belief, alcohol's effect on sexual arousal is not mediated through a physiological process but through a psychological process in which

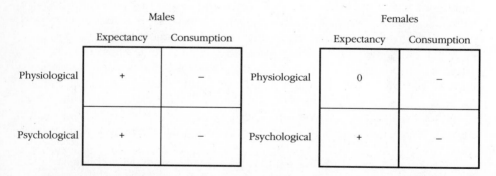

Figure 5-1 Summary of alcohol expectancy and consumption effects on physiological and psychological sexual arousal in college males and females.

one's expectancies are more critical, at least at low dosages. The correspondence between physiological and psychological sexual arousal is much weaker for women than it is for men. Wilson and Lawson (1978) suggested that social and anatomical factors could account for this difference. Men may form stronger associations between genital sensations and cognitive information such as the type of beverage consumed because it may be easier for males to label or identify penile arousal than it is for females to detect vaginal arousal.

Crowe and George (1989) speculated that the pattern of results from laboratory studies of alcohol effects on sexual arousal was compatible with the excuse function of alcohol use. Sexual arousal may be increased by alcohol expectancy in situations where excuses are needed—that is, when inhibition may exist. Thus, in one study (George & Marlatt, 1986), subjects were allowed to view slides showing erotic, violent, and violent-erotic content, materials that presumably create inhibition in the participants in a research study. Both the amount of viewing time and self-reported sexual arousal were higher for the group that expected alcohol than the group that did not, especially for a set of slides depicting highly deviant behaviors. Viewing of such stimuli, especially in an experiment conducted at a university, is a type of "deviant" activity that is likely to generate inhibition. Therefore, the expectancy of alcohol should disinhibit or enhance sexual arousal.

Crowe and George also noted the importance of considering the cultural context when interpreting the pattern of findings. Society imposes a double standard, with greater tolerance of sexual arousal and deviance among men than among women; it should not be surprising, then, that alcohol expectancy generally produces less sexual arousal among women than among men.

The fact that alcohol at higher dosages can often increase sexual responsiveness even when it is socially unacceptable may be due to the impairment of cognitive processing. Steele and Southwick (1985) proposed a model of alcohol-related disinhibitory effects in which higher doses disrupt cognitive judgment and awareness of inhibitory cues that ordinarily restrain antisocial behaviors such as sexually inappropriate behaviors. Evidence for the model came from previous studies of the effects of alcohol that were classified in terms of whether the observed behavior/situation involved high or low conflict. A method known as meta-analysis was used by Steele and Southwick to combine results from different studies to evaluate the effects of alcohol consumption and expectancy for low-conflict and high-conflict contexts. Consistent with their model, expectancy effects exceeded consumption effects in low-conflict situations, but the opposite was found for high-conflict situations.

Conclusions

Alcohol is popularly viewed as a disinhibitor, so it is not surprising that its use is associated with behaviors that are ordinarily inhibited or restrained in most circumstances, such as violence or sexual arousal and intimacy. Legal and moral control of these behaviors may be less effective after drinking occurs because alcohol may restrict attention and reduce the salience of inhibiting cues. Higher cognitive controls in the forms of self- and social criticism that ordinarily restrain behaviors may also be weakened under the influence of alcohol, which disrupts awareness of cues that ordinarily inhibit antisocial behaviors.

Although naturalistic evidence shows a greater use of alcohol associated with many forms of violent behaviors and crimes, the relationship may be inflated because as Murdoch, Pihl, and Ross (1990) noted, the intoxicated offenders may be more likely to be apprehended.

An analysis of the alcohol-violence correlation must distinguish between situations where only the offender was drinking, only the victim was drinking, and where both were drinking. The first situation implicates alcohol as a possible cause of violence, but the second situation is contrary to a causal interpretation, and the third situation is ambiguous about causality (Murdoch, Pihl, & Ross, 1990). Thus, if both parties to an assault had been drinking, it is difficult to determine whether alcohol instigated violence on the part of the offender or the victim or both. Also, in some cases, it may not be certain which party was offender and which, victim. Or consider the example of acquaintance rape where both parties had been drinking. A number of processes could have been affected by drinking (Abbey, 1991). For example, did the alcohol increase the male's expectation of consenting sexual intimacy and/or did it lower the female's initial resistance?

Laboratory studies allow controlled observation to help rule out alternative explanations. Alcohol generally releases aggression in laboratory studies, although the situation is also an important factor. The more conflict is involved in the situation, the more likely it is that alcohol will make a difference. However, since drinking levels in an experiment are assigned on a random basis, the role of the participants' own drinking levels are not evaluated as factors.

Sexual activity is also affected by alcohol consumption. Anxiety, fear, and guilt, which might be inhibitors of sexual behavior, might be reduced by alcohol consumption. Alcohol use also can serve as an "excuse" later if sexual activities are condemned.

Among alcoholics, alcohol use has been found to be associated with sexual dysfunction. Due to the correlational nature of the evidence, however, it is unclear whether the alcohol abuse produced the sexual impairment or vice versa.

Laboratory studies of the effects of alcohol on sexual arousal are limited to relatively small doses given on single occasions to a select group of college students who are willing to volunteer for studies that most students might not volunteer for. While the generalizability is questionable, these studies demonstrate the power of alcohol expectancies to increase sexual arousal.

Aggression and sexual activity are similar in that they are both often highly restricted behaviors. When alcohol is consumed at levels and in circumstances that narrow the attention of the drinker, inhibitors are less effective in restraining either of these behaviors.

References

Abbey, A. (1991). Acquaintance rape and alcohol consumption on college campuses: How are they linked? *Journal of American College Health, 39,* 165–169.

Amir, M. (1967). Alcohol and forcible rape. *British Journal of Addiction, 62,* 219–232.

Beckman, L. J. (1978a). Sex-role conflict in alcoholic women: Myth or reality? *Journal of Abnormal Psychology, 87,* 408–417.

Beckman, L. J. (1978b). The self-esteem of women alcoholics. *Journal of Studies on Alcohol, 39,* 491–498.

Beckman, L. J. (1979). Reported effects of alcohol on the sexual feelings and behavior of women alcoholics and nonalcoholics. *Journal of Studies on Alcohol, 40,* 272–282.

Bushman, B. J., & Cooper, H. M. (1990). Effects of alcohol on human aggression: An integrative research review. *Psychological Bulletin, 107,* 341–354.

Coles, R., & Stokes, G. (1985). *Sex and the American teenager.* New York: HarperCollins.

Collins, J. J. (1986). The relationship of problem drinking to individual offending sequences. In A. Blumstein, J. Cohen, J. A. Roth, & C. Visher (Eds.), *Criminal careers and "career criminals"* (pp. 89–120). Washington, DC: National Academy Press.

Collins, J. J., & Schlenger, W. E. (1988). Acute and chronic effects of alcohol use on violence. *Journal of Studies on Alcohol, 49,* 532–537.

Crowe, L. C., & George, W. H. (1989). Alcohol and human sexuality: Review and integration. *Psychological Bulletin, 105,* 374–386.

Farkas, G., & Rosen, R. C. (1976). The effects of ethanol on male sexual arousal. *Journal of Studies on Alcohol, 37,* 265–272.

Fillmore, K. M. (1985). The social victims of drinking. *British Journal of Addiction, 80,* 307–314.

Flanagan, B., McLean, A., Hall, C., & Propp, V. (1990). Alcohol use as a situational influence on young women's pregnancy risk-taking behaviors. *Adolescence, 25,* 205–214.

Frieze, I. H., & Knoble, J. (1980, Sept.). *The effect of alcohol on marital violence.* Paper presented at the annual convention of the American Psychological Association, Montreal, Canada.

Frieze, I. H., & Schafer, P. C. (1983). Alcohol use and marital violence: Female and male differences in reactions to alcohol. In S. C. Wilsnack & L. J. Beckman (Eds.), *Alcohol problems in women: Antecedents, consequences, and intervention* (pp. 260–279). New York: Guilford Press.

Gebhard, P. H., Gagnon, J. H., Pomeroy, W. B., & Christianson, C. V. (1965). *Sex offenders.* New York: Harper & Row.

Gelles, R. J. (1972). *The violent home: A study of physical aggression between husbands and wives.* Newbury Park, CA: Sage.

George, W. H., & Marlatt, G. A. (1986). The effects of alcohol and anger on interest in violence, erotica, and deviance. *Journal of Abnormal Psychology, 95,* 150–158.

Gerson, L. W. (1978). Alcohol-related acts of violence: Who was drinking and where the acts occurred. *Journal of Studies on Alcohol, 39,* 1294–1296.

Hingson, R. W., Strunin, L., Berlin, B. M., & Heeren, T. (1990). Beliefs about AIDS, use of alcohol, drugs, and unprotected sex among Massachusetts adolescents. *American Journal of Public Health, 80,* 295–299.

Hull, J. G., & Bond, C. F. (1986). Social and behavior consequences of alcohol consumption and expectancy: A meta-analysis. *Psychological Bulletin, 99,* 347–360.

Jones, B. M., & Jones, M. (1976). Women and alcohol: Intoxication, metabolism, and the menstrual cycle. In M. Greenblatt & M. A. Schuckit (Eds.), *Alcoholism problems in women and children* (pp. 103–136). New York: Grune & Stratton.

Josephs, R. A., & Steele, C. M. (1990). The two faces of alcohol myopia: Attentional mediation of psychological stress. *Journal of Abnormal Psychology, 99,* 115–126.

Kinsey, A. W., Pomeroy, W. B., Martin, C., & Gebhard, P. (1953). *Sexual behavior in the human female.* Philadelphia: W. B. Saunders.

Klassen, A. D., & Wilsnack, S. C. (1986). Sexual experiences and drinking among women in a U.S. national survey. *Archives of Sexual Behavior, 15,* 363–392.

Leigh, B. W. (1990). Alcohol and unsafe sex: An overview of research and theory. In D. Seminara, A. Pawlowski, & R. Watson (Eds.), *Alcohol, immunomodulation, and AIDS* (pp. 35–46). New York: Alan R. Liss.

Leigh, B. C., & Morrison, D. M. (1991). Alcohol consumption and sexual risk-taking in adolescents. *Alcohol Health and Research World, 15,* 58–63.

Lemere, F., & Smith, J. W. (1973). Alcohol-induced sexual impotence. *American Journal of Psychiatry, 130,* 212–213.

Leonard, K. E., Bromet, E. J., Parkinson, D. K., Day, N. L., & Ryan, C. M. (1985). Patterns of alcohol use and physically aggressive behaviour in men. *Journal of Studies on Alcohol, 46,* 279–282.

Lohrenz, L. J., Connelly, J. C., Coyne, L., & Spare, K. E. (1978). Alcohol problems in several Midwestern homosexual communities. *Journal of Studies on Alcohol, 39,* 1959–1963.

MacAndrew, C., & Edgerton, R. B. (1969). *Drunken comportment: A social explanation.* Chicago: Aldine.

Masters, W. H., & Johnson, V. E. (1966). *Human sexual response.* Boston: Little, Brown.

Mayfield, D. (1976). Alcoholism, alcohol, intoxication and assaultive behavior. *Diseases of the Nervous System, 37,* 288–291.

McKirnan, D. J., & Peterson, P. L. (1989). Alcohol and drug use among homosexual men and women: Epidemiology and population characteristics. *Addictive Behaviors, 14,* 545–553.

Miller, B. A., Downs, W. R., & Gondoli, D. M. (1989). Spousal violence among alcoholic women as compared to a random household sample of women. *Journal of Studies on Alcohol, 50,* 533–540.

Murdoch, D., Pihl, R. O., & Ross, D. (1990). Alcohol and crimes of violence: Present issues. *International Journal of the Addictions, 25,* 1065–1081.

Orford, J., Guthrie, S., Nicholls, P., Oppenheimer, E., Egert, S., & Hensman, C. (1975). Self-reported coping behaviour of wives of alcoholics and its association with drinking outcome. *Journal of Studies on Alcohol, 36,* 1254–1267.

Paul, J. P., Stall, R., & Bloomfield, K. A. (1991). Gay and alcoholic: Epidemiologic and clinical issues. *Alcohol and Health Research World, 15,* 151–160.

Pernanen, K. (1976). Alcohol and crimes of violence. In B. Kissin & H. Begleiter (Eds.), *The biology of alcoholism* (pp. 351–444). New York: Plenum Press.

Pernanen, K. (1981). Theoretical aspects of the relationship between alcohol use and crime. In J. J. Collins (Ed.), *Drinking and crime: Perspectives on the relationships between alcohol consumption and criminal behavior* (pp. 1–69). New York: Guilford Press.

Robertson, J. A., & Plant, M. A. (1988). Alcohol, sex, and risks of HIV infection. *Drug and Alcohol Dependence, 22,* 75–78.

Steele, C. M., & Southwick, L. (1985). Alcohol and social behavior I: The psychology of drunken excess. *Journal of Personality and Social Psychology, 48,* 18–34.

Straus, M., & Gelles, R. J. (1986). Societal change and change in family violence from 1975 to 1985 as revealed by two national surveys. *Journal of Marriage and the Family, 48,* 465–479.

Taylor, S. P., & Leonard, K. E. (1983). Alcohol and human physical aggression. In R. G. Geen & E. I. Donnerstein (Eds.), *Aggression: Theoretical and empirical reviews. Vol. 2. Issues in research.* New York: Academic Press.

Van Hasselt, V. B., Morrison, R. L., & Bellack, A. S. (1985). Alcohol use in wife abusers and their spouses. *Addictive Behaviors, 10,* 127–135.

Welte, J. W., & Abel, E. L. (1989). Homicide: Drinking by the victim. *Journal of Studies on Alcohol, 50,* 197–201.

Wilsnack, S. C. (1973). Sex role identity in female alcoholism. *Journal of Abnormal Psychology, 82,* 253–261.

Wilson, G. T., & Lawson, D. W. (1976a). The effects of alcohol on sexual arousal in women. *Journal of Abnormal Psychology, 85,* 489–497.

Wilson, G. T., & Lawson, D. W. (1976b). Expectancies, alcohol, and sexual arousal in male social drinkers. *Journal of Abnormal Psychology, 85,* 587–594.

Wilson, G. T., & Lawson, D. M. (1978). Expectancies, alcohol, and sexual arousal in women. *Journal of Abnormal Psychology, 87,* 358–367.

Wolchik, S. A., Braver, S. L., & Jensen, K. (1985). Volunteer bias in erotica research: Effects of intrusiveness of measure and sexual background. *Archives of Sexual Behavior, 14,* 93–107.

Zucker, R. A., Battistich, V. A., & Langer, G. B. (1981). Sexual behavior, sex-role adaptation, and drinking in young women. *Journal of Studies on Alcohol, 42,* 457–465.

Theories of Drinking

What are the factors that lead people to drink alcohol? Why are some drinkers more likely to become intoxicated? Why do some drinkers develop alcoholism while others seem to avoid problems stemming from alcohol use? To what extent is alcohol use governed by internal versus external factors? What are the relative roles of physiological and cognitive factors in drinking? These are some of the intriguing questions that arise about the psychological bases of alcohol use and abuse.

In this chapter, we will examine major theories about the nature of the processes underlying alcohol consumption and its consequences. We will describe the processes proposed by each theory as well as discuss the evidence from research designed to evaluate its validity. The theories to be presented focus variously on physiological, affective, cognitive, and social psychological factors. Because all of these factors are involved in motivating the use of alcohol, no single theory can be regarded as complete. Instead, it may be useful to think of the theories as complementing each other in giving us a full picture of alcohol consumption.

Theories of alcohol use must direct attention to processes that precede the onset of drinking: the developmental process of beginning drinkers as well as the specific instigations of experienced drinkers. Social learning theory, which emphasizes beliefs and expectancies about the effects of alcohol, is relevant for understanding this stage. How does alcohol use serve drinkers after drinking has become an established habit? The effect of alcohol on interpersonal interactions can often involve the use of socially learned strategies such as those depicted in excuse and self-handicapping theories. Tension reduction and self-awareness reduction models emphasize processes occurring mainly within the individual, such as the use of alcohol for coping with stress. Theories such as stress-response dampening theory and the opponent-process model focus on the physiological and affective changes caused once alcohol has been consumed.

Theories about drinking must also address the question of what happens to terminate drinking episodes. What happens to the drinker following cessation of drinking? Finally, the transition from normal or social drinking to alcoholic patterns of consumption is a crucial process that must also be explained.

Social Learning Theory

Social learning theory (Bandura, 1969) holds that we form expectancies about the effects of alcohol through observation. A number of beliefs about drinking are acquired in this manner. First, social norms or frequencies of different drinking behaviors and outcomes are noted. Observers see how much drinking is permissible in various situations and what kinds of behavior typically occur with different drinking patterns.

The knowledge we acquire, whether it pertains to drinking or to other behaviors, can influence our feelings of *self-efficacy*. One's level of self-efficacy, the belief that one can control outcomes regarding an activity, affects the motivation for engaging in that behavior (Bandura, 1977). Thus, a poor student would be more likely to drop out of school than a good student because of lesser feelings of

self-efficacy in academic endeavors. To increase feelings of s
dividual may try a variety of solutions ranging from more study
the use of alcohol or drugs. If, for example, our hypothetical studen̪.
people who drank alcohol seemed to be more academically competent, have ı̣.̣
fun socially, or cope with stressors better, these expectations about alcohol might
lead to drinking in hopes of achieving greater feelings of self-efficacy. Conversely,
observation that drinking leads to poorer academic achievement, interpersonal
tension, or inadequate coping with stressors should create expectations that drinking reduces feelings of self-efficacy.

Social learning theory focuses on the expectations held about the ability to
cope with a stressor, but the theory also recognizes the role of affect. Thus, when
we experience negative affective states, we often have lesser feelings of self-efficacy
in dealing with problems. If we believe that alcohol can reduce the negative affect,
we might try to "drink our troubles away." In situations such as a party where
positive affect prevails, our expectations that alcohol will lower inhibitions and
allow positive feelings to occur can also stimulate drinking.

Social learning theory is also concerned with the relationship of coping skills
to drinking. Individuals who have adequate coping skills and high self-esteem are
able to drink at socially acceptable levels and to develop friendships with others
who also avoid alcohol abuse so that a mutual or reciprocal influence develops. In
contrast, those who will probably develop into problem drinkers and alcoholics
are those with poor coping skills in general for dealing with life problems.
Consequently, they may turn to alcohol as a means to reduce tension, escape from
problems, and feel better. But such excessive use of alcohol will only serve to
isolate them from those with acceptable drinking levels. Eventually they will
affiliate increasingly with similar alcohol abusers, and they will mutually reinforce
this lifestyle, so that a reciprocal influence exists among members of this group as
well.

The social context of drinking can also affect an observer's responses to
drinking by others (MacAndrew & Edgerton, 1969). Collins, Parks, and Marlatt
(1985) conducted an experiment in which subjects were paired with accomplices
who drank either a small or a large amount. They found that the observers' own
level of drinking was correlated with that of their drinking models. The nature of
the social interaction between the model and the observer also affected drinking
level. The more a sociable model drank, the more the observer drank. In contrast,
subjects who observed unsociable models, regardless of their drinking levels,
drank more, presumably to relieve the tension of the social situation.

Beliefs and Expectancies

Alcohol is a drug and produces physiological effects, but the individual's psychological experiences may also be important in reactions to drinking. All drinkers
have certain beliefs and expectations about the effects of alcohol, many of which
are acquired during childhood before ever having drunk a drop of alcohol.
Vicarious learning from movies and television as well as observation and conversa-
tion provide ample opportunity for children to acquire strong expectations. Thus,

Miller, Smith, and Goldman (1990) found positive alcohol expectancies in young children that increased with age. However, children from alcoholic families showed less positive expectancies.

The Alcohol Expectancy Questionnaire (AEQ) developed by Brown, Goldman, Inn, and Anderson (1980)* assesses expectancies and beliefs regarding the effects of alcohol. These researchers had college students rate a set of positive expectancies about alcohol use. They identified six basic expectancies, listed here along with a sample item for each:

1. global positive transforming effect ("Alcohol seems like magic")
2. social/physical pleasure ("Drinking makes me feel good")
3. sexual enhancement ("I often feel sexier after I've had a few drinks")
4. arousal/power/aggression ("If I'm feeling restricted in any way, a few drinks make me feel better")
5. increased social assertiveness ("A few drinks make it easier to talk to people")
6. relaxation/tension reduction ("Alcohol helps me sleep better")

After drinking begins, the original expectations may be revised in line with each individual's actual experience, as determined by factors as varied as alcohol sensitivity and tolerance, amounts consumed, and the conditions or context of drinking.

The AEQ-A, a version of the scale developed with adolescents, yielded factors (Christiansen, Goldman, & Inn, 1982) similar to those on the AEQ. A comparison of expectancies before drinking started with those held a year later showed only slight differences, suggested that psychological factors are the major determinants of early drinking, while pharmacological factors fine tune the expectations. It is likely that higher positive expectancies will promote future drinking. Thus, Brown, Creamer, and Stetson (1987), using the AEQ-A, found higher positive expectancies about alcohol effects among adolescent problem drinkers than among nondrinkers.

A study of seventh- and eighth-grade adolescents (Christiansen, Roehling, Smith, & Goldman, 1989) showed that those who had higher expectancies of enhanced social functioning and improved cognitive and motor functioning were more likely to be drinking at the time of the initial survey as well as a year later. Thus, alcohol expectations play an important role in motivating people to begin as well as to continue drinking.

The relationship of expectations to drinking among college students was examined by Brown, Goldman, and Christiansen (1985) using the AEQ. They found that alcoholics had greater positive expectancies than the college students on all factors except for tension reduction. Mooney, Fromme, Kivlahan, and Marlatt (1987) reported that college males who drank more frequently had higher expectations of social and physical pleasure, global positive changes, and sexual enhancement. In contrast, for females more frequent drinking was related to

* From "Do alcohol expectancies mediate drinking patterns of adults?" by S. A. Brown, M. S. Goldman, A. Inn, and L. R. Anderson in *Journal of Consulting and Clinical Psychology, 1980, 48,* 419–426. Copyright © 1980 by American Psychological Association.

expectations of reduced tension or relaxation. Higher expectations of social and physical pleasure and social assertion was related to a greater amount of drinking for both sexes.

Negative Expectancies.   Although widely used, the AEQ has some limits because it examines only positive expectancies. *Negative* expectancies about alcohol effects should also be tested as predictors of drinking. Some negative expectations may have weaker effects because they involve distal or delayed consequences—for example, hangovers that may not occur until the morning after drinking. Leigh (1987a) found that heavier drinkers expected less impairment, but more nastiness and disinhibition, from drinking than did lighter drinkers.

A survey by Southwick, Steele, Marlatt, and Lindell (1981) assessed both positive and negative beliefs about alcohol effects. In addition, they took into account the *biphasic* nature of alcohol effects, in which the effects eventually reverse due to adaptation and metabolism of the alcohol consumed. Southwick et al. found that expectancies in the initial phase of alcohol effect were positive, especially for heavy drinkers. But as time after drinking passed, in phase 2 there was a return to neutral expectancies for light drinkers and a shift to negative expectancies for heavy drinkers.

Drinking Parameters.   The AEQ does not assess expectancies as a function of different dose levels, allowing respondents to rate only their typical drinking levels. Furthermore, the situation or context of the drinking is not specified on the instrument so that only generalized expectancies are assessed.

Dose level is an important determinant of expectancies. Southwick et al. (1981) found that moderate doses were associated with expectations of pleasurable disinhibition whereas higher doses were expected to impair behavior.

Many studies have shown only a modest positive correlation between the magnitude of alcohol expectancies and the extent of drinking, more so with respect to quantity than to frequency of drinking (for example, Leigh, 1987b). Apparently, the quantity consumed per occasion matters more than the frequency of drinking episodes in determining expected effects.

Heavy versus Light Drinkers.   As noted earlier, Southwick et al. (1981) found different expectancies for different types of drinkers. In order to understand why heavy and light drinkers have different expectancies, it may be important to examine the conditions that prompt them to begin their drinking episodes. Marlatt (1987) suggested that the typical light drinker is in a positive mood when drinking starts. The drinking might take place at a party or celebration where a festive mood prevails, and the drinking is intended to enhance the good time already existing. This mood coupled with alcohol's ability initially to enhance mood accentuates the good effect. After drinking ends, negative effects occur but they are offset by the positive affect experienced in phase 1, so there is a gradual decline to a state of neutral feeling or mildly negative states. In short, a restoration of balanced emotions occurs.

In contrast, heavy drinkers more often drink when they are in a negative mood already. They may be depressed, lonely, or angry, and they seek alcohol to improve their mood. In phase 1, alcohol may work to counter the negative moods they start out with. A few extra strong drinks gulped down quickly may give a momentary positive lift. However, in phase 2, after drinking ends and the effects of alcohol wear off, negative feelings and fatigue arise. These conditions are apt to prompt drinking episodes in the near future that repeat the cycle just described with increasing frequency and severity.

Heavier drinkers are more lenient in their attitudes, not surprisingly, and believe less than lighter drinkers in the likelihood of adverse effects. In part, this leniency could be a self-serving rationalization for their own drinking, but it might be that heavier drinkers have adapted to heavy use and actually experience less negative impact from their drinking.

Sex Differences. Different expectancies have also been reported for men and women. In a study by Critchlow (1983), men expected a greater impact of alcohol on personality than women did. However, since men typically drink more heavily than women do, that factor is confounded with sex per se. It is possible that men may use intoxication as an excuse for unacceptable behaviors more than women do. They would find it to their advantage to regard alcohol effects as more potent than women would. Women, who are often the victims of alcohol's effects on men, may attribute such behaviors to the influence of alcohol rather than to personality changes in the male drinkers.

Processes Underlying Expectancy Effects

What is the nature of the underlying mechanisms by which expectancy can actually evoke physical or psychological responses? A strictly pharmacological basis might involve classical conditioning. By this reasoning, past association of alcohol consumption with certain effects should allow the mere belief that one has consumed alcohol to elicit the same types of effects to some degree.

Leigh (1989) noted the lack of a theoretical understanding of the observed relationships between expectancies and drinking. She called for research on how these beliefs and drinking affect each other. If expectancies motivate drinking, she argued, then those who value more highly the expected outcomes should be more likely to drink. Also, each individual may have a number of expectancies about alcohol effects that may affect drinking, and these expectancies differ not only in saliency within each person but also across individuals.

Additionally, research must examine how the situation in which the drinking takes place can modify expectancies. Thus, drinking at a party might be expected to enhance good times, whereas drinking in the classroom might be expected to lead to a number of negative consequences. Research is also needed to test the implication that if expectancies (or values) are modified, then drinking changes will also follow. Any occurrence of the opposite effect—that is, a change in drinking patterns without any corresponding changes in expectancies, would suggest that additional factors are involved in the motivation of drinking behavior.

Since most expectancy studies have been cross-sectional in design, they are inconclusive as to questions of causality. Thus, it is possible that the expectancies are the effect, not the cause, of the drinking. Longitudinal studies in which the expectancies are measured first and correlated with later drinking are needed to resolve this question. Findings in one such study (Bauman, Fisher, Bryan, & Chenoweth, 1985) support the view that expectancies and drinking are related in a complex reciprocal manner, with initial expectancies determining drinking, and drinking outcomes then modifying those expectancies, and so on.

Alcohol as an Excuse

Oscar Levant, the eccentric pianist, once lamented, "I envy people who drink—at least they know what to blame everything on." Not uncommonly, when people drink they attribute some of their behavior to the effects of alcohol, especially if they might otherwise be blamed or criticized for their misconduct while drinking. People learn that being under the influence of alcohol is widely accepted by others as a social excuse. MacAndrew and Edgerton (1969) held that when individuals have had alcohol to drink they may use it as an excuse for their socially unacceptable behaviors.

Hull and Bond (1986) predicted that this excuse mechanism would be invoked more frequently for deviant social behaviors such as some forms of aggression or sexual misconduct but less often for nonsocial behaviors such as mood changes or memory lapses, where there might be less need for an excuse. They reanalyzed findings from 34 different published experiments by other investigators that used the balanced placebo design and estimated the effects of alcohol consumption, alcohol expectancy, and the interaction of these two factors on the attributions people gave for their behavior following the receipt of alcohol or a placebo. Both consumption and expectancy effects were found in various studies, showing that it is important to consider the role of the psychological factor of expectancy as well as that of the pharmacological factor of alcohol.

More important, as they predicted, the effects of alcohol consumption were more likely to exceed those of alcohol expectancy with nonsocial behaviors, while the opposite pattern tended to occur for deviant social behaviors. This pattern of findings supports the view that alcohol acts as an excuse, with expectancy effects occurring only for socially deviant behaviors. Interactions of the two variables (for example, the expectancy effect exceeding the consumption effect if the person was expecting alcohol, but not if no alcohol was expected) were rarely observed.

Self-Handicapping and Alcohol Use

The use of alcohol as an excuse for one's failings is related to the intriguing phenomenon of making excuses *prior* to an anticipated shortcoming as a strategy to protect self-esteem. Jones and Berglas (1978) referred to excessive use of alcohol as a type of self-handicapping strategy when one expects failure or when past success creates anxiety about the likelihood of continued achievement. To test their theory, Berglas and Jones (1978) devised an anagram test. They presented some subjects with unsolvable anagrams. These subjects did not know the anagrams had no solutions but they were told they had succeeded on some of the problems. Another group of subjects succeeded on solvable anagrams. It was predicted that subjects with the unsolvable problems, some of which they apparently had "solved," would perceive a greater threat to self-esteem when given a second similar task than would the subjects with solvable anagrams. Prior to the second task, subjects were offered a drug that would supposedly either impair or improve performance (no drug was actually given, as the experiment ended after the choice was made). It was predicted and found that the subjects with unsolvable problems would choose the "harmful" drug more often than those with the solvable problems. By choosing the performance-impairing drug, the subjects with the inexplicable success on the first task provided themselves with a self-handicap or excuse for the poor performance that they expected would occur on the second task.

Tucker, Vuchinich, and Sobell (1981) conducted two experiments to further test the Jones and Berglas hypothesis. Subjects were informed that the purpose of the study was to examine the effects of drinking on cognitive performance. They took an intellectual performance test twice, with the opportunity to drink alcohol during a 15-minute break between the two tests. In one study, subjects also had study materials available that the experimenter said would help their performance on the task. Given this alternative means for coping with the task, subjects used the time to study, providing little support for the self-handicapping theory. However, in a second experiment where the study materials were not provided, the findings did match the predictions of self-handicapping theory. Thus, self-handicapping with alcohol may occur as a last resort rather than as a preferred coping method.

Self-Awareness Reduction Theory

A popular conception about drinking, often the theme of heartbreak songs, is that it can help one escape or forget troubles. Jay Hull (1981; 1987) proposed the self-awareness reduction model, which holds that drinking can impair cognitive processes and hence reduce awareness about one's own situation. Not only is access to previously acquired memories reduced, but acquisition of new information is disrupted to an even greater extent, according to Birnbaum and Parker (1977). It is presumed that alcohol interferes with storage of new information by disrupting organizational strategies (Birnbaum, Parker, Hartley, & Noble, 1978).

Self-awareness is generally heightened by the ability to encode and classify information that is relevant to the individual. Alcohol, by preventing awareness of an individual's own values and beliefs about proper conduct, can lead to disinhibitory effects on some usually inhibited behaviors.

Effects on Self-Awareness

Hull, Levenson, Young, and Sher (1983) gave subjects a moderate dose of an alcoholic or placebo beverage and recorded their self-references in assigned speeches about their physical self-perceptions. Self-relevant pronouns such as *I*,

me, myself, my, and *mine* were less frequent for the alcoho'
lowering of self-awareness due to alcohol consumption.
pectancy of consuming alcohol rather than the actual consumptio.
have produced this effect was ruled out in a second study in which
consumption and expectancy were varied with the balanced placebo desi
self-reference occurred in the groups consuming alcohol than in those groups
only expected alcohol.

Effects on Self-Relevant Encoding

How does alcohol reduce self-awareness? Hull et al. (1983) hypothesized that alcohol disrupts processing of information about the self. They gave an alcoholic beverage or a placebo to subjects of either high or low levels of self-consciousness. It was assumed that persons with high self-consciousness would process self-relevant information at a deeper cognitive level and be able to recall it better. Subjects were presented with a list of 30 common words and asked to classify the words as to structural features (is it short or long?), semantic aspects (is it meaning-ful?), and self-relevance (does it describe you?). Later, they received an unexpected recall test to see how many words they remembered.

It was predicted and found that with a placebo, the highly self-conscious subjects had better recall of the self-relevant than the nonrelevant words. However, as predicted, recall of self-relevant words after consuming alcohol was poorer for subjects with high self-consciousness than for those with low self-consciousness.

Strategic Avoidance of Self-Awareness

Use of alcohol can help one deliberately avoid self-awareness. When one is experiencing success, feedback should be welcome, but when failure occurs alcohol may be used to prevent self-awareness. Hull and Young (1983) provided, on a random basis, fake feedback of either success or failure to subjects working on tasks that resembled an intelligence test. Subjects were then placed in an apparent-ly unrelated second study in which they had to rate the taste of wines and then their mood. Conditions allowed them to drink as much or as little as they liked in forming their taste ratings. In each group, subjects were further divided on the basis of a personality scale to determine high versus low levels of self-conscious-ness.

According to the hypothesis, failure should evoke more negative affective moods, especially for those high in self-consciousness, and these individuals should drink more wine in the taste testing. The results confirmed the predicted interaction, with failure leading to more drinking by highly self-conscious subjects only.

Hull, Young, and Jouriles (1986) applied the model to account for relapse among treated alcoholics. They examined relapse among male alcoholics after three and also after six months following detoxification and found that among those who scored high on self-consciousness there were more self-relevant life events with negative outcomes.

Self-Awareness and Self-Regulation

The self-awareness reduction theory is related to the excuse theory of alcohol use. Lowered self-awareness created by alcohol's impairment of cognitive processing may give drinkers an excuse for violating social norms. By reducing self-awareness, alcohol could also reduce compliance with one's typical standards of appropriate behavior, leading to varying degrees of socially unacceptable behaviors.

The Tension Reduction Hypothesis

A commonsense view of the reason people drink alcohol is known as the tension reduction hypothesis. According to this hypothesis, people believe that alcohol can relieve aversive states such as tension and anxiety. When tension is unpleasantly high, people may drink, expecting that the alcohol will lower the tension. If this expectation is upheld, their tendency to resort to alcohol as a future means of coping with tension should be increased by this reinforcing experience.

Tension Reduction as an Effect of Drinking

The tension reduction view has been examined by research that dates from the 1940s. It is consistent with behavioristic models such as those of Conger (1951) and Clark Hull (1943). According to Hull's learning theory, any response that reduces drive states such as hunger, thirst, or anxiety becomes reinforced and associated with that situation in the future. The next time an organism is in a similar situation it should be likely to perform the same response that was previously successful in lowering the drive state.

Masserman and Yum (1946) tested this theory using cats that received an aversive air puff when they were in front of the food dish. It was assumed and found that alcohol reduced tension because when cats received alcohol in advance they were more likely to approach the food in spite of the aversive air puff. Other animal learning tests were used by other investigators but yielded less conclusive support for the tension reduction theory (Cappell & Herman, 1972).

Evidence for the theory is even more mixed in studies with humans. Alcohol might increase rather than lower tension in some situations and possibly add to drinking tendencies. Although self-report and clinical observation might suggest that alcohol reduces tension, controlled studies (for example, Nathan, 1976) have indicated that anxiety is generally not alleviated by alcohol for social drinkers or alcoholics. Laboratory studies by Mendelson (1964) in which alcoholics received alcohol under carefully monitored conditions found that tension increased with drinking.

Furthermore, expectancies about alcohol effects in different settings may not be the same for any one person. Thus, the laboratory findings that alcohol consumption increases tension could possibly be due to the artificiality of such drinking conditions. In the case of alcoholics in treatment who may or may not want to stop drinking, the therapists' reminding them of the adverse effects of drinking might increase the likelihood that their subsequent drinking would

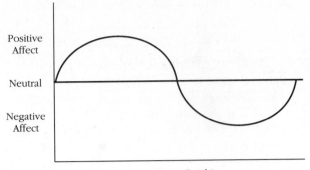

Figure 6-1 A diagram of the biphasic nature of the effect of alcohol on affective experience as a function of time since drinking. Positive affect rises to a peak, followed by a return to neutral, an increase in negative affect to a peak, and then an eventual return to neutral.

increase tension. In contrast, drinking might lower tension at a social gathering where most drinkers seem to be enjoying themselves.

Finally, Marlatt noted that alcohol effects are biphasic, leading only initially to tension reduction and positive feelings such as relief and pleasure. This positive state might continue and rise to a peak as either heavier doses are taken or as the blood alcohol content from a given dose increases over time, as illustrated in Figure 6-1. With further passage of time, however, the tension may reverse and start to increase along with feelings of discomfort and anxiety, reaching a peak and then returning to a state of neutrality. Thus, alcohol can produce both positive and negative affective states, with the dose level and temporal factors being important determinants of the direction of affect.

Tension as a Cause of Drinking

In addition to being modified by alcohol use, stress and tension may actually cause drinking. It seems reasonable that if people believe alcohol reduces tension, even if it does not directly do so, stress will be a primary motivator of drinking, unless they eventually learn that it is not effective.

While laboratory studies afford better control than anecdotal or naturalistic evidence for testing the effects of stress on drinking, one problem is that subjects may be suspicious of receiving alcohol in such a setting and respond to the alcohol differently from the way they normally would. Higgins and Marlatt (1973) used a taste rating task to disguise the true purpose of administering alcohol. Subjects were led to believe that they were sampling different wines to assess their taste preferences; in actuality, the goal was to see if subjects sampled a larger quantity of alcohol when higher stress was induced by the experimental task. Although none of the subjects actually received a shock, one group of males was told they would later encounter a painful shock to see how it affected taste reactions, whereas another group of males was told they would receive a mild shock for the same purpose.

It was predicted that the high fear condition should lead to more alcohol consumption if alcohol were, in fact, expected to relieve tension. However, no such effect was found with either social drinkers or a group of male alcoholics. One problem with this study is that the rather unusual threat of electric shock might not reflect the sorts of tensions people ordinarily attempt to relieve by drinking.

In a further study using the taste rating task, Higgins and Marlatt (1975) examined the effects of social evaluation on drinking by telling male students that they would soon be interacting with females who would be evaluating them on their personal attractiveness. Control subjects were not led to expect these subsequent evaluations. During the 15-minute tasting test, the group expecting to be evaluated drank about twice as much as the group that did not expect evaluation. Thus, in this situation tension appeared to induce drinking.

Volpicelli (1987) noted that when stress is present, drinking may often be inhibited, but after the stress is over, drinking may increase. For example, Pihl and Yankofsky (1979) had male social drinkers work unsolvable anagrams but gave false feedback that their performance was among either the top 15 percent or the bottom 15 percent of participants. Drinking decreased after the feedback for those given stressful negative feedback, suggesting that the presence of tension did not facilitate drinking. For those receiving positive feedback, which relieved stress, increased drinking occurred.

Volpicelli hypothesized that stress may deplete endorphins (Davis & Walsh, 1970), a type of opioid substance released in the brain to help counter pain. Consequently, drinking may increase following such depletion to stimulate endorphin production. Over time, individuals may increasingly turn to alcohol following stressful experiences to compensate for the endorphin deficiency.

Alcohol use, it should be pointed out, is not the only possible response available for relieving tension in many situations. If other responses are available that can lower the tension, use of alcohol may not be necessary. Thus, in one study (Marlatt, Kosturn, & Lang, 1975) male subjects were angered by an accomplice of the experimenter. Then, half of the subjects had a chance to administer shocks to the accomplice on a task. No shocks were actually given. Finally, on a taste-rating task the subjects allowed to "shock" the accomplice consumed less alcohol than did the group that did not have this means of "getting even." But Marlatt suggested that tension reduction may not be the primary motive for drinking. Instead, feelings of power and control resulting from drinking may be more important. In fact, when the tired worker comes home and has a drink to relax, it probably creates physiological arousal but is paradoxically interpreted as "relaxation" instead of as excitation.

This view is akin to that of McClelland, Davis, Kalin, and Wanner (1972), who maintained that drinking leads to fantasies of power. Situations where no alternatives for coping with tension exist may increase the chance that alcohol will be used in hopes of producing a feeling of power. Ironically, excessive alcohol use may produce adverse consequences that eventually increase rather than lower tension. In contrast, if there are other alternatives for reducing tension, the likelihood of alcohol use may be lower.

Stress-Response Dampening Theory

Sher and Levenson (1982) regarded stress as a determinant of drinking, but not as a necessary or sufficient one. Their stress-response dampening model focuses on the pharmacological effects of alcohol. It assumes there is a complex psychophysiological response to alcohol, especially due to factors such as individual differences and social context. This theory of drinking gives less emphasis to cognitive factors such as expectancies. Thus, although social drinkers *expect* a reduction in tension when they consume alcohol, in this model such expectancies are not as important as psychophysiological factors are.

Stress-response dampening theory (Sher, 1987) is a pared-down version of the tension reduction hypothesis discussed earlier. Alcohol typically dampens or *reduces* stress, especially cardiovascular reactions, so that alcohol consumption is reinforcing. Thus, alcohol moderates the reaction to stress.

However, it is possible that alcohol does not dampen all bodily reactions to stress. Fowles (1980) extended a model of drug effects that involves the postulation of a behavior inhibitory system (BIS) and a behavior activation system (BAS), as proposed by Gray (1978). Fowles proposed that electrodermal response as indexed by the galvanic skin response reflects the activation of the BIS in aversive situations to inhibit responding. In contrast, the BAS is assumed to activate appetitional or goal-directed activity. Heart rate is used as an index of such activation. Alcohol, as well as many other drugs, may inhibit behavior. One question is whether such effects apply equally to situations involving aversive consequences and those associated with appetitional behavior.

Alcohol Effects on Psychophysiological Indexes

Many studies have shown that alcohol reduces heart rate response levels (for example, Cummings & Marlatt, 1983; Sher & Levenson, 1982), whereas the evidence about its effect on electrodermal indexes of stress such as the galvanic skin response is less consistent (for example, Cummings & Marlatt, 1983; Sher & Levenson, 1982). This pattern suggests that alcohol does not have a generalized dampening effect but acts selectively on the cardiovascular responses.

Moderators of Stress-Dampening Effects

Dose Level. One determinant of whether alcohol dampens stress is the amount of alcohol consumed. To reduce cardiovascular responding levels, high doses of alcohol equivalent to four or five drinks within an hour (for example, .75 to 1 g/kg) are typically needed.

Type of Stressor. The type of stressor—physical versus psychological—is also a factor that determines the effect of alcohol. Most people do not use alcohol to reduce all types of stresses because they realize that it would only add to stress in some situations—for example, drinking at the office. Instead, they may selectively use alcohol for only those stressors that they believe will be alleviated by drinking.

Individual Differences. Individual differences may exist in the magnitude of the stress-dampening effect. For women, expectations of consuming alcohol was found to be stress inducing, rather than reducing, perhaps due to the perceived negative social consequences of intoxication for women. Among social drinkers, Sher and Levenson (1982) found greater stress-response dampening (using a relatively large dose of 1 g/kg) for those who showed prealcoholic personality traits.

Availability of Alternatives to Alcohol. One of the most important findings from the stress-induced drinking literature is that the degree to which a stressor elicits drinking is in part a function of the availability of alternative coping responses, such as relaxation and retaliation. Stress itself may be neither sufficient nor necessary for drinking to occur; if no alternative exists and the probability of punishment is low, then drinking is more likely to take place.

Opponent-Process Theory

Solomon (1980) proposed the opponent-process theory as a general model of addictive behaviors, not one limited to alcoholism. It is based on the role of two opposing affective reactions to the receipt and termination of strong stimuli. Since the model distinguishes between early and later stages of affective experiences, it is suited for explaining the transition from normal to addictive drinking.

Alcohol itself is a strong stimulus that produces an affective state, A, as shown in Figure 6-2, which reflects the greater magnitude of a over b, the underlying opponent processes. When this effect dissipates, an affective aftereffect, B, occurs

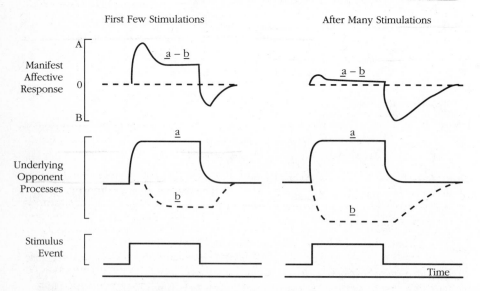

Figure 6-2 The opponent-process model of addiction.

Source: From "The opponent-process theory of acquired motivation: The costs and pleasure and benefits of pain," by R. L. Solomon in the *American Psychologist, 1980, 35,* 691–712. Copyright © by the American Psychological Association. Reprinted by permission.

that is opposite in emotional tone to that produced by the consumption of alcohol because a is now smaller than b. If the alcohol produced positive affect, its removal or termination leaves a feeling of negative tone. Taken together, the two states represent opponent processes. The process is similar to that involved in producing visual aftereffects; if we look at a red light constantly for a few minutes and then close our eyes, we may see the complementary or opposite color, green.

Early versus Later Stages

The opponent-process theory explains why the relationship between the two opposing affective states shifts over time as the drinker becomes more experienced with alcohol. For beginning or light drinkers, a small amount of alcohol is capable of producing a strong positive affect (state A) while the negative aftereffect (state B) is relatively weak. However, as drinking continues and becomes heavier, tolerance develops. The small dose that originally was capable of producing a given amount of positive affect now generates a weaker A state. When the experienced heavy drinker does not have access to alcohol, the drinker's misery is compounded as the negative opponent process or B state is now much stronger than it was in the past when drinking was lighter. The typical "solution" adopted by the heavy drinker is to try to forestall both the loss of positive affect and the occurrence of the negative aftereffect by increasing the quantity and frequency of alcohol consumption. Unfortunately, this strategy backfires and further entraps the drinker into a cycle of deepening addiction.

Conditioning Processes

By adding concepts from classical conditioning theory, the opponent-process theory can account for the difficulty of reducing addictions such as alcoholism. In the famous experiments on classical conditioning by Pavlov (1927), dogs were trained to salivate to the sound of a tone that had been presented in conjunction with meat powder on a number of prior trials. Alcohol, like the meat powder can be considered an unconditioned stimulus (UCS) that produces certain inherent reactions called unconditioned responses (UCR), just as Pavlov's dogs responded to the meat powder with salivation, as shown in Figure 6-3.

A stimulus such as the tone, originally neutral with respect to the meat powder, can become a conditioned stimulus (CS) by association with an unconditioned stimulus (UCS) and substitute for it to elicit the salivation, which would then be the conditioned response (CR). Similarly, the sight, smell, or other cues that are paired with alcohol (UCS) can come to elicit the reactions that ordinarily occur in response to alcohol. When a newly learned stimulus (CS) acquires this ability, the reaction is referred to as a conditioned response (CR) although it is often highly similar to the UCR. Thus, the sight, name, or other cues associated with alcohol could become a stimulus (CS) that might trigger the urge or craving to drink (CR) if alcohol's effects (UCR) are desired. The potential number of environmental cues for drinking in our society are substantial and make it very difficult for someone who is trying to stop drinking to avoid being tempted to resume or continue. Many people have friends who drink. Many of the places that one visits may be sites

Pavlov's Classical Conditioning Paradigm	
Event	Reaction

Before Conditioning

Conditioned stimulus (CS) ————————▶ None related to food
(tone)

Unconditioned stimulus (UCS) ————▶ Unconditioned response (UCR)
(food powder)   (salivation)

After Conditioning

Conditioned stimulus (CS) ————————▶ Conditioned response (CR)
(tone)   (salivation)

Alcohol and Classical Conditioning	
Event	Reaction

Before Conditioning

Conditioned stimulus (CS) ————————▶ None related to alcohol
(alcohol drinking context cues)

Unconditioned stimulus (UCS) ————▶ Unconditioned response (UCR)
(alcohol)   (degrees of intoxication)

After Conditioning

Conditioned stimulus (CS) ————————▶ Conditioned response (CR)
(alcohol drinking context cues)   (craving)

Figure 6-3 The role of classical conditioning in alcohol consumption.

where drinking occurred previously. In addition, advertising and mass media portrayals rely heavily on presentations of drinking.

Moreover, the aversive B state that follows the end of the pleasant A state occurs in the presence of environmental cues that may also be conditioned to the B state (not shown in Figure 6-3). Later these powerful conditioned stimuli can activate uncomfortable feelings and cravings for alcohol and hence trigger renewed drinking. Thus, the alcoholic is caught in a viselike grip of both the conditioned stimuli associated with the pleasant feelings of drinking in the A state and those associated with the unpleasant B state sensations that occur after drinking ends. In view of the abundance of conditioned stimuli available, it is hardly surprising that the road to recovery for someone wishing to achieve and maintain abstinence is very difficult, as we will see again in a discussion of the causes of relapse in Chapter 13.

Conclusions

A diversity of theories about the causes and effects of alcohol use have been proposed, some focusing on physiological factors, some on cognitive and affective experiences, and others on social determinants. All of these factors are important, and they can influence each other. Expectations about the effects of alcohol can affect the physiological response just as the emotional reactions can alter the cognitive processes occurring while drinking. Thus, these theories should be viewed as complementary rather than as competing, as suggested by Figure 6-4. No single theory can account for all aspects of drinking and its effects, but considered together, these theories can account for a variety of phenomena related to drinking.

Social learning theory emphasizes cognitive factors, such as expectancies about alcohol, as determinants of drinking. Drinkers learn from watching others, and from past experiences, what effects alcohol can produce. They adjust their drinking according to their own needs and values. These expectancies exist for most people before they ever take their first drink. Hence, cognitive factors are initially much more important than physiological determinants of drinking. However, with continued drinking, the pharmacological effects may assume greater importance than social factors for later drinking, especially among heavy drinkers and alcoholics.

Social consequences of excessive drinking are sometimes negative. Drinkers are held accountable for clearly illegal and harmful consequences of their drinking, but they are sometimes excused for milder social transgressions. Drunkenness is often used by drinkers as an excuse for otherwise unacceptable behaviors largely

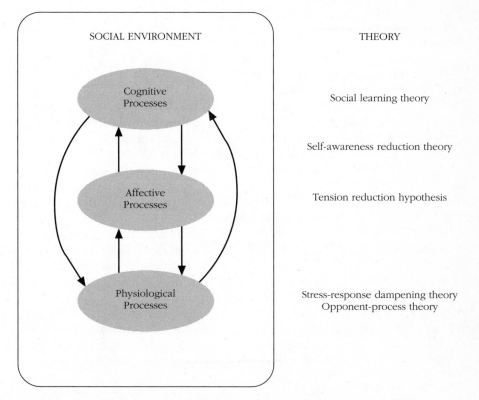

Figure 6-4 Interrelationship of theories about alcohol use and its effects.

because others hold drinkers less responsible for certain behaviors attributed to the influence of alcohol. Consequently, drinkers sometimes may avoid punishment for these behaviors. However, excuses can backfire as when drinkers use alcohol as a self-handicap and consequently increase the likelihood that their performance will be inadequate.

At a phenomenological level, drinkers report that they drink when under stress because it alleviates tension or helps them forget their problems. Tension reduction theory assumes a direct pharmacological influence of alcohol, such as relaxation, whereas self-awareness theory assumes an indirect process in which alcohol reduces awareness of distressful situations. Self-awareness reduction theory accounts for the way information processing is impaired by alcohol. Although drinkers may seek to reduce stress and self-awareness by drinking, sometimes the opposite effect may actually occur due to the impaired functioning and social criticism created by excessive drinking. Drinking may ironically increase tension— as a result of social rejection and disapproval or interpersonal conflicts, for example.

Other theories focus on the physiological processes underlying alcohol effects. Cardiovascular responses, in particular, and other physiologic stress reactions have been found to be dampened or reduced by use of alcohol. If alcohol dampens stress responses, drinking behavior under stress should be reinforcing. Those for whom these effects occur should be more likely to drink to cope when under stress. But stress-response dampening is not the only process involved when drinking typically occurs. This model focuses on how the physiological responses to alcohol affect stress. If responses other than drinking are available, they may determine the effect of drinking or even whether drinking occurs in the face of stress.

The opponent-process model directs attention to affective and conditioned determinants of drinking without considering cognitive factors. It is able to account for the development of tolerance as well as the difficulty of eliminating addictions to substances that evoke strong initial affective states.

A variety of methods, naturalistic and experimental, have been devised to test implications of each theory. Researchers attempting to reach definitive answers often prefer controlled studies. Experiments on the effects of alcohol conducted under controlled laboratory conditions sometimes suggest a different picture about the effects of alcohol than that held by the layperson. For example, if someone drinks and then becomes aggressive, is this outcome due to the alcohol per se or to the expectation derived from previously formed beliefs that alcohol transforms one into an aggressive person? With experiments, it is possible to separate effects of alcohol from the influence of beliefs about alcohol's effects to determine how much each factor contributes to the observed behavior. By equating groups through randomization on all factors except for the amount of alcohol consumed, an experiment can also test the argument that the observed differences are not caused by alcohol but merely reflect the possibility that those who tend to drink more may also be more aggressive.

But on the negative side, experiments are artificial and the behavior may not be reflective of behavior outside the laboratory. Sampling is limited to a small number of subjects as well as to unrepresentative samples of the general population; observations are of short duration, and subjects know their behavior is being observed. In laboratory settings, subjects drink on cue, quite unlike the situation in real life when the person decides when to have a drink.

However, it is important to have research using both naturalistic and laboratory methods to capitalize on the strengths of each type of evidence. We hope to ultimately understand real-life drinking behaviors, but too many uncontrollable variables may limit our comprehension. Laboratory studies afford us a more precise form of observation, but at the cost of reduced generalizability. Using evidence from both methods may enable us to gradually refine our models and derive more valid conclusions from our observations.

References

Bandura, A. (1969). *Principles of behavior modification*. New York: Holt, Rinehart & Winston.

Bandura, A. (1977). *Social learning theory*. Englewood Cliffs, NJ: Prentice-Hall.

Bauman, K. E., Fisher, L. A., Bryan, E. S., & Chenoweth, R. L. (1985). Relationship between subjective expected utility and behavior: A longitudinal study of adolescent drinking behavior. *Journal of Studies on Alcohol, 40,* 272–282.

Berglas, S., & Jones, E. E. (1978). Drug choice as a self-handicapping strategy in response to noncontingent success. *Journal of Personality and Social Psychology, 36,* 405–417.

Birnbaum, I. M., & Parker, E. S. (1977). Acute effects of alcohol on storage and retrieval. In I. M. Birnbaum & E. S. Parker (Eds.), *Alcohol and human memory* (pp. 99–108). Hillsdale, NJ: Lawrence Erlbaum.

Birnbaum, I. M., Parker, E. S., Hartley, J. T., & Noble, E. P. (1978). Alcohol and memory: Retrieval processes. *Journal of Verbal Learning and Verbal Behavior, 17,* 325–335.

Brown, S. A., Creamer, V. A., & Stetson, B. A. (1987). Adolescent alcohol expectancies in relation to personal and parental drinking patterns. *Journal of Abnormal Psychology, 96,* 117–121.

Brown, S. A., Goldman, M. S., & Christiansen, B. S. (1985). Do alcohol expectancies mediate drinking patterns of adults? *Journal of Consulting and Clinical Psychology, 53,* 512–519.

Brown, S. A., Goldman, M. S., Inn, A., & Anderson, L. R. (1980). Expectations of reinforcement from alcohol: Their domain and relation to drinking patterns. *Journal of Consulting and Clinical Psychology, 48,* 419–426.

Cappell, H., & Herman, C. P. (1972). Alcohol and tension reduction: A review. *Journal of Studies on Alcohol, 33,* 33–64.

Christiansen, B. A., Goldman, M. S., & Inn, A. (1982). Development of alcohol-related expectancies in adolescents: Separating pharmacological from social learning influences. *Journal of Consulting and Clinical Psychology, 50,* 336–344.

Christiansen, B. A., Roehling, P. V., Smith, G. T., & Goldman, M. S. (1989). Using alcohol expectancies to predict adolescent drinking behavior after one year. *Journal of Consulting and Clinical Psychology, 57,* 93–99.

Collins, R., Parks, G., & Marlatt, G. A. (1985). Social determinants of alcohol consumption: The effects of social interaction and model status on the self-administration of alcohol. *Journal of Consulting and Clinical Psychology, 53,* 189–200.

Conger, J. J. (1951). The effects on alcohol on conflict behavior in the albino rat. *Quarterly Journal of Studies on Alcohol, 12,* 1–29.

Critchlow, B. (1983). Blaming the booze: The attribution of responsibility for drunken behavior. *Personality and Social Psychology Bulletin, 9,* 451–473.

Critchlow, B. (1986). The powers of John Barleycorn: Beliefs about the effects of alcohol on social behavior. *American Psychologist, 41,* 751–764.

Cummings, C., & Marlatt, G. A. (1983, August). *Stress-induced alcohol consumption in high-risk drinkers.* Paper presented at the annual meeting of the American Psychological Association, Anaheim, CA.

Davis, V. E., & Walsh, M. J. (1970). Alcohol, amines, and alkaloids: A possible biochemical basis for alcohol addiction. *Science, 167,* 1005–1107.

Fowles, D. (1980). The three-arousal model: Implications of Gray's two-factor learning theory for heart rate, electrodermal activity, and psychopathy. *Psychophysiology, 17,* 87–104.

Goldman, M. S., Brown, S. A., & Christiansen, B. A. (1987). Expectancy theory: Thinking about drinking. In H. T. Blane & K. E. Leonard (Eds.), *Psychological theories of drinking and alcoholism* (pp. 181–226). New York: Guilford Press.

Gray, J. (1978). The neuropsychology of anxiety. *British Journal of Psychology, 69,* 417–434.

Higgins, R. L., & Marlatt, G. A. (1973). Effects of anxiety arousal on the consumption of alcohol by alcoholics and social drinkers. *Journal of Consulting and Clinical Psychology, 41,* 426–433.

Higgins, R. L., & Marlatt, G. A. (1975). Fear of interpersonal evaluation as a determinant of alcohol consumption in male social drinkers. *Journal of Abnormal Psychology, 84,* 644–651.

Hull, C. (1943). *Principles of behavior.* New York: Appleton-Century-Crofts.

Hull, J. (1981). A self-awareness model of the causes and effects of alcohol consumption. *Journal of Abnormal Psychology, 90,* 586–600.

Hull, J. (1987). Self-awareness model. In H. T. Blane & K. E. Leonard (Eds.), *Psychological theories of drinking and alcoholism* (pp. 272–304). New York: Guilford Press.

Hull, J., Levenson, R. W., Young, R. D., & Sher, K. J. (1983). Self-awareness reducing effects of alcohol. *Journal of Personality and Social Psychology, 44,* 461–473.

Hull, J., & Young, R. D. (1983). Self-consciousness, self-esteem, and success-failure as determinants of alcohol consumption in male social drinkers. *Journal of Personality and Social Psychology, 44,* 1097–1109.

Hull, J., Young, R. D., & Jouriles, E. (1986). Applications of the self-awareness model of alcohol consumption. *Journal of Personality and Social Psychology, 51,* 790–796.

Hull, J. G., & Bond, C. F. (1986). Social and behavioral consequences of alcohol consumption and expectancy: A meta-analysis. *Psychological Bulletin, 99,* 347–360.

Jones, E. E., & Berglas, S. (1978). Control of attributions about the self through self-handicapping strategies: The appeal of alcohol and the role of underachievement. *Personality and Social Psychology Bulletin, 4,* 200–206.

Leigh, B. C. (1987a). Beliefs about the effects of alcohol on self and others. *Journal of Studies on Alcohol, 48,* 467–475.

Leigh, B. C. (1987b). Evaluations of alcohol expectancies: Do they add to prediction of drinking patterns? *Psychology of Addictive Behaviors, 1,* 135–139.

Leigh, B. C. (1989). In search of the seven dwarves: Issues of measurement and meaning in alcohol expectancy research. *Psychological Bulletin, 105,* 361–373.

MacAndrew, C., & Edgerton, R. B. (1969). *Drunken comportment: A social explanation.* Chicago: Aldine.

Marlatt, G. A. (1987). Alcohol, the magic elixir: Stress, expectancy, and the transformation of emotional states. In E. Gottheil, K. A. Druly, S. Pashko, & S. P. Weinstein (Eds.), *Stress and addiction.* New York: Brunner/Mazel.

Marlatt, G. A., Kosturn, C. F., & Lang, A. R. (1975). Provocation to anger and opportunity for retaliation as determinants of alcohol consumption in social drinkers. *Journal of Abnormal Psychology, 84,* 652–659.

Masserman, J. H., & Yum, K. S. (1946). An analysis of the influence of alcohol on experimental neurosis in cats. *Psychosomatic Medicine, 8,* 36–52.

McClelland, D. C., Davis, W. N., Kalin, R., & Wanner, E. (1972). *The drinking man.* New York: Free Press.

Mendelson, J. H. (1964). Experimentally induced chronic intoxication and withdrawal in alcoholics. *Quarterly Journal of Studies on Alcohol, Suppl. No. 2.*

Miller, P. M., Smith, G. T., & Goldman, M. S. (1990). Emergence of alcohol expectations in childhood: A possible critical period. *Journal of Studies on Alcohol, 51,* 343–349.

Mooney, D. K., Fromme, K., Kivlahan, D. R., & Marlatt, G. A. (1987). Correlates of alcohol consumption: Sex, age, and expectancies relate differently to quantity and frequency. *Addictive Behaviors, 12,* 235–240.

Nathan, P. E. (1976). Alcoholism. In H. Leitenberg (Ed.), *Handbook of behavior modification.* New York: Appleton-Century-Crofts.

Pavlov, I. P. (1927). *Conditioned reflexes.* London: Oxford University Press.

Pihl, R. O., & Yankofsky, L. (1979). Alcohol consumption in male social drinkers as a function of situationally induced depressive affect and anxiety. *Psychopharmacology, 65,* 251–257.

Sher, K. J. (1987). Stress response dampening. In H. T. Blane & K. E. Leonard (Eds.), *Psychological theories of drinking and alcoholism* (pp. 227–271). New York: Plenum Press.

Sher, K. J., & Levenson, R. W. (1982). Risk for alcoholism and individual differences in the stress-response-dampening effect of alcohol. *Journal of Abnormal Psychology, 91,* 350–368.

Solomon, R. L. (1980). The opponent-process theory of acquired motivation: The costs of pleasure and the benefits of pain. *American Psychologist, 35,* 691–712.

Southwick, L., Steele, C., Marlatt, A., & Lindell, M. (1981). Alcohol-related expectancies: Defined by phase of intoxication and drinking experience. *Journal of Consulting and Clinical Psychology, 49,* 713–721.

Tucker, J. A., Vuchinich, R. E., & Sobell, M. B. (1981). Alcohol consumption as a self-handicapping strategy. *Journal of Abnormal Psychology, 90,* 220–230.

Volpicelli, J. R. (1987). Uncontrollable events and alcohol drinking. *British Journal of Addiction, 82,* 381–392.

SEVEN

Alcohol Use Disorders: Definition and Prevalence

Although the majority of drinkers usually consume alcohol without negative consequences, alcohol use still presents major problems for society. The three major areas of concern related to the adverse impact of alcohol are: excessive alcohol consumption, alcoholism or alcohol dependence, and alcohol-related problems. Although these areas overlap, it is important to note their distinct aspects in developing intervention and prevention strategies.

After distinguishing between these three areas, this chapter will examine the complex problem of defining alcoholism or alcohol dependence. Major formulations will be described to show how the definition has evolved, and is continuing to evolve from using subjective criteria toward more reliance on objective criteria. Then, the major methods and findings of epidemiological studies about the prevalence rates of alcoholism in the United States will be examined to illustrate how the estimates vary, depending on the definition that is used.

Approaches to Alcohol Use Disorders

Excessive Alcohol Consumption

Excessive consumption of alcohol leads to intoxication. The amount of alcohol that produces this condition will vary with many factors such as the individual's past drinking experience, physical size, and health. This impaired condition may lead to aggression, accidents, and other adverse psychological and social consequences as well as to medical problems. Consequently, some previous efforts to solve this type of alcohol problem have assumed that restriction or prohibition of the availability of the substance would be an effective solution. Yet, this is a simplistic approach because those who otherwise would have abused alcohol might readily find another dangerous substance to abuse. Finding acceptable means to minimize or eliminate the disruptive effects of excessive alcohol consumption is a major objective.

Alcohol Dependence

Some drinkers become dependent on alcohol so that drinking takes over their lives and disrupts their ability to function normally. Since most drinkers seem able to drink without developing such dependence, commonly referred to as alcoholism, some other factor besides alcohol itself must be implicated. Does some predisposing factor or underlying process exist that increases the likelihood of eventual alcoholism in certain people? Posing this question focuses attention on the physiological and/or psychological aspects of the drinker as the problem. From this perspective, the important tasks include finding ways to prevent potential alcoholics from developing dependence on alcohol and to treat those who develop alcoholism despite the efforts of society to prevent this outcome.

Alcohol-Related Problems

Concern about alcohol use also stems from "alcohol-related problems" created by the behavior of individuals under the influence of alcohol, problems such as

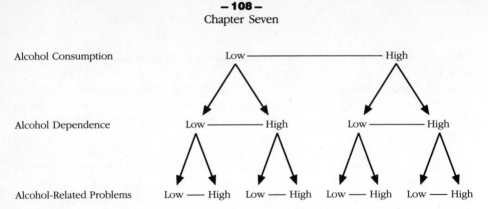

Figure 7-1 The relationship among three different aspects of alcohol use: consumption level, dependence, and alcohol-related problems.

physical impairment, driving accidents, domestic violence, birth defects, work impairment, and financial problems. One does not have to be an alcoholic or even drink excessively on a single occasion to experience these adverse effects of alcohol, which may occur even for light and occasional drinkers. These problems may be reduced through a variety of approaches: education to increase awareness of the link between alcohol use and problems such as birth defects; stronger enforcement of legal controls such as those related to drinking and driving; and social policy changes to "deglamorize" drinking by restricting alcohol advertising content.

How Alcohol Use Disorders Interrelate

Thus, the problems associated with alcohol in our society are multiple and interrelated. A focus on one problem, without recognition of the other aspects of alcohol's impact on society, yields an incomplete picture. Each of the three problems, and different combinations of them as shown in Figure 7-1, are unique and should not be considered equivalent to one of the others. Some individuals might have only one or two of these three problems. Thus, one person might engage in heavy alcohol consumption, suffer alcohol-related problems, and yet not show dependence. Another person might be alcohol dependent as well as have alcohol-related problems, despite a low consumption level. Yet another person might drink heavily and be dependent but not show much evidence of other alcohol-related problems. Finally, some drinkers may suffer from all three problems.

Definitions of Alcoholism

Of the three problems just described, alcoholism or alcohol dependence receives the most attention. The general public holds an image, created and reinforced by mass media, of the alcoholic as the stereotypical skid-row bum, though alcoholics exist at all socioeconomic levels and in all walks of life. As with most complex constructs, it is not easy to achieve a clear and precise definition of alcoholism.

Several different formulations have been proposed, and we will describe the major ones here. Controversies in the field have stemmed from this lack of agreement about the nature of alcoholism, so that resolution of disputes over the causes of alcoholism or the preferred treatment may hinge on which definition of alcoholism is used.

The Disease Conception of Alcoholism

As noted in Chapter 1, the disease conception of alcoholism proposed by Jellinek (1960) has had a major influence on the way most people think of alcoholism to this day. A central tenet of his model is that alcoholism involves a loss of control over drinking, an inability to stop drinking after only one or two drinks. Similarly, a major criterion of an alcoholic for AA is the self-perception that one is "powerless" or has lost control over drinking. This is a highly subjective rather than a scientific or medical definition. Jellinek identified stages and subtypes of alcoholism.

Stages of Alcoholism. Jellinek (1946) analyzed responses of 98 AA members who completed a questionnaire in the *Grapevine*, the AA newsletter that had a circulation of about 1,600, about the course of development of their drinking problems. From this limited data, AA had him propose a model of alcoholism by identifying a syndrome of symptoms to describe its temporal course. A larger sample of about 2,000 AA members was used to refine the model later (Jellinek, 1952). Figures 7-2 and 7-3 show the similarity of the popular Temperance era view

Figure 7-2 "The drunkards' progress from the first drink to the grave."
Source: from Rutgers University Center for Alcohol Studies by N. Currier. Reprinted by permission.

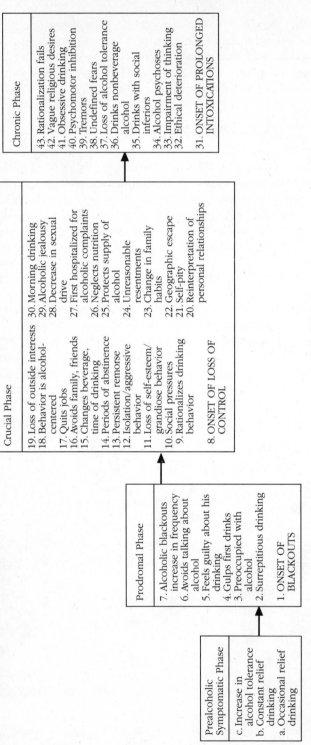

Figure 7-3 The natural history of alcoholism according to Jellinek's model based on male members of AA.

Source: from "The epidemiology of alcoholism," by M. Russell in *Alcoholism: Consequences, Intervention* by N. J. Estes and M. E. Heineman (Eds.). Copyright © 1987 by C. V. Mosby. Reprinted by permission.

of drunkards and Jellinek's classic model of the progressive nature of the disease of alcoholism.

In the early stage, referred to as the *prealcoholic phase,* social factors often lead to drinking for relief from tension. Eventually, tolerance to alcohol develops so that a larger dose is needed to produce the same level of relief previously generated by a smaller amount. The disease enters the *prodromal phase* with the occurrence of blackouts, a type of amnesia for events experienced during drinking episodes, especially when the drinker is physically fatigued. Later, when sober, the drinker may not recall experiences encountered during previous drinking bouts. The character portrayed by Jane Fonda in the movie *The Morning After* vividly illustrates this phase. Surreptitious drinking begins in which the alcoholic sneaks drinks to prevent others from knowing. Preoccupation with drinking develops so that the alcohol takes on a greater importance than previously.

In the third phase, the *crucial phase,* loss of control occurs in which drinking is difficult to stop once it begins. There may still be control over whether to start drinking on a specific occasion. As drinking takes over, the alcoholic begins to rationalize his or her drinking more frequently, often with defensiveness and hostility. Other major changes occur in the life of the alcoholic—family frictions, loss of friends, work impairment, poor nutrition, and medical problems—which might also increase drinking.

Finally, in the fourth phase, the *chronic phase,* prolonged periods of intoxication or "benders" occur, along with a reversal in tolerance for alcohol so that less alcohol is needed to produce impairment than previously. When alcohol is not available, withdrawal reactions occur involving pronounced physical discomfort, anxiety, shakes, tremors, and irritability. Although the length of the phases may vary with the individual and other factors, Jellinek proposed that the sequence of the phases is universal.

This model, proposed by one of the leading alcohol researchers of the time, was important because it provided a disease model as an alternative to the prevailing moral model that held that alcoholics drank because they lacked willpower. Instead of condemning the alcoholic and denying compassion and treatment, the disease model called for a nonjudgmental response and treatment just as for any other physical disease.

The views of AA and Jellinek were not developed independently of each other, because as noted earlier, Jellinek relied heavily on the personal experiences of AA members. It should hardly be surprising, then, if the self-reports of self-labeled alcoholics fit the primary model proposed by Jellinek and AA very closely. Interestingly, it also may be noted that none of the interview responses of females were included since, according to Fingarette (1988), they often differed from those provided by males.

Subtypes of Alcoholics. If other types of alcoholics than those studied by Jellinek in AA exist, the disease model may have less validity for them. In his formulation derived from interviews with AA members, Jellinek (1960) did describe several types of alcoholics, distinguishing among them by using Greek letter designations. The *gamma* alcoholic, characterized by psychological and physical dependence as well as loss of control, was the type most commonly seen by AA and assumed to be the prototypical American male alcoholic. This type of alcoholic loses control over drinking and is unable to voluntarily stop; the alcoholism is chronic and progressive.

Jellinek also proposed the existence of several other types. The *alpha* alcoholic is a purely psychologically dependent case and presumably does not exhibit loss of control or show evidence of physical addiction to alcohol. In contrast, the *beta* alcoholic, an infrequent variety, shows only organic damage and nutritional deficiencies, probably due to heavy drinking, but no psychological or physical dependence. The *delta* alcoholic is similar to the gamma alcoholic, but without loss of control. This drinker seems to drink continuously throughout the day but not in quantities that typically produce intoxication. This type is more commonly observed in wine-consuming nations such as France. Finally, there is the *epsilon* or periodic alcoholic, who would be described as an infrequent binge drinker, but one who shows no chronic physical dependence. This type of alcoholic can go for long periods without drinking, but when drinking occurs, it is excessive. Although the types seem to be mutually exclusive, Jellinek did allow that individuals drink in different patterns at different times and hence might be classified as different types on various occasions.

Instead of acknowledging some type of variation among alcoholics, following either Jellinek's or some other taxonomy, many views about alcoholism assume that all alcoholics are alike and that an individual can readily be identified as either an alcoholic or a nonalcoholic. Jellinek's typology has generally been ignored and alcoholism has been viewed as a disease shared by a somewhat homogenous group. The value of examining subtypes of alcoholics should be recognized since it may provide a better understanding of both the origins of and treatments for the different types of alcoholisms than possible under a unitary model of the disease.

In contrast to the concept of alcoholism proposed by Jellinek and AA, which involves a high degree of subjectivity because it requires the alcoholic to label himself or herself as an alcoholic, three other major conceptions have relied to a greater extent on objective criteria for defining alcoholism. We now turn to these alternative conceptions.

The NCA Diagnostic Criteria

In 1944 a voluntary association of state and local groups interested in alcoholism problems formed the National Council on Alcoholism (NCA), which sponsors programs for increasing public awareness and action on alcohol issues. It should not be confused with the federally funded agency established in 1970, the National Institute on Alcohol Abuse and Alcoholism (NIAAA), which provides federal programs for basic research and treatment as well as social policy recommendations concerning alcohol issues. In 1972, working with alcoholism experts, the NCA published a detailed set of physiological and psychological criteria for use in diagnosis of alcoholism. The criteria were in two major "tracks": track 1, which is physiological and clinical, and track 2, which is psychological, behavioral, and attitudinal. The criteria were assigned three levels of importance for purposes of diagnosis. In addition to these major criteria such as tolerance, dependence and withdrawal, and continued drinking despite adverse social and legal consequences, which are considered to be conclusive evidence of alcoholism, each track also contains some minor criteria such as some medical problems and complaints of loss of control that are considered only suggestive symptoms. Individuals with one or more of the major criteria of diagnostic level 1 would be considered alcoholic, especially if other information such as laboratory tests and physical examination provided corroboration.

This description of alcoholism is based on the clinical experience of experts but it still has required testing by other practitioners in applying it to additional patients. No empirical data were provided by NCA about the reliability or validity of the criteria.

A study in Germany by Ringer, Kufner, Antons, and Feuerlein (1977) discovered problems with these criteria when they were applied to 120 male alcoholics and 80 hospital patient controls matched for age. Although the NCA criteria correctly identified all the alcoholics, they also classified almost half the control group as alcoholics. This high incidence of "false positives" suggested that the criteria are overinclusive, raising questions about their utility. Besides the stigma that might be experienced by false positive cases, the cost of treating the false positives for alcoholism would be wasteful and unnecessary.

On the other hand, Ringer et al. recognized that some unknown number of these false positives might really be alcoholics that clinicians had failed to correctly diagnose. If one takes this view, then the treatment of these cases for alcoholism would be justified. It depends on whether we have more faith in the validity of the psychiatric classification or the NCA criteria for alcoholism.

The NCA criteria, as intended, have served as an objective diagnostic checklist for physicians. The usefulness of the criteria for research has been limited. Furthermore, they have not furthered understanding about the psychological causes or effects of alcoholism.

The Alcohol Dependence Syndrome Formulation

Edwards and Gross (1976), at the Addiction Research Unit of the London Institute of Psychiatry, formulated a description of the alcohol dependence syndrome (ADS). Instead of relying on the drinker's self-perception to define alcoholism, the ADS formulation contains the components as shown in the box.

Reports by Davies (1962) and other researchers that alcoholics could be taught to drink without loss of control showed the need for an alternative model to the traditional AA conception of alcoholism. The ADS formulation emphasizes a *continuum* of alcohol drinking rather than the dichotomy implied by the alcoholic/nonalcoholic distinction. The separation between physical and psychological dependence is blurred under this conception. *Impaired control* of drinking, rather than a *loss of control,* is postulated by the ADS formulation to reflect that the phenomenon is not an all-or-none experience.

The ADS formulation represents a bi-axial model consisting of alcohol dependence and alcohol-related *problems,* disorders that may or may not be associated

— Factors in the Alcohol Dependence Syndrome —

1. *Narrowing of the drinking repertoire:* Increasing severity of dependence is marked by increasingly stereotyped drinking with little day-to-day variability of beverage choice; drinking is scheduled so as to maintain a high blood alcohol level.
2. *Salience of drink-seeking behavior:* Increasing severity of dependence is marked by the individual granting highest priority to maintaining alcohol intake, with a failure of negative social consequences to deter drinking behavior.
3. *Increased tolerance:* Increasing severity of dependence is marked by the individual functioning at blood alcohol levels that would incapacitate the nontolerant drinker. In later stages, the individual begins to lose previously acquired tolerance because of liver damage, aging, and/or brain damage.
4. *Repeated withdrawal symptoms:* With increasing severity of dependence, the individual manifests more frequent and severe withdrawal symptoms; four key symptoms are tremor, nausea, sweating, and mood disturbance.
5. *Relief avoidance of withdrawal symptoms:* With increasing severity of dependence, the individual drinks earlier in the day and may even awaken in the middle of the night to drink.
6. *Subjective awareness of a compulsion to drink:* With increasing severity of dependence, the individual experiences a sense of "loss of control" or impaired control over alcohol intake and a subjective sense of craving or desire to drink. Cues for craving may include the feeling of intoxication, withdrawal, affective discomfort, or situational stimuli.
7. *Reinstatement after abstinence:* With increasing severity of dependence, the individual feels "hooked" within a few days of starting to drink and drinking will revert to the old stereotyped pattern. The six elements of the syndrome rapidly reappear.

Source: from *Seventh Special Report to U.S. Congress on Alcohol,* 1990, Washington, DC: U.S. Government Printing Office.

with dependence. A drinker who is alcohol-dependent may be somewhat free from physical, economic, or social problems related to the drinking. Also, a drinker with physical damage from heavy drinking may not necessarily be alcohol-dependent.

In contrast to AA's conception, according to the ADS model, all drinkers who develop alcohol dependence will not go through a progression of stages or phases with certain symptoms. The World Health Organization (1978) included the alcohol dependence syndrome (ADS) in its ninth revision of the *International Classification of Diseases* (ICD-9).

The concept of alcohol dependence was proposed as an improvement over the disease concept because it does not place as much emphasis on the physiological basis of alcohol problems but instead recognizes psychological and sociological factors. However, critics of the construct such as Heather and Robertson (1981) maintain that it still is not sufficiently different from the disease conception.

The DSM-III and DSM-III-R Criteria

The American Psychiatric Association has developed its own set of criteria for defining major psychological disorders known as the *Diagnostic and Statistical*

Manual of Mental Disorders (DSM). The third version of these criteria, DSM-III (American Psychiatric Association, 1980), is based on symptoms associated with various syndromes or disorders. This descriptive approach uses objective criteria that should be more reliable than subjective indexes. DSM-III uses five independent dimensions, or axes, for classifying patients: (1) alcohol abuse and dependency; (2) personality disorder; (3) physical disorder; (4) psychosocial stress; (5) adaptive functioning. In contrast, earlier versions such as DSM-II viewed alcoholism as a part of a psychiatric disorder, but in DSM-III there is an allowance that primary alcoholism may exist without other psychiatric disorders, as alcohol abuse and dependency are viewed as different dimensions from that of personality disorder. One benefit presumed to occur from this classification is the destigmatization of alcoholism.

DSM-III defines *alcohol abuse* in terms of three criteria: (1) pathological use in terms of inability to stop or control use, (2) impairment in social or occupational functioning such as job disruption, interpersonal conflict, or aggression, and (3) duration of disturbance exceeding one month. If psychiatric disorder is involved, any alcoholism may be viewed as a secondary form.

In addition to the preceding DSM-III criteria for alcohol abuse, *alcohol dependence* involves either *physiological* tolerance or withdrawal reactions. *Tolerance* refers to the diminished impact of a given amount of alcohol as the drinker becomes adapted to that dose. Withdrawal involves a syndrome of adverse reactions such as irritability, anxiety, and hallucinations when alcohol is withheld or not available to a drinker who has developed tolerance to alcohol. The DSM-III definitions imply that abuse is less serious than dependence.

The goal of the DSM-III criteria is to facilitate the proper choice of treatment rather than to prove any particular theoretical model of alcoholism. Factors associated with the disease conception of alcoholism such as loss of control, irreversible and progressive disorder, and craving are not easily identifiable or measurable, so they are not included as part of the DSM-III definition. It should be noted that the term *alcoholism* is not even used in the DSM-III formulation. In its place, the concept of *alcohol dependence* has been substituted, thus paralleling the formulation in England of the ADS described earlier.

In the revised DSM-III-R (American Psychiatric Association, 1987), definitions of *alcohol abuse* and *dependence* have been modified. For a diagnosis of alcohol abuse, a drinker has to have either a maladaptive pattern of drinking or recurrent use in physically hazardous situations during the past year lasting at least one month or occurring repeatedly over a longer period. To be classified as alcohol-dependent, the drinker has to meet any three of a set of nine criteria, with symptoms meeting at least two of these criteria occurring two or more times in the past year. These criteria are listed in Table 7-1.

DSM-III-R also groups together all forms of psychoactive substance abuse and dependence because the behavioral impairments created by each of them have many similarities. Although the DSM-III-R approach offers some important improvements in the reliable diagnosis of alcoholism, Niaura and Nathan (1987) expressed concern that it may still be too vague to allow differential selection for treatment, which is the primary goal of the classification. The expertise of clinicians and use of other assessment instruments is still necessary to improve plans for successful treatment.

Both the 10th revision of the *International Classification of Diseases* (ICD-10) proposed for 1994 (World Health Organization, 1990) and the DSM-III-R have placed emphasis on the term *alcohol dependence* rather than *alcoholism* as shown in Table 7-1, but definitional issues are still in need of improvement. Caetano (1987a) noted that both formulations are vague in their wording with terms such as *often* and *frequent* or *progressive neglect*. Moreover, no clear time frame exists for making diagnoses, with ICD-10 specifying that the symptoms should have been

Table 7-1 Correspondence between DSM-III-R and ICD-10 Criteria for Diagnosis of Alcohol Dependence

DSM-III-R	ICD-10
1. *Compulsion:* Substance often taken in larger amounts or over a longer period than the person intended.	
2. *Readdiction liability:* Persistent desire or one or more unsuccessful efforts to cut down or control substance use.	
3. *Compulsion:* A great deal of time spent in activities necessary to get the substance, taking the substance or recovering from its effects.	
4. *Salience:* Frequent intoxication or withdrawal symptoms when expected to fulfill major role obligations at work, school, or at home or when substance use is physically hazardous.	
5. *Salience:* Important social, occupational or recreational activities given up because of substance use.	1. Progressive neglect of alternative pleasures or interests in favor of substance use.
6. *Salience:* Continued substance use despite knowledge of having a persistent or recurrent social, psychological, or physical problem that is caused or exacerbated by the use of the substance.	2. Persisting with drug use despite clear evidence of overtly harmful consequences.
7. *Tolerance:* Need for markedly increased amounts of the substance (i.e., at least 50% increase) in order to achieve intoxication or desired effect, or markedly diminished effect with continued use of the same amount.	3. Evidence of tolerance such that increased doses of substance are required in order to achieve effects originally produced by lower doses.
8. *Withdrawal:* Characteristic withdrawal symptoms.	4. A physiological withdrawal state.
9. *Compulsion:* Substance often taken to relieve or avoid withdrawal symptoms.	5. Substance use with the intention of relieving withdrawal symptoms and with awareness that this strategy is effective.

(continued)

Table 7·1 (*continued*)

DSM-III-R	ICD-10
	6. A narrowing of the personal repertoire of patterns of drug use, e.g., a tendency to drink alcoholic beverages in the same way on weekdays and weekends and whatever the social constraints regarding appropriate drinking behavior.
	7. Evidence that return to drug use after a period of abstinence leads to a more rapid reinstatement of other features of the syndrome than occurs with non-dependent individuals.
	8. Subjective awareness of an impaired capacity to control drug taking behavior in terms of its onset, termination or level of use.
	9. Strong desire or sense of compulsion to take drugs.

Source: from "What I would most like to know: When will we have a standard concept of alcohol dependence?" by R. Caetano in the *British Journal of Addiction, (1987), 82,* pp. 601–605. Copyright © 1987 by the Society for the Study of Addiction to Alcohol and Other Drugs. Reprinted by permission.

present in the last six months and DSM-III-R vaguely requiring that the symptoms last for at least one month or occur repeatedly over "a longer period." Remission of dependence is also vaguely defined.

To understand why disagreement among definitions exists, it is necessary to examine the origins, functions, and goals of these major classification systems. Kendall (1991) pointed out some of the major differences. The ICD-9 is a more comprehensive classification covering all "diseases, injuries, and causes of death" and the proposed ICD-10 (World Health Organization, 1990) deals with all "diseases and related health problems," whereas the DSM is limited to mental and psychiatric disorders. The ICD deals with a broader audience of health professionals than does the DSM and it must be accepted in 140 countries and in at least eight languages. The DSM is directed more to mental health professionals and emphasizes problems that are more prominent in Western society than in other cultures (for example, some types of sexual dysfunctions and eating disorders).

Widiger, Frances, Pincus, Davis, and First (1991) traced the history of both taxonomies. In 1948 the sixth edition of ICD included for the first time a classification of mental disorders, but it did not meet the needs of American psychiatrists, who developed their own nomenclature in 1952 with the first version of the DSM. Since then, the two organizations have revised their taxonomies several times in the light of new thinking and evidence. Although converging in their definitions, the two approaches still differ. These classification systems are advances over prior systems because they have been empirically tested, with data available on the reliability and validity of diagnostic categories. Both are periodically revised, with the newest version of the DSM due in 1993 and the ICD in 1994. The hope is that eventually the definitions will converge.

Chapter Seven

How Many Alcoholics Are There?

One of the most frequent questions raised in discussions of alcoholism is, How many alcoholics are there? Unfortunately, estimates from different sources are not in agreement. One reason why epidemiological studies offer a wide variety of estimates is that the definition is not the same for all researchers. We will examine the various sources of data and then focus on specific estimates.

Sources of Data

Methods for identifying patterns of alcohol use and abuse in the general population do not usually involve direct observation but instead rely on inferences based on several different sources of information.

Official Records.   One method uses official records or social indicators such as mortality statistics, hospital admission records, data on arrests for drunkenness, alcohol sales figures, and tax revenues from alcohol sales. Another method uses an equation known as the Jellinek formula to determine the number of deaths due to liver cirrhosis. Although objective, each of these indexes still has its particular limitations. Thus, sales and tax revenue figures provide one means of determining trends in the total volume of alcohol sold each year but do not reveal patterns of actual individual consumption. The purchaser of alcohol is not always the actual consumer; the term *apparent consumption* is used to reflect that difference. This index is computed by dividing the total amount of alcohol sold by the number of persons aged 14 and over.

Another problem in using sales statistics to infer consumption levels is that there is often a temporal lag between purchase and consumption. While increased sales might imply heavier drinking if the number of drinkers stays the same or decreases during that interval, an opposite interpretation is called for if the number of drinkers increases over that period.

Treatment Data.   Another index of the extent of alcoholism is more direct: using data from hospital *treatment* statistics to determine the number of alcoholics. However, because economic and psychological barriers to utilization of health care facilities exist (poorer and less educated alcoholics might be less likely to use treatment facilities), this index identifies a biased and unrealistically small sample of those with alcohol problems.

General Population Surveys.   Surveys administered to random samples of the general population provide large sets of data obtained with standard instruments that allow estimates of the prevalence of alcoholism for different subgroups.

Specific Estimates

For purposes of comparison, we will examine the estimates of the number of alcoholics in the United States arrived at by four major general population surveys done in the 1980s.

The National Alcohol Survey.   Based on data from the 1984 National Alcohol Survey, Hilton (1989) estimated the number of alcoholics in the United States at from 3.7 to 8 million males and from 1.5 to 4 million females, depending on whether two or four criteria out of a list of 13 were used to classify a drinker as alcoholic.

The NIAAA Survey.   The figures from the NIAAA reported by Williams, Stinson, Parker, Harford, and Noble (1987) using DSM-III criteria indicated there are 7.1 million male and 3.3 million female alcoholics, representing 4 to 5 percent of the U.S. population.

The Epidemiologic Catchment Area Survey.   A large-scale study of various aspects of mental health conducted across the United States by the National Institute of Mental Health at five major regional research centers with over 20,000 participants included survey items pertaining to alcohol use and associated con-sequences. The Epidemiologic Catchment Area (ECA) study reported by Myers et al. (1984) and by Robins et al. (1984) used carefully planned questionnaires to allow classification of respondents according to the DSM-III criteria for alcohol abuse and dependence as well as for various major psychiatric categories. An estimated 13.6 percent of respondents in the ECA study were classified as alcohol abusers and/or for alcohol dependent (Helzer & Burnam, 1991), with a 5:1 ratio of higher rates for men (23.8 versus 4.6 percent) than for women. For the year preceding the assessment, a similar ratio existed, with 11.9 percent of the men and 2.2 percent of the women classified as alcohol abusers and/or dependents.

The National Health Interview Survey.   Grant et al. (1991) estimated the U.S. prevalence of alcohol dependence and alcohol abuse using the DSM-III-R criteria. They examined self-reported alcohol use from 43,809 interviews collected from respondents aged 18 and over in all 50 states and the District of Columbia in 1988 as part of the National Health Interview Survey conducted by the National Center for Health Statistics. They found that 8.63 percent of the population could be classified as either alcohol dependent (6.25 percent) or alcohol abusers (2.38 percent). These estimates translate to a total of 15.2 million Americans aged 18 and over.

Figure 7-4 provides a breakdown of the one-year prevalence rates of alcohol abuse and alcohol dependence found by this survey for men and women by age, separately for whites and nonwhites. As the figure shows, males had about three times more abuse and dependence than females. However, the male-to-female ratio was smallest for the youngest age group, possibly reflecting increased drink-ing among young females. Whites showed almost twice the prevalence shown by nonwhites. The youngest age grouping showed the highest prevalence for both males and females, with each successively older group showing lower rates. While whites of either gender had a greater prevalence than nonwhites for the youngest groups, this ethnic difference declined for older groups and reversed for the oldest groups.

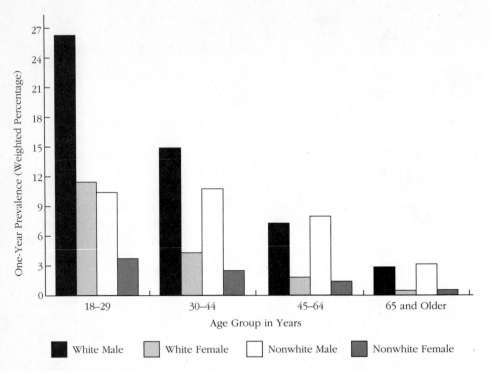

Figure 7-4 Prevalence of DSM-III-R alcohol abuse and alcoholism by age, sex, and ethnicity: United States, 1988.

Source: from "Prevalence of DSM-III-R alcohol abuse and alcoholism: United States, 1988. Epidemiologic Bulletin No. 27," by B. F. Grant, T. C. Harford, P. Chou, R. Pickering, D. A. Dawson, F. S. Stinson, and J. Nobel in *Alcohol Health and Research World, 1991, 15,* 91–96.

Where Do These Estimates Leave Us?

As we have seen, the estimates of the number of alcohol-dependent or alcoholic individuals vary across four major studies, even though the studies were conducted within the space of a few years. Hilton (1989) warned that the question of the number of alcoholics is predicated on the disease model of alcoholism in which a person either is or is not an alcoholic. There are numerous criteria for defining and diagnosing alcoholics, and each set will generate a different number. We will never agree on how many alcoholics there are because definitions differ across studies and change across time. Given that there are undoubtedly too many, the more important tasks appear to be to understand the causes and effects of alcoholism and to develop better ways to treat and prevent it. Semantic disputes over the precise definition and sociopolitical arguments about the number of alcoholics are perhaps unavoidable, unfortunately, but they should not be allowed to make us lose sight of other important issues.

Conclusions

Since the 1930s, several major sets of criteria have been developed to define alcoholism. In the mind of the public, the disease conception is the best known due to its widespread dissemination through AA. This definition involves a specific sequence of symptoms that occurs over the course of the development of alcoholism. It entails a theoretical account of the origins of the disease of alcoholism in terms of physical factors, although it also recognizes that alcoholism involves a spiritual "disease" as well. Ultimately, AA's definition requires a self-recognition of alcoholism on the part of the individual.

In contrast, professionally developed criteria such as the NCA diagnostic criteria, the ADS formulation, and DSM-III-R do not agree with the disease conception, nor do they concur among themselves. However, unlike the highly subjective definition of alcoholism proposed by the disease conception of Jellinek and held by AA, the professional definitions are objective and standardized. They describe the symptoms rather than explain the origins of alcoholism.

A high percentage of the general population (Blum, Roman, & Bennett, 1989; Caetano, 1987b) agrees with AA's view that alcoholism is a disease rather than a moral shortcoming and that abstinence is necessary for recovery. Whereas in the 1940s only about 20 percent held this view, in the 1980s about 90 percent of the respondents in a northern California survey (Caetano, 1987b) accepted the view that alcoholism is an illness. However, the disease conception held by the public is not identical with that proposed by Jellinek (1960), as 40 percent also believed that alcoholics drank because they "wanted to." Caetano concluded that a moral attitude toward alcoholism, stemming from the temperance movement, still exists in America. A survey in Georgia (Blum et al., 1989) also found that the public held ambivalent attitudes toward the disease conception of alcoholism. The results showed alcoholism was regarded as a disease for which humane treatment should be given, but they also suggested that the public expects victims of chronic diseases to assume some responsibility for their own recovery.

Fingarette (1988) and Peele (1989) have attempted to discredit the disease concept of alcoholism as a myth. In their view, alcoholism is not a disease but a strong habit or lifestyle in which heavy drinking has become a dominant factor, much to the alcoholic's detriment. Fingarette (1988) insisted that the alcoholic does need a type of willpower or act of commitment to change his or her lifestyle, although admittedly willpower is insufficient. Treatment techniques that consider the individual pattern and history of each drinker can be developed to help reduce the heavy drinking of the alcoholic. In addition, environmental changes that include social policies that limit and discourage adverse drinking levels and effects are needed.

The lack of accord about the definition of alcoholism creates a dilemma. Alcoholism, like other constructs, is an abstraction rather than a concrete or tangible object with objectively measurable dimensions. Since substantial agreement on the criteria for alcoholism does not exist, how can we identify alcoholics for research purposes or diagnose those who need treatment? Conclusions drawn by one set of investigators using one set of criteria to define alcoholics might not be accepted by other researchers who follow a different definition of alcoholism. Those with one approach to alcoholism might fail to replicate or simply reject the findings of rival approaches on the argument that their models were not based on observations of "true" alcoholics.

Unfortunately, the conceptual disagreement among researchers creates much confusion. As there is not yet a single definition of alcoholism that is universally accepted, it is important to consider the particular definition used in each individual study when comparing and interpreting findings across studies. It may be useful to think of alcoholism, as Jellinek (1960) did, as involving a number of subtypes, all of which have some common features as well as some unique characteristics. The causes and methods for treating each subtype may vary. To this way of thinking, controversies and conflicting findings only arise when clinicians and researchers view all subtypes as if they were the same.

References

American Psychiatric Association. (1980). *Diagnostic and statistical manual of mental disorders* (3rd ed.). Washington, DC: Author.

American Psychiatric Association. (1987). *Diagnostic and statistical manual of mental disorders* (3rd ed., rev.). Washington, DC: Author.

Blum, T. C., Roman, P. M., & Bennett, N. (1989). Public images of alcoholism: Data from a Georgia survey. *Journal of Studies on Alcohol, 50,* 5–14.

Caetano, R. (1987a). What I would most like to know: When will we have a standard concept of alcohol dependence? *British Journal of Addiction, 82,* 601–605.

Caetano, R. (1987b). Public opinions about alcoholism and its treatment. *Journal of Studies on Alcohol, 48,* 153–160.

Davies, D. L. (1962). Normal drinking in recovered alcohol addicts. *Quarterly Journal of Studies on Alcohol, 23,* 94–104.

Edwards, G., & Gross, M. M. (1976). Alcohol dependence: Provisional descriptions of a clinical syndrome. *British Medical Journal, 1,* 1058–1061.

Fingarette, H. (1988). *Heavy drinking: The myth of alcoholism as a disease.* Berkeley, CA: University of California Press.

Grant, B. F., Harford, T. C., Chou, P., Pickering, R., Dawson, D. A., Stinson, F. S., & Noble, J. (1991). Prevalence of DSM-III-R alcohol abuse and alcoholism: United States, 1988. Epidemiologic Bulletin No. 27. *Alcohol Health and Research World, 15,* 91–96.

Heather, N., & Robertson, I. (1981). *Controlled drinking.* London: Methuen.

Helzer, J. E., & Burnam, M. A. (1991). Epidemiology of alcohol addiction: United States. In N. S. Miller (Ed.), *Comprehensive handbook of drug and alcohol addiction* (pp. 9–38). New York: Marcel Dekker.

Hilton, M. E. (1989). What I would most want to know: How many alcoholics are there in the U.S.? *British Journal of Addiction, 84,* 459–460.

Jellinek, E. M. (1946). Phase in the drinking history of alcoholics: An analysis of a survey conducted by the official organ of Alcoholics Anonymous. *Quarterly Journal of Studies on Alcohol, 7,* 1–88.

Jellinek, E. M. (1952). Phases of alcohol addiction. *Quarterly Journal of Studies on Alcohol, 13,* 673–684.

Jellinek, E. M. (1960). *The disease conception of alcoholism.* New Brunswick, NJ: Hillhouse Press.

Kendall, R. E. (1991). Relationship between the DSM-IV and the ICD-10. *Journal of Abnormal Psychology, 100,* 297–301.

Myers, J. K., Weissman, M. M., Tischler, G. L., Holzer, C. E. III, Leaf, P. J., Orvaschel, H., Anthony, J. C., Boyd, J. H., Burker, J. D., Jr., Kramer, M. D., Stoltzman, R. (1984). Six month prevalence of psychiatric disorders in three communities. *Archives of General Psychiatry, 41,* 959–967.

National Council on Alcoholism. (1972). Criteria for the diagnosis of alcoholism. *American Journal of Psychiatry, 129,* 127–135.

Niaura, R. S., & Nathan, P. E. (1987). DSM-III and the addictive behaviors. In T. D. Nirenberg & S. A. Maisto (Eds.), *Developments in the assessment and treatment of addictive behaviors* (pp. 31–48). Norwood, NJ: Ablex.

Peele, S. (1989). *Diseasing of America: Addiction treatment out of control.* Lexington, MA: Lexington.

Ringer, C., Kufner, H., Antons, K., & Feuerlein, W. (1977). The NCA criteria for the diagnosis of alcoholism: An empirical validation study. *Journal of Studies on Alcohol, 38,* 1259–1273.

Robins, L. N., Helzer, J. E., Weissman, M. M., Orvaschel, H., Gruenberg, E., Burker, J. D., Jr., & Regier, D. A. (1984). Lifetime prevalence of specific psychiatric disorders in three sites. *Archives of General Psychiatry, 41,* 949–958.

U.S. Department of Health and Human Services. (1990). *Seventh Special Report to the U.S. Congress on Alcohol and Health.* Washington, DC: U.S. Government Printing Office.

Widiger, T. A., Frances, A. J., Pincus, H. A., Davis, W. W., & First, M. B. (1991). Toward an empirical classification for the DSM-IV. *Journal of Abnormal Psychology, 100,* 280–288.

Williams, G. D., Stinson, F. S., Parker, D. A., Harford, T., & Noble, J. (1987). Demographic trends, alcohol abuse and alcoholism. Epidemiologic Bulletin No. 15. *Alcohol Health and Research World, 11,* 80–83, 91.

World Health Organization. (1978). *Mental disorders: Glossary and guide to their classification in accordance with the ninth revision of the International Classification of Diseases.* Geneva: Author.

World Health Organization. (1990). *Proposed 10th revision of the International Classification of Diseases. Diagnostic Criteria for Research. (ICD-10).* Geneva: Author.

EIGHT

Alcoholism: The Role of Heredity and Environment

The observation that other members of an alcoholic's family are often also likely to have drinking problems suggests that heredity might be a determinant of alcoholism. But because family members usually share a common environment as well as a common heredity, this type of evidence can also be explained in environmental terms. Through observation and modeling of an alcoholic parent, children may acquire attitudes and norms about drinking that may increase their susceptibility to similar drinking styles. Alternatively, but with the same eventual effect on drinking, the children may develop poor self-esteem, experience abuse or neglect, and later as adults turn to drinking to cope with stressors, not as a consequence of modeling of parental drinking but as a form of escape.

The relative contributions of heredity and environment to alcoholism are the focus of this chapter. We will examine the evidence from several types of studies used to determine the influence of heredity and environment.

Family Studies

In research on possible familial links to alcoholism, the term *proband* is used to refer to those individuals assumed to be at risk for alcoholism due to having an alcoholic biological parent. A review by Cotton (1979) of 39 studies collectively covering thousands of alcoholics in psychiatric treatment, confirmed that alcoholics were about five times more likely than nonalcoholics to have an alcoholic relative. It must be pointed out, however, that in the studies reviewed by Cotton, anywhere from 45 to 80 percent of the alcoholics did *not* have an alcohlic relative. Therefore, other factors must be involved, since a large percentage of children of *non*alcoholic families still become alcoholic without the genetic factors that are assumed to contribute to alcoholism and problem drinking for children in alcoholic families.

Amark (1951) examined the family drinking patterns for the relatives of alcoholic probands and noted that the first-degree male, but not female, relatives were more likely to be alcoholic than for the general population. Later studies (Reich, Cloninger, Van Eerdewegh, Rice, & Mullaney, 1988; Winokur, Reich, Rimmer, & Pitts, 1970) have found similar tendencies. The findings of Reich et al. (1988) in Table 8-1 show that the fathers, brothers, and sons of both male and female alcoholics were more at risk to be alcoholic than were the first-degree female relatives such as mothers, sisters, and daughters. In addition, the wives of alcoholic men were less likely than the husbands of alcoholic women to also have alcoholism. Although women were at lower risk for alcoholism, Winokur et al. (1970) found that the female relatives were at greater risk than the male relatives for affective or mood disorders such as depression.

Although relatives of alcoholics share some common genetically transmitted tendencies for different emotional or affective reactions to stressors, societal and cultural conditions may allow different forms of expression for males and females. Since most societies tolerate and even encourage more drinking by males, these tendencies may lead to heavier use of alcohol for them, whereas females who traditionally are restricted from drinking may turn to other drugs such as tranquilizers to deal with stress.

Table 8-1 Frequency of Alcoholism in Interviewed Spouses and First-Degree Relatives of 300 Alcoholic Probands

	Male Probands			Female Probands		
	N	% Affected	Mean Age	N	% Affected	Mean Age
Fathers	80	37.5	54.1	13	38.5	61.2
Mothers	125	20.8	51.2	27	3.7	59.3
Brothers	192	56.8	29.3	36	52.8	36.7
Sisters	196	14.8	31.1	49	20.4	35.3
Sons	28	32.1	23.8	20	50.0	26.3
Daughters	47	19.1	23.1	18	16.7	24.9
Spouses	100	13.0	35.9	25	56.0	41.0

Source: from T. Reich, C. R. Cloninger, P. Van Eerdewegh, J. P. Rice, and J. Mullaney, "Secular trends in the familial transmission of alcoholism," *Alcoholism: Clinical and Experimental Research, 1988, 12,* 456–466. Copyright © 1988 by The Research Society on Alcoholism. Reprinted by permission.

Reich et al. (1988) also found that transmissibility, or the influence of family history of alcoholism, was greater for males. Furthermore, they found that this effect was greater for more recently born cohorts in terms of a higher lifetime prevalence as well as earlier age of onset of alcoholism. These cohort effects may reflect changes in society that increase drinking or encourage drinking at an earlier age.

Twin Studies

One traditional strategy used by researchers trying to marshal evidence for heredi-tarian views, originating with Sir Francis Galton in the late 1800s, has been the study of twins. Concordance rates, or the extent to which both members of a set of twins show the same outcomes, are compared among identical or monozygotic twins, fraternal or dizygotic twins, and siblings. Scandinavian countries, with their extensive and thorough registries of birth and medical treatments and temperance board records of alcohol problems, have provided an excellent source of data for testing theories about the role of heredity in alcoholism as well as other conditions. Concordance rates of alcoholism were often found to be higher among identical twins than in the other groups in the studies by Jonsson and Nilsson (1968) and by Partanen, Bruun, and Markham (1966), a finding that has been used to argue in favor of a genetic factor. Nonetheless, as with studies of the role of heredity in other behaviors, greater concordance of alcoholism in identical than in fraternal twins could still be attributed to the likelihood that they have a more similar environment than fraternal twins do, as well as to their shared genetic background.

A Finnish study by Kaprio et al. (1987) of more than 2,800 pairs of male twins between 24 and 49 years of age examined the relationship of genetic factors and social contact between twins and drinking patterns and consequences. Although the obtained higher concordance of alcoholism among identical than among fraternal twins supported a genetic explanation, it was also found that the frequency of social contact was greater between identical twins than between fraternal twins. Thus, the higher concordance of their drinking patterns may also be partly attributable to their more frequent social contact.

Heath, Jardine, and Martin (1989) located almost 2,000 female twins in Australia using a birth registry. They found that concordance of alcoholism was higher among the identical than the fraternal twins; frequency of social contact between twins did not seem to affect the alcoholism concordance rates, as had been the case in the Finnish study of Kaprio et al. Thus, their findings are more convincing evidence for a genetic basis for alcoholism.

However, a surprising finding was that marital status interacted with genetic factors. Regardless of age, concordance of alcoholism was stronger for identical than for fraternal twins among unmarried twins. If one assumes that unmarried identical twins may maintain more social contact with each other than would married ones, this finding might be interpreted as due to the influence of both genetic and environmental similarity being higher among the unmarried twins.

Pickens, Svikis, McGue, Lykken, Heston, and Clayton (1991) studied both male and female same-sexed twins at alcoholism treatment centers. The differences in alcoholism concordance rates varied somewhat with the type of diagnosis based on the DSM-III Criteria. The largest difference in alcoholism rates of monozygotic twins over dizygotic twins was for alcohol-dependent clients, with rates of .59 versus .36 for male twins and .25 versus .05 for female twins. Pickens et al. concluded that the evidence of a genetic basis for alcoholism is stronger for men than for women.

However, research by Kendler, Heath, Neale, Kessler, and Eaves (1992) with female twins identified through the Virginia Twin Registry indicated stronger evidence that there may be a genetic basis for alcoholism in women as well. Based on 1,030 sets of female twins, Kendler et al. found that the likelihood of monozygotic twins being alcoholic was greater than for dyzgotic twins. Concordance rates of monozygotic twins were four to five times the rate for women in the general population, but concordance rates of dizygotic twins had only one and one-half to two times the rate of women in the general population. Kendler et al. concluded that there is a genetic factor involved in the transmission of alcoholism for women.

Insofar as they did not include male twins from the general population, however, it is difficult to know if the monozygotic-dyzotic twin rate differences are comparable to those in men. The differences in findings could reflect some important methodological factors. Kendler et al. used a much larger sample than most previous investigators did. Also important is the fact that earlier studies used treatment populations to identify twins so that in all pairs, at least one twin was alcoholic. This type of sample may be an unrepresentative segment of the twin population as a whole. In contrast, a general population study such as Kendler et al. includes sets of twins where neither is alcoholic, a subset that may be at lower risk. Since treatment and general population samples are not equivalent, it may be misleading to make quantitative comparisons between studies that differ in their source of participants.

Chapter Eight

Adoption Studies

When children grow up in the homes of alcoholic birth parents, it is not possible to isolate the impact of genetic and environmental factors on their chances of becoming alcoholics themselves as adults. In contrast, a "natural experiment" exists when children of alcoholic parents are adopted by nonalcoholics at an early age. If alcoholism has a strong genetic basis, these children should still be likely to become alcoholics as adults. On the other hand, if environment plays a greater role in alcoholism, they should have a lower probability of becoming alcoholics. This analytical advantage afforded by adoption studies has led to several influential investigations using this paradigm, notably in Scandinavia.

Danish Adoption Studies

Male Adoptees.   Goodwin, Schulsinger, Hermansen, Guze, and Winokur (1973), using adoption records from Denmark, were able to locate male offspring of 55 alcoholic parents, primarily fathers, who were adopted during the first few weeks of life by nonalcoholic families. Comparisons of the adult alcoholism rates of these 55 alcoholic probands with 78 control adoptees from nonalcoholic parents revealed a 4:1 ratio of more alcoholism among those adoptees who had at least one alcoholic parent.

Thus, the male alcoholic probands became alcoholics as adults at a higher rate and at an earlier age than did sons of nonalcoholics, even though adopted into apparently nonalcoholic environments. They also had a much higher rate of divorce than the sons of nonalcoholics, a factor that in addition to any genetic influence could have contributed to their alcohol problems. Comparisons on other factors such as psychiatric disorder did not show differences.

A second phase of the study by Goodwin et al. (1974) was possible since 20 of the probands had a total of 35 brothers who were not adopted out but grew up in the homes of their alcoholic biological parent. The nonadopted and adopted-out siblings did not differ in alcoholism rates, suggesting that being raised in an alcoholic home of the biological parent did not add to the risk of alcoholism among persons known to be at risk biologically. Thus, the biological factor appeared to be the major factor responsible for determining alcoholism rates.

Female Adoptees.   A third phase of the same research examined biological factors involved in alcoholism among women. In contrast to the results of the study of males, Goodwin, Schulsinger, Moller, Mednick, and Guze (1977) failed to find differences in alcoholism for 49 female adoptees from alcoholic biological parents in comparison to 48 control adoptees from nonalcoholic parents. Actually, the observed alcoholism rate of 4 percent was higher than that found in the general population for females in Denmark, a finding that was not expected for the controls.

The studies of Goodwin and his colleagues were pioneering and highly influential, but they are not without a number of problems. The foster parents who adopted the children showed high rates of psychiatric problems as well as a high divorce rate; these problems might have added to the influence that any genetic factor of alcoholism would have had. Although alcoholism rates were higher among adopted sons of alcoholics, it should be noted that only about 20 percent of the probands had become alcoholic at the time they were studied. And when the two heaviest drinking categories, alcoholics and problem drinkers, are combined, there is little difference between the adoptees from alcoholic and nonalcoholic parentage. Finally, the total sample of 55 alcoholic probands used is a rather small number upon which to base strong generalizations.

Searles (1988) also pointed out that the majority of the alcoholic parents were the fathers, but no information was obtained about the mothers' status regarding alcoholism. It is not unreasonable to expect that some of them were alcoholic as well or at least drinking during pregnancy. If so, this prenatal factor complicates the interpretation of genetic influence.

Swedish Adoption Studies

Later studies in Sweden with larger samples corroborate the conclusions from the Danish studies. Studying persons born out of wedlock and adopted before the age of 3 by nonrelatives, Bohman (1978) examined alcoholism rates in adoptees and their biological parents. Alcohol abuse was defined in an objective but nonstandard fashion, being based on the number of times an individual had been registered for insobriety with the Swedish Temperance Board and whether or not treatment had been recommended. Three levels of severity of abuse were defined with this type of information rather than any clinical or psychiatric criteria. It is improbable that more commonly accepted criteria would have yielded the same classification.

Adopted sons with alcoholic biological fathers were found to be three times as likely to be alcoholic as adopted sons of nonalcoholic fathers. The ratio was still 2:1 if the alcoholic parent in question was the mother. The proportions of alcoholism for adopted-out daughters did not seem to be a function of parental alcoholism.

Cloninger, Bohman, and Sigvardsson (1981) studied 862 male adoptees with alcohol problems. The overall prevalence rate of alcoholism for men was about 18 percent. They distinguished two types of heritable alcoholism, *milieu-limited* and *male-limited,* as outlined in Table 8-2.

When both biological parents engaged in mild but untreated alcohol abuse, the alcoholism in adopted-out offspring was defined as milieu-limited alcoholism (Type 1), because alcohol abuse by both sons and daughters varied in proportion to the number of environmental demands they faced. This form of alcoholism, which emerges at a later age and in a less severe form, represented about 13 percent of the sample. These drinkers did not engage in much aggressive behavior when drinking but did show problems with loss of control or psychological dependence on alcohol along with guilt and fear about this outcome.

If the biological fathers had severe alcoholism, the alcoholic adopted-out offspring were defined as male-limited alcoholics (Type 2), because this type seemed absent among women. Variations in their environment did not affect the number of abusers. This type of alcoholism occurred for 4 percent of the sample. These adoptees engaged in moderate alcohol abuse usually, but such abuse often

Table 8-2 Differences in Type 1 and Type 2 Alcoholics

	Type of Alcoholism	
Characteristic Features	*Type 1*	*Type 2*
	Alcohol-Related Problems	
Usual age of onset (years)	after 25	before 25
Spontaneous alcohol-seeking (inability to abstain)	infrequent	frequent
Fighting and arrests when drinking	infrequent	frequent
Psychological dependence (loss of control)	frequent	infrequent
Guilt and fear about alcohol dependence	frequent	infrequent
	Personality Traits	
Novelty seeking	low	high
Harm avoidance	high	low
Reward dependence	high	low

Source: from "Neurogenetic adaptive mechanisms in alcoholism," by C. R. Cloninger in *Science, 1987, 236*, 410–416. Copyright © 1987 by the American Association for the Advancement of Science. Reprinted by permission.

led to fighting and aggression without much psychological dependence or guilt. The male-limited alcoholic (Type 2) typically developed before the age of 25, whereas the milieu-limited alcoholic (Type 1) generally developed after 25. In summary, while both types involved heritable factors, environmental conditions played an additional role with the milieu-limited type but not with the male-limited variety of alcoholism.

Cloninger (1987) also proposed that these two types may differ on three personality traits—*novelty seeking, harm avoidance,* and *reward dependence*—which may be important precursors of the differences in drinking patterns. Milieu-limited alcoholics (Type 1) were postulated to be inhibited individuals concerned with avoidance of harm. They would engage in low levels of novelty seeking and show high concern for rewards from others. In contrast, male-limited alcoholics (Type 2) would be persons, primarily males, who showed high novelty seeking through impulsive and excitable responses, low harm avoidance as reflcted by uninhibited and aggressive actions, and low dependence on rewards manifested by their distant social relationships.

As noted in Table 8-3, Cloninger proposed a neuropsychological model in which levels of different neurotransmitters mediated the different behavior patterns exhibited by the two types of alcoholics. Novelty-seeking levels were postulated to be higher when dopamine was low. Inhibitory behaviors such as harm avoidance were expected to occur in the absence of serotonin. Finally, a tendency to be dependent on rewards was assumed to reflect a lack of norepinephrine.

A similar analysis of the relationship between parental and offspring alcoholism using 913 female adoptees (Bohman, Sivardsson, & Cloninger, 1981) showed an overall prevalence of alcoholism of around 4 percent. The risk of alcoholism was four times greater if the biological mother, but not the father, was alcoholic. The level of alcohol abuse of the foster parents in the adoptive environment did not play as great a role as the alcohol abuse of the parents. Thus, this study supported a possible genetic influence for alcoholism in women.

Table 8-3 A Temperament Model of Personality and Alcoholism

Brain System (Related Temperament Dimension)	Principal Monoamine Neuromodulator	Relevant Stimuli	Behavioral Response
Behavioral activation (novelty seeking)	Dopamine	Novelty Potential rewards or their conditioned signals	Exploratory pursuit Appetitive approach
		Potential relief of: punishment or monotony or their conditioned signals	Escape Active avoidance
Behavioral inhibition (harm avoidance)	Serotonin	Conditioned signals for: punishment, novelty, or frustrative nonreward	Passive avoidance Extinction
Behavioral maintenance (reward dependence)	Norepinephrine	Conditioned signals for reward or relief of punishment	Resistance to extinction

Source: from "Neurogenetic adaptive mechanisms in alcoholism," by C. R. Cloninger in *Science, 1987, 236*, 410–416. Copyright © 1987 by the American Association for the Advancement of Science. Reprinted by permission.

Searles (1988) noted a number of qualifications to the validity of the Swedish data. First, he noted that estimated alcoholism rates for both men and women are much higher in Sweden than in the United States. Moreover, if it is likely that those who put their children up for adoption differ in important ways, such as alcoholism, from those who do not, comparisons of adoptees and nonadoptees may be invalidated. There was no control group of nonadoptees from families that did not put any children up for adoption to determine the degree to which being adopted affects alcoholism rates. Nor was any comparison made of alcoholism between biologically related and unrelated members of the adopting families, a common comparison made to see the effects of a common environment. The lack of a standard criterion in these studies for classifying alcoholism severity is also a serious problem.

In addition to these limitations, one important anomaly in the data calls the generalizability of the results into question. Unlike most studies examining age where an increase in alcoholism is found for the ages of 23 to 43, the study of the Swedish adoptees did not find such an age effect.

U.S. Adoption Studies

Although the documentation about the biological parents of adoptees is less complete in the United States and the criteria for adoption involve nonrandom assignment of adoptees to homes, adoption studies conducted in Iowa show agreement with the Scandinavian research about the relationship of alcoholism in parents and adopted children. Cadoret and Gath (1978) examined male and female adoptees separated at birth from parents with psychiatric disturbance in comparison to adoptees with parents without mental disturbances. The psychiatric background of the parent was not associated with adoptee alcoholism status. Although alcoholism rates were low among the adoptees, there was nonetheless a pattern suggesting that adoptees with alcoholism were more likely to have an alcoholic biological parent than those without alcoholism. However, the criteria for diagnosing parental alcoholism were subjective and based on ratings by social workers rather than by psychiatrists.

High-Risk Sample Studies

Regardless of how well controlled an adoption study is, it is obvious that the vast majority of children in the general population are not adoptees, so that the generalizability of conclusions based on samples of adoptees can be questioned. In recent years there has been increased interest in high-risk populations, defined as those individuals who come from families with a history of alcoholism (designated FH+). These individuals are compared with individuals from families with histories free of alcoholism (designated FH−) on a number of demographic variables and other factors that might affect drinking. The FH designation is based on drinking levels of family members, not drinking levels of the offspring, who may or may not be alcohol abusers themselves at the time of the study.

Unlike adoption studies, high-risk sample studies do not permit a separation of hereditary and environmental contributions. Instead, they assess the joint influences of heredity and environment on the drinking behaviors and psychological well-being of children from alcoholic and nonalcoholic families. The assumption is that both genetic and home environment factors represent a higher risk for alcoholism in FH+ than in FH− families. However, the genetic and environmental factors may offset each other in some families. As depicted in Figure 8-1, there may be families where a genetic factor favoring alcoholism is opposed by a home environment that lowers the risk of alcoholism, and other families where a low genetic potential for alcoholism is offset by a home environment that raises the risk of alcoholism.

In other words, the vulnerability or susceptibility of an individual to alcoholism is based on a combination of *both* genetic and environmental factors. If either factor is sufficiently strong, alcoholism may occur even if the other factor is weak. For children of alcoholics, both factors are generally assumed to be high. However, it is conceivable that although children of alcoholics may have a high genetic potential for alcoholism, some may have an environment that does not foster alcoholism. Similarly, although children of nonalcoholics may have a low genetic potential for alcoholism, some of them may live in an environment that fosters alcoholism.

Retrospective Studies

Studies based on retrospective recall of alcoholics, typically assessed during treatment, generally depict a negative impact of parental alcoholism on children.

Alcoholism: The Role of Heredity and Environment

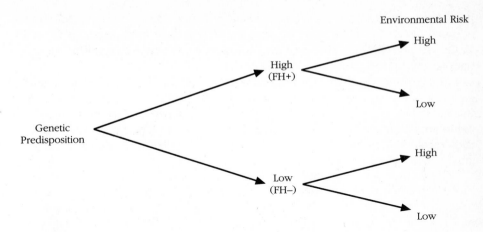

Figure 8-1 Joint effects of hereditary and environmental factors on risk of alcoholism.

Self-reports of alcoholics who had an alcoholic parent imply that alcohol may have had a stronger effect for them when they first started drinking than for alcoholics who did not have an alcoholic parent. For example, Penick et al. (1987) found that alcoholics with an alcoholic parent or grandparent recalled having started drinking at a younger age and having had more problems due to alcohol than either alcoholics without a drinking parent or alcoholics whose drinking relative was someone other than a parent or grandparent. Thus, the individual's own level of alcohol abuse and a family history of alcoholism appear to produce independent and additive effects. Either factor places one at higher risk and having both factors increases the likelihood of alcoholism even more.

The inclusion by Penick et al. of FH+ subjects who were not alcoholic as a control group in this study allowed an evaluation of the effects of family history of alcoholism on persons not yet afflicted by alcoholism. Since FH+ subjects were found to be more susceptible to problems on most measures than the FH– controls, it appears that a family history of alcoholism places one at higher risk for a variety of psychological and physical health impairments.

Glenn and Parsons (1989a, 1989b) reported a variety of adverse effects associated with a family history of alcoholism, defined in this study as having one first-degree relative treated for alcoholism or considered by several family members to have a drinking problem. They studied 148 middle-aged alcoholics in treatment, about half of whom had an FH+ background and half of whom had an FH– background. Control groups of matched nonalcoholics were included, again with about half FH+ and half FH– backgrounds. This study is unusual in the inclusion of both alcoholic and nonalcoholic groups as well as both males and females.

Glenn and Parsons (1989b) predicted that a family history of alcoholism would be related to poorer physical health, trauma and injury history, drug use history, and alcohol-related disorders. In general, health was worse for alcoholics, but to a greater extent among those from FH+ backgrounds where at least one first-degree relative was an alcoholic. Even among nonalcoholic controls, however, health was poorer for those with an FH+ background. Finally, there were few differences in health between males and females that could be attributed to alcoholism per se as opposed to biological and sex-role differences.

Another analysis using the same samples (Glenn & Parsons, 1989a) examined psychosocial correlates of family history of alcoholism for the alcoholics and nonalcoholic controls. Five categories of measures were employed, including demographic, marital, and occupational background; drinking practices; and psychological functioning. Retrospective reports of childhood behavior problems and family psychopathology were also obtained.

Glenn and Parsons (1989a) found that family history as well as the subject's own alcoholism status affected scores on most variables. Those with either a family history of alcoholism or alcoholism themselves had poorer occupational levels and more turnover, greater family psychopathology, more marriages, and greater anxiety and depression. Similarly, these groups reported more childhood behavior problems such as hyperactivity and conduct problems. Contrary to predictions, men differed significantly from women only on this latter category.

Retrospective studies are often based on clinical samples of individuals seeking help for problems not necessarily related to alcohol. These subjects may be likely to search earlier memories for signs of family problems such as parental alcoholism to explain their own problems; this tendency is particularly problematic since most studies rely on self-report of family history rather than objective or independent assessment. This tendency might produce overestimates of the extent of alcoholism in family backgrounds. It is also likely that clinical samples are an atypical sample of the general population.

Prospective Studies

Prospective studies assess subjects prior to the onset of alcoholism and follow them afterward. These before-after comparisons of individuals from FH+ and FH– backgrounds offer a stronger basis for inferences about the effects of FH background on the offspring than do retrospective studies.

In contrast to retrospective studies, prospective studies show less support for the adverse effects of an alcoholic family background. Pandina and Johnson (1989) compared an FH+ group of adolescents who had a parent who had been treated for alcoholism, another FH+ group who had at least one parent with heavy drinking, and two groups of FH– background offspring. They conducted a prospective study of a community, rather than a clinical population, over three years with about 1,400 high school students. They found no differences in alcohol problems such as escape drinking, early onset of intoxication, or frequency of intoxication, but did report that children of alcoholics were more likely to have other problems related to alcohol and drugs sooner. A related study on the same sample (Pandina & Johnson, 1990) also failed to find that family history affected alcohol use but did report more FH+ students experiencing alcohol-related problems.

A study by Harwood and Leonard (1989) examining the relationship of problem drinking to self-reported family history of alcoholism and antisocial behavior involved 123 first-time DWI (driving while intoxicated) offender males. If any family member was reported to have been a frequent heavy social drinker or alcoholic, the individual was considered to be FH+. If more than 4 of a list of 18 deviant behaviors were reported to have occurred before the age of 18, he was classified as positive for antisocial behaviors.

Approximately half of the group was FH+ and half FH–. Antisocial tendencies existed in about 60 percent of the sample. The results suggested that neither consumption levels nor alcohol-related problems were related to either family history or antisocial behavior levels, although family history was associated with earlier age of drinking onset, preoccupation with alcohol, and physical dependence.

Johnson, Leonard, and Jacob (1989) also failed to find any differences in drinking behavior, attitudes and reasons for drinking, drinking context, or consequences between adolescent children of alcoholics and two control groups, one consisting of children of normals and the other consisting of children of depressives. However, children of alcoholics did report more use of drugs such as marijuana, hashish, speed, and cocaine than did children of depressives and children of normals.

Savoie, Emory, and Moody-Thomas (1988) found that alcohol may have a more arousing effect on children from FH– than those from FH+ families. They speculated that this difference might explain why FH+ background children were likely to consume alcohol in higher quantities and/or more frequently. Perhaps some biochemical metabolic differences underlie these effects. However, when younger children were actually administered small doses of alcohol, no differences were found in objective or subjective indexes of intoxication as a function of FH+ and FH– background.

Problems with High-Risk Sample Studies

Overall, then, the evidence is mixed about whether children from FH+ backgrounds are more likely to use more alcohol or to develop alcohol problems. One problem with both retrospective and prospective studies is the wide variation in the criteria used to define family histories as positive or negative for alcoholism. Some studies use stringent criteria such as a parent diagnosed and treated for alcoholism, while other studies rely on vague and uncorroborated criteria such as the offspring's judgment that a parent had drinking problems sometime in the past. Thus, in some studies, the magnitude of the difference between the FH+ and FH– conditions is rather small and unreliable.

As suggested by Figure 8-2, the likelihood of finding differences between FH+ and FH– groups should vary with the criteria used for defining the two groups. Figure 8-2 depicts a continuum of drinking that ranges from nondrinking through moderate to heavy drinking. If groups selected from drinking levels 2 and 3 on the diagram are used to represent FH– and FH+ groups respectively, there should be

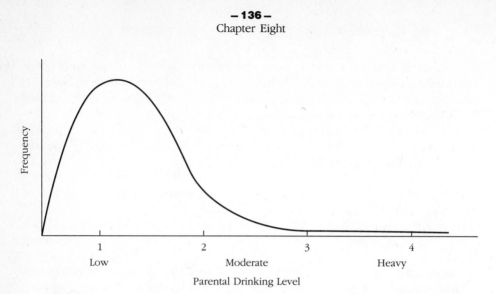

Parental Drinking Level

Figure 8-2 Comparisons of FH+ and FH– groups will yield different results depending on the criteria used to classify subjects. Studies that use extreme groups (level 1 to represent FH– and level 4 to represent FH+) will be more likely to show differences than studies that use intermediate groups (level 2 to represent FH– and level 3 to represent FH+).

less chance of finding differences than if groups are selected from drinking levels 1 and 4.

For example, strong evidence of more alcohol use, greater conduct behavior problems, and symptoms such as depression among FH+ than FH– groups obtained in two carefully planned studies may have been due to their choice of widely different groups in their comparison. Chassin, Rogosch, and Barrera (1991) carefully recruited and screened 454 adolescent participants from the community rather than using volunteers or clinical samples. They excluded apparent FH– individuals whom they had reason to suspect had parents with alcohol problems. Inclusion of these subjects would have reduced the differences between the FH+ and FH– groups.

Chassin et al. used face-to-face interviews with the parents and applied the rigorous DSM-III-R criteria for distinguishing alcoholic and nonalcoholic parents. This procedure provided a more stringent definition than the subjective criterion used in many studies based only on the child's feeling that one or both of the parents had drinking problems. In addition, Chassin et al. recruited a larger sample than most other studies comparing FH+ and FH– individuals to provide a more powerful assessment.

A comparison of 253 FH+ and 237 FH– college students over their four years of college by Sher, Walitzer, Wood, and Brent (1991) also used rigorous measures to define family history of alcoholism. Unlike in the study by Chassin et al., the drinking history of the parents was not assessed directly but based on the student's description. Measures of parental comorbidity (the presence of other psychological disorders often found among alcoholics) were taken so that conclusions about the specific effect of parental alcoholism could be made.

The results revealed that a family history of alcoholism is associated with more alcohol and drug problems, stronger expectancies for alcohol use, more behavioral undercontrol, and more psychiatric distress. In addition, FH+ students showed poorer academic performance and lower verbal ability. These differences were present for both men and women for most variables.

In conclusion, the findings of Sher et al. (1991), like those of Chassin et al. (1991), suggest that when more stringent criteria are used to ensure that the groups being compared do represent extremes of parental alcoholism, FH+ do not fare as well as FH– individuals on a number of important aspects of psychological well-being and functioning.

Another problem in comparisons of FH+ and FH– individuals is that researchers have not generally reported the levels of alcohol use in any absolute or standard units that can be compared across studies. The reported lack of differences could reflect either equally low *or* high drinking by FH+ and FH– groups. It is conceivable that any effect of family drinking history among young samples is masked by the tendency for FH– individuals to drink because of adolescent curiosity about alcohol and from peer pressure to drink. If other factors such as these influences combine with family drinking history to determine alcohol use levels, no clear-cut effect of family drinking history will be found. Finally, the studies, thus far, may not show strong relationships between parental and offspring drinking simply because they cannot rule out the possibility of future alcoholism in the children.

Marker Studies

Another strategy for predicting the risk of alcoholism is to search for marker variables, factors that might distinguish persons from FH+ and FH– backgrounds. A *marker* is not necessarily a cause but is a factor that helps identify individuals who are likely to differ from others in some respect. In marker studies, the offspring need not be alcoholic yet themselves. The goal is to compare the children of FH+ and FH– families to see if they already differ on factors that might point toward future differences in drinking behavior. If, as assumed by a genetic model, children of FH+ backgrounds are more likely to develop drinking problems, perhaps some genetic, physical, biochemical, or neurophysiological differences exist even prior to the development of drinking problems. Furthermore, some types of markers, such as indicators of differences in ethanol metabolism, may play a causal role in producing differences in reactions to alcohol. Thus far, the research, as the following overview shows, has produced a set of conflicting findings.

Genetic Markers

A search for metabolic differences relating to alcoholism risk between FH+ and FH– groups has not proved fruitful so far (Schuckit, 1981). While some evidence by Schuckit (1984) showed that FH+ males had higher acetaldehyde levels after consuming alcohol than matched FH– males, other studies with young males

(Behar et al., 1983) have not confirmed this result. Contrary to expectations about a genetic basis for differences in metabolism, no differences between FH+ and FH– subjects in rates of absorption of ethanol have been found (Nagoshi & Wilson, 1987; Schuckit, 1981).

Biochemical Markers

Monoamine oxidase (MAO) is a genetically controlled enzyme that is involved with mood states through its regulation of the levels of neurotransmitters such as dopamine and norepinephrine. MAO levels in blood platelets have been found to be lower in alcoholics even after they abstain for long periods. Members of alcoholic families also show lower platelet MAO levels than those from nonalcoholic families. Studies (Pandey, Fawcett, Gibbons, Clark, & Davis, 1988; Von Knorring, Bohman, Von Knorring, & Oreland, 1985) suggest that the MAO level differences between normals and alcoholics are limited to what Cloninger et al. (1981) termed Type 2 or male-limited alcoholics, but do not appear with Type 1 or milieu-limited alcoholics whose alcoholism is influenced more by environmental factors.

Similarly, the neurotransmitter serotonin has been found to be low in alcoholics, possibly prior to the development of alcoholism (Ballenger, Goodwin, Major, & Brown, 1979) and may also serve as a marker variable.

Electrophysiological Markers

Differences in brain wave patterns have been observed between FH+ and FH– groups. For example, the P300 wave, a measure of electrical brain activity assumed to reflect attention when stimuli are presented, is smaller for FH+ groups given a dose of alcohol than for FH– groups (Volavka, Pollack, Gabrielli, & Mednick, 1985). Similar results were found for young boys by Begleiter, Porjesz, Bihari, & Kissin (1984). These findings, although challenged by later studies summarized by Tarter, Moss, and Laird (1990), imply that sons of alcoholics may suffer attentional or perceptual processing deficits.

Neuropsychological and Cognitive Markers

Some studies such as one by Nagoshi and Wilson (1987) have suggested that offspring of alcoholics have impaired cognitive abilities in comparison to controls, prior to, but not after, consuming a moderate dose of alcohol.

After controlling for age, intelligence, and level of drinking, cognitive differences between FH+ and FH– groups were not found by Hesselbrock, Hesselbrock, and Stabenau (1985). Similarly, Workman-Daniels and Hesselbrock (1987) found no major differences in performance of FH+ and FH– groups on a number of cognitive tests assumed to reflect different levels of neuropsychological functioning.

Psychological Markers

Schuckit (1987) suggested that sons of alcoholics may differ from sons of nonalcoholics in their sensitivity or reaction to ethanol. He found that sons of alcoholics had a lower arousal from a moderate dose of alcohol than sons of nonalcoholics did, a difference that might be part of the basis for why alcoholics need to drink larger amounts of alcohol. However, other research by Nagoshi and Wilson (1987), using both male and female children, found that FH+ subjects tend to show more sensitivity to (more disruption effect from) a dose of alcohol than FH– subjects.

Problems with Marker Studies

Overall, the evidence on markers for alcoholism has been inconsistent. One ignored factor throughout this research that may contribute to the conflicting array of findings is the time of measurement following alcohol administration. Newlin and Thomson (1990) proposed that FH+ and FH– sons may differ in their sensitivity to alcohol in different ways, depending on whether the blood alcohol level is ascending or descending at the time of observation, as depicted in Figure 8-3.

Specifically, their differentiator model proposed that sons of alcoholics (SOAs) may experience more positive arousal than sons of nonalcoholics (SONAs) on the ascending limb, which would give them more incentive to drink. In addition, they may also differ on the descending limb in that SOAs may have greater acute tolerance within the test session and return to baseline levels more quickly than the SONAs, a difference that would lead to less anxiety and also promote more drinking by SOAs. During about the first 30 minutes after a drink, the SOAs would show more intoxication and physiological changes than SONAs, but as time since drinking passed, they would show fewer negative effects of intoxication as compared with the SONAs.

This model may reconcile some of the confusing results in past research on markers if different studies assessed the effects of alcohol at different times of the day. Newlin and Thomson pointed out that alcohol doses in laboratory studies are typically administered at the convenience of the researcher's schedule rather than at times corresponding to when the subjects typically drink. For example, Schuck-

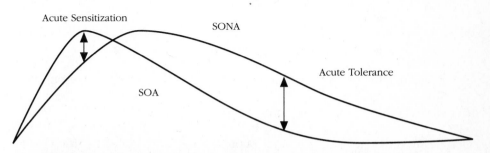

Figure 8-3 Schematic diagram of differentiator model. Note the greater acute sensitization during the ascending limb of the blood alcohol curve in sons of alcoholics (SOAs) and the greater acute tolerance in SOAs during the falling limb of the curve. This is indicated by a more rapid and robust onset of the effect of alcohol and more rapid return to baseline of the falling blood alcohol curve.

Source: from "Alcohol challenge with sons of alcoholics: A critical review and analysis," by D. B. Newlin and J. B. Thomson in *Psychological Bulletin, 1990, 108,* 383–401. Copyright © 1990 by American Psychological Association. Reprinted by permission.

it's numerous studies in which alcohol is given to subjects have generally tested at 9 A.M. Light drinkers typically become nauseous when drinking at this atypical time, so that some of the differences between FH+ and FH– individuals may be due to nausea rather than to alcohol sensitivity differences per se. Also, subjects are usually tested in the presence of an experimenter so that social interaction is required. Thus, differences in reaction could be affected by social factors as well as by alcohol.

Even where markers seem to have been found, there is no clearly formulated theory to account for the findings. How do markers act as contributors to or as "causes" of alcohol consumption? For example, Tarter, Moss, and Laird (1990) pointed out that morphological characteristics such as body size could be viewed as markers since boys who are physically larger for their age might start drinking sooner because they can more easily be perceived as older. We would not conclude that large body size was a direct cause of drinking differences. Instead, it may be that body size has an indirect effect on drinking levels as a factor that is sociologically and psychologically conducive to drinking.

Conclusions

The question of the relative influence of genetic and environmental factors on the development of alcoholism has generated considerable interest and controversy. An explanation emphasizing heredity is more fatalistic since it implies that the "die has already been cast" and the offspring cannot alter or control their destiny. Environmental explanations are more optimistic in the sense that interventions can be attempted to counteract or reduce the damage. Children of alcoholics might receive earlier counseling or be placed under foster care, for example. Another possibility would be more education and counseling of parents as to the dangers of parental alcoholism.

At the level of the individual, the answer to this issue would have implications for assignment of blame or responsibility between parents and children. If alcoholism were regarded as primarily of genetic origin, the alcoholic would seemingly be absolved of personal responsibility for the problem. At the societal level, the answer to the question carries implications for social attitudes and social policy. If genetic factors were assumed to be the primary determinants of alcoholism, society would be more tolerant than if the alcoholic was seen to be personally responsible.

The major evidence that first led to increased awareness about the role of heredity as a risk factor for alcoholism was the adoption studies conducted in the 1950s in Denmark and subsequently in Sweden. However, the generalizability of findings from adoptees to the larger population must be evaluated. The circumstances and the types of individuals who put children up for adoption and accept adopted children are likely to be significantly different from the more general population. For example, infants placed for adoption are not a random sample of infants but often come from unwed mothers, probably adolescent girls. They may have lower income, poor nutrition, and so on. The types of individuals who apply to adopt children are not a random sample of the general population either, being screened by social agencies to ensure that they can afford to care for the child and appear to be psychologically stable. Certainly the types of individuals involved may vary in different countries and eras, depending on social and legal conditions and cultural attitudes related to adoptions.

Much research on the heredity-environment issue has shifted toward the study of children who grow up in the homes of their biological parents, comparing those whose parents vary in their level of alcoholism. Although these comparisons cannot address the question of the relative role of heredity and environment as adoption studies can, they can be generalized to a much larger segment of the total population. Differences between children from FH+ and FH– families would have to be viewed as due to the joint or combined effects of heredity and environment.

Such studies are beginning to test the widely held view that children who grow up in alcoholic families are at risk not only for alcoholism but for other types of psychological and behavioral problems as well. Clinical observations have provided some provocative hypotheses, but few carefully controlled studies have been done. Thus far, there is weak research support for the conclusion that children of alcoholics are different from children of nonalcoholics. Overall, the children of alcoholics and nonalcoholics do not differ with respect to their own drinking practices or drinking's effect on personality. Some of the contradictory findings across different studies about the relationship of parental alcoholism and characteristics of their children may be due to the variety of criteria used to define an alcoholic parent in different studies. It is also possible that under some conditions, or for some types of individuals, the potentially adverse effects of alcoholism in parents can be offset, but the nature of these protective factors is not yet fully understood. Finally, because alcoholism may require a number of years to become manifest, continued follow-up over another 10 or 20 years could possibly show wider differences.

References

Amark, C. (1951). A study in alcoholism: Clinical, social-psychiatric and genetic investigations. *Acta Psychiatrica et Neurologica Scandinavica, 70*(Suppl. 70), 1–283.

Ballenger, J. C., Goodwin, F. K., Major, L. F., & Brown G. (1979). Alcohol and central serotonin metabolism in man. *Archives of General Psychiatry, 36,* 224–227.

Begleiter, H., Porjesz, B., Bihari, B., & Kissin, B. (1984). Event-related potentials in boys at risk for alcoholism. *Science, 225,* 1493–1496.

Behar, D., Berg, C. J., Rapoport, J. L., Nelson, W., Linnoila, M., Cohen, M., Bozevich, C., & Marshall, T. (1983). Behavioral and physiological effects of ethanol in high-risk and control children: A pilot study. *Alcoholism: Clinical and Experimental Research, 7,* 404–410.

Bohman, M. (1978). Some genetic aspects of alcoholism and criminality: A population of adoptees. *Archives of General Psychiatry, 35,* 269–276.

Bohman, M., Sivardsson, S., & Cloninger, C. R. (1981). Maternal inheritance of alcohol abuse: Cross fostering analysis of adopted women. *Archives of General Psychiatry, 38,* 965–969.

Cadoret, R. J., & Gath, A. (1978). Inheritance of alcoholism in adoptees. *British Journal of Psychiatry, 132,* 252–258.

Chassin, L., Rogosch, F., & Barrera, M. (1991). Substance use and symptomatology among adolescent children of alcoholics. *Journal of Abnormal Psychology, 100,* 449–463.

Cloninger, C. R. (1987). Neurogenetic adaptive mechanisms in alcoholism. *Science, 236,* 410–416.

Cloninger, C. R., Bohman, M., & Sigvardsson, S. (1981). Inheritance of alcohol abuse: Cross fostering analysis of adopted men. *Archives of General Psychiatry, 38,* 861–868.

Cotton, N. S. (1979). The familial transmission of alcoholism: A review. *Journal of Studies on Alcohol, 40,* 89–116.

Glenn, S. W., & Parsons, O. A. (1989a). Alcohol abuse and familial alcoholism: Psychosocial correlates in men and women. *Journal of Studies on Alcohol, 50,* 116–127.

Glenn, S. W., & Parsons, O. A. (1989b). Effects of alcohol abuse and familial alcoholism on physical health in men and women. *Health Psychology, 8,* 325–341.

Goodwin, D. W., Schulsinger, F., Hermansen, L., Guze, S. B., & Winokur, G. (1973). Alcohol problems in adoptees raised apart from biological parents. *Archives of General Psychiatry, 28,* 238–243.

Goodwin, D. W., Schulsinger, F., Moller, N., Hermansen, L., Winokur, G., & Guze, S. B. (1974). Drinking problems in adopted and nonadopted sons of alcoholics. *Archives of General Psychiatry, 31,* 164–169.

Goodwin, D. W., Schulsinger, F., Moller, N., Mednick, S., & Guze, S. B. (1977). Psychopathology in adopted and nonadopted daughters of alcoholics. *Archives of General Psychiatry, 34,* 1005–1009.

Harwood, M. K., & Leonard, K. E. (1989). Family history of alcoholism, youthful antisocial behavior and problem drinking among DWI offenders. *Journal of Studies on Alcohol, 50,* 210–216.

Heath, A. C., Jardine, R., & Martin, N. G. (1989). Interactive effects of genotype and social environment on alcohol consumption in female twins. *Journal of Studies on Alcohol, 50,* 38–48.

Hesselbrock, V. M., Hesselbrock, M. N., & Stabenau, J. R. (1985). Alcoholism in men patients subtyped by family history and antisocial personality. *Journal of Studies on Alcohol, 46,* 59–64.

Johnson, S., Leonard, K. E., & Jacob, T. (1989). Drinking, drinking styles and drug use in children of alcoholics, depressives and controls. *Journal of Studies on Alcohol, 50,* 427–431.

Jonsson, E., & Nilsson, T. (1968). Alcohol konsumption hos monozygota och dizygota tvillingpar. *Nordisk Hygienisk Tidskrift, 49,* 21–25.

Kaprio, J., Koskenvuo, M., Langinvaino, H., Ramonov, K., Sarna, S., & Rose, R. J. (1987). Genetic influences on use and abuse of alcohol: A study of 5,638 adult Finnish twin brothers. *Alcoholism: Clinical and Experimental Reearch, 11,* 349–356.

Kendler, K. S., Heath, A. C., Neale, M. C., Kessler, R. C., & Eaves, L. J. (1992). A population-based twin study of alcoholism in women. *Journal of the American Medical Association, 268,* 1877–1882.

Nagoshi, C. T., & Wilson, J. R. (1987). Influence of family alcoholism history on alcohol metabolism, sensitivity, and tolerance. *Alcoholism: Clinical and Experimental Research, 11,* 392–398.

Newlin, D. B., & Thomson, J. B. (1990). Alcohol challenge with sons of alcoholics: A critical review and analysis. *Psychological Bulletin, 108,* 383–402.

Pandey, G. N., Fawcett, J., Gibbons, R., Clark, C. D., & Davis, J. M. (1988). Platelet monoamine oxidase in alcoholism. *Biological Psychiatry, 24,* 15–24.

Pandina, R. J., & Johnson, V. (1989). Familial drinking history as a predictor of alcohol and drug consumption among adolescent children. *Journal of Studies on Alcohol, 50,* 245–253.

Pandina, R. J., & Johnson, V. (1990). Serious alcohol and drug problems among adolescents with a family history of alcoholism. *Journal of Studies on Alcohol, 51,* 278–282.

Partanen, J., Bruun, K., & Markham, T. (1966). *Inheritance of drinking behavior.* New Brunswick, NJ: Rutgers University Center for Alcohol Studies.

Penick, E. C., Powell, B. J., Bingham, S. F., Liskow, B. I., Miller, N. S., & Read, M. R. (1987). A comparative study of familial alcoholism. *Journal of Studies on Alcohol 48,* 136–146.

Pickens, R. W., Svikis, D. S., McGue, M., Lykken, D. T., Heston, L. L., & Clayton, P. J. (1991). Heterogeneity in the inheritance of alcoholism. A study of male and female twins. *Archives of General Psychiatry, 48,* 19–28.

Reich, T., Cloninger, C. R., Van Eerdewegh, P., Rice, J. P., & Mullaney, J. (1988). Secular trends in the familial transmission of alcoholism. *Alcoholism: Clinical and Experimental Reseach, 12,* 458–464.

Savoie, T. M., Emory, E. K., & Moody-Thomas, S. (1988). Acute alcohol intoxication in socially drinking female and male offspring of alcohlic fathers. *Journal of Studies on Alcohol, 49,* 430–435.

Schuckit, M. (1981). Peak blood alcohol levels in men at high risk for future development of alcoholism. *Alcoholism: Clinical and Experimental Research, 5,* 64–66.

Schuckit, M. (1984). Prospective markers for alcoholism. In D. W. Goodwin, K.T.V. Dusen, & S. A. Mednick (Eds.), *Longitudinal research in alcoholism* (pp. 147–169). Boston: Kluwer-Nijhoff.

Schuckit, M. (1987). Biological vulnerability to alcoholism. *Journal of Consulting and Clinical Psychology, 55,* 301–309.

Searles, J. S. (1988). The role of genetics in the pathogenesis of alcoholism. *Journal of Abnormal Psychology, 97,* 153–167.

Sher, K. J., Walitzer, K. S., Wood, P. K., & Brent, E. E. (1991). Characteristics of children of alcoholics: Putative risk factors, substance use and abuse, and psychopathology. *Journal of Abnormal Psychology, 100,* 427–448.

Tarter, R. E., Moss, H., & Laird, S. B. (1990). Biological markers for vulnerability to alcoholism. In R. L. Collins, K. E. Leonard, & J. S. Searles (Eds.), *Alcohol and the family: Research and clinical perspectives* (pp. 79–106). New York: Guilford Press.

Volavka, J., Pollack, V., Gabrielli, W. F., & Mednick, S. A. (1985). The EEG in persons at risk for alcoholism. In M. Galanter (Ed.), *Recent developments in alcoholism* (pp. 21–36). New York: Plenum Press.

Von Knorring, A. L., Bohman, M., Von Knorring, L., & Oreland, L. (1985). Platelet MAO activity as a biological marker in subgroups of alcoholism. *Acta Scandinavica, 72,* 51–58.

Winokur, G., Reich, T., Rimmer, J., & Pitts, F. N. (1970). Alcoholism III: Diagnosis and family psychiatric illness. *Archives of General Psychiatry, 23,* 104–111.

Workman-Daniels, K. L., & Hesselbrock, V. M. (1987). Childhood problem behavior and neuropsychological functioning in persons at risk for alcoholism. *Journal of Studies on Alcohol, 48,* 187–193.

Family Dynamics and Alcoholism

*"Mid pleasures and palaces, though we may roam,
Be it ever so humble, there's no place like home."*

The well-known last line of this couplet about the security and comfort of home actually comes from a lament about the domestic ravages of alcoholism entitled "Ruined by Drink," by Nobil Adkisson, composed around 1860. It goes on to describe the domestic scene: "But the father lies drunk on the floor, / The table is empty, the wolf's at the door, / And mother sobs loud in her broken-back'd chair, / Her garments in taters, her soul in despair."

Beyond any genetic influence children may suffer from parental alcoholism, the family environment of alcoholic homes may also affect their eventual level of drinking and possibly their future personality. Observational learning in the home affects the formation of attitudes and behaviors. Children form standards of evaluation from their observations as to what are considered acceptable or appropriate behaviors. Social learning theory (Bandura, 1977) suggests that parents act as models in determining how children may perceive alcohol's role, since children imitate the values and behavior of parents. Thus, for children who grow up in the homes of alcoholic biological parents, it is likely that experiences related to drinking by alcoholic parents as well as biologically inherited factors may combine to adversely affect them. These negative experiences may be psychologically disruptive and in some cases may increase the likelihood that the children will develop their own alcohol problems as adults.

In earlier approaches to the study of alcoholism, the focus was on the alcoholic, although it was recognized that nonalcoholic family members were adversely affected by the problem of family alcoholism. Still, relatively little study of the effects of alcoholism on the family has been done, especially focusing on the underlying process for such effects such as the nature of interaction patterns among family members. The preceding chapter discussed research on family history, but for the most part these studies have focused on the resulting differences between offspring of alcoholics and nonalcoholics rather than the family dynamics that might produce such differences. Many early studies used clinical observations based on small samples that were unrepresentative of the alcoholic population. Poor measurement instruments yielded observations that were often unreliable and invalid. This chapter focuses on more recent research that examines the process by which alcoholic home environments affect the children.

Direct Paths of Family Influence

According to social learning theory (Bandura, 1977), sex-role identification involves observational learning, through which boys will be likely to model their behavior after masculine models such as their fathers while girls will likely model their behavior after feminine models such as their mothers.

One study (Harburg, Davis, & Caplan, 1982), based on a larger longitudinal investigation of health behavior known as the Tecumseh Community Health Study, examined the relationship between the level of fathers' and mothers' drinking with that of their sons and daughters. The results generally upheld the social learning theory prediction. The heavier the drinking was in a parent, the heavier the drinking was for the offspring, up to a point, after which there was a divergence as shown in Figure 9-1. For the two different measures shown, as parental drinking levels rise, offspring drinking levels fall off, especially in relationship to opposite-sex parent drinking.

Thus, the relative amount of alcohol consumed by sons tended to parallel that of their fathers, but fell behind when fathers were very heavy drinkers. The same trend emerged with respect to drinking of daughters in relation to drinking of their mothers. Weaker correspondences occurred between offspring and their opposite-sex parents. This pattern shows the strong sex-role identification influence for both sexes who imitate the same-sex parent more than the opposite-sex parent. The results also show that excessive drinking by parents, especially those of the opposite sex, tend to have a reverse effect, lowering the drinking level of offspring.

Webster, Harburg, Gleiberman, Schork, and DiFranceisco (1989), in a follow-up study, compared the relationship between drinking of parents when their children were young and the current levels of drinking by their children as young adults. Unlike most studies that rely on retrospective reports by the child about what they can remember of their parents' drinking pattern many years earlier, this study used self-reports of drinking obtained 17 years earlier from the parents

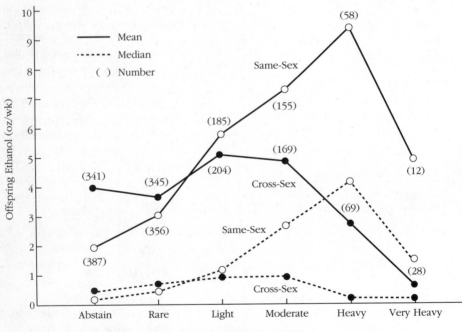

Figure 9-1 Mean and median ethanol intake (in ounces per week) of offspring by same- or cross-sex parent's drinking habit.

Source: Reprinted with permission from *Journal of Studies on Alcohol,* Vol. 43, pp. 497–516, 1982. Copyright by Journal of Studies on Alcohol, Inc., Rutgers Center for Alcohol Studies, New Brunswick, N.J. 08903

themselves in conjunction with a larger study. The study was based on 420 sets of mothers, fathers, and adult offspring. The level of the parents' self-reported drinking in 1960 was compared with the current drinking level reported by their adult offspring in 1977.

Drinking levels of offspring were found to be related to earlier paternal use levels. If parents were lifelong abstainers, offspring drank less. Parents who drank heavily had offspring, especially daughters, who drank heavily. Sons' drinking was more similar to fathers' than to mothers'. Overall, offspring drinking levels resembled parents' drinking levels, but still a high percentage of children did not imitate their parents' drinking patterns.

Webster et al. proposed that two processes, *aversion* and *polarization,* may develop in children of alcoholics and reduce the similarity between drinking of parents and children for heavily drinking parents. Aversion to drinking may occur and lead to abstinence if the child finds the parent's heavy drinking to be unacceptable. Thus, 56 percent of the low-volume male drinkers had a heavily drinking mother whose drinking violated cultural norms. Polarization refers to the child's drinking at extremes of the continuum in reaction to the parents' drinking, either abstaining or engaging in heavy drinking. Because heavily drinking parents may often be abusive toward their children, for example, the tendency of the children to model after the drinking of such parents may be reduced. Daughters of heavily drinking parents were found to be more likely to show the polarization effect.

Webster et al. also found that abstinent parents were likely to have children who were abstinent, perhaps because these parents had religious motivations and convictions against drinking that they conveyed strongly to their children.

Harburg, DiFranceisco, Webster, Gleiberman, and Schork (1990) analyzed other aspects of the follow-up of the Tecumseh study. They found that aversion effects were more likely when the opposite-sex parent was a heavy drinker *with alcohol-related problems*. However, daughters often imitated the drinking levels of heavily drinking fathers without problems related to their drinking. Daughters showed a polarization effect if their mothers were heavy drinkers, with most of them being abstainers and a sizable minority becoming heavy drinkers themselves. Overall, the highest correspondence of drinking levels between parents and children occurred for abstaining parents, especially if the father was abstinent.

Orford and Velleman (1991) found that the relationship of heavy parental drinking to the drinking of offspring also varied with the interpersonal relationship between drinking parent and child. Daughters were more likely to have drinking problems if they had a close relationship with their heavily drinking fathers. Sons were more likely to have drinking problems if they had heavily drinking mothers *and* poor relations with their fathers. These findings, similar in many respects to those of Harburg et al., suggest that the impact of heavy drinking by parents on the drinking of their children is greater for offspring of the opposite sex.

Indirect Paths of Family Influence

A less direct influence of parental drinking involves the emotional strife and turmoil found in many alcoholic homes that may have an adverse effect on the psychological development of children and increase their own future likelihood of using alcohol to cope.

A study by Reich, Earls, and Powell (1988) compared the home environments of children of alcoholics and nonalcoholics. More marital conflict, parent-child conflict, psychiatric problems among the children, and poor adaptive functioning by parents were observed in the alcoholic homes.

These conflictual and stressful family environments may interfere with the development of the children's self-esteem. However, conflict and stress are by no means specific or limited to alcoholic homes but occur in families with nonalcoholic psychiatric problems as well. Thus, any impairments observed in children of alcoholics may reflect the effects of growing up in a dysfunctional family rather than of alcoholism per se.

Children of Alcoholics (CoAs)

Various forms of psychopathology among children of alcoholics (CoAs), even after they have become adults, have been noted by many clinicians. Woititz (1983) sees CoAs having problems that range from insecurity and low self-esteem to an extreme tendency to please others and to rescue the family. They judge themselves without mercy, feel different from other people, and have difficulty having fun.

In his moving memoir about growing up with an alcoholic father, Sanders (1989) describes how the children kept the family secret and "never breathed a word of it beyond the four walls of our house. To this day, my brother and sister rarely mention it" (p. 70). Tension permeated the home when his father was drinking, for "the more he drank, the more obsessed Mother became with stopping him. She hunted for bottles, counted the cash in his wallet, sniffed at his breath" (p. 70). He goes on to describe how each sibling reacted to these circumstances: "My brother became a rebel, my sister retreated into shyness, I played the stalwart and dutiful son who would hold the family together. If my father was unstable, I would be a rock. If he squandered money on drink, I would pinch every penny. If he wept when drunk—and only when drunk—I would not let myself weep at all" (p. 75).

These poignant personal observations are supported by clinical observations of CoAs that the dysfunctional parents create a dysfunctional family (Black, 1981). The children react in a variety of ways, with anger and resentment or even suppression of feelings. Some children cope by withdrawal while others may try to placate and mediate. Many children may come to blame themselves for the problem.

Wegsheider (1981) proposed four general types in her taxonomy of adult children of alcoholics. The *hero* is the child who rescues the family by stepping in to assume the responsibilities vacated by the alcoholic. Wegsheider suggested that the hero learns to stay out of trouble by keeping negative feelings inside and by expressing many positive feelings. Above all, this child tries to keep from others the family secret of the alcoholic parent's drinking. This child is successful in life as a means of avoiding the strife of an alcoholic home. However, the price for these achievements is high as the hero feels inadequacy and guilt over the inability to rescue the family. The *mascot* is the child who tries to mediate disputes and relieve tension in the family. Like the hero, the mascot expresses positive feelings and evokes laughter from others by being cute and showing off. But the defense of immaturity adopted by the mascot against family alcoholism limits growth and fosters feelings of inadequacy. The *scapegoat* is the child who acts out and eventually becomes delinquent. Wegsheider suggests that this role may occur because an older child has already assumed the hero role, so that by default the scapegoat is unable to get attention from parents. Since the family does not seem to care, the scapegoat responds with the same apparent indifference about the family and acts in a manner opposite to that of the hero by bringing disgrace to the family. The *lost child* also feels like an outsider and copes by detaching from the turmoil of the alcoholic home into a world of fantasy. This child is often a loner, unable to form friendships because no human warmth was experienced from the family. Wegsheider believes that none of these different reactions are healthy in the long run and are only adaptations to a dysfunctional family situation that will eventually entail serious psychological cost to the well-being of the child.

Comparisons of Children of Alcoholics and Nonalcoholics

Miller and Jang (1977) conducted a 20-year longitudinal study with a sample from the lower socioeconomic level and found more alcohol abuse, school dropouts, and delinquency among those with an alcoholic parent. However, numerous other differences between the alcoholic and nonalcoholic families also existed, with more divorce and welfare assistance for the alcoholic families. These factors may also have played a role in causing the problems of the children. Alternatively, these differences may have been *effects* of parental alcoholism.

West and Prinz (1987) examined a number of areas to determine the extent to which parental alcoholism affects the children. Weak support was found in six of seven reviewed studies for the idea that children of alcoholics are more hyperactive. How to interpret these findings is unclear. Since hyperactivity involves attention deficit and is related to aggression, hyperactivity rather than alcoholism could be the basis for the relationship between parental alcoholism and problems in the children. Moreover, a number of questions are raised. For example, how much of any observed differences could be due to prenatal factors? Is the impairment the same for children living with an alcoholic mother, with an alcoholic father, or with two alcoholic parents? When one parent is alcoholic, what difference does it make whether the nonalcoholic parent also lives in the home?

Children from alcoholic families have been found to use health care more, to have more mental health problems (Moos & Billings, 1982), and to engage in substance abuse more often (Beardslee, Son, & Vaillant, 1986), but other variables such as socioeconomic status cannot be ruled out as alternative causes of these problems. Although Clair and Genest (1987) found a poorer family home environment among children of alcoholics than among controls, they also noted that many of these children functioned as well as or better than children from the nonalcoholic control families.

Roosa, Sandler, Beals, and Short (1988) found that adolescent children of alcoholics have lower self-esteem, more depression, and heavier drinking in comparison to controls from nonalcoholic families, but the evidence is based mostly on self-report and ignores other causes such as physical abuse and other family psychopathologies. Sampling may also be biased since only those children of alcoholics seeking counseling are included and they may have other problems not directly derived from the parents' alcoholism.

Why Do Some but Not Other CoAs Become Alcoholic?

For those CoAs who do become alcoholic, what is the underlying mechanism? Roosa et al. (1988) suggested that the lower self-esteem of some CoAs derives from the greater number of life stresses experienced in the home, which in turn leads to depression and other symptoms. Eventually, this process might increase the risk of alcohol abuse as a means of coping with the low self-esteem. However, for those children in alcoholic homes who do not experience as many threats to their self-esteem, parental alcoholism may have a weaker impact.

The family environment may sometimes affect the likelihood of CoAs becoming alcoholic as adults in complex ways. McCord (1988), in a follow-up of the classic longitudinal study of adolescent boys started in the 1940s, examined factors that affected the drinking of sons of alcoholics. If the mother held the alcoholic father in high esteem, the sons were more likely to show alcoholic tendencies. In nonalcoholic families where sons became alcoholics, a better predictor was the extent to which the sons were undercontrolled during adolescence. Thus, different pathways to alcoholism may exist in different families.

Invulnerables

More variability exists among children of alcoholics than the formulations of self-help mutual aid organizations such as Adult Children of Alcoholics would suggest. A large percentage of these children seem to function ably, and it would be worthwhile to examine the factors that enable them to do so well while others do not. All alcoholic parents are not equal in the severity of their alcoholism, and the alcoholism does not lead to divorce or splitting up of the family in all cases. The age of the child when the parent develops alcoholism, the child's relationship in general with parents, the size of the family, and other forms of parental psychopathology are added factors that might prove important in determining how detrimental the alcoholism of a parent is to the mental health of the children.

An illustrative example of invulnerables can be found in research by Werner (1986), who over 18 years conducted a prospective study of a multiracial group of children of alcoholics in Kauai, one of the Hawaiian Islands. Although alcoholism of parents did adversely impact some children, Werner found evidence of resiliency in a majority of the children. Those who coped well had an achievement orientation, responsible attitudes, and positive self-concept, as well as a more stable early home environment. However, the sample was small and came from a population that is highly dissimilar to that of the general population, so caution is needed in making generalizations.

The fact that some children of alcoholic parents do not develop drinking problems is viewed as one exception to the belief that parental modeling is a major influence on children. Another exception is represented by children from nonalcoholic parents who nonetheless develop alcohol problems.

Such discrepancies force us to search for other factors that may interact with parental influences on children. As suggested by Figure 9-2, other major life events may either add to or offset the impact of parental alcohol abuse. Thus, a child with one or both alcoholic parents may be beset by events outside the home that also jeopardize self-esteem. Strong negative stresses such as poor academic achievement, economic adversity, and such, that may lower self-esteem can also affect a child from a nonalcoholic home and possibly lead to drinking later as a means of coping, despite the lack of parental models for such coping behavior. In contrast, the child might be fortunate enough to encounter some sources of rewarding experiences at school or in the community that may offset an alcoholic home situation, and thus the child may be less likely to develop low self-esteem.

Another set of factors involves other persons such as other relatives, especially older siblings, and friends, who may either add to or offset the negative impact of the alcoholic parent on the child's developing self-esteem. Thus, a child of alcoholic parents may still develop a sense of self-worth through associations with nonalcoholic friends and other relatives, whereas a child of nonalcoholics could end up associating with peers who encourage abusive drinking.

The drinking levels of parents should be viewed as only one of the possible determinants of the eventual drinking levels of the children, a factor that may be offset by counterforces. Unfortunately, however, the forces are probably not independent for most families in that alcoholic parents may also have older children who abuse alcohol, and excessive drinking in the home may create a variety of

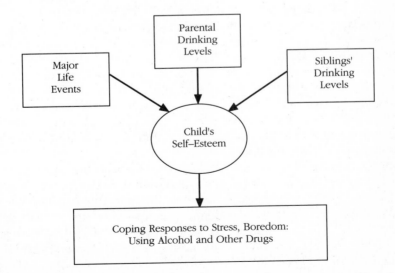

Figure 9-2 A model of other influences on a child's drinking in addition to parental drinking.

negative consequences ranging from family arguments and conflicts to job loss to problems with health to trouble with finances and the law.

A Critique of CoA Studies

Heller, Sher, and Benson (1982) pointed out the risk of overgeneralizations being made based on children of alcoholics who were receiving counseling. Those offspring of alcoholics who do not have adjustment problems are overlooked. Similarly, Blane (1988) lamented the lack of controlled research to evaluate the validity of these typologies and called for research involving comparisons between alcoholic and nonalcoholic families. Such comparisons are not easy because as Searles and Windle (1990) noted, the definition of an alcoholic parent is often vague and varies widely across different studies. In studies where nonalcoholic controls are included, only small differences in psychological functioning and well-being have been found between children of alcoholics and nonalcoholics.

For example, Tweed and Ryff (1991) compared 114 adults who were children of alcoholics with 125 adults of nonalcoholics. Although the children of alcoholics showed higher anxiety and depression scores than the children of nonalcohlics (possibly due to their awareness of the risks of growing up in an alcoholic home), no differences were found in the overall functioning of the two groups. One reason why Tweed and Ryff's results do not agree with many earlier studies is that they used community rather than clinical samples. Thus, it is possible that the home environment may be more harmful for children coming from families where the alcoholic parent needs treatment than for those coming from homes where the alcoholic parent does not go into treatment.

Moreover, research evaluating various types of interventions is sorely needed. It is important to determine whether different types of programs are needed, depending on the age of the child. In fact, it has been suggested by Burk and Sher (1988) that psychological interventions might even have harmful effects for some children of alcoholics, especially if the labeling of such individuals promotes self-fulfilling prophecies. Studies (Burk & Sher, 1990) have demonstrated that adolescents hold more negative stereotypes of "children of alcoholics" than they hold of "typical teenagers." In a second study, Burk and Sher showed mental health professionals a brief videotape of an adolescent with a sound track describing the home background. They gave more negative evaluations when the adolescent was labeled as a child of an alcoholic than of a nonalcoholic, regardless of whether the description of the adolescent was positive or negative.

Most naturalistic and clinical studies of adolescent and adult children of alcoholics are retrospective, relying on inferences and self-reports about earlier events (Sher, 1991). The implication is that the present characteristics differentiating adult children of alcoholics versus nonalcoholics can be attributed to this factor alone. Actually, objective and thorough comparisons of early life events experienced by children of alcoholics and those of nonalcoholics are rarely available and are difficult to obtain.

Many observational studies first identify alcoholic parents, usually in treatment, and then compare their children with those of nonalcoholic parents. One problem with the use of a sample of alcoholic parents in treatment is that as a group they may not be comparable in their alcoholism with *nontreated* alcoholics, who could be either more or less impaired. Similarly, the children of treated alcoholics may not be equivalent to those of nontreated alcoholics.

Other studies focus first on the identification of problem children and then examine drinking levels of the parents in comparison with that of parents of nonproblem children. This method and the one described in the preceding paragraph may not produce the same results since it is unlikely that all of the parents with drinking problems identified with the second method would be receiving treatment for alcohol problems, whereas with the first method all of them are. If one assumes that treatment benefits the alcoholic and the family, the children identified with the first method may show fewer problems than those selected under the second approach.

Another major problem with these methods, which both involve *cross-sectional* designs comparing different groups at one point in time, is the difficulty of establishing causal inferences. If a correlation exists between the drinking levels of the parents and children, it could be that the parents' alcoholism is producing the problems in their children, or vice versa, or that both processes are involved. The use of *longitudinal* designs, in which measures are taken of the same individuals at different points in time, would permit such inferences, but these methods are expensive and obviously require a longer time frame. Hence, it is hardly surprising that they are rarely used.

It might also be important to differentiate among alcoholic families where one versus both parents are alcoholic. If both parents are alcoholic, it might appear that it would be worse for the children than if only one were. On the other hand, if one parent is alcoholic and the other is not, there might be more conflicts between the two parents. When only one parent is alcoholic, comparisons of the effect of the sex of the alcoholic might prove important. Furthermore, the effect of the alcoholic parent could very well differ for sons and daughters. Whether the alcoholic parent is the same or the opposite sex may have different implications for different children. Unfortunately, little research has examined these aspects of the alcoholic parent-child relationship.

Alcoholic Family Interactions

Observation of the interactions of members of alcoholic families may provide important insights about the process of family disruption from the alcoholic's drinking. Studies correlating parent and child behaviors do not examine the actual dynamics of family interaction.

Due to the fallibility and unreliability of self-report about these interactions, some researchers bring families into the clinic or the laboratory and observe their interactions directly. This type of research is expensive and time-consuming but offers the advantage that the observations are made directly by the researchers. One shortcoming is that the clinic may involve a biased sample of families and that the laboratory or the clinic may yield artificial or atypical family interactions.

However, direct observation of families in their own homes is obviously difficult to achieve due to the amount of time required and the intrusiveness of the observers, which may distort the typical behaviors. Any families that might allow such observation may be quite different from those that would not participate in such research. It is also possible that expectations and biases of the observers might distort their observations. Nonetheless, research involving direct observation of families such as that by Steinglass, Bennett, Wolin, and Reiss (1987) and by Wolin, Bennett, Noonan, and Teitelbaum (1980) offers the advantage of studying family interaction patterns as they actually occur.

Wet versus Dry Interactions

One strategy has been to compare interactions when the alcoholic has been and has not been drinking (Jacob & Seilhamer, 1989). An early example of this approach is a study by Herson, Miller, and Eisler (1973) that examined verbal interchanges and found that the nonalcoholic spouse paid more attention to the alcoholic when intoxicated than when sober, suggesting that the nonalcoholic might be unwittingly reinforcing the drinking. Similarly, Jacob, Ritchey, Cvitkovic, and Blane (1981) compared discussions by alcoholic and control families and found more negative affect by both the alcoholic and nonalcoholic spouse when the alcoholic had been drinking. Husbands in nonalcoholic families were more influential than their wives in problem-solving communications while the opposite was found for alcoholic couples.

Steinglass, working from a series of studies of direct observations of family interactions, suggested that the use of alcohol may act as a stabilizer for the alcoholic family that has developed a homeostasis centered around the drinking of the alcoholic. In one study described by Steinglass (1981), an alcoholic who was being treated in a residential facility volunteered to be a research participant. He was reluctant to give up alcohol and had stated his intention to resume drinking following discharge. He agreed to be observed in an interview session while sober along with his wife and two teenage children and a psychiatrist. The session was marked by confrontations between him and the other family members, who attacked his behavior.

A week later, another interview occurred with one important difference. Prior to the interview, the alcoholic was allowed to drink six ounces of alcohol and told he could drink during the interview. Family members were informed about this procedure and agreed to participate as part of a research project. The alcoholic was less depressed than in the first interview and was assertive with his family. Similarly, the family members were more animated, whereas in the first interview they had sat rigidly in their seats avoiding eye contact with each other. Verbal interactions increased dramatically. Surprisingly, there was also considerable laughter among all members even when references were made to some of the alcoholic's past alcoholic behaviors.

In part, some of the differences could be due to the fact that the family members felt more at ease in the second or alcohol interview, but Steinglass felt that most of the difference could not be due to that factor. He maintained that there is a cycle between behaviors associated with sobriety and those related to intoxication. The family acts as if it believes that certain behaviors are caused by the alcohol, behaviors that do not occur when the alcoholic is sober. These intoxicated state behaviors are highly predictable over drinking occasions for any given family, although they may not be the same for all alcoholic families.

More important than their regularity is that these behaviors serve the function of *short-term* problem-solving strategies for dealing with family problems—for example, feelings, role conflicts, sexual difficulties, or problems external to the family such as neighbors or work issues. Thus, alcohol might act to make one person assertive in dealing with a problem when assertion is desirable or it might lead another person to withdraw from conflict where such retreat helps promote interpersonal harmony. Such habits or strategies inspired by alcohol become stronger over time. Steinglass allowed that the family is not typically aware of this function served by the alcohol. In fact, the family usually views the alcoholism as the problem rather than as their strategy for coping with everyday problems. Although alcohol may work for short-term solutions, it does not work in the long run and also creates the additional problems of alcoholism and its disintegrative effects on the family.

Steinglass and his colleagues observed 31 families from a wide variety of backgrounds on nine separate four-hour home visits spread over six months. Two observers made systematic records about minute-by-minute verbal and nonverbal interaction patterns. These findings may not be specific to alcoholic families, as no observations of families with other psychopathologies were made. Steinglass (1981) found that different patterns of family interaction occurred when the alcoholic had been drinking from when he or she had not. Moreover, although observed families showed dramatically different behavior patterns when the alcoholic member was "wet" versus "dry," the nature of the difference between the "wet" and the "dry" state interactions was not universal but varied across families.

Episodic versus Steady Drinkers

According to Jacob and Leonard (1988), a distinction between *episodic* (binge) and *steady* (regular pattern) drinkers is needed to improve our understanding of the effects of alcoholism on family interactions. They suggested that drinking comes to serve as a strategy for facilitating problem solving among steady drinkers. In contrast, it functions as a means of avoidance that allows episodic drinkers to express hostility when they are faced with conflictual situations. Their observations of sober interactions showed no differences between these two types of alcoholics. However, after drinking had occurred, more problem solving as well as greater negativity was found for couples with a steady drinker but not for those with an episodic drinker. Overall, these studies suggest that alcoholic family interactions when the alcoholic is drinking differ from those observed during sobriety, but the exact pattern may differ for acoholics with different drinking styles.

Family Rituals

Wolin, Bennett, and Jacobs (1988) reported on the role of alcoholism in family rituals. A ritual is a valued routine that a family engages in around some important activity such as dinner, holidays, and vacations. Rituals are stable behavior patterns repeated regularly with each family member having a consistent role to play. Alcoholism may either disrupt (subsume) or not interfere with these rituals. The research examined the extent to which alcohol abuse subsumed family rituals and took over as the central theme of family life. Wolin et al. hypothesized that transmission of alcoholism across generations is more likely to the extent that the alcoholism disrupts such rituals. They found that if the adult offspring of alcoholics are "deliberate" in rejecting alcohol as a central theme of their family life by forming new, nonalcoholic rituals or by marrying a nonalcoholic, they may avoid some of the adverse effects of growing up in an alcoholic home.

Codependency

The focus of the discussion thus far has been the family environment of an alcoholic home as it might affect the children and nonalcoholic members of the family. It is assumed that the family wants the drinking to stop or be reduced and that the family will try to influence the alcoholic in this direction. However, it is also important to examine the possibility that the reactions of the nonalcoholics may paradoxically contribute to or enable the *continued* or *increased* drinking of the alcoholic.

Attention was directed by Ackerman (1958) and Bowen (1974), among others, toward examination of the family interactions among members of alcoholic families. They proposed a systems theory view of the family that focuses on the influence of each member's behavior on other members. These models hold that, in general, families achieve a balance or homeostasis from which they resist change.

In the case of alcoholic families, the alcoholism becomes the focal point to which adjustments are made, and family interactions can become highly dysfunctional in maintaining this equilibrium, according to Steinglass, Weiner, and Mendelsohn (1971). The concept of *codependency* (Wegsheider, 1981) refers to this reciprocal relationship between the alcoholic and one or more nonalcoholics who may unwittingly aid and abet the alcoholic's excessive drinking as well as irresponsible nondrinking behaviors created by the drinking.

Jackson (1954) observed that there is a developmental process within the family as it adjusts to the drinking problem. There is an understandable tendency for the nonalcoholic family members to deny there is a problem for a long time. The alcoholic becomes the focus of the family and adjustments are made to the alcoholic. Thus, the codependents sacrifice their own independence and autonomy by reacting to the alcoholic's behavior in a futile attempt to regain control. By covering up and excusing the alcoholic's shortcomings, the coalcoholic becomes an accomplice.

Due to the stigma of alcoholism, it is not surprising that many nonalcoholic family members would be inclined to hide the fact of alcoholism from the outside world by making up excuses for the alcoholic when necessary. In addition, they may blame themselves or be blamed by others for their role in facilitating and maintaining the drinking of the alcoholic member.

Codependent behavior, however, has not been generally seen in a negative light until recently. Indeed, in the past a heroic vision of the martyred family members of the alcoholic has been a more prevalent portrayal. However, the view that the nonalcoholic members of a family could be contributing to maintaining the alcoholic's drinking has gained acceptance, and codependency is increasingly regarded as a problem in its own right (Cermak, 1986; Woititz, 1983). By continually adjusting to and reacting to the alcoholic's drinking, but without success, the codependent suffers a loss of self-esteem and experiences a mixture of depression, helplessness, and self-blame. As the alcoholic becomes less able to perform his or her family roles, the codependent may try to "rescue" the family and assume the responsibility by trying to perform the alcoholic's tasks in addition to his or her own. Adult Children of Alcoholics, the self-help organization mentioned earlier, has actively called attention to the dysfunctional aspects of codependency among coalcoholics and encouraged them to toss aside the need to control the lives of others.

This line of thinking is not limited to alcoholism but also has been applied to a spectrum of addictions, including dependency on other people as well as on substances. The pop psychology and self-help books of the past decade called for codependents to recognize and overcome their codependent relationships. It is too soon to determine the extent to which this development is a fad or part of a tendency to blame one's current problems on past relationships with other people. Clinical observation and anecdotal evidence have attested to the nature of codependency, but relatively few rigorous scientific investigations have been conducted to validate these impressions, identify correlates, and determine consequences.

Wives of Alcoholics

Alcoholism has often been referred to as a family disease in the sense that all members are adversely affected. It was not until the 1950s that the family dynamics of alcoholism began to receive attention. Ablon (1984) noted that the early focus came from clinical studies of alcoholic men and their nonalcohlic wives. At that time, it was suspected that the wife may have often been a factor causing the alcoholic to drink because she was frequently observed to have psychological problems. Thus, the alcoholism of the husband was blamed on the wife, as if her psychological disturbances somehow "drove him to drink" or she had some characteristics that facilitated her husband's drinking.

A different type of explanation for the correlation between the husband's drinking and the wife's psychological problems assumes that certain types of people are attracted to each other. *Assortative mating,* as it is termed, may be involved, leading to matches between antisocial and rebellious men who are prone to drink excessively and women who have psychological problems, as Stewart and deBlois (1981) found.

Yet another explanation is that the psychological problems of the wife of an alcoholic might result from living with an alcoholic husband, as was recognized by

Jackson (1962). She proposed a seven-stage model to describe how the wives of alcoholics might cope, starting with denial and ending with recovery as the final stage, although it was not assumed that all families would successfully reach recovery. Her formulation was based on observation of Al-Anon meetings. Al-Anon membership is comprised of the family members of alcoholics who feel the need to find support from persons facing the same problems. In many respects the philosophy parallels that of AA in that members must recognize that they are powerless over the alcoholic and that they need to accept a higher power. The goal is not to cure the alcoholic, whom they are told to "release with love," but to find a means of dealing with their own feelings and to stop trying to save the alcoholic, who has usually led the wives and other family members to engage in irrational and dysfunctional models of behavior as they cope with the alcoholic family member.

Lemert (1960) furthered this approach by examining the model in relation to five widely different sources of wives of alcoholics: state hospital commitments, welfare clients, divorce court cases, police probation cases, and Al-Anon participants. He was unable to find a common pattern of adjustment, which is not surprising given the diversity of the samples. These findings were interpreted as reflecting the need to take the cultural context into consideration, since the meanings and reactions to the same types of events differ with socioeconomic background.

Conclusions

In addition to any genetic influence from alcoholic parents, children living in alcoholic family environments may be affected in several ways by the alcoholism of one or both parents. Direct effects during early development may occur as the parents' drinking behavior serves as a model for the children to imitate later. However, it appears that for some children, there is a drop-off in the tendency to imitate the cross-sex parent's drinking if it is heavy. In addition to influencing children's drinking patterns as they become older, parental alcoholism may result in neglect or abuse of children, the effects of which may eventually lead to excessive drinking.

Indirect paths of influence are also possible, as when alcoholism leads to domestic strife or divorce, which could create a home environment that might impair children's development of self-esteem, regardless of whether they eventually develop drinking problems. The belief that children of alcoholics have interpersonal difficulty, perhaps due to a need to be in control, has been fostered in the writings of therapists who have worked with children from alcoholic homes. It seems plausible that children of alcoholics might be afraid or embarrassed to bring friends home and might be unable to relate well with others. Living in an alcoholic home has been thought to make CoAs insecure "people pleasers" who want to be liked and accepted; on the other hand, there is evidence that some CoAs may be "invulnerable" to these effects of the stressful alcoholic home. However, controlled research in this area is rare. West and Prinz (1987) concluded that when control groups of children of nonalcoholic parents who are in therapy are compared with the children of alcoholics, differences are not as strong as commonly assumed.

Direct observations of interactions of families in clinical treatment reveal that the family members behave differently when the alcoholic is dry versus sober, but the nature of the differences may vary with the family or whether the alcoholic is a binge or steady drinker. Alcohol may function as a short-term coping response for problems that eventually fails in the long run. Alcoholic drinking may disrupt established family rituals or established patterns of interaction. These studies are based on small samples who agree to be observed; thus, the findings may not be generalizable to other families, but they offer important opportunities to develop hypotheses about the impact of alcoholism on family interactions.

Nonalcoholic family members may inadvertently contribute to or "enable" the alcoholic's drinking. By adjusting their behavior to accommodate that of the alcoholic, they may hope to avoid conflict and arguments. Codependency may develop so that the nonalcoholic family members try to please, or not annoy, the alcoholic. Thus, the blame is shifted, partially at least, from the alcoholic to the nonalcoholic family members, who are encouraged to seek help to learn how to break their codependent addictive relationship with the alcoholic.

References

Ackerman, N. W. (1958). *The psychodynamics of family life.* New York: Basic Books.

Ablon, J. (1984). Family research and alcoholism. In M. Galanter (Ed.), *Recent developments in alcoholism* (pp. 383–395). New York: Plenum Press.

Bandura, A. (1977). *Social learning theory.* Englewood Cliffs, NJ: Prentice-Hall.

Beardslee, W. R., Son, L., & Vaillant, G. E. (1986). Exposure to parental alcoholism during childhood and outcome in adulthood: A prospective longitudinal study. *British Journal of Psychiatry, 149,* 584–591.

Black, C. (1981). *It will never happen to me.* Denver: MAC.

Blane, H. T. (1988). Prevention issues with children of alcoholics. *British Journal of Addictions, 83,* 793–798.

Bowen, M. (1974). Alcoholism as viewed through family systems theory and family psychotherapy. *Annals of the New York Academy of Sciences, 128,* 115–122.

Burk, J. P., & Sher, K. J. (1988). The "forgotten children" revisited: Neglected areas of COA research. *Clinical Psychology Review, 8,* 285–302.

Burk, J. P., & Sher, K. J. (1990). Labeling the child of an alcoholic: Negative stereotyping by mental health professionals and peers. *Journal of Studies on Alcohol, 51,* 156–163.

Cermak, T. L. (1986). *Diagnosing and treating co-dependency: A guide for professionals.* Minneapolis: Johnson Institute.

Clair, D., & Genest, M. (1987). Variables associated with the adjustment of offspring of alcoholic fathers. *Journal of Studies on Alcohol, 48,* 345–358.

Harburg, E., Davis, D. R., & Caplan, R. (1982). Parent and offspring alcohol use: 1. Imitative and aversive transmission. *Journal of Studies on Alcohol, 43,* 497–516.

Harburg, E., DiFranceisco, W., Webster, D., Gleiberman, L., & Schork, A. (1990). Familial transmission of alcohol use: II. Imitation of and aversion to parent drinking (1960) by adult offspring (1977)—Tecumseh, Michigan. *Journal of Studies on Alcohol, 51,* 245–256.

Heller, K., Sher, K. J., & Benson, C. S. (1982). Problems associated with risk overprediction in studies of offspring of alcoholics: Implications for prevention. *Clinical Psychology Review, 2,* 183–200.

Herson, M., Miller, P. M., & Eisler, R. M. (1973). Interactions between alcoholics and their wives: A descriptive analysis of verbal and nonverbal behavior. *Quarterly Journal of Studies on Alcohol, 34,* 516–520.

Jackson, J. K. (1954). The adjustment of the family to the crisis of alcoholism. *Quarterly Journal of Studies on Alcohol, 15,* 562–586.

Jackson, J. K. (1962). Alcoholism and the family. In J. Pittman & C. R. Snyder (Eds.), *Society, culture, and drinking patterns* (pp. 472–492). New York: Wiley.

Jacob, T., & Leonard, K. (1988). Alcoholic-spouse interaction as function of alcoholism subtype and alcohol consumption. *Journal of Abnormal Psychology, 97,* 231–237.

Jacob, T., Ritchey, D., Cvitkovic, J., & Blane, H. (1981). Communication styles of alcoholic and nonalcoholic families when drinking and not drinking. *Journal of Studies on Alcohol, 43,* 466–482.

Jacob, T., & Seilhamer, R. A. (1989). Alcoholism and family interaction. In M. Galanter (Ed.), *Recent developments in alcoholism* (pp. 129–145). New York: Plenum Press.

Lemert, E. M. (1960). The occurrence and sequence of events in the adjustment of families to alcoholism. *Quarterly Journal of Studies on Alcohol, 21,* 679–697.

McCord, J. (1988). Identifying developmental paradigms leading to alcoholism. *Journal of Studies on Alcohol, 49,* 357–362.

Miller, D., & Jang, M. (1977). Children of alcoholics: A 20-year longitudinal study. *Social Work Research and Abstracts, 13,* 23–29.

Moos, R. H., & Billings, A. G. (1982). Children of alcoholics during the recovery process: Alcoholic and matched control families. *Addictive Behaviors, 7,* 155–163.

Orford, J., & Velleman, R. (1991). The environmental intergenerational transmission of alcohol problems: A comparison of two hypotheses. *British Journal of Medical Psychology, 64,* 189–200.

Reich, W., Earls, F., & Powell, J. (1988). A comparison of the home and social environments of children of alcoholic parents. *British Journal of Addiction, 83,* 831–839.

Roosa, M. W., Sandler, I. N., Beals, J., & Short J. (1988). Risk status of adolescent children of problem drinking parents. *American Journal of Community Psychology, 16,* 225–239.

Sanders, S. R. (1989, November). Under the influence: Paying the price of my father's booze. *Harper's,* pp. 68–75.

Searles, J. S., & Windle, M. (1990). Introduction and overview: Salient issues in the children of alcoholics literature. In M. Windle & J. S. Searles (Eds.), *Children of alcoholics: Critical perspectives* (pp. 1–8). New York: Guilford Press.

Sher, K. J. (1991). *Children of alcoholics: A critical approach to theory and research.* Chicago: University of Chicago Press.

Steinglass, P. (1981). The alcoholic family at home. Patterns of interaction in dry, wet, and transitional stages of alcoholism. *Archives of General Psychiatry, 38,* 578–584.

Steinglass, P., Bennett, L. A., Wolin, S. J., & Reiss, D. (1987). *The alcoholic family.* New York: Basic Books.

Steinglass, P., Weiner, S., & Mendelsohn, J. H. (1971). A systems approach to alcoholism: A model and its clinical application. *Archives of General Psychiatry, 24,* 401–408.

Stewart, M. A., & deBlois, C. S. (1981). Wife abuse among families attending a child psychiatry clinic. *Journal of the American Academy of Child Psychiatry, 20,* 845–862.

Tweed, S. H., & Ryff, C. D. (1991). Adult children of alcoholics: Profiles of wellness. *Journal of Studies on Alcohol, 52,* 133–141.

Webster, D. W., Harburg, E., Gleiberman, L., Schork, A., & DiFranceisco, W. (1989). Familial transmission of alcohol use: I. Parent and adult offspring alcohol use over 17 years— Tecumseh, Michigan. *Journal of Studies on Alcohol, 50,* 557–566.

Wegsheider, S. (1981). *Another chance: Hope and health for the alcoholic family.* Palo Alto, CA: Science and Behavior Books.

Werner, E. E. (1986). Resilient offspring of alcoholics: A longitudinal study from birth to age 18. *Journal of Studies on Alcohol, 47,* 34–40.

West, M. O., & Prinz, R. J. (1987). Parental alcoholism and childhood psychopathology. *Psychological Bulletin, 102,* 204–218.

Woititz, J. (1983). *Adult children of alcoholics.* Deerfield Beach, FL: Health Communications.

Wolin, S. J., Bennett, L. A., & Jacobs, J. (1988). Assessing family rituals in alcoholic families. *Rituals in families and family therapy.* New York: Norton.

Wolin, S. J., Bennett, L. A., Noonan, D. L., & Teitelbaum, M. A. (1980). Disrupted family rituals: A factor in the intergenerational transmission of alcoholism. *Journal of Studies on Alcohol, 41,* 199–214.

Personality and
Alcoholism

Is there an "alcoholic personality," some pattern of traits typically found among alcoholics? As noted in Chapter 7, alcoholics represent a heterogeneous group and the factors leading to alcohol abuse may differ widely for different individuals. Nonetheless, the strong tendency to adopt stereotypes about members of a group fosters the idea that some set of personality traits may differentiate alcoholics from nonalcoholics. If such differences could be identified, it might be possible to plan better methods of intervention, treatment, and prevention. Consequently, researchers have devoted much effort to the search for personality factors. The concern of this chapter is whether such personality differences exist and how they are related to alcoholism.

Personality Differences: Cause or Effect?

If an "alcoholic personality" were determined, there would be the question of whether these characteristics preceded alcoholism and possibly contributed to its development, or whether these traits were primarily the consequences of being alcoholic. Further complicating the issue is the likelihood that some personality correlates might be *both* causes and effects of alcoholism rather than one or the other.

As suggested by the overview presented in Figure 10-1, some general personality variables such as temperament differences discussed in Chapter 8 may exist *before* the development of drinking. Such inherited differences may predispose some persons to either drink or drink with adverse physical and social consequences. Although these personality differences might be viewed as potential factors leading to alcohol problems, they may not be sufficient alone to cause alcoholism. Numerous subsequent factors such as parental modeling, peer influences, coping skills, and types and amounts of stress encountered may moderate the influence of temperament. In other words, the interaction between inherited general personality traits and specific life experiences determines an individual's likelihood of alcohol abuse and its problems.

In addition, Figure 10-1 suggests that the reactions of others to the drinking behavior also affect the "alcoholic personality." For example, as an individual's drinking becomes heavier and more frequent, with its attendant loss of social status, financial, social, and psychological deterioration, embarrassment, ostracism, and social rejection may occur. Consequently, additional personality differences that distinguish alcoholics from nonalcoholics may begin to emerge. Such personality differences could be viewed as the consequences, rather than the antecedents, of alcoholism.

Theoretical Approaches to the "Alcoholic Personality"

We will examine two contrasting approaches to theorizing about personality differences underlying alcoholism. The psychoanalytic approach emphasizes often

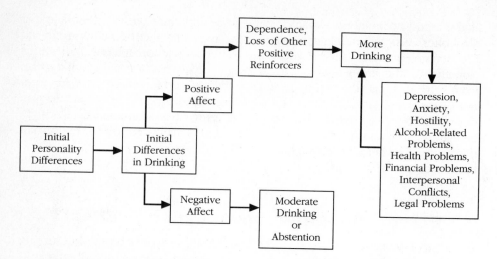

Figure 10-1 A model showing how initial personality differences may pre-dispose individuals to differences in initial levels of drinking. Those who have positive affect from drinking may develop dependence and drink more until they start having negative consequences such as negative emotions and alcohol-related problems, which lead to even more drinking. Those who have initial negative affect from drinking may keep their drinking levels at moderate levels or even abstain from alcohol completely.

unconscious motives for excessive use of alcohol while the biological vulnerability approach focuses on differences in physiological reactivity to alcohol that may produce variations in the effects of alcohol.

Psychodynamic Theory

Early psychological theories of alcoholism were of psychoanalytic origin. Cox (1987) suggested that this emphasis was perhaps due to the fact that many alcoholics sought therapy from psychoanalytically-oriented psychiatrists. As with psychoanalytic views about many other forms of psychopathology, psychoanalytic explanations of alcoholism focused on unresolved early childhood conflicts of an unconscious nature. They suggested that perhaps due to fixation at the oral stage of psychosexual development as proposed by Freud (1905), a need for alcohol developed as a means of achieving immediate oral gratification and pleasure. Alcoholics were depicted as being immature, dependent, and unable to delay gratification. Use of alcohol was seen as a means to feel good immediately or to achieve a feeling of power.

A classic study conducted by McCord and McCord (1960) using juvenile delinquents tested the dependency view of alcoholism. A comparison of those who later became alcoholics with those who did not led to the conclusion that it is *conflict* about dependency, not dependency per se, that underlies alcoholism for male alcoholics. Society demands that males be independent and fulfill the masculine role of being aggressive. Such a role encourages males to drink alcohol. However, if potential male alcoholics are fixated at the oral stage and have unresolved dependency needs that are not in keeping with the male role, a dilemma exists. Drinking heavily on occasion enables them to fulfill one aspect of masculine role behavior; at the same time, this drinking behavior causes them to be dependent on others without censure because this dependency is attributed to the influence of alcohol. Consequently, they try to fulfill both needs of independence and dependence simultaneously through heavy drinking.

McClelland, Davis, Kalin, and Wanner (1972) developed a power theory of alcoholism. They proposed a general model of the motivation for drinking rather than one limited to the drinking of alcoholics. The independence and aggressiveness often seen in male drinkers was interpreted as a direct manifestation of a drive for power rather than a reaction against dependency. Drinking enables one to engage in fantasies and feelings of power. Thus, it is lack of power that leads to drinking. A series of studies measuring fantasies and imagery in projective test situations before and after the consumption of alcohol was a major line of evidence used to support the theory. As larger amounts of alcohol were consumed, the fantasies involved greater degrees of personal power.

Wilsnack (1974) extended the approach of McClelland et al. to the analysis of drinking among women. In contrast to the model proposed for men, she proposed that drinking served to reduce rather than elicit fantasies of power among women. Wilsnack depicted women as having more fantasies about engaging in traditionally feminine activities after drinking. Alcoholic women were assumed to be more likely to have anxieties about their womanliness. According to Wilsnack (1973), they might turn to alcohol to help them cope with these feelings of inadequacy.

One problem with psychoanalytic theories about the personality processes involved in drinking is that the formulations are difficult to test since they involve assumptions about early experiences about which there is usually no objective evidence. Also, as with the dependency and power formulations, the predictions are sometimes diametrically opposed.

Biological Vulnerability Models

In contrast to the intrapsychic processes postulated by psychoanalytic theories, other theories focus on the biological factors that contribute to alcohol use. Tarter, Alterman, and Edwards (1985) suggested that there may be important inherited biological characteristics that may influence the likelihood of alcohol problems, at least for males. They noted that temperamental factors such as activity level (high), attention span (short), emotional expressivity (labile), ability to calm following stress (slow), and sociability (high) are associated with greater likelihood of alcohol problems for males.

Based on such findings, Tarter, Moss, and Laird (1990) proposed a neuropsychological model of differences in *biological vulnerability* to account for higher risk for alcoholism, at least for early-onset heavily drinking males with antisocial tendencies. This model is similar to the view of Cloninger (1987), discussed in Chapter 8, in which male-limited alcoholics (Type 2) were found to be high on genetically determined traits such as novelty seeking, a factor that promotes impulsivity and excitability. Recall that Cloninger also believed that Type 2 alcoholics were likely to engage in these behaviors due to genetically based low tendencies to avoid harmful situations. Finally, possibly due to inherited tendencies to have a low dependence on rewards, they had distant social relations.

Pihl, Peterson, and Finn (1990) also proposed a comprehensive model of the interrelationship among inherited tendencies toward alcoholism, localized brain functions, childhood behavior problems, and alcohol abuse. The model, depicted in Figure 10–2, assumes that sons of male alcoholics have inherited tendencies that limit cognitive functioning and attention during information-processing tasks. Such cognitive deficits initiate consequences that place these children at higher risk for future alcohol abuse. First, these deficits harm learning and academic performance by disrupting attention and preventing the learning of conceptual rules, abstract categories, and rules of social behavior. A second factor that may predispose these children toward conduct disorders, and eventual alcohol abuse, is poor socialization about rules of social behavior since these children often come from families with low socioeconomic status, hostility, and alcohol and drug abuse (Hinshaw, 1987). As a consequence, these children may be hyperactive and act out with conduct disorders at school. In turn, the use of alcohol may be reinforcing for these children by reducing anxiety in times of stress. However, extended use of alcohol may further disrupt cognitive functions, leading to additional problem behavior, creating a vicious cycle of more drinking and impairment.

Pihl et al. developed the model using a wide array of evidence from biochemical studies; investigations of the function of specific brain areas such as the prefrontal cortex, which is involved with organization and categorization; neuropsychological studies of information processing; and childhood behavior problems such as hyperactivity. In their tests of the validity of the model, Pihl and his colleagues focused on young sons of male alcoholics because this group seems to have more risk of alcohol abuse than do daughters of male alcoholics or offspring of either sex when the mother is the alcoholic parent. They have conducted laboratory experiments with tasks involving threats such as a signal followed in a few seconds by electric shock. Sons of alcoholics and a control group of sons of nonalcoholics receive either a dose of alcohol or a placebo before being compared in their reactions to the task. Psychophysiological measures such as heart rate, evoked potentials, and EEG waves are recorded.

Finn and Pihl (1987, 1988) found that subjective reports of alcohol effects did not differ appreciably for sons of male alcoholics and nonalcoholics, but the psychophysical indicators suggest that sons of male alcoholics are hyperactive when sober but after consuming alcohol achieve a calmer state. In contrast, sons of nonalcoholics are less active when sober but more reactive upon intoxication. There are also biochemical differences, with sons of male alcoholics showing lower monoamine oxidase and deficits in serotonin (5-HT).

Pihl and his associates acknowledged that their model may apply better to *early* stages of drinking than to later stages of drinking. As drinking increases over an extended period, other factors such as social criticism and alienation may occur and further increase drinking behavior. They recognized that their model is largely untested and many of their neuropsychological assumptions are conjectural and

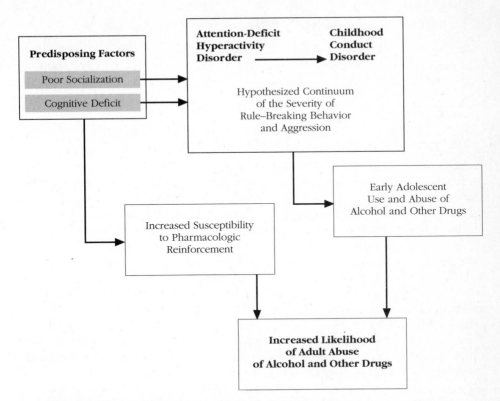

Figure 10-2 Possible paths to adult alcoholism. Note that it is the poorly socialized and aggressive child, with the diagnosis of childhood conduct disorder, who is at greatest risk for developing alcoholism later in life.

Source: from "Attention-deficit hyperactivity disorder, childhood conduct disorder, and alcoholism," by R. O. Pihl and J. B. Peterson in *Alcohol Health and Research Work, 1991, 15(1),* 25–31.

open to a variety of alternative interpretations. Nonetheless, their model does tie together many differences observed between sons of male alcoholics and controls in behavioral, neurophysiological, and biochemical reactions to alcohol challenge tests. Their model provides a useful framework for developing and testing hypotheses about the bases for differences in response to alcohol.

In summary, neuropsychological differences in personality are not the only determinants of drinking levels but rather should be viewed only as predisposing factors. The development of alcoholism still depends on the later occurrence of other determinants such as psychosocial factors. Thus, the fact that these predispositions are found among men but not among women may reflect the different social norms and attitudes about the role of drinking for men and women. Since women are not encouraged to drink at a level comparable to that for men, any genetically determined temperamental characteristics that might increase the risk of excessive drinking among women is countered by these sex-role expectations in our society.

Chapter Ten

Research Evidence

Studies of the relationship of personality to alcoholism differ in terms of whether the personality assessments are made before (prospective) or after (retrospective) the onset of alcoholism. As we will see, each type of research design has strengths and weaknesses and both are valuable methods for studying this problem.

Retrospective Studies

Many research studies designed to test theories about the personality of alcoholics have examined alcoholics *after* they have become alcoholic. Inferences are often based mainly on their retrospective recall of earlier aspects of their lives. Interviews with adult alcoholics may often reveal a chaotic childhood, but distortions of memory, selective recall, or deliberate misrepresentation renders this type of evidence of uncertain validity. Therefore, questions of whether an "unhappy" childhood, unresolved dependency needs, parental conflicts, or such contributed to alcoholism may not be tested accurately with this procedure.

The retrospective study of the personality of alcoholics has centered on clients in clinical settings, where there is an overrepresentation of less educated individuals from lower socioeconomic levels of the population. Most of these studies have included no comparisons of males and females. Indeed, most studies have been of males only, and when both sexes have been studied, the results are typically combined across sex, obscuring any differences that might exist.

Prospective Studies

In contrast to retrospective studies, prospective studies use evidence about the prealcoholic years obtained prior to the appearance of alcoholism. For example, McCord and McCord (1960) were able to use archival records to determine personality measures of alcoholic males that had been collected many years earlier during adolescence, before their development of alcoholism. They identified more antisocial factors among those male adolescents who later became alcoholics than among those who did not. However, it must be recognized that this study used juvenile delinquents and the results may not be generalizable to a general population.

Some studies of samples of adolescents more representative of the general population (Jessor & Jessor, 1975; Kandel, 1978; Zucker, 1979) have administered personality tests to students *before* they initiated alcohol drinking. A few years later when it was possible to identify two subgroups, those who had and had not developed drinking problems, they could compare them for predrinking personality differences. Generally, adolescents who developed alcohol drinking problems were found to be more independent, aggressive, nonconformist, antisocial, impulsive, and hyperactive than those who did not, even prior to having problems with drinking. Importantly, adolescents prior to having drinking problems later, did not show negative personality attributes such as anxiety or depression. Thus, even though alcoholics may show these negative mood states, they do not appear have been predisposing factors toward drinking for most adolescents.

Evidence from *archival* studies (Cox, Lun, & Loper, 1983; Jones, 1968, 1971; Loper, Kammier, & Hoffman, 1973) has provided a similar profile. Archival studies involve opportunistic situations where a set of current observations is made on a sample for whom there fortuitously exist other data collected earlier for a reason totally unrelated to the purpose of the later study. Present subgroups, varying in their level of alcohol use, can then be compared to test hypotheses about possible causal realtionships between differences on earlier measures and the present drinking status of the subgroups. The availability of such archival data gives the researcher the chance to go back in time in a sense and "collect" data about variables that had not been planned for the present purpose. Thus, with archival data, groups of alcoholics and nonalcoholics presently under study can be compared on their characteristics before any of them ever began drinking.

Jones (1968, 1971) examined scores of adolescents on the California Personality Inventory, which was included as part of a developmental study when no drinking problems were yet evident. A comparison of those male adolescents with subsequent alcohol problems and a control group without such problems showed that male problem drinkers had been more rebellious and extraverted *prior* to the beginning of drinking.

Jones (1971), however, found different antecedents of problem drinking among females. Middle-aged females were interviewed and classified into five levels of drinking ranging from abstainer to problem drinker. An examination was made of their personality traits that had been measured during adolescence prior to the use of alcohol. Those who were presently heavy drinkers differed from those without problem drinking but in different ways from those observed among males. The heavily drinking women had been more pessimistic, withdrawn, and less independent as adolescents than their lighter-drinking counterparts.

In the study by Loper et al. (1973), it was possible to examine Minnesota Multiphasic Personality Inventory (MMPI) scores of men in their early 30s with and without alcohol problems who had completed these tests 13 years earlier as a requirement for freshman students at the University of Minnesota. Based on MMPI test scores, they concluded that those students who later became alcoholic were likely to have been more impulsive, nonconforming, and gregarious, but not any more maladjusted, than those who did not become alcoholic.

Mediator versus Moderator Variables

Explanations about alcohol use involving personality factors generally assume some characteristics are underlying or *mediating* mechanisms bridging past experiences of individuals and their current drinking behaviors. The so-called "alcoholic personality" is some set of characteristics that presumably leads some people to have more problems with alcohol than others do. Thus, as noted in Chapter 8, biological vulnerability or temperamental differences (Cloninger, 1987; Tarter et al., 1985) have been proposed as a type of personality factor that is predictive of problems with alcohol. Individuals who are undercontrolled, impulsive, and aggressive are assumed to encounter poorer school achievement and more problem behaviors that might place them at greater risk for alcohol abuse (Cox, Lun, & Loper, 1983). Personality factors for this example act as mediating variables, factors that contribute to the differences in drinking behavior.

A different view of personality as a determinant of behavior involves *moderator variables* (Baron & Kenny, 1986). When the strength of the effect of one factor on drinking differs, depending on the level of some other factor, that factor is said to be a moderator variable. Thus, if family history is related to alcoholism for some, but not for others, on some personality variable, this dimension is a moderator of the effect of family history.

Rogosch, Chassin, and Sher (1990) hypothesized that differences in the personality trait of self-awareness, the extent to which individuals are conscious of their own behavior and feelings, might function as a moderator variable of the influence of family history of alcoholism on drinking. They reasoned that individuals who were high in self-awareness might react to alcohol cautiously if they came from a family with a history of alcohol problems and hence minimize the chances that they would develop alcohol problems themselves. In contrast, individuals with a similar family history of alcoholism, but low in self-awareness, would not react defensively to their family history and thereby be more likely to develop drinking problems.

Rogosch et al. studied 979 students at a predominantly white high school and identified their family history for alcohol problems; self-awareness levels; scores on personality dimensions, such as impulsivity and risk taking, known to be risk factors for alcohol problems; and quantity-frequency drinking scores. The presumed personality risk characteristics for drinking problems were not related to actual drinking levels; hence, these personality variables do not appear to be *mediating* variables.

However, dividing the positive family history subjects into two groups on the basis of level of self-awareness, they found that high self-awareness students had less drinking and fewer problems with alcohol than low self-awareness individuals did. Hence, there was a *moderating* effect of self-awareness levels on drinking levels and adverse social consequences. Individuals with high self-awareness may restrict their drinking because they want to avoid the anticipated adverse consequences of drinking.

When the effects of the presumed personality risk factors were examined, another moderating variable was found. Students with high personality risk factor levels were more likely to drink more and have more problems related to alcohol if they also had a family history of alcohol abuse. In contrast, drinking patterns and consequences of those who were low in the presumed personality traits were not related to family drinking history. Thus, the combination of high levels of personality factors presumed to lead to drinking problems and a family history of alcohol problems magnify the chances of alcohol problems.

"Alcoholic Personality" as the Effect of Alcoholism

A contrasting view of personality differences between alcoholics and nonalcoholics proposed by Vaillant and Milofsky (1982) held that the majority of such differences are the *results* rather than the causes of their differences in drinking behavior. They gathered evidence from 55-year-old white males who had been part of a classic study by Glueck and Glueck (1950) of juvenile delinquents. The original control group of 456 inner-city nondelinquent students was also contacted. Blind ratings were made of their alcohol use, personality, and sociopathy. They examined the relationships between adult alcoholism levels and extensive data collected 33 years earlier about their infant health problems, childhood emotional well-being, social and academic competence, family drinking levels, and various demographic factors.

Judgments about adult alcohol use and interviews were possible for 367 men. Some had died before the age of 40 and were not included in the analysis, leaving 260 social drinkers and 71 alcoholics. Alcoholism was defined by two methods, the DSM-III classification and the problem drinking criteria of Cahalan (1970). In addition, they developed a problem drinking scale that combined the two indexes.

The results showed no differences between these two groups with regard to most of the boyhood factors such as emotional well-being or family demographics. However, the alcoholics were more likely as adults to have more unemployment, lower education and health, and lower social class status. They concluded then that because boyhood competence had been comparable for the two groups, it could not have been the major factor responsible for the differences observed later in life, differences concluded to be the *effects* of alcoholism.

In addition, heredity, as indexed by alcoholism among parents, ancestors, and the individual's cultural background, predicted adult alcoholism better than childhood psychological and sociopathological variables did. When ethnicity and heredity were statistically controlled and equated, the childhood factors did not predict adult alcohol problems, although they did predict adult mental health. Furthermore, factors such as delinquency of parents, childhood environmental weaknesses, and school problems predicted adult sociopathy but not alcoholism levels. Overall, the pattern supports the role of heredity rather than environment as influencing alcoholism.

Zucker and Gomberg (1986), however, challenged Valliant and Milofsky's interpretation of the findings, especially since the data about early childhood experiences had not actually been collected during those years but later, when the boys were already 14 years old. In other words, this information about early childhood was based on *retrospective* recall and could have been inaccurate or distorted. Zucker and Gomberg regarded the early environment as more critical than heredity as a factor in subsequent alcoholism. In support of their view, they noted that previous family studies have generally shown correlations between adult alcoholism and early environmental factors such as (1) childhood antisocial personality, (2) poor childhood achievement, (3) parental divorce, and (4) parental alcoholism.

Atheoretical Approaches to the "Alcoholic Personality"

A different approach to the study of the personality of alcoholics has been descriptive rather than aimed at testing predictions derived from theories. In these studies, alcoholics complete standard personality tests that are not selected on the basis of any particular theory about the nature of alcoholism. Personality characteristics that distinguish alcoholics in treatment from nonalcoholic controls may be identified. These characteristics must be interpreted cautiously since they could either be antecedents or consequences, or even both, of being alcoholic.

It is also possible that some observed traits may not be specific to alcoholics but may also exist among samples with other forms of psychopathology. Alcoholics may suffer from other psychological disorders such as depression or anxiety, aside from their problems with drinking, and these personality variables may reflect those problems rather than drinking per se, as will be discussed in more detail later.

Another problem is that, unfortunately, many studies of the personality of alcoholics have drawn misleading conclusions because of the lack of a control group of nonalcoholics. Indeed, it is difficult to determine what constitutes an adequate control group. Even studies of institutionalized alcoholics that include a comparison with some other nonalcoholic but institutionalized groups may be suspect because they may be primarily identifying some of the correlates of being institutionalized. Finally, most of these studies are dealing with alcoholics receiving some form of treatment, mostly males from lower socioeconomic levels, and these subjects may differ from alcoholics who are not yet in treatment or with different backgrounds.

The more complete research designs have used three groups: alcoholics, another psychiatric sample without alcoholism, and a noninstitutionalized control group of "normals." Without the inclusion of the institutionalized nonalcoholics, there is the possibility that any impairments found in the alcoholics in comparison to the normals may have been due to the effects of being institutionalized rather than to alcoholism per se.

Several alcoholism scales derived from the Minnesota Multiphasic Personality Inventory (MMPI) have been developed to assess alcoholics. Hampton (1953) developed the *Al* scale, while Button (1956) proposed the *Am* scale, and Hoyt and Sedlacek (1958) developed the *Ah* scale. All of these researchers found that scores on their scales distinguished between alcoholics and nonalcoholic controls.

However, MacAndrew and Geertsma (1964) had poor discriminability when they compared alcoholics and nonalcoholic psychiatric controls on these same three MMPI-based scales. Since they also found little difference between alcoholics and the psychiatric control group where general adjustment level was presumably more comparable, the results may have reflected the lower general adjustment level of alcoholics rather than the effects of alcoholism per se.

The MacAndrew scale (MacAndrew, 1965) is a widely used measure consisting of 49 of the 566 items on the MMPI that differentiated male alcoholic outpatients from male nonalcoholic psychiatric outpatients. It should be noted, however, that the average age was around 42 for the alcoholics but only about 35 for the psychiatric controls, so that some differences might be due to this factor. A serious problem with the scale is that it misclassified about 15 percent of nonalcoholics as alcoholics and another 15 percent of alcoholics as nonalcoholics. Uecker (1970), using inpatient populations, found that the psychiatric controls actually scored higher than the alcoholic patients in MacAndrew's study. This finding implies that the scale makes many false positive identifications of alcoholics.

Gottesman and Prescott (1989) pointed out that the MacAndrew scale is even less useful for identifying alcoholics among women, adolescents, and minority groups. Furthermore, no evidence was obtained about the alcohol and drug use of the psychiatric controls nor was there any information about the psychological adjustment of the alcoholics. It is highly unlikely that there would be no overlap between the two groups—that is, we would expect that some psychiatric patients abuse alcohol and some alcoholics have psychological disturbances. Lack of such information limits the generalizability of the scale to other populations.

The MMPI, as well as other standardized self-report inventories, has shown negative affect and low self-esteem in alcoholics entering treatment. However, as treatment progresses, these characteristics are reduced, implying that they may have been reactions to alcohol problems rather than causes. If they had been "causes" of alcoholism, they should have been less likely to change through treatment for alcoholism.

Graham and Strenger (1988) reviewed previous MMPI studies of alcoholics. Although alcoholics have been found to score high on certain scales such as scale 4 (psychopathic deviate), they concluded that there was no evidence of a single MMPI profile that could characterize an "alcoholic personality." They felt more attention should be directed toward differences on the MMPI among subgroups.

Personality Differences in Motivational Factors

Cox and Klinger (1988) proposed a motivational model based on affective consequences of drinking as a basis for understanding how personality differences might be related to different amounts of alcohol consumption.

The amount of alcohol, the drinking context, and the personality of the drinker may affect the response to drinking. Thus, as Sher and Levenson (1982) noted, male students who are outgoing, extraverted, and antisocial seem to derive more positive affect from their drinking episodes than others when they *first* begin drinking. Interestingly, these traits are similar to those identified in eventual alcoholics prior to the onset of their drinking problems.

The irony is that alcohol comes to be associated increasingly with negative affect for drinkers as they become alcoholics. When alcohol is consumed at this stage, negative feelings follow. In addition, drinkers are apt to evoke negative responses from others. And when alcohol is absent, alcoholics also experience discomfort.

In summary, prealcoholics may be the kind of persons who drink to achieve positive affect rather than mainly to escape negative affect. Those who eventually develop serious drinking problems may be those who find alcohol more reinforcing in terms of producing greater positive affective reactions, at least when they first begin drinking. However, as tolerance for alcohol develops, these potential alcoholics must consume greater amounts of alcohol to achieve the level of positive affect previously experienced. At this point negative affect begins to assume a greater role in motivating drinking. Due to the adverse consequences of frequent and heavy drinking such as loss of self-esteem, negative reactions from others, and physical and social debilitation, the alcoholic is apt to feel chronic depression and other negative emotions. When alcohol is not available, the physical withdrawal symptoms experienced may create added anxiety and tension. Unfortunately, the solution adopted by the alcoholic to deal with these overpowering negative affects is to drink more alcohol, hoping to escape the harsh reality. Thus, a reversal in the nature of the affective states governing drinking occurs as the social drinker is transformed into the alcoholic.

Psychopathology and Alcoholism

Although alcoholism itself can be viewed as a form of psychopathology, it can also be related to *other* forms of psychopathology such as antisocial personality, depression, anxiety, and affective disorders. Thus, Helzer and Pryzbeck (1988) found evidence of comorbidity of alcoholism and psychiatric disorders. About half of the 13 percent of the general population that had experienced alcohol abuse or dependence during their lives also had received an additional psychiatric diagnosis. Women with alcohol problems were more likely than women in the general population to have diagnoses of depression (19 versus 7 percent), but there was not much difference in depression between men with alcohol problems and men in the general population (5 versus 3 percent). In contrast, alcohol-dependent men were much more likely to have antisocial personality disorder diagnoses than in the general population (15 versus 4 percent). An even larger difference was found for women (10 versus 0.8 percent).

When correlations between alcoholism and psychopathology are observed, at least two different interpretations can be made. First, alcoholism might be viewed as one of the "causes" of other forms of psychopathology—that is, the alcoholism is *primary*. Due to the excessive drinking, the alcoholic may become antisocial or depressed, for example. Second, there is the view that alcoholics are premorbidly pathological or addiction-prone, a condition that may lead them to develop alcoholism (*secondary*) eventually. According to this argument, the alcoholic has some form of psychopathology that precedes, and perhaps contributes toward, alcoholism. This is a view favored by psychiatry. For example, the association between alcoholism and antisocial personality might involve this pattern. Past studies have found antisocial personality in approximately 15 to 50 percent of alcoholics. Antisocial personality is a DSM-III category, formerly referred to as sociopathy, and is found mostly in males. It involves dysphoric moods, sensation seeking, a history of childhood misconduct, and underachievement.

Is psychopathology a risk factor for alcoholism? There is no simple answer to this question since the *relative* frequency of a characteristic or behavior influences its accuracy as a predictor. To the extent that the predictor in question is common in a given group, it should be less of a risk factor for the pathology. But for more extreme (that is, less common) behaviors—for example, use of illicit drugs—there will be a stronger link between psychopathology and that predictor. Thus, heavy drinking may not be viewed as a sign of psychopathology in France because drinking is commonplace there. In contrast, it would be a predictor of psychopathology among Jews, for whom heavy drinking is less prevalent.

Conclusions

Alcoholics have been observed to differ from nonalcoholics in many aspects of their personalities, suggesting the possibility that there is an "alcoholic personality." One important question, assuming such a profile can be identified, is whether these differences existed prior to the onset of alcoholism and hence were part of the causal process leading to the outcome of alcoholism or whether the differences primarily reflect the consequences of chronic alcohol abuse and its damaging effects on the physical, psychological, and social well-being of alcoholics.

Longitudinal studies that obtain measures of personality prior to, as well as subsequent to, the development of alcoholism have suggested that some *general* personality characteristics exist that distinguish the future alcoholic from the nonalcoholic. These factors may not directly affect drinking but probably operate indirectly over a period of time. Thus, the rebellious and adventuresome youth is more likely to experiment with drinking than the law-abiding and moral youth, who may conform to social norms by not drinking or delaying until a later age. While many youth who experiment with alcohol may curb or control excesses and never develop dependence on alcohol or engage in other forms of socially disapproved behaviors, others may find that alcohol is a means of coping with life's adversities or providing excitement and stimulation. However, instead of solving problems, their drinking may create additional and larger problems such as academic difficulties, financial woes, interpersonal conflicts, or problems with the law. These unpleasant consequences may further accelerate a dependence on alcohol for dealing with stressors, until eventually alcohol abuse and alcoholism is the consequence.

This model appears to account for the origins of differences in behaviors leading to alcohol dependence. In a sense, these personality differences could be considered a "prealcoholic personality." In addition, a complementary model suggests that the alcoholic's stigmatized existence and associated psychological dysfunction may be responsible for creating *additional* personality differences between alcoholics and nonalcoholics. These differences reflect the effects of alcoholism on personality.

References

Baron, R. M., & Kenny, D. D. (1986). The moderator-mediator distinction in social psychological research: Conceptual, strategic and statistical considerations. *Journal of Personality and Social Psychology, 51,* 1173–1182.

Button, A. D. (1956). A study of alcoholics with the Minnesota Multiphasic Personality Inventory. *Quarterly Journal of Studies on Alcohol, 17,* 263–281.

Cahalan, D. (1970). *Problem drinkers: A national survey.* San Francisco: Jossey-Bass.

Cloninger, C. R. (1987). Neurogenetic adaptive mechanisms in alcoholism. *Science, 236,* 410–416.

Cox, W. M. (1987). Personality theory and research. In H. T. Blane & K. E. Leonard (Eds.), *Psychological theories of drinking and alcoholism* (pp. 55–89). New York: Guilford Press.

Cox, W. M., & Klinger, E. (1988). A motivational model of alcohol use. *Journal of Abnormal Psychology, 97,* 168–180.

Cox, W. M., Lun, K., & Loper, R. G. (1983). Identifying prealcoholic personality characteristics. In W. M. Cox (Ed.), *Identifying prealcoholic personality characteristics* (pp. 5–17). San Francisco: Jossey-Bass.

Finn, P. R., & Pihl, R. O. (1987). Men at high risk for alcoholism: The effect of alcohol on cardiovascular reactivity and sensitivity to alcohol. *Journal of Abnormal Psychology, 96,* 230–236.

Finn, P. R., & Pihl, P. O. (1988). Risk for alcoholism: A comparison between two different groups of sons of alcoholics on cardiovascular reactivity and sensitivity to alcohol. *Alcoholism: Experimental and Clinical Research, 12,* 742–747.

Freud, S. (1905). Three essays on the theory of sexuality. In J. Strachey (Ed. and Trans.), *The complete psychological works.* New York: Norton.

Glueck, S., & Glueck, E. (1950). *Unraveling juvenile delinquency.* New York: The Commonwealth Fund.

Gottesman, I. I., & Prescott, C. A. (1989). Abuses of the MacAndrew MMPI alcoholism scale: A critical review. *Clinical Psychology Review, 9,* 223–242.

Graham, J. R., & Strenger, V. E. (1988). MMPI characteristics of alcoholics: A review. *Journal of Consulting and Clinical Psychology, 56,* 197–205.

Hampton, P. J. (1953). The development of a personality questionnaire for alcoholics. *Genetic Psychology Monographs, 48,* 55–115.

Helzer, J. E., & Pryzbeck, T. R. (1988). The co-occurrence of alcoholism with other psychiatric disorders in the general population and its impact on treatment. *Journal of Studies on Alcohol, 49,* 219–224.

Hinshaw, S. P. (1987). On the distinction between attention deficits/hyperactivity and conduct problems/aggression in child psychopathology. *Psychological Bulletin, 101,* 443–463.

Hoyt, D. P., & Sedlacek, G. M. (1958). Differentiating alcoholics from normals and abnormals with the MMPI. *Journal of Clinical Psychology, 14,* 69–74.

Jessor, R., & Jessor, S. L. (1975). Adolescent development and the onset of drinking: A longitudinal study. *Journal of Studies on Alcohol, 36,* 27–51.

Jones, M. C. (1968). Personality antecedents and correlates of drinking patterns in adult males. *Journal of Consulting and Clinical Psychology, 32,* 2–12.

Jones, M. C. (1971). Personality antecedents and correlates of drinking patterns in women. *Journal of Consulting and Clinical Psychology, 36,* 61–69.

Kandel, D. (1978). *Longitudinal research on drug use: Empirical findings and methodological issues.* Washington, DC: Hemisphere.

Loper, R. G., Kammier, M. L., & Hoffman, H. (1973). MMPI characteristics of college freshman males who later become alcoholics. *Journal of Abnormal Psychology, 82,* 159–162.

MacAndrew, C. (1965). The differentiation of male alcoholic outpatients from nonalcoholic psychiatric outpatients by means of the MMPI. *Quarterly Journal of Studies on Alcohol, 26,* 238–246.

MacAndrew, C., & Geertsma, R. H. (1964). An analysis of responses of alcoholics to scale 4 of the MMPI. *Quarterly Journal of Studies on Alcohol, 24,* 23–38.

McClelland, D. C., Davis, W. N., Kalin, R., & Wanner, E. (1972). *The drinking man.* New York: Free Press.

McCord, W., & McCord, J. (1960). *Origins of alcoholism*. Stanford, CA: Stanford University Press.

Pihl, R. O., Peterson, J., & Finn, P. (1990). Inherited predisposition to alcoholism: Characteristics of sons of male alcoholics. *Journal of Abnormal Psychology, 99,* 291–301.

Rogosch, F., Chassin, L., & Sher, K. J. (1990). Personality variables as mediators and moderators of family history for alcoholism: Conceptual and methodological issues. *Journal of Studies on Alcohol, 51,* 310–318.

Sher, K. J., & Levenson, R. W. (1982). Risk for alcoholism and individual differences in the stress-response-dampening effect of alcohol. *Journal of Abnormal Psychology, 91,* 350–368.

Tarter, R. E., Alterman, A. I., & Edwards, K. L. (1985). Vulnerability to alcoholism in men: A behavior-genetic perspective. *Journal of Studies on Alcohol, 46,* 329–356.

Tarter, R. E., Moss, H., & Laird, S. B. (1990). Biological markers for vulnerability to alcoholism. In R. L. Collins, K. E. Leonard, & J. S. Searles (Eds.), *Alcohol and the family: Research and clinical perspectives* (pp. 79–106). New York: Guilford Press.

Uecker, A. E. (1970). Differentiating male alcoholics from other psychiatric patients. *Quarterly Journal of Studies on Alcohol, 31,* 379–383.

Vaillant, G. E., & Milofsky, E. S. (1982). The etiology of alcoholism: A prospective viewpoint. *American Psychologist, 37,* 494–503.

Wilsnack, S. (1973). Sex role identity in female alcoholism. *Journal of Abnormal Psychology, 82,* 253–261.

Wilsnack, S. C. (1974). The effects of social drinking on women's fantasy. *Journal of Personality, 42,* 43–61.

Zucker, R. A. (1979). Developmental aspects of drinking through the young adult years. In H. T. Blane & M. E. Chafetz (Eds.), *Youth, alcohol, and social policy* (pp. 91–146). New York: Plenum Press.

Zucker, R. A., & Gomberg, E. L. (1986). Etiology of alcoholism reconsidered: The case for a biopsychosocial process. *American Psychologist, 41,* 783–793.

ELEVEN

Self-Help and Alcoholism Recovery

Many drinkers fortunately never develop physical or psychological problems from their consumption, but a sizable number of others experience serious impairment as a consequence. As noted in earlier chapters, no one type of alcoholic or single pattern of development exists, but alcoholics are alike in that their drinking produces some form of disruption of their lives. Unfortunately, the alcoholic is often the last to recognize the problem, so that his or her drinking deteriorates from bad to even worse. The alcoholic, adept at denial of a drinking problem, fails to recognize the harmful effects of the drinking on himself or herself as well as on family and friends.

Denzin (1987) provided an interesting look at the mind of the alcoholic, offering an inside perspective of the irrational thought processes that allow the alcoholic to defend his or her drinking. The alcoholic, according to Denzin, could be said to hold a "lay theory" of drinking that centers around denial. Alcoholics believe that alcohol conveys power and control; any challenge to their drinking evokes powerful rationalizations and defenses of their drinking. They often shift the blame from themselves to others such as nondrinking spouses, who allegedly "made" them drink. Instead of viewing alcohol use as the *problem,* the alcoholic reverses things and regards alcohol as the *solution.* Even alcoholics in treatment may nostalgically recall earlier days when their drinking was associated with positive outcomes, a tendency that may sustain the denial. The alcoholic may think that he or she can still regain the power to indulge in "successful drinking," despite the present setbacks associated with drinking.

Sooner or later many individuals who drink alcohol excessively will develop problems that necessitate intervention and treatment. They may experience physical symptoms such as craving and withdrawal and/or suffer alcohol-related health problems. In addition or alternatively, some may manifest antisocial or violent behavior, poor work performance, depression, or hostility. Eventually they will be referred to, or in some cases mandated by legal authorities to submit to, some form of alcoholism treatment and counseling.

As noted in Chapter 7, many different definitions and criteria are used to define an alcoholic or alcohol-dependent person. Regardless of the particular definition used, until the alcoholic is diagnosed as such, the process of treatment and rehabilitation cannot begin. Even then, there is often much resistance.

In some instances a professional counselor, physician, psychiatrist, or other authority makes the diagnosis of alcoholism. For others, a "self-diagnosis" may occur, where the drinker comes to the eventual recognition that, in the words of AA, their "lives had become unmanageable" due to alcohol. However, because denial is usually a stronger characteristic of persons with drinking problems, it is likely that this self-realization that alcohol is the problem will be difficult. In extreme cases, such as when acute intoxication is involved, the alcohol abuser may enter treatment first as a medical emergency requiring detoxification or "drying out" before being treated from a psychological perspective.

An estimate of the number of alcoholics under treatment in the United States can be obtained from the National Drug and Alcoholism Treatment Unit Survey, which was started in 1974 by the National Institute on Drug Abuse (NIDA) and has been jointly conducted since 1979 with the National Institute on Alcoholism and

Alcohol Abuse (NIAAA). All private and public alcohol and drug treatment facilities in the United States are surveyed periodically to determine the number and type of treatment facilities and the extent to which they are utilized. Only the statistics for alcoholics will be examined here. The 1989 report (NIDA/NIAAA, 1990) showed that about 80 percent of the capacity of the 6,493 facilities was currently utilized by 383,000 alcoholic clients. The vast majority, 86 percent, were seen on an outpatient basis in these facilities, of which 64 percent were privately supported. During the 12 months prior to the survey, a total of 1,450,000 patients were in treatment at a cost estimated to be $1.7 billion. About 25 percent of those receiving outpatient and about 22 percent receiving inpatient treatment were female. About 17 percent were over 45 years of age while only about 6 percent were under 18 years of age. Blacks and Hispanics represented 26 percent of the clientele and whites comprised about 71 percent.

A variety of approaches exist for the treatment of alcoholism and alcohol abuse, but they can be grouped in three major categories: Alcoholics Anonymous, psychotherapy, and behavioral programs. It is not uncommon for some combination of approaches to be used. In this chapter the focus is on informal treatment through Alcoholics Anonymous, and the following chapter will examine more formal treatment approaches involving professionally trained therapists.

Alcoholics Anonymous

Interestingly, the most widely known "treatment" for alcoholism did not develop originally as a formal treatment method. Alcoholics Anonymous (AA), a recovery program unique because of its self-help orientation and philosophy that alcoholics can best help other alcoholics to recover, has offered hope to countless alcoholics. The concepts underlying Alcoholics Anonymous are not entirely original, having been used by earlier social reformers (Trice & Staudemeier, 1989). The 19th-century temperance movement in the United States produced one of the forerunners of AA in the mid-1800s: the Washingtonians, a group of alcoholics who took a pledge of abstinence and relied on mutual support and hope as a means of recovery. A later movement of a quasi-religious nature, called the Oxford group, emphasized the importance for alcoholics of recognizing or admitting their powerlessness over alcohol. As with the Washingtonians who preceded and AA which followed, the Oxford group strongly believed in the value of mutual support and help.

The AA Program

AA involves a program based on the Twelve Steps, a set of practices designed to help the alcoholic achieve a lasting recovery. The Twelve Steps (Alcoholics Anonymous World Services, 1985) are as follows:

1. We admitted we were powerless over alcohol—that our lives had become unmanageable.

2. Came to believe that a power greater than ourselves could restore us to sanity.
3. Made a decision to turn our will and our lives over to the care of God as we understood Him.
4. Made a searching and fearless moral inventory of ourselves.
5. Admitted to God, to ourselves and to another human being the exact nature of our wrongs.
6. Were entirely ready to have God remove all these defects of character.
7. Humbly asked Him to remove our shortcomings.
8. Made a list of all persons we had harmed, and became willing to make amends to them all.
9. Made direct amends to such people wherever possible, except when to do so would injure them or others.
10. Continued to take personal inventory and when we were wrong, promptly admitted it.
11. Sought through prayer and meditation to improve our conscious contact with God as we understood Him, praying only for knowledge of His will for us and the power to carry that out.
12. Having had a spiritual awakening as the result of these steps, we tried to carry this message to alcoholics and to practice these principles in all our affairs.*

Source: Reprinted with permission of A.A. World Services, Inc.

Although not based on any formal religion, the Twelve Steps encompass a number of concepts and processes that resemble features of many religious ceremonies and rituals. First and foremost is the recognition that the alcoholic is powerless over alcohol, because the belief of control over drinking ensures defeat by it. The alcoholic must move from arrogance and pride to humility. Unless this first step is achieved the prognosis for improvement is poor, because individuals will feel that others are imposing the treatment on them for a nonexistent problem. In contrast, once they can change their self-perception and admit frailty, progress can begin.

Alcoholics are then encouraged to believe that a higher power (Step 2) can restore them to sanity, and next in Step 3 to decide to turn their lives over to the care of the higher power or God "as we understand Him." These two steps often repesent major hurdles for those who do not believe in the concept of God, even though AA expands the definition of God to allow even nonreligious conceptions. A spiritual awakening and an attitude of surrender to a higher power infuses this step in which the drinker seeks and accepts help.

A number of the Twelve Steps involve highly specific behavioral objectives, starting with the making of a "fearless moral inventory" (Step 4) to increase awareness of one's strengths and weaknesses, followed by a confession not only to

*The Twelve Steps are reprinted with permission of Alcoholics Anonymous World Services, Inc. Permission to reprint this material does not mean that AA has reviewed or approved the contents of this publication, nor that AA agrees with the views expressed herein. AA is a program of recovery from alcoholism *only*—use of the Twelve Steps in connection with programs and activities which are patterned after AA, but which address other problems, does not imply otherwise.

oneself and a higher power but also to another person of wrongs committed against others (Step 5).

Knowledge of one's faults is not enough. Steps 6 and 7 call for the readiness for change with the help of a higher power. They entail submission or humility because the alcoholic must admit to needing the assistance of the higher power.

Step 8 calls for a commitment to make amends wherever possible to persons who the alcoholic has harmed, while Step 9 requires actual fulfillment of these good intentions. These acts of self-examination and reform are not a single action but a set of activities to continue into the future. Hence Step 10 reminds the alcoholic to continue taking personal inventory and admitting errors.

Step 11 invokes a religious tone, reminding the alcoholic of the importance of prayer and meditation to maintain contact with the higher power and to determine what His will is for the alcoholic. This step is spiritual and urges the alcoholic not to pray for what he or she wants but for insight into what the higher power wants. By working the Twelve Steps of the program, the alcoholic achieves humility and atonement and eventually carries forth the message to help other alcoholics, as specified in Step 12.

AA's method contains features that could easily be related to a variety of theoretical approaches. A behaviorist would notice the use of self-monitoring, social learning, and covert sensitization, whereas a psychotherapist might focus on the development of insight or the reliance on realistic goal setting as exemplified in the AA attitude of "one day at a time."

The tenets of the program developed by AA are set forth in a number of publications widely available to members. These guides, such as *Alcoholics Anonymous* (Alcoholics Anonymous World Services, 1976), are not abstract or theoretical but contain specific advice and admonitions, case histories, and spiritual inspiration.

The founders of AA also established "Twelve Traditions" (Alcoholics Anonymous World Services, 1985) or goals for AA to follow to ensure its integrity and viability as an organization. One tradition established that the sole goal of AA is to help those who sincerely desire to stop drinking. Another tradition is that there is no membership fee so that help is available to anyone who needs and wants it. The tradition of being financially self-supported through voluntary contributions helps keep the organization from going astray with commercial or political entanglements that might jeopardize the goal of helping alcoholics achieve sobriety.

Members attend free AA group meetings as often as they wish. These meetings are held in most communities throughout the week in public facilities such as churches, community centers, and hospitals. Some meetings are open to any interested person with or without a personal drinking problem, while other meetings are closed to nonmembers. During the typical meeting one or more recovering alcoholics will make a personal statement about their own life and how it was adversely affected by drinking before they came to AA. They then relate how their lives were changed through "working the program" of AA to achieve sobriety. The speaker typically greets the audience with a self-labeling statement—"Hi, my name is __. I'm an alcoholic"—to which the accepting audience warmly responds, "Hi, __." There is a formal structure beginning with an inspirational reading from an AA publication and ending with a prayer.

Although self-identification as an alcoholic is recognized as a central process for members of AA, Skinner, Glaser, and Annis (1982) found few differences in demographic or personality characteristics in a sample of 225 individuals referred for alcoholism treatment between those drinkers who accept the "alcoholic" label and those who do not. They speculated that those problem drinkers who had suffered more adverse effects from their drinking may find themselves attending AA at a higher rate than similar drinkers who have not yet suffered such consequences, but that the difference between an "alcoholic" and a "nonalcoholic" problem drinker is mainly one of degree rather than kind.

Beckman (1980) proposed an attributional analysis of some of the benefits of AA attendance. She argued that participation in AA enables alcoholics to modify their attributions of responsibility for their drinking. The realization of alcoholics that many drinkers do not suffer the harmful effects of alcohol experienced by alcoholics leads them to blame themselves for their plight. The feeling that "I'm a no-good drunk" adds to their burden and maintains the drinking. By affiliating with AA members instead, alcoholics reinforce each other's belief that the disease of alcoholism, not their own doing, is responsible for their condition. Acceptance of AA ideology allows a shift of attributions about their drinking from internal to external factors, a change that may be helpful in reducing their self-blame and facilitating recovery.

Critics and skeptics have often rejected the religious connotation of many tenets of AA, especially the notion of a surrender to God, even though AA allows considerable latitude in defining God or a power greater than ourselves. By using the term "God, as we came to know Him," AA broadened the concept so that it need not be a religious deity at all. Nevertheless, the view that AA is a type of religious cult with rigid rules and ideas dies hard and is often an obstacle to newcomers. Skeptics also ridicule AA participants for their excessive smoking and coffee drinking, arguing that even if they give up alcohol they are still addicts to other substances or to AA meetings themselves.

Evaluation of AA's Effectiveness

Glaser and Ogbourne (1982) examined research, or the lack of it, on the effectiveness of AA. Due to the anonymous nature of AA participation, a feature designed to facilitate the seeking of help by protecting individuals with this highly stigmatized problem, it is not possible to obtain scientifically rigorous evidence about the benefits of AA (Ogbourne, 1989). Little is known about who attends AA and drops out or continues but does not benefit. Of course, an abundance of testimonials and anecdotal evidence attest to the many positive changes achieved through AA, so it is likely that benefits are real and substantial for large numbers of participants. Nonetheless, without more thorough information it is difficult to understand the underlying basis for improvement. The possibility that AA works only for certain types of alcoholics or for those from some backgrounds but not for others cannot be assessed.

Bradley (1988) studied the findings from evaluations of AA made by its own anonymous survey of participants. These surveys, conducted every three years, are not based on random samples and may involve some biased samples of those who choose to complete them. The 1987 report (Alcoholics Anonymous World Services, 1987) showed 36 percent of members reporting that professional treatment helped lead them to AA. This cooperation between professionals and AA is not surprising, given that about 60 percent of therapists are also members of AA. The AA surveys reported an increased number of members with three or more months of attendance, but this includes many who already have achieved sobriety but may be coming to meetings for "booster shots."

One strategy for evaluating the effectiveness of AA involves comparing alcoholics in a treatment program who have and have not participated in AA. A serious problem, however, is that these two groups may differ in many other respects such as severity of their alcoholism or motivation for improvement, so that interpretations must be cautious.

The fact that many participants do benefit and achieve abstinence might reflect a selective process in which those who are more motivated or ready to accept the goal of abstinence are more likely to attend AA meetings than those who are not. However, none of the demographic variables examined by Emrick (1989) distinguished between those who did or did not benefit from AA participation. This analysis of AA survey responses by Emrick showed that degree of AA involvement— before, during, or after a treatment program—was not related to drinking levels.

Controlled studies (Brandsma, Maultry, & Welsh, 1980; Ditman, Crawford, Forgy, Moskowitz, & MacAndrew, 1967) have assessed the effectiveness of AA. They have found that alcoholics assigned randomly to AA and several other types of formal treatment did not differ in the level of improvement. However, these studies may have underestimated the effects of treatment since they used poorly motivated clients referred to AA by the courts, as evidenced by high dropout rates.

Bradley (1988) maintained that the difficulty in evaluating AA is not just due to anonymity of participants or to methodological problems but also to vague definitions and concepts. These problems contribute to the lack of progress in understanding how AA works.

The scientific approach to evaluating AA attempts to measure processes of disease and recovery with objective methods. However, the approach of AA is holistic and phenomenological, not scientific. Thus, the "outcome" is not achieved at a specific, measurable point in time. Dropouts should not be viewed as "failures" because the definition of *dropout* can be relative, as "someone not ready" at that point for AA, rather than absolute. Researchers may need to come to view AA with the cultural anthropologist's attitudes in order to see the truths that AA holds rather than trying to dissect AA.

An indirect method of assessing the effects of AA membership was used by Smart, Mann, and Anglin (1989), who examined relationships between liver cirrhosis rates and AA membership levels from 1974 to 1983 in Canada and found no significant relationship. They noted that different patterns emerged for two different types of alcohol problems—driving while intoxicated (DWI) and public drunkenness—with increases in AA membership associated with a decline in DWI but an increase in public drunkenness. They speculated that convicted DWI offenders are more likely to be periodic binge drinkers who are more similar to AA members and less likely to develop cirrhosis. In contrast, steady drinkers, more prone to develop cirrhosis, will more typically be skid-row alcoholics who are also less likely to be attracted to AA.

Different Functions of AA

The evaluation of AA must also recognize the distinction among a number of different goals or functions that may be served by AA participation (Bradley, 1988).

AA as a Treatment Adjunct. When AA is used in conjunction with a more formal method, as is often the case, it is not possible to obtain a "clean" test of AA's effect since it is confounded by the client's chosen other treatment.

AA as Primary Intervention. A pure test of AA can be made when the participants are not using any other treatment, but it must be noted that conclusions may be limited or restricted to a population highly motivated to stop drinking. No comparison has been made to dropouts from AA or an untreated group. Retrospective studies by AA on primary participants show one-year abstinence rates of 26 to 50 percent (comparing favorably with other treatments).

AA as Pretreatment. Participation in AA may be helpful if it can focus on the benefits of sobriety such as improved health and family relationships, break down the resistance and denial of the alcoholic, and facilitate acceptance of formal treatment. Mixed results have been obtained about how effective prior experience with AA is in getting alcoholics into formal treatment.

AA as Aftercare. Perhaps the most successful manner in which AA might function is to provide an inexpensive, long-term, and readily available aftercare for formal treatment programs. Many studies have shown that alcoholics who attend AA after treatment have more success staying sober (Bradley, 1988).

AA as Part of a Multimodal Treatment. Studies have shown that those who attend AA get better treatment results. However, variations in baseline drinking levels prior to treatment, outcome measures, and length of follow-up exist between attenders and nonattenders and make treatment evaluation difficult.

Who Goes to AA?

It should not be assumed that everyone referred to AA attends regularly or at all. Brandsma et al. (1980) found that only around 20 percent of those referred to AA actually go. Ogbourne and Glaser (1981) presented a profile of the AA member as typically being male, over 40, white, from the middle upper class, with an authoritarian personality, strong affiliative needs, susceptibility to guilt, external locus of control, field dependence, cognitive simplicity, formalistic thinking, low conceptual level, high autokinesis, religious orientation, existential anxiety, and a tendency to conform.

However, later studies such as one by Emrick (1987) refuted this negative profile by showing there was no relationship between AA involvement and socio-economic status, social competence, social stability, or religion. Gianetti (1981) found AA members to be more internal, hold more positive treatment expectations, and have less existential anxiety than alcoholics not participating in AA. Hurlburt, Gade, and Fuqua (1984) found that treated alcoholics who were AA members were psychologically healthier than those whose treatment did not include AA.

These conflicting views could all be tenable if the nature of AA membership has changed over the years. Although the membership surveys conducted by AA do not assess psychological dimensions of participants, they do indicate a shift in demographic features. Surveys by AA indicate more female members, increasing from 30 to 34 percent from 1984 to 1987, and more members under the age of 30 than in the past. Thus, the male over-40 group represented only about 45 percent of participants in 1987, whereas in previous years the majority was overwhelmingly male. These shifts in the composition of AA membership may be due in part to changing drinking norms and demographic changes. In addition, the reputation of AA as a successful program has led to many treatment facilities and social agencies referring alcohol-dependent individuals to AA who in the past would not have chosen to attend.

Treating the Family

It was noted in Chapter 9 that family members are seriously damaged by the drinking of the alcoholic member of the family and are often in need of counseling and psychological treatment. A program for treatment of the family members *separately* from the treatment of the alcoholic has been developed that borrows heavily from AA concepts. This program is called Al-Anon.

The Al-Anon Program

Al-Anon is a recovery program related to AA in approach that was developed for the significant others of alcoholics. Started in 1935 by Lois Wilson, the wife of the cofounder of AA, its philosophy closely mirrors that of AA and its Twelve Steps. Al-Anon (Al-Anon, 1984, 1986) encourages its members to admit their powerlessness over their alcoholic and the unmanageability of their lives as the first step toward recovery. Without this first step of detachment, members might continue to try to find ways to stop the alcoholic from drinking and/or feel guilty that they had failed.

Al-Anon holds that nonalcoholic family members need to be concerned about their own recovery from strong tendencies to be overcontrolling and assuming too much responsibility for the lives of others. Before the term *codependency* was coined, Al-Anon was dealing with the underlying phenomenon in which the nonalcoholic unintentionally enables or contributes to the maintenance of the alcoholic's drinking. Many nonalcoholic wives try to prevent their alcoholic husband from drinking, using a variety of means such as hiding the bottles or emptying them down the sink. These attempts to control the drinking of the alcoholic are rarely effective in changing the drinking, so that eventually the codependent feels despair, resentment, and a sense of hopelessness. At the same time, codependents deny that alcoholism exists in their family. They are embarrassed by the stigma associated with alcoholism. They also "cover up" and clean up after the alcoholic despite the physical and psychological damage created by the drinking. Because the alcoholic is spared some of the adverse effects of the drinking, the alcoholic is unlikely to assume responsibility for the drinking.

Al-Anon recognizes that nonalcoholic wives have problems, separate from those of the alcoholics, and that in order to solve those problems, it is first necessary for them to recognize that they are not personally responsible or to blame for their alcoholic's drinking or for getting the alcoholic to stop drinking. As in AA, the alcoholic's drinking is viewed as a disease, not a willful act. The task of stopping the drinking, according to Al-Anon, can only be undertaken by the alcoholic, while the tasks of the nonalcoholic or codependent are to learn to "release with love" and to stop overcontrolling their alcoholic. After the first step of detachment, the codependent is urged to turn the matter over to a higher power. As with AA, members of Al-Anon gain support from each other to facilitate recovery through a 12-step program of self-improvement and personal growth based on similar concepts developed by AA.

Evaluation of Al-Anon's Effectiveness

Cermak (1989) noted that a 1984 survey conducted across the United States by Al-Anon showed that the majority of participants were white (96 percent) and female (88 percent). They were mostly middle-aged, with about half of them having had some college education. There may have been some bias in the types of persons who completed the survey, so this demographic portrait of membership may only be a rough approximation.

As is true of AA, little objective evaluation of the effectiveness of Al-Anon participation has been done. Gorman and Rooney (1979) examined self-reports of wives who participated in Al-Anon. These wives claimed to have reduced their enabling behaviors—making excuses, covering up, checking up on the spouse's drinking—as well as emotional outbursts and nagging about the spouse's drinking. However, even assuming these self-reports are valid, it is not possible to conclude that such changes reduced the husband's drinking behavior.

Conclusions

Alcoholics Anonymous is the best known and most widely publicized approach to recovery from alcoholism and alcohol abuse. Although it describes itself as a program of spiritual recovery more than as a "treatment" for alcoholism, nonetheless AA's philosophy and methods have exerted a strong influence on formal treatment programs. Through self-evaluation and mutual support, AA members engage in a spiritual program to abstain from alcohol as they rebuild their lives. Countless numbers of individuals have attended AA group meetings all over the world. The Twelve Steps, beginning with an admission of powerlessness over alcohol, comprise a structured program of self-examination and improvement that will help overcome alcoholism.

Due to its informal and subjective nature, the program of AA is difficult to evaluate thoroughly and objectively with regard to its effectiveness. Nevertheless, professional or formal treatments often involve AA participation as an adjunct to a treatment package consisting of education and counseling as well as more specialized components that differ across programs. The failure to include control groups makes it impossible to determine the relative effectiveness of different parts of a treatment package. AA's reputation as an effective means of recovery from alcoholism, although difficult to rigorously evaluate, has led to the development of similar organizations for other types of psychological problems.

Al-Anon is a self-help organization for family and friends of alcoholics. It is modeled after AA in concept, and offers a similar 12-step program for codependents to help them realize that they are powerless over the drinking of their alcoholic. It is believed that this first step of detachment is needed before codependents can begin to recover from their own addiction to trying to control their alcoholic's drinking. Alcoholism is viewed as a family disease, not limited to the alcoholic member, because the nonalcoholic family members are also dysfunctional. The codependents must be led to focus primarily on their own recovery, not that of the alcoholic.

References

Al-Anon. (1984). *Al-Anon family groups*. New York: Al-Anon Family Group Headquarters, Inc.

Al-Anon. (1986). *First steps: Al-Anon . . . 35 years of beginnings*. New York: Al-Anon Family Group Headquarters, Inc.

Alcoholics Anonymous World Services. (1976). *Alcoholics Anonymous: The story of how many thousands of men and women have recovered from alcoholism* (3rd ed.). New York: Author.

Alcoholics Anonymous World Services. (1985). *Twelve steps and twelve traditions*. New York: Author.

Alcoholics Anonymous World Services. (1987). *AA membership survey*. New York: Author.

Beckman, L. J. (1980). An attributional analysis of Alcoholics Anonymous. *Journal of Studies on Alcohol, 41,* 714–726.

Bradley, A. M. (1988). Keep coming back: The case for a valuation of Alcoholics Anonymous. *Alcohol Health and Research World, 12,* 192–201.

Brandsma, J. M., Maultry, M. C., & Welsh, R. J. (1980). *Outpatient treatment of alcoholism: A review and comparative study*. Baltimore, MD: University Park Press.

Cermak, T. L. (1989). Al-Anon and recovery. In M. Galanter (Ed.), *Recent developments in alcoholism: Emerging issues in treatment Vol. 7* (pp. 91–104). New York: Plenum Press.

Denzin, N. (1987). *The alcoholic self*. Newbury Park, CA: Sage.

Ditman, K., Crawford, G., Forgy, E., Moskowitz, H., & MacAndrew, C. A. (1967). Controlled experiment on the use of court probation for drunk arrests. *American Journal of Psychiatry, 124,* 160–163.

Emrick, C. (1987). Alcoholics Anonymous: Affiliation processes and effectiveness as treatment. *Alcoholism: Clinical and Experimental Research, 11,* 416–423.

Emrick, C. D. (1989). Alcoholics Anonymous: Membership characteristics and effectiveness as treatment. In M. Galanter (Ed.), *Recent developments in alcoholism: Emerging issues in treatment Vol. 7* (pp. 37–53). New York: Plenum Press.

Gianetti, V. (1981). Alcoholics Anonymous and the recovering alcoholic: An exploratory study. *American Journal of Drug and Alcohol Abuse, 8,* 363–370.

Glaser, F., & Ogbourne, A. C. (1982). Does AA really work? *British Journal of Addiction, 77,* 123–129.

Gorman, J. M., & Rooney, J. F. (1979). The influence of Al-Anon on the coping behavior of wives of alcoholics. *Journal of Studies on Alcohol, 40,* 1030–1038.

Hurlburt, G., Gade, G., & Fuqua, D. (1984). Personality differences between Alcoholics Anonymous members and nonmembers. *Journal of Studies on Alcohol, 45,* 170–171.

National Institute on Drug Abuse/National Institute on Alcoholism and Alcohol Abuse (NIDA/NIAAA). (1990). *National Drug and Alcoholism Treatment Unit Survey (NDATUS) 1989: Main findings report.* Rockville, MD: Author.

Ogbourne, A. C. (1989). Some limitations of Alcoholics Anonymous. In M. Galanter (Ed.), *Recent developments in alcoholism: Emerging issues in treatment Vol. 7* (pp. 55–65). New York: Plenum Press.

Ogbourne, A., & Glaser, F. (1981). Characteristics of affiliates of Alcoholics Anonymous. *Journal of Studies on Alcohol, 42,* 661–675.

Skinner, H. A., Glaser, F. B., & Annis, H. M. (1982). Crossing the threshold: Factors in self-identification as an alcoholic. *British Journal of Addiction, 77,* 51–64.

Smart, R. G., Mann, R. E., & Anglin, L. (1989). Decreases in alcohol problems and increased Alcoholics Anonymous membership. *British Journal of Addiction, 84,* 507–513.

Trice, H. M., & Staudemeier, W. J. (1989). A sociocultural history of Alcoholics Anonymous. In M. Galanter (Ed.), *Recent developments in alcoholism: Emerging issues in treatment Vol. 7* (pp. 11–35). New York: Plenum Press.

—TWELVE—

Treatment of Alcoholism

Psychotherapeutic Approaches

Behavioral Approaches
   Classical Conditioning
   Operant Conditioning
   Social Learning

Family Therapy Approaches

A Typical 28-Day Treatment Program

Treatment Goals: Abstinence versus Moderation
   The Sobells' Study Controversy
   The Rand Study

Evaluation of Treatment Programs
   Controls
   Outcomes
   Attrition
   Success Rate
   Type of Treatment
   Duration of Treatment
   Inpatient versus Outpatient Treatment

Other Issues
   Brief Therapy
   Early Detection
      Screening
      Matching
   The Role of Motivation in Treatment
   Natural Recovery

Conclusions

References

In marked contrast to the grassroots or lay orientation of Alcoholics Anonymous and Al-Anon, formal treatment of alcoholism requires specialized professional knowledge. As we will see in this chapter, most formal treatment programs involve a combination of techniques and approaches including psychotherapy, aversive conditioning, medication, hypnosis, physical exercise, and social skills training rather than a single technique (Institute of Medicine, 1990).

Three general categories—pharmacological, psychotherapeutic, and behavioral—encompass most approaches. Our focus will be on psychotherapeutic and behavioral approaches, although this distinction is often blurred because they overlap or are used together. Little attention will be given to pharmacological approaches except to recognize that drugs are used to treat alcoholism primarily to ensure the physical safety of intoxicated patients undergoing the adverse effects of withdrawal reactions. Another application is the use of drugs such as disulfiram (Antabuse) to block the elimination of acetaldehyde, a toxic byproduct of alcohol metabolism by the liver. This approach is assumed to prevent drinking because alcohol consumption while taking this medication produces strong unpleasant physical reactions. Finally, drugs are used as an adjunct to relieve anxiety and depression to facilitate the psychological treatment of patients.

Psychotherapeutic Approaches

Psychotherapy comes in many forms but most rely on verbal communication between patient and therapist, either in individual or group settings. The nature and goals of the communication vary with the orientation of the therapist but generally focus on the patient's background, current life situation, motives, and consequences of drinking. According to some approaches, if the patient can come to an understanding of the causes of the drinking, he or she can achieve control over the drinking problem. Other approaches emphasize the impact of drinking on the present and future rather than searching for past causes.

Psychodynamic schools of thought interpret alcoholic drinking as a reflection of some conflicts (often unconscious) or characterological defects in earlier stages of development. For example, psychoanalytic views hold drinking to be a sign of a negative fixation at the oral stage of development (Freud, 1905) due to negative experiences associated with feeding during infancy. The alcoholic is regarded as adept at the use of defense mechanisms such as denial, rationalization, and projection to cope with the threat represented by the excessive drinking. Interpretation of the past by the therapist is assumed to break down defenses, provide insight to the patient, and facilitate recovery. However, Wallace (1985) cautioned that it may be unwise to strip away too early in the therapeutic process the "preferred defense structure" developed by alcoholics. These defenses, although maladaptive in the long run, are the only means of coping that the alcoholic has, and the alcoholic must develop other methods before he or she can give up these defenses.

It is beyond the scope of this analysis to review different psychotherapeutic methods in detail. One example, rational-emotive therapy (RET), will be outlined to serve as a contrast to the psychodynamic approach. RET places more emphasis on increasing the client's awareness of present and future motivators of drinking than on past or unconscious factors. Based on the views of Albert Ellis (Ellis, McInerney, DiGiuseppe, & Yeager, 1988) that many psychological problems stem from irrational beliefs, the therapist attempts to dispel and correct misconceptions about alcoholism held by the client. By continually questioning and confronting the alcoholic with evidence, the therapist aims to help the client realize the illogical and erroneous views he or she has. Denial is often the reaction of alcoholics to such confrontation; many seem to think, "I can't be alcoholic because I don't drink in the morning" or "I only drink wine and beer."

Later, after facts are presented that convince the alcoholic that he or she has a drinking problem, the goal is to help the client realize why he or she is drinking and how to find alternative ways of achieving such goals. RET also helps the client understand the need for abstinence and learn how to overcome irrational beliefs such as "I need alcohol to relax" or "I am too weak to handle the situation without a drink." Abstinence may be difficult to maintain because of other irrational beliefs such as "No one will like me if I don't drink" or "I'll never have fun anymore without alcohol." The therapist tries to modify these cognitions by helping the client obtain disconfirming evidence.

Behavioral Approaches

Behaviorists use a variety of techniques based on classical conditioning including relaxation training, covert desensitization, counterconditioning, and aversive conditioning. In addition, techniques involving operant conditioning such as contingency contracting are used. Learning theory, the theoretical basis underlying these techniques, assumes that reinforcements of prior associations and habits are responsible for the development of most human behaviors, including alcohol consumption. It further assumes that the same processes can be employed to "unlearn" prior habits or to develop new ones.

Classical Conditioning

Classical conditioning, a major tradition of learning theory pioneered by Pavlov (1927), involves a relatively passive role for the individual. According to classical conditioning, a subject develops associations between neutral stimuli and consequences so that eventually those stimuli acquire the ability to elicit a response. Applying this paradigm, alcoholism treatment pairs aversive stimuli with alcohol or alcohol-related stimuli so that eventually the latter elicit negative reactions on their own. The pioneering 18th-century American physician Benjamin Rush observed that mixing a tartar emetic with rum produced an aversion to alcohol in a man who loved to drink (Jellinek, 1943). It is assumed that repeated pairing of alcohol, or its taste and visual cues, with a negative or painful stimulus will make alcoholics want to avoid it in the future.

Aversive conditioning (Rachman & Teasdale, 1969) builds upon classical conditioning by repeatedly pairing strong negative stimuli such as electric shock or nausea-producing drugs called emetics with the drinking of alcoholic beverages to reduce the attractiveness of such drinking. Following a series of trials in which alcohol drinking is immediately paired with one of these noxious stimuli, the drinker will experience negative feelings at the very thought of drinking and will eventually avoid alcohol because of the expected noxious outcomes. This paradigm has been the basis for commercial use of aversive conditioning in alcoholism treatment.

In a large-scale study of the treatment of several thousand alcoholics, Lemere and Voegtlin (1950) used emetine, a drug that induces vomiting and nausea as a unconditioned stimulus presented in association with the sight, taste, and smell of alcohol. Although the success rate was high after a year, it should be noted that no control groups were used.

A similar failure to include a control group makes it difficult to assess the findings of Wiens and Menustik (1983), who evaluated the effectiveness of aversion conditioning with emetine for 685 alcoholics. They found a 63 percent abstinence rate one year after the end of treatment although it dropped to only about 33 percent after three years.

Chaney, O'Leary, & Marlatt (1978) did include a control group of chronic alcoholic inpatients for comparison with an aversive conditioning group. At follow-up after 3 months, the aversive conditioning group showed a higher rate of abstinence, but at a follow-up 15 months after treatment, the advantage for the aversive conditioning group had dissipated. Cannon, Baker, & Wehl (1981) found that chemical aversion and a standard psychological treatment did not differ in their rates of success over a year, although both were superior to a no-treatment control group. A review of research on aversive conditioning led Wilson (1987) to conclude that the benefits of chemical aversion conditioning are low in comparison to the physical risks involved. A different conclusion was reached by Elkins (1991), who found that emetic conditioning was achieving a success rate of around 60 percent in private hospitals.

Irrespective of the effectiveness of aversive conditioning, not all alcoholics are willing to accept this type of treatment, and success may be limited to those who are motivated to participate. Aside from queasiness about the discomfort involved, there is also the real danger of physical harm if the noxious stimuli are too strong.

Operant Conditioning

Another major tradition in learning theory, operant conditioning, holds a view of the learner as an active participant in behavior change. Trial-and-error behavior (Thorndike, 1911) may be involved in which the learner comes to identify which responses lead to which outcomes. The outcomes serve as reinforcers (Skinner, 1938) that are contingent on the responses being made by the individual. Drinking alcohol is similar to any other behavior in the sense that it can be reinforced by consequences of that behavior. The drinker initially finds that alcohol leads to positive or pleasurable outcomes and begins to drink more often or more heavily.

In theory, drinking should be reduced if it leads to negative consequences. Yet, alcoholics often experience severe negative physical and social consequences from their drinking but do not easily reduce their drinking. One reason for this failure of negative consequences to decrease the drinking behavior is the long temporal gap between the beginning of the drinking episode and the unpleasant consequences.

Some treatment programs have employed contingency contracting to reinforce alcoholics when they abstain and for program participation. For example, Pomerleau, Pertschuk, Adkins, and Brady (1978) reported that a requirement of sizable monetary deposits from patients, which they would forfeit if they did not complete the program, was effective in improving attendance. Use of employment opportunities as a consequence of sobriety was found by Nathan (1984) to be another effective form of contingency management for alcohol self-regulation.

Social Learning

Social learning theory (Bandura, 1977), discussed in Chapter 6, focuses on cognitive processes that allow learning through observation of consequences to others. Thus, we might notice that those who reduce their drinking receive desirable reinforcers such as privileges or social approval. Alcoholism treatment based on this theory attempts to reduce drinking through the use of appropriate social reinforcers.

All of these behavioristic approaches focus on the *behavior* of the alcoholic, especially the drinking. It is assumed that drinking, like other behaviors, is a set of learned responses. Accordingly, treatment applies learning principles to teach drinkers to change their drinking behavior by changing the outcomes or contingencies of alcohol consumption. In addition, the alcoholic is taught alternative coping behaviors for reducing stress through relaxation training and stress management techniques.

Family Therapy Approaches

In contrast to Al-Anon's focus on treating the family members separately from any treatment of the alcoholic as described in Chapter 11, other approaches to family treatment call for the treatment of the nondrinking spouse, or even the entire family, to be integrated with the alcoholic's own treatment.

Family therapy, an approach that shifted the focus of therapy from the individual to the family, has grown rapidly since the 1950s. Originally developed for a variety of psychological problems including schizophrenia, it has also been used for treating the alcoholic family. There is no single type of family therapy, with such contrasting emphases as psychodynamic and behavioristic approaches.

Ackerman (1958) was a pioneer in family therapy who came from a Freudian psychoanalytic orientation, which emphasizes unconscious intrapsychic conflicts and defense mechanisms. He recognized the need to work with the entire family as an interrelated system in treating any type of psychological problem. Each member of a family system has a role and there are boundaries or rules that more or less define each member's function. When conflicts arise among family members, communication may break down. Family members may become defensive, anxious, and unable to deal with each other. Ackerman felt that the therapist must help the family overcome resistance and achieve a new balance of roles among members after its homeostasis has been disrupted by disturbances such as alcoholism.

Bowen (1971; 1978) also viewed many psychological problems as rooted in family interrelationships. Tensions between any two family members may spread to include a third member, a process Bowen termed *triangulation*. When two persons have a breakdown of communication, one party may draw into the conflict a third family member, who may take sides. This process may be repeated so that more interlocking triangles are created until eventually all family members are enmeshed in the problem.

The therapist also can be regarded as part of a triangle. To be effective, Bowen cautions, the therapist must not take sides but must maintain emotional contact with both parties in a conflict. Placing more emphasis on cognitive than on emotional reactions, Bowen felt the therapist must help individuals differentiate between their intellect and emotional feelings. If they fail to do so, they will be less adaptable when faced with stress and be overwhelmed by their emotions. In addition to this intrapsychic goal, individuals need to differentiate "self" from the other family members of "undifferentiated family ego mass." If they succeed, they can freely express their own feelings and not be dominated by the feelings of other family members.

In the case of alcoholism, Bowen posits that family members who have the greatest dependence on the alcoholic member are the most overly anxious about the problem. This anxiety may lead to criticism of the drinker and emotional isolation from the drinker, factors that might increase the drinking, creating an escalating cycle of events. The family therapist's task is to interrupt and reverse this process by helping family members lower their anxiety and restore emotional contact with the alcoholic member.

Despite clinical evidence of the usefulness of family therapy, the comparative effectiveness of different approaches to family therapy has not been determined (Kaufman, 1985) and controlled evaluations are rare (Thomas, 1989). One problem in comparing studies of family therapy is that there are so many variables in family composition, such as marital status, number of children, living arrangements, and number of drinkers in the family. Also, there is the generalizability issue of whether families willing to enter family therapy are similar to those who do not (Institute of Medicine, 1990).

Behavioral treatment methods for family therapy (McCrady, 1989) focus on the reciprocal reinforcement system between spouses. One example given by McCrady (1992) was a wife who would call her husband at work asking when he would be home, with the hope that the call would bring him home soon. Discussion in therapy revealed that the husband resented the call and it made him want to start drinking. McCrady suggested that such feedback is needed to help the spouse learn which behaviors are effective and which are ineffective in dealing with the husband's drinking.

Behavioral treatment might be useful as a method of rehabilitation. The goal of behavioral intervention has typically been to develop improved positive communications, relying on the nondrinking spouse to provide reinforcement to the alcoholic for achieving sobriety. Spouses are taught how to reinforce nondrinking as well as how to cope with the spouse when drinking does occur.

A controlled study of 33 couples by McCrady et al (1979) compared individualized therapy against couples treatment, either with or without joint hospitalization. This study found better drinking outcomes for the spouse-involved group, but a four-year follow-up by McCrady et al (1982) showed no differences.

Studies comparing recovering alcoholics with nonalcoholic controls from the community by Moos and his colleagues suggested that marital therapy can be effective in improvement of the psychological functioning of spouses and children. Moos, Finney, and Chan (1981) compared the family environments of alcoholics two years after marital therapy with those of nonalcoholic community controls. Two subgroups of alcoholics were identified, the remitted group that had maintained sobriety and the relapsed group that had not. Cohesive, expressive environments relatively free of conflict were found in the homes of both the remitted alcoholics and controls. In contrast, the home environments of relapsed alcoholics were not cohesive, expressive, organized, or free of conflict. Remitted patients were similar to controls in some respects such as depression and physical symptoms but they still did more poorly in other respects such as more use of medical treatment and greater anxiety. The relapsed patients did most poorly on all dimensions.

Finney and Moos (1991, 1992) followed up on the 83 members of the original sample of 113 alcoholics who were alive ten years later. Many of the findings observed at the two-year follow-up held up at the ten-year follow-up. For over two thirds of the patients at ten years, their drinking status, remission or relapse, was the same as it had been at two years after treatment.

Alcoholics with more cohesive families, experiencing lower life stress, and using active cognitive coping at the two-year follow-up were more likely to have better ten-year outcomes. At ten years, those who showed remission functioned at a level comparable to the matched community control group, and both were superior to the relapsed group.

Moos, Finney, and Gamble (1982) examined the predominantly female spouses of the alcoholics who had undergone remission. In comparison to the spouses of relapsed alcoholics and the community controls, no differences in social competence and coping skills were found but there was more stress among spouses of relapsed alcoholics.

Unfortunately, evaluative studies such as these, especially those involving random assignment, low attrition rates, and adequate follow-ups, are rare. As more systematic research is conducted, a better understanding of the factors affecting the usefulness of family therapy will be achieved.

A Typical 28-Day Treatment Program

Although individual variations exist among treatment programs, most 28-day inpatient alcoholism treatment programs share some common features. Many programs adhere to the Minnesota model of rehabilitation (Institute of Medicine,

1990). First, if the patient enters the hospital in a crisis due to excessive drinking, detoxification for several days up to a week is needed to "dry out" the alcoholic before counseling and psychotherapy can begin. Severe withdrawal reactions may occur due to the sudden unavailability of alcohol. Medical supervision, drug treatment with benzodiazapines, and nutritional treatment with vitamins is required to safely manage the detoxification phase.

Then, a mixture of individual counseling and group therapy is used along with didactic films and lectures about the physical effects of alcohol. There is some question as to how much of the cognitive information is comprehended since even after detoxification, cognitive processes are impaired for a period of weeks (McCrady, 1987).

These standard components of the treatment program are often supplemented by recreational and occupational therapy. AA meetings are recommended as supplements, especially after the patient is discharged from the inpatient program.

Treatment Goals: Abstinence versus Moderation

An emotionally charged treatment issue is the question of whether alcoholism treatment should require abstinence or only reduced drinking to moderate or controlled levels. AA ideology clearly insists on abstinence as the goal because "one drink is too many and a thousand is not enough" for an alcoholic. Behaviorists, on the other hand, have argued that more alcoholics might undergo treatment if they were allowed to drink moderately rather than give up alcohol completely. AA might reply that it is a false hope for alcoholics to think they can control their drinking and that relapse would be more likely if drinking were allowed than if abstinence were rigorously followed.

The argument as just stated centers on philosophical issues. However, some clinical studies by Davies (1962) and by Lovibond and Caddy (1970) provided evidence that suggests it is "possible" for alcoholics to achieve controlled drinking, contrary to the views held by AA. The alcoholics studied seemed to be able to function normally on jobs without relapse even though they had on the average up to five ounces of absolute alcohol daily; this seems to refute the assertion that abstinence is a necessary goal for recovery.

Advocates of abstinence hold that it is dangerous for recovering alcoholics to drink at all because they might lose control. Whether recovering alcoholics *should* drink, even at a moderate level, and whether they *can* drink moderately are separate questions. Jellinek (1960) argued that once an alcoholic drinks, the alcohol activates loss of control physiologically. In contrast, in the 1960s psychologists with a behavioristic orientation (Marlatt, 1983; Roizen, 1987) challenged the disease conception of alcoholism that held that alcoholics had to achieve abstinence before treatment could be successful. Behaviorists had applied operant conditioning techniques to reinforce contingencies between desired behaviors and rewarding consequences in many areas other than alcoholism. They felt the same techniques should work with drinking behavior, as illustrated by laboratory studies of reinforcement of drinking responses by Nathan, Lowenstein, Solomon, and Rossi

(1970). Behaviorists insisted that the issue of whether recovering alcoholics can drink moderately be resolved empirically by comparison of alcoholics treated under the two different criteria of abstinence and controlled drinking.

Lovibond and Caddy (1970) reported that alcoholics, contrary to Jellinek's view, could be trained to control drinking of alcohol at levels that did not lead to problems. They conducted a rigorously controlled experiment in Australia and found that alcoholics could maintain moderate drinking levels even after periods of up to two years after treatment.

The Sobells' Study Controversy

Sobell and Sobell (1973) also presented evidence of controlled drinking with alcoholics under treatment in an inpatient hospital setting. Their research was widely cited because it appeared to be a controlled and carefully executed study with a large sample. A total of 70 male alcoholics were randomly assigned to one of four groups, two of which were experimental groups and two of which were control groups.

The two experimental groups received a package of treatments termed individualized behavior therapy, with one group given a criterion of abstinence while the other had a goal of controlled drinking. This treatment included a set of procedures such as blood alcohol content discrimination training, aversive conditioning, assertion training, and counseling. The two control groups received the conventional programs used in the past at the hospital, again with one having a controlled drinking goal and one given an abstinence criterion. The program lasted for four weeks.

At both the six-month and one-year follow-ups, the treated experimental groups appeared to show better improvement than the control groups. Importantly, the abstinent groups were no better off than the groups that had been allowed to drink moderately under the controlled drinking criterion.

At first, it appeared that the Sobell and Sobell study was decisive evidence and represented the largest and most convincing demonstration that controlled drinking was possible for alcoholics. Eventually, however, the Sobells' study became the center of public as well as scientific controversy of major magnitude. In the public arena, AA advocates and others reacted negatively and hostilely toward the findings, because they felt the findings were dangerous and would tempt many recovering alcoholics to abandon their abstinence and to experiment with controlled drinking, a situation with potentially disastrous consequences for their continued sobriety.

At the professional level, researchers such as Pendery, Maltzman, and West (1982) doubted the reported findings and challenged the authenticity of the data, accusing the Sobells of faulty findings and possible misrepresentation. Pendery et al. conducted their own investigation with a follow-up of the controlled drinking patients who had been in the Sobells' study ten years earlier. Their critique revealed a high number of relapses in the first year among this group. Also, their follow-up revealed that several of the treated alcoholics in this group had relapsed into alcoholic drinking, while four had died of alcohol-related complications.

Eventually, allegations of fraud were raised against the Sobells (Boffey, 1982) and the highly respected Addiction Research Foundation of Canada formed a special committee of independent investigators to study the evidence (Dickens, Doob, Warwick, & Winegard, 1982). They concluded, after a thorough evaluation, that no proof of fraud could be established.

Pendery et al. (1982) did *not* follow up on the Sobells' control group, making it impossible to interpret meaningfully the relapse rate found in the experimental group. The argument of Pendery et al. would have been more damning if it could have shown that the relapse rate in the experimental group had exceeded that of the control group.

The Rand Study

The second and somewhat related controversy involved a study known as the Rand report (Armor, Polich, & Stambul, 1978). This research involved the analysis of data from a study of a sample of 8 of the 44 federally funded alcoholism treatment centers located across the nation. This study of a random sample of more than 1,300 male alcoholics found that six months after treatment, some of the alcoholics had resumed "controlled" drinking, defined at a somewhat high level of three to five ounces on a typical day, but were not experiencing any problems. In comparison to an untreated control group of alcoholics who had a remission rate of 50 percent, the treated alcoholics, overall, showed a 70-percent remission rate a year later. However, a controversial finding was that the relapse rates at 18 months after treatment were no different among those who had been engaged in controlled drinking and those who were totally abstinent when assessed at 6 months after treatment ended. The implication was that it did not make any difference whether or not alcoholics were abstinent or drinking in moderation 6 months after treatment ended, because relapse was at the same rate for both groups 18 months after treatment ended.

AA advocates and others attacked the study on a number of grounds, including the charge that even if the results were true, it was irresponsible to publish them because it might undermine the recovery of many alcoholics who would try to drink in moderation but not succeed. It was also held that the alcoholics tested were not really alcoholics, only heavy drinkers. In other words, critics of controlled drinking defined alcoholics as drinkers who cannot drink in moderation. By this definition, any evidence that some alcoholics can drink moderately can simply be dismissed on the grounds that this sample could not really consist of alcoholics. Thus, circular definitions prevent the issue from being tested. An objective definition of *alcoholic* is needed but there is no consensus on this issue.

Polich, Armor, and Braiker (1981) performed a four-year follow-up to further study 922 of the male alcoholics of the first Rand study (Armor et al., 1978). Relapse was found in 41 percent of the alcoholics who had been drinking in moderation 18 months after treatment ended as compared with only 30 percent of alcoholics who were abstinent 18 months after treatment ended. In other words, when a longer time period than the 18-month interval of the original Rand study is used, abstinence does appear to have been more successful in preventing relapse. Polich et al. (1981) suggested that alcoholism is not a condition that involves a steady progression, as is popularly thought, but rather one of unstable fluctuation; therefore, use of too short a period for defining abstinence may lead to inaccurate and unreliable measurement. Treatment outcomes should be conceptualized as unstable, and longer periods of evaluation following treatment are needed to measure accurately the effects of treatment.

A review of 22 independent studies by Miller (1983) found only one in which controlled drinking was unsuccessful for large percentages of varying types of patients throughout the country. In contrast, Helzer, Robins, and Taylor (1986) found that less than 5 percent of alcoholics examined were able to exercise controlled drinking. But these researchers did not teach techniques for monitoring drinking to these patients as part of their treatment, so the findings are difficult to interpret as evidence that controlled drinking cannot work.

In one of the few studies that has directly compared controlled drinking and abstinence goals, Foy, Nunn, and Rychtarik (1984) found that controlled drinking was associated with more alcohol abuse at a six-month follow-up, but there was no difference at one year after treatment. A follow-up of the clients after five to six years (Rychtarik, Foy, Scott, Lokey, & Prue, 1987) also found no difference between the two treatment criteria, but interestingly, there was controlled drinking by about a fifth of the patients. In contrast, Nordstrom and Berglund (1987) found in a follow-up about 20 years later of 60 Swedish male alcoholics that controlled drinking was associated with fewer relapses.

How can the conflicting evidence be reconciled? One possibility is that severity of alcoholism is a factor, with controlled drinking working only for those with less dependence and abstinence being more effective for those with severe dependence. Miller, Leckman, Delaney, and Tinkcom (1992) found that an abstinence treatment goal was more effective than a moderate drinking criterion only for drinkers with severe dependence. However, neither Rychtarik et al. (1987) nor Nordstrom and Berglund (1987) found that severity of dependence affected whether alcoholics would be abstinent or controlled drinkers at follow-up. A better predictor of type of remission, according to studies by Orford and Keddie (1986) and Elal-Lawrence, Slade, and Dewey (1986), was the beliefs and expectations of the clients about which treatment goal would work for them.

In recent years, the controversy over and interest in controlled drinking appears to have diminished. Abstinence appears to be the primary treatment goal. Nathan (1992), who was an early advocate of controlled drinking, has maintained that the evidence has not upheld the original promise it offered in the 1970s. Peele (1992), however, has charged that the politically charged atmosphere intimidated the controlled drinking proponents from further evaluation of the potential of controlled drinking.

Evaluation of Treatment Programs

As is the case with AA, formal treatment programs do not generally include controlled evaluation of the effectiveness of procedures or identification of the underlying processes that may be involved in any improvement in the patients. Instead, many psychotherapists rely on clinical experience and expertise to measure the treatment's success.

The goals of clinical practitioners who conduct psychotherapy with alcoholics are not the same as those of research-oriented evaluators of treatment outcomes. The therapists, based on years of training and actual practice in dealing with alcoholics, may be convinced that an effective program does not need scientific evaluation. Although effective treatment may indeed occur in the absence of objective and rigorous evaluation, such scrutiny is vital to scientific researchers and their efforts to isolate effective from ineffective, or even harmful, treatments.

Controls

In practice, sound evaluation of treatment programs is difficult for a number of reasons. A researcher might want to use an experimental design in which some alcoholics in a control group do not receive treatment while others in an experimental group do. However, most treatment facilities do not permit untreated control groups, partly because they assume their program is valid and cannot justify withholding it from persons in need. Ethical concerns would prevent the formation of untreated control groups, whereas research goals would require their inclusion to achieve scientific rigor.

Moreover, even when different treatments are compared, patients (and therapists) are usually *not* randomly assigned to the difficult treatment conditions. Instead, some selective bias may be involved in deciding who works with whom. This process is not necessarily wrong from a practical perspective. If people are more motivated when they perceive a choice in their treatment, that may be an important factor that makes treatment more effective. On the other hand, this bias compromises evaluation of the factors responsible for the treatment outcomes and limits the generalizability of outcomes.

Figure 12-1 presents a model illustrating how treatment outcomes are affected jointly by various aspects of the treatment, such as its length, setting, or technique, as well as by client characteristics, such as drinking patterns, physical and psychological attributes, and social background. A focus on either treatment or client variables to the exclusion of the other can present an incomplete picture of the determinants of success or failure from treatment.

Another problem in evaluating treatment is identifying the most effective procedures within a program. Treatments usually involve a "package" or set of components, so that it is often impossible to determine what each component contributes to the outcome. As already noted, a typical program may include group psychotherapy and individual counseling, exercise, nutrition, and educational films and lectures. If changes occur following treatment, can we determine how much each component contributed to the changes? It is conceivable that some of the components may have even had adverse effects that were hidden by the beneficial effects of other components.

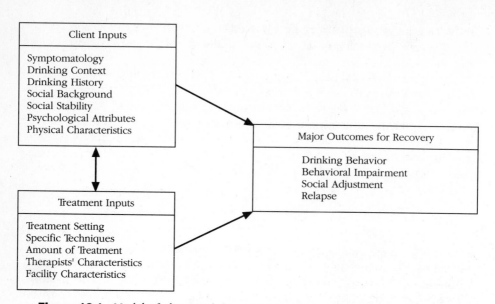

Figure 12-1 Model of client and therapist inputs into treatment outcomes.
Source: from *Alcoholism and Treatment* by D. J. Armor, J. M. Polich, and H. B. Stambul.
Copyright © 1978 by Rand Corporation. Reprinted by permission.

Outcomes

In evaluating treatment effectiveness, one must specify one or more outcomes that are expected to occur. What should be the criteria for success of a program? While it would seem obvious that reduction or cessation of drinking is necessary, it is important to include other criteria such as psychological well-being, work productivity, interpersonal relationships, and family behavior. If drinking stops but other problems persist, it would be difficult to conclude that success has occurred.

And, if drinking is the focus, is the criterion of success total abstinence or a reduction to a lower level of consumption (controlled drinking)? Over what period of time must the improvement last before the treatment is considered successful?

Attrition

Clients may drop out before the end of a program, creating some difficulties of interpretation. If the more severe cases drop out, leaving cases that are more amenable to improvement, one may conclude erroneously that the treatment was the sole factor responsible for the success of those who improved. Differential dropout rates from several programs being compared might lead to faulty conclusions about the relative merits of the programs (Baekeland & Lundwall, 1975).

Long-term follow-ups, essential for evaluation, are difficult to conduct for alcoholic populations. Once released from treatment, some alcoholics who have no families to return to or steady employment opportunities may become transients with little chance of being relocated later. If contacted, they may have little interest in participating in research, especially if they have suffered relapse from their treatment gains.

Success Rate

Emrick and Hansen (1983) searched for factors that might influence the success rate of treatment. First, they noted that widely divergent claims of treatment success exist. They found advertisements of individual hospital treatment programs claiming success rates as high as 90 percent, while a much less optimistic estimate of 7 percent was made in the Rand study (Polich et al., 1981). Closer examination of the two reports showed self-selection bias occurred in the treatment program with the 90 percent success rate, but the evaluation was based on only the 10 percent of the patients who participated in aftercare programs. The high success rate may also have been due to the fact that about one third of the patients were treated twice before they achieved success. Moreover, the evaluation interview may have been open to interviewer bias.

In the Rand study showing only a 7-percent success rate, more thorough assessment with objective procedures was used. Random samplings of 474 patients at eight different NIAAA-funded programs were studied over 4.5 years. Less attrition occurred, with about 85 percent of the original patients located for reinterview or found to be deceased. In addition, independent measures of drinking levels were obtained and checked against blood alcohol content readings. Emrick and Hansen concluded that the 7-percent success rate in the Rand study was more realistic, while the 90-percent estimate in the first study was more of a fantasy.

They concluded from their review of previous research that the success rate in psychotherapy for alcoholics is highly dependent on factors such as context, patient sample, time frame, attrition rate, and method of evaluation, among other factors.

Type of Treatment

A review of 26 published evaluation studies by Maisto and Carey (1987) avoided the problem of selective bias affecting assignment of subjects to treatment conditions. They included only studies involving either random assignment of clients to two or more treatment groups or studies in which clients in different treatment groups were matched on variables related to the outcome measures. A wide variety of treatment approaches was represented in this set of studies. The treatments were usually added as supplements to other prior forms of treatment. Furthermore, pretreatment measures were obtained before administering the treatments. The evaluation was made from 1 to 19 or more months later, depending on the study, with the modal period being 12 months.

The review revealed that the *type* of treatment was not a factor in effectiveness. Observed improvements across the 26 studies were stable over the observed period of one to two years. One conclusion might be that improvement was due to a few common aspects embedded throughout the variety of methods used and that some of the differences in treatment were not having any effect. However, Maisto and Carey (1987) suggested that the lack of differences in improvement may reflect a "ceiling effect," in that the level of improvement was already approaching the maximum when these supplemental treatments were imposed. Another explanation involves the failure to try to match patients to the type of therapy. Treating all alcoholics with the same treatment method may have masked some genuine effects (Finney & Moos, 1986). Thus, if some alcoholics benefit more from one technique while others improve more with a different procedure, the overall results obtained with a single method applied to both populations would show a less impressive averaged effect.

Duration of Treatment

Treatment programs vary in duration, with most ranging from a few weeks to one or two months. Does the duration or amount of treatment affect treatment outcomes? Treatment effectiveness is often measured by abstinence rates at follow-up after intervals of from a few months to one or two years after treatment. Examination of success across programs of varying duration has shown more abstinence with longer treatment programs (Welte, Hymes, Sokolow, & Lyons, 1981a). However, it is not clear that length of treatment is responsible for these outcomes, because those who can afford lengthier treatment may improve for other reasons.

Similarly, conclusions from comparisons of treatment duration within a given treatment program must also be qualified. Those who receive shorter treatment may have dropped out because they were less motivated or not showing improvement, while those who remained for the full treatment may have been less severe cases (Chapman & Huygens, 1988; Welte, Hynes, Sokolov, & Lyons, 1981b). Smart (1978) reviewed research on this issue and found that those who received longer treatment showed better outcomes, but since the duration of treatment was not randomly assigned to clients, causal interpretations of the effects of length of treatment are not warranted.

Studies that have employed random assignment of alcoholics to different durations of treatment have failed to show that longer treatment is any more effective than briefer treatment. Walker, Donovan, Kivlahan, and O'Leary (1983) randomly assigned alcoholics to two or seven weeks of hospital treatment and found no differences in the amount of improvement. Those who did continue with weekly aftercare meetings for nine months, however, were more likely to remain abstinent. Powell, Penick, Read, and Ludwig (1985) used random assignment of male alcoholics to one of three outpatient treatments that varied in intensity. All groups improved but none was superior.

Inpatient versus Outpatient Treatment

Treatment may involve inpatient (residential) or outpatient (nonresidential) care. One advantage of inpatient care is the continual supervision of the patient by a staff of professionals; but the cost for the typical 28-day hospital stay for alcoholism often exceeds $10,000, while outpatient treatment typically costs about 10 percent of that amount. An important question is whether the substantially greater cost of inpatient over outpatient programs is worthwhile in terms of more effective treatment.

Miller and Hester (1986a) conducted a review of controlled studies of treatment and concluded that the more costly residential programs did not show more effective treatment. Inpatient programs varying in duration of stay did not show any differences in success either. Some studies have indicated otherwise, finding that longer stays led to less remission, but such studies are typically confounded by factors such as higher motivation or socioeconomic status of patients undergoing lengthier and more costly treatment.

Other Issues

Other issues relating to treatment of alcoholism include the question of the effectiveness of brief therapy, the importance of early detection, the role of motivation in treatment, and the possibility of natural recovery.

Brief Therapy

In addition to the major approaches to therapy already discussed, some forms of "brief therapy" may be effective, at least for some individuals. For example, a provocative study of 99 married male alcoholics was reported by Orford and Edwards (1977) suggesting that conventional treatment involving abstinence for a randomly selected subgroup was no more effective than a *single session of advice and counseling* regarding the need to reduce drinking. Each couple in the advice group met with a psychiatrist who told them that the husband had alcoholism and should abstain from drinking and that it was up to them to handle the problem. In the treatment group, couples were offered a year-long program including AA and access to prescription drugs to reduce withdrawal symptoms. By the end of the treatment only 11 of the total sample were abstainers, and there was no difference between the advice and treatment groups. On the surface, this study would appear to suggest that at least some types of alcoholics can achieve effective change with the briefest of treatments. However, it would be dangerous to generalize this conclusion to all types of alcoholics. This effect may be limited to alcoholics who have milder levels of alcohol dependence. Furthermore, how long-lasting was the effectiveness of this brief therapy?

Other forms of brief therapy include *bibliotherapy,* a term referring to the use of a handbook or manual instructing the alcoholic how to manage his or her own drinking levels. Miller and Taylor (1980) have provided such self-therapy guides to help problem drinkers achieve controlled drinking through a variety of self-monitoring activities and stress-reduction exercises. Sanchez-Craig, Leigh, Spivak, and Lei (1989) compared men and women problem drinkers who were randomly assigned to three forms of brief therapy based on cognitive and behavioral change. Two therapy programs involved self-help manuals, while the other employed a therapist teaching the same concepts. Females were found to benefit more, especially with the self-help versions of the therapy.

Early Detection

For any type of psychological disorder, early detection allows early participation in treatment. A major goal of alcoholism treatment, therefore, has been to find ways of early detection in hopes that more severe problems can be prevented from occurring.

Screening. For instance, if individuals simply complete a short written questionnaire and self-diagnose the extent to which they may be having alcohol problems, it might help identify alcohol problems at an earlier stage. Such an instrument would be inexpensive and readily available so that large numbers of people could, if they wished, be tested. Early screening, if accurate, could facilitate early intervention.

The Michigan Alcoholism Screening Test (MAST) shown in Figure 12-2 developed by Selzer (1971) was one of the first such surveys. It consists of 25 items dealing with questions of drinking, opinions of friends and relatives about the respondent's drinking, alcohol-related problems, and symptoms related to alcohol dependence. Use of the MAST with alcoholics in treatment has been effective in accurately identifying a high percentage of them as alcoholic. However, the test requires that honest answers be given, and it is easy to fake since it is obvious which answers indicate alcohol problems. Treated alcoholics have already come to admit or accept their diagnosis of alcoholism; however, whether the scale would be as successful in identifying alcoholics who are in denial and not yet in treatment is a different issue. Another question is the level of false positives, individuals who are erroneously classified as alcoholics. Screening may also be used to identify alcoholics who are at later stages of dependence but who have not been receiving treatment.

Matching. Matching is a form of screening to identify which alcoholics are more likely to be successful in treatment, so that those who are unlikely to benefit do not receive resources that might be more appropriately given to others (Miller & Hester, 1986c). This approach might appear inhumane since it would exclude cases in dire need of treatment. However, to the extent that the screening is valid, nothing would be gained by trying to treat those who probably would not benefit from a specific program and, if resources are scarce, such screening might allow someone who could benefit to have access to treatment that would otherwise be unavailable to her or him.

Ideally, however, some other form of treatment would be available for those who do not seem likely to benefit from the program being offered. Thus, instead of exercising exclusion, matching patients to treatments allows for individual differences to prescribe the optimal therapy.

A comparison of several treatment programs for VA patients by McLellan, Luborsky, Woody, O'Brien, and Druley (1983) found that severity of psychiatric disturbance could be matched to effectiveness of various treatments. Alcoholics

Points	Question	YES	NO
	0. Do you enjoy a drink now and then?	——	——
(2)	*1. Do you feel you are a normal drinker? (By normal we mean you drink less than or as much as most other people.)	——	——
(2)	2. Have you ever awakened the morning after some drinking the night before and found that you could not remember a part of the evening?	——	——
(1)	3. Does your wife, husband, a parent, or other near relative ever worry or complain about your drinking?	——	——
(2)	*4. Can you stop drinking without a struggle after one or two drinks?	——	——
(1)	5. Do you ever feel guilty about your drinking?	——	——
(2)	*6. Do friends or relatives think you are a normal drinker?	——	——
(2)	*7. Are you able to stop drinking when you want to?	——	——
(5)	8. Have you ever attended a meeting of Alcoholics Anonymous (AA)?	——	——
(1)	9. Have you gotten into physical fights when drinking?	——	——
(2)	10. Has your drinking ever created problems between you and your wife, husband, a parent, or other relative?	——	——
(2)	11. Has your wife, husband (or other family members) ever gone to anyone for help about your drinking?	——	——
(2)	12. Have you ever lost friends because of your drinking?	——	——
(2)	13. Have you ever gotten into trouble at work or school because of drinking?	——	——
(2)	14. Have you ever lost a job because of drinking?	——	——
(2)	15. Have you ever neglected your obligations, your family, or your work for two or more days in a row because you were drinking?	——	——
(1)	16. Do you drink before noon fairly often?	——	——
(2)	17. Have you ever been told you have liver trouble? Cirrhosis?	——	——
(2)	**18. After heavy drinking have you ever had Delirium Tremens (D.T.'s) or severe shaking, or heard voices or seen things that really weren't there?	——	——
(5)	19. Have you ever gone to anyone for help about your drinking?	——	——
(5)	20. Have you ever been in a hospital because of drinking?	——	——
(2)	21. Have you ever been a patient in a psychiatric hospital or on a psychiatric ward of a general hospital where drinking was part of the problem that resulted in hospitalization?	——	——
(2)	22. Have you ever been seen at a psychiatric or mental health clinic or gone to any doctor, social worker, or clergyman for help with any emotional problem, where drinking was part of the problem?	——	——
(2)	***23. Have you ever been arrested for drunk driving, driving while intoxicated, or driving under the influence of alcoholic beverages? (IF YES, How many times?_____)	——	——
(2)	***24. Have you ever been arrested, or taken into custody, even for a few hours, because of other drunk behavior? (IF YES, How many times?_____)	——	——

*Alcoholic response is negative.
**5 points for Delirium Tremens.
***2 points for *each* arrest.
SCORING SYSTEM: In general, five points or more would place the subject in an "alcoholic" category. Four points would be suggestive of alcoholism, three points or less would indicate the subject was not alcoholic.

Figure 12-2 Michigan Alcoholism Screening Test (MAST).

Source: from *Seventh Special Report to U.S. Congress on Alcohol, 1990,* Washington, DC: U.S. Government Printing Office.

with moderate impairment showed better success with inpatient than outpatient treatment, while no difference was found for those at the extreme ends. Patients with low severity of disturbance did well in both programs, while highly disturbed patients did most poorly in both programs.

Babor, Kranzler, and Lauerman (1989) used a battery of tests including a physical exam, lab tests, diagnostic interviews, personality tests, and two self-report inventories administered to alcoholic and nonalcoholic males and females in an attempt to determine if any one screening test worked best. Scores on these tests correlated reasonably well with established screening tests such as the MAST and MacAndrew scales. Self-report items dealing specifically with alcohol content were best at differentiating among males but were less effective at identifying high-risk females. There may be no one best method for screening, because the purpose of the screening and the characteristics of the sample must also be considered.

A study by Kadden, Getter, Cooney, and Litt (1989) illustrated the usefulness of matching alcoholics with either a coping skills treatment or an interactional group therapy treatment. The coping skills treatment attempted to teach behavioral skills for coping with situations that lead to drinking, while the interactional group therapy treatment promoted cohesive groups involved in emotional closeness and self-disclosure. Male and female alcoholics were randomly assigned to one of the approaches. Coping skills training was more successful for alcoholics considered high in sociopathy and psychopathology, whereas interactional group therapy was more effective for those low in sociopathy.

Following their review of studies on the effects of matching, Mattson and Allen (1991) concluded that matching has potential benefits, but they also cautioned that the best variables to use for matching are not yet known. Moreover, the improvement in treatment outcomes with matching has been modest, typically around 10 percent. In view of the added costs and effort, it remains to be seen whether many treatment providers will undertake the changes involved in offering more individualized treatment programs for different types of clients.

The Role of Motivation in Treatment

When treatment fails, it is often attributed to the client's lack of motivation, not to the lack of therapist skill or the inappropriateness of the treatment. In keeping with the general view of the alcoholic as someone with inadequate coping skills or low self-esteem, this accusation of low motivation is not surprising. Miller (1985) noted the danger of self-fulfilling prophecies whereby the therapists' expectation that the alcoholic will not be motivated increases the likelihood that treatment will fail. Of course, those patients who do successfully complete treatment are credited with high motivation. The definition of motivation, then, is circular and irrefutable, and hardly useful as an explanation.

Natural Recovery

Tuchfield (1981) described the natural recovery or remission of some alcoholics who did not receive formal treatment but still managed to end their drinking excesses. Ludwig (1986) also interviewed alcoholics who experienced spontaneous recovery. They reported that certain life events motivated change, but such events ranged from social pressure to major life changes, on the one hand, to "strangely trivial" events on the other (Knupfer, 1972).

Benjamin Rush, the physician mentioned earlier in this chapter, described several cases of natural recovery in his discourse on the effects of alcohol (Jellinek, 1943). In one instance, a farmer who was habitually drunk happened to rush home from the local tavern one day due to an impending storm before he had had a chance to become intoxicated. Surprised by his unusual sobriety, his 6-year-old son announced his father's arrival to his mother, emphasizing that he was not drunk. Shamed by his realization of how he was regarded by his son, the farmer suddenly reformed his drinking habits.

Another tale of natural recovery involved a drunkard who was followed one day to the tavern by his goat, whom he proceeded to drench with liquor so that they both had to stagger home. The next day, the loyal goat again followed the master to the tavern, but balked at the entrance despite the master's entreaties to enter. The apparently greater intelligence of the goat so shamed the master that from that point he ceased to drink liquor.

Whether these anecdotes are authentic or apocryphal, they suggest that sudden changes in drinking attitudes and behaviors can occur. Overall, however, not much attention has been given to such natural recoveries. Sobell, Sobell, and Toneatto (1991) suggested that natural recoveries may be much more frequent than suspected. They called for attention to reaching problem drinkers who may not need formal treatment, especially since the majority of them needing treatment do not seek or receive it (Nathan, 1989).

Sobell et al. recruited 120 ex-drinkers through newspaper ads, asking "Have you successfully overcome a drinking problem without formal treatment?" After screening, 71 were found to be abstinent and 49 nonabstinent. In addition, another group of 28 abstinent alcoholics were discovered who had had some formal treatment but did not consider it as a factor in their recovery.

Unlike in previous studies of natural recoveries, a control group of problem drinkers was included by recruiting 62 drinkers with newspaper ads asking "Do you have a drinking problem now?" The ad indicated that this was a research study to obtain information to help those with problems and seeking treatment but that participants in this study would not be given a treatment program. Only those who had never sought formal treatment were studied.

More than 96 percent of the 182 participants in the study met the DSM-III-R criteria for alcohol dependence, although only 21 percent were considered highly dependent. The demographic profile of the participants was similar to that found for alcoholics in seven major outcome studies (for example, Foy et al., 1984).

In the first phase of the study, Sobell et al. identified the variables related to stopping and maintaining the cessation of drinking, distinguishing between those who achieved abstinent and nonabstinent (controlled drinking) recovery. The reasons for choosing abstinent or controlled drinking were related to the respondents' self-confidence that they could control their drinking, with those choosing abstinence being less optimistic.

Not seeking formal treatment was related to embarrassment, no perception of a problem, unwillingness to share the problem with others, and stigma. Almost all claimed that they felt they could handle the problem themselves. Paradoxically, they also admitted having a drinking problem. Sobell et al. concluded that the failure to identify with the stereotype of an alcoholic was often a barrier to seeking treatment. They urged that more attempts to offer programs for those who recognized that they have a drinking problem but do not want formal treatment.

Conclusions

A variety of treatment approaches have been developed for alcoholism. It is difficult to evaluate the effectiveness of many treatments objectively because the goals and methods of scientific researchers and clinical practitioners differ. Treatment outcomes depend not only on the treatment method and its setting but also on client variables such as drinking history, other forms of psychopathology, and demographic factors. Evaluation studies yield divergent results.

A thorough review of American alcoholism treatment programs and their effectiveness (Miller & Hester, 1986b) found that there has been a rigid adherence to a standard treatment approach involving components that have not been demonstrated with controlled studies to be effective. This review identifies such widely used approaches as AA, confrontation with alcoholics over their denial, individual counseling, group therapy, and alcohol education. The tendency has been to favor highly expensive inpatient programs based on the disease model, although these have not been any more effective than lower cost outpatient programs. At the same time, there has been slow acceptance of techniques for which controlled evidence of effectiveness does exist, such as stress management, social skills training, behavioral self-control, marital and family therapy, some aversion therapies, and community-based programs involving social, family, and vocational reinforcement.

The hotly debated issue of whether the treatment criterion should be abstinence or controlled drinking pits one of AA's central tenets about the nature of alcoholism against the skepticism of the empirically oriented behaviorist. The answer to this question hinges very much on one's definition and conception of alcoholism, an issue that was noted in Chapter 7 to be highly controversial in its own right. This question may have no scientific answer and the political fallout from the controversy may serve only to distract researchers and practitioners from more immediate concerns that can be evaluated empirically.

The controversy resides primarily in whether abstinence is a *necessary* condition for recovery, not whether it is a highly effective approach. Behaviorists feel that AA is dogmatic and that demonstrations of controlled drinking by alcoholics disprove AA's assumption that alcoholics inevitably undergo loss of control. AA believes that the controlled drinkers probably were not really "alcoholics." Furthermore, they regard the laboratory demonstrations of controlled drinking as highly artificial and point out that the controlled drinking may not hold up for alcoholics when they return to the community.

Although these rival approaches have been bitter opponents in their perspectives on the nature of alcoholism and how to promote recovery, there are some areas of overlap and agreement between them that may be overlooked because of differences in terminology. The social learning focus on the acquisition of coping skills to reduce stress is not incompatible with the methods of AA. The Twelve Steps call for changes in attitude, behavior, and outlook, all of which can relieve stress.

The alcoholic member's drinking disrupts family functioning and is harmful to the well-being of family members, but family members may contribute to the alcoholic member's drinking. Recognition of the reciprocal influence between the alcoholic and other members of the family system is growing. Use of family therapy where the nonalcoholic family members undergo therapy with the alcoholic member is growing and offers a promising approach.

Most treatment methods probably work for some alcoholics, but no single method seems to be effective for every alcoholic. Alcoholics vary in their psychological and sociological backgrounds, factors that may determine which treatment method, type of therapist, or amount of treatment will be most effective. Miller (1990) rejected the myth that "everything works about equally well" as well as the myth that "there is one superior treatment." It is important that we eventually identify the type of alcoholic that each technique can help in the hope that we can match each alcoholic to the appropriate treatment.

References

Ackerman, N. (1958). *The psychodynamics of family life*. New York: Basic Books.

Armor, D. J., Polich, J. M., & Stambul, H. B. (1978). *Alcoholism and treatment*. New York: Wiley.

Babor, T. F., Kranzler, H. R., & Lauerman, R. J. (1989). Early detection of harmful alcohol consumption: Comparison of clinical, laboratory, and self-report screening procedures. *Addictive Behaviors, 14,* 139–157.

Baekeland, F., & Lundwall, L. (1975). Dropping out of treatment: A critical review. *Psychological Bulletin, 82,* 738–783.

Bandura, A. (1977). *Social learning theory*. Englewood Cliffs, NJ: Prentice-Hall.

Boffey, P. M. (1982, June 28). *Alcoholism study under new attack*. New York Times, p. A12.

Bowen, M. (1971). Family therapy and family group therapy. In H. Haplan & B. Sadock (Eds.), *Comprehensive group psychotherapy*. New York: Williams and Wilkins.

Bowen, M. (1978). Alcoholism and the family. In M. Bowen (Ed.), *Family therapy in clinical practice*. New York: Jason Aronson.

Cannon, D. S., Baker, T. B., & Wehl, C. K. (1981). Emetic and electric shock alcohol aversion therapy: Six- and twelve-month follow-up. *Journal of Consulting and Clinical Psychology, 49,* 360–368.

Chaney, E., O'Leary, M., & Marlatt, G. A. (1978). Skill training with alcoholics. *Journal of Consulting and Clinical Psychology, 46,* 1092–1104.

Chapman, P.L.H., & Huygens, I. (1988). An evaluation of three treatment programmes for alcoholism: An experimental study with 6- and 18-month follow-ups. *British Journal of Addiction, 83,* 67–81.

Davies, D. L. (1962). Normal drinking in recovered alcohol addicts. *Quarterly Journal of Studies on Alcohol, 23,* 94–104.

Dickens, B. M., Doob, A. N., Warwick, O. H., & Winegard, W. C. (1982). *Report of the committee of enquiry into allegations concerning Drs. Linda and Mark Sobell*. Toronto, Canada: Addiction Research Foundation.

Elal-Lawrence, G., Slade, P. D., & Dewey, M. E. (1986). Predictors of outcome type in treated problem drinkers. *Journal of Studies on Alcohol, 47,* 41–47.

Elkins, R. L. (1991). An appraisal of chemical aversion (emetic therapy) approaches to alcoholism treatment. *Behaviour Research and Therapy, 29,* 387–418.

Ellis, A., McInerney, J. F., DiGiuseppe, R., & Yeager, R. J. (1988). *Rational-emotive therapy with alcoholics and substance abusers.* New York: Pergamon Press.

Emrick, C. D., & Hansen, J. (1983). Assertions regarding effectiveness of treatment for alcoholism: Fact or fantasy? *American Psychologist, 38,* 1078–1088.

Finney, J. W., & Moos, R. H. (1986). Matching patients with treatments: Conceptual and methodological issues. *Journal of Studies on Alcohol, 47,* 122–134.

Finney, J. W., & Moos, R. H. (1991). The long-term course of treated alcoholism: I. Mortality, relapse and remission rates and comparisons with community controls. *Journal of Studies on Alcohol, 52,* 44–54.

Finney, J. W., & Moos, R. H. (1992). The long-term course of treated alcoholism: II. Predictors and correlates of 10-year functioning and mortality. *Journal of Studies on Alcohol, 53,* 142–153.

Foy, D. W., Nunn, L. B., & Rychtarik, R. G. (1984). Broad-spectrum behavioral treatment for chronic alcoholics: Effect of training controlled drinking skills. *Journal of Consulting and Clinical Psychology, 52,* 218–230.

Freud, S. (1905). Three essays on the theory of sexuality. In J. Strachey (Ed. and Trans.), *The complete psychological works.* New York: Norton.

Helzer, J. E., Robins, L. E., & Taylor, J. R. (1986). Moderate drinking in ex-alcoholics: Recent studies. *Journal of Studies on Alcohol, 47,* 115–120.

Institute of Medicine. (1990). *Broadening the base of treatment for alcohol problems.* Washington, DC: National Academy Press.

Jellinek, E. M. (1943). Benjamin Rush's "An inquiry into the effects of ardent spirits upon the human body and mind, with an account of the means of preventing and of the remedies for curing them. *Quarterly Journal of Studies on Alcohol, 4,* 321–341.

Jellinek, E. M. (1960). *The disease conception of alcoholism.* New Brunswick, NJ: Hillhouse Press.

Kadden, R. M., Getter, H., Cooney, N. L., & Litt, M. D. (1989). Matching alcoholics to coping skills or interactional therapies: Posttreatment results. *Journal of Consulting and Clinical Psychology, 57,* 698–704.

Kaufman, E. (1985). Family therapy in the treatment of alcoholism. In T. E. Bratter & G. G. Forrest (Eds.), *Alcoholism and substance abuse: Strategies for clinical intervention* (pp. 376–397). New York: Free Press.

Knupner, G. (1972). Ex-problem drinkers. In M. Roff, L. Robins, & M. Pollack (Eds.), *Life history research in psychopathology* (pp. 256–280). Minneapolis, MN: University of Minnesota Press.

Lemere, F., & Voegtlin, W. (1950). An evaluation of the aversion treatment of alcoholism. *Quarterly Journal of Studies of Alcohol, 11,* 199–204.

Lovibond, S., & Caddy, G. (1970). Discriminated aversive control in the moderation of alcoholics' drinking behaviour. *Behavior Therapy, 1,* 437–444.

Ludwig, A. M. (1986). Pavlov's "bells" and alcohol craving. *Addictive Behaviors, 11,* 87–91.

Maisto, S. A., & Carey, K. B. (1987). Treatment of alcohol abuse. In T. D. Nirenberg & S. A. Maisto (Eds.), *Developments in the assessment and treatment of addictive behaviors* (pp. 173–212). Norwood, NJ: Ablex.

Marlatt, G. A. (1983). The controlled-drinking controversy: A commentary. *American Psychologist, 38,* 1097–1110.

Mattson, M. E., & Allen, J. P. (1991). Research on matching alcoholic patients to treatments: Findings, issues, and implications. *Journal of Addictive Diseases, 11,* 33–49.

McCrady, B. S. (1987). Implications of neuropsychological research findings for the treatment and rehabilitation of alcoholics. In O. A. Parsons, N. Butter, & P. E. Nathan (Eds.), *Neuropsychology of alcoholism: Implications for diagnosis and treament* (pp. 381–391). New York: Guilford Press.

McCrady, B. S. (1989). Outcomes of family-involved alcoholism treatment. In M. Galanter (Ed.), *Recent developments in alcoholism* (pp. 165–182). New York: Plenum Press.

McCrady, B. S. (1992). Behavioral treatment of the alcoholic marriage. In E. Kaufman & P. Kaufmann (Eds.), *Family therapy of drug and alcohol abuse* (pp. 190–210). Boston: Allyn Bacon.

McCrady, B. S., Moreau, J., Paolino, T. J., Jr., & Longabaugh, R. L. (1982). Joint hospitalization and couples therapy for alcoholism: A four-year follow-up. *Journal of Studies on Alcohol, 43,* 1244–1250.

McCrady, B. S., Paolino, T. J., Jr., Longabaugh, R. L., & Rossi, J. (1979). Effects of joint hospital admission and couples treatment for hospitalized alcoholics: A pilot study. *Addictive Behaviors, 4,* 155–165.

McLellan, A. T., Luborsky, L., Woody, G. E., O'Brien, C. P., & Druley, K. A. (1983). Predicting response to alcohol and drug abuse treatments. *Archives of General Psychiatry, 40,* 620–625.

Miller, W. (1983). Controlled drinking: A history and a critical review. *Journal of Studies on Alcohol, 44,* 68–82.

Miller, W. R. (1985). Motivation for treatment: A review with special emphasis on alcoholism. *Psychological Bulletin, 98,* 84–107.

Miller, W. R. (1990). Alcohol treatment alternatives: What works? In H. B. Milkman & L. I. Sederer (Eds.), *Treatment choices for alcoholism and substance abuse.* Lexington, MA: Lexington.

Miller, W. R., & Hester, R. K. (1986a). Inpatient alcoholism treatment: Who benefits? *American Psychologist, 41,* 794–805.

Miller, W. R., & Hester, R. K. (1986b). The effectiveness of alcoholism treatment: What research reveals. In W. R. Miller & N. Heather (Eds.), *The addictive behaviors: Processes of change* (pp. 121–174). New York: Plenum.

Miller, W. R., & Hester, R. K. (1986c). Matching problem drinkers with optimal treatments. In W. R. Miller & N. Heather (Eds.), *The addictive behaviors: Processes of change* (pp. 175–203). New York: Plenum.

Miller, W. R., Leckman, A. L., Delaney, H. D., & Tinkcom, M. (1992). Long-term follow-up of behavioral self-control training. *Journal of Studies on Alcohol, 53,* 249–261.

Miller, W. R., & Taylor, C. A. (1980). Relative effectiveness of bibliotherapy, individual and group self-control training in the treatment of problem drinkers. *Addictive Behaviors, 15,* 13–24.

Moos, R. H., Finney, J. W., & Chan, A. D. (1981). The process of recovery from alcoholism: I. Comparing alcoholic patients and matched community controls. *Journal of Studies on Alcohol, 42,* 383–402.

Moos, R., Finney, J., & Gamble, W. (1982). The process of recovery from alcoholism: II. Comparing spouses of alcoholic patients and matched community controls. *Journal of Studies on Alcohol, 43,* 888–909.

Nathan, P. E. (1984). Alcohol prevention in the workplace. In P. M. Miller & T. D. Nirenberg (Eds.), *Prevention of alcohol abuse* (pp. 387–406). New York: Plenum.

Nathan, P. E. (1989). Treatment outcomes for alcoholism in the U.S.: Current research. In T. Lorberg, W. R. Miller, P. E. Nathan, & G. A. Marlatt (Eds.), *Addictive behaviors: Prevention and early intervention* (pp. 87–101). Amsterdam: Swets & Zeitlinger.

Nathan, P. E. (1992). Peele hasn't done his homework—again: A response to "Alcoholism politics, and bureaucracy: The consensus against controlled-drinking therapy in America." *Addictive Behaviors, 17,* 63–65.

Nathan, P. E., Lowenstein, L. M., Solomon, P., & Rossi, A. M. (1970). Behavioral analysis of chronic alcoholism. *Archives of General Psychiatry, 22,* 419–430.

Nordstrom, G., & Berglund, M. (1987). A prospective study of successful long-term adjustment in alcohol dependence: Social drinking vs. abstinence. *Journal of Studies on Alcohol, 48,* 95–103.

Orford, J., & Edwards, G. (1977). *Alcoholism: A comparison of treatment and advice, with a study of the influence of marriage.* Oxford: Oxford University Press.

Orford, J., & Keddie, A. (1986). Abstinence or controlled drinking: A test of the dependence and persuasion hypotheses. *British Journal of Addiction, 81,* 495–504.

Pavlov, I. P. (1927). *Conditioned reflexes.* London: Oxford University Press.

Peele, S. (1992). Alcoholism, politics, and bureaucracy: The consensus against controlled-drinking therapy in America. *Addictive Behaviors, 17,* 49–62.

Pendery, M., Maltzman, I., & West, J. (1982). Controlled drinking by alcoholics? New findings and a reevaluation of a major affirmative study. *Science, 217,* 169–175.

Polich, J. M., Armor, D. J., & Braiker, H. B. (1981). *The course of alcoholism: Four years after treatment.* New York: Wiley.

Pomerleau, O., Pertschuk, M., Adkins, D., & Brady, J. P. (1978). A comparison of behavioral and traditional treatment for middle-income problem drinkers. *Journal of Behavioral Medicine, 1,* 187–200.

Powell, B. J., Penick, E. C., Read, M. R., & Ludwig, A. M. (1985). Comparison of three outpatient treatment interventions: A twelve-month follow-up of men alcoholics. *Journal of Studies on Alcohol, 46,* 309–312.

Rachman, S., & Teasdale, J. (1969). *Aversion therapy: Appraisal and status.* Coral Gables, FL: University of Miami Press.

Roizen, R. (1987). The great controlled-drinking controversy. In M. Galanter (Ed.), *Recent developments in alcoholism* (pp. 245–279). New York: Plenum Press.

Rychtarik, R. G., Foy, D. W., Scott, T., Lokey, L., & Prue, D. M. (1987). Five–six year follow-up of broad-spectrum behavioral treatment for alcoholism: Effects of training controlled drinking skills. *Journal of Consulting and Clinical Psychology, 55,* 106–108.

Sanchez-Craig, M., Leigh, G., Spivak, K., & Lei, H. (1989). Superior outcome of females over males after brief treatment for reduction of heavy drinking. *British Journal of Addiction, 84,* 395–404.

Selzer, M. L. (1971). The Michigan Alcoholism Screening Test: The quest for a new diagnostic instrument. *American Journal of Psychiatry, 127,* 1653–1658.

Skinner, B. F. (1938). *The behavior of organisms.* New York: Appleton-Century-Crofts.

Smart, R. G. (1978). Do some alcoholics do better in some types of treatment than others? *Drug and Alcohol Dependence, 3,* 65–75.

Sobell, M. B., & Sobell, L. C. (1973). Individualized behavior therapy for alcoholics. *Behavior Therapy, 4,* 49–72.

Sobell, L. C., Sobell, M. B., & Toneatto, T. (1991). Recovery from alcohol problems without treatment. In N. Heather, W. R. Miller, & J. Greeley (Eds.), *Self-control and addictive behaviors* (pp. 198–242). New York: Pergamon Press.

Thomas, J. C. (1989). An overview of marital and family treatments with substance abusing populations. *Alcoholism Treatment Quarterly, 6,* 91–102.

Thorndike, E. L. (1911). *Animal intelligence.* New York: Macmillan.

Tuchfield, B. S. (1981). Spontaneous remission in alcoholics: Empirical observations and theoretical implications. *Journal of Studies on Alcohol, 42,* 626–640.

Walker, R. D., Donovan, D. M., Kivlahan, D. R., & O'Leary, M. R. (1983). Length of stay, neuropsychological performance, and aftercare: Influence on alcohol treatment outcome. *Journal of Consulting and Clinical Psychology, 51,* 900–911.

Wallace, J. (1985). Critical issues in alcoholism therapy. In S. Zimberg, J. Wallace, & S. B. Blume (Eds.), *Practical approaches to alcoholism psychotherapy* (pp. 37–49). New York: Plenum.

Welte, J., Hynes, G., Sokolov, L., & Lyons, J. P. (1981a). Effect of length of stay in inpatient alcoholism treatment on outcome. *Journal of Studies on Alcohol, 42,* 483–491.

Welte, J., Hynes, G., Sokolov, L., & Lyons, J. P., (1981b). Comparison of clients completing inpatient alcoholism treatment with clients who left prematurely. *Alcoholism: Clinical and Experimental Research, 5,* 393–399.

Wiens, A. N., & Menustik, C. E. (1983). Treatment outcome and patient characteristics in an aversion therapy program for alcoholism. *American Psychologist, 38,* 1089–1096.

Wilson, G. T. (1987). Chemical aversion conditioning as a treatment for alcoholism: A re-analysis. *Behavior Research and Therapy, 25,* 503–515.

THIRTEEN

Relapse and Alcoholism Treatment

One of the most frustrating and frequent obstacles to successful treatment and recovery is the high likelihood of relapse, not only among alcoholics but for individuals suffering from any addictive behavior. Following treatment that produces abstinence or even reduced drinking, alcoholics may eventually suffer "cravings" for a drink, insidious experiences in which temptation is strong. The argument often made both by the alcoholic and by those who cannot enjoy drinking when someone else is abstaining, is that "one drink can't hurt." The inability to cope with the temptations that frequently confront the treated patient jeopardizes the maintenance of recovery. Hunt and Matarazzo (1973) estimated that relapse rates of 50 to 90 percent occur for treatment programs within six months following treatment for a variety of addictions ranging from alcoholism to smoking to heroin use.

Brownell, Marlatt, Lichenstein, and Wilson (1986) maintained that little research has been done about the causes of relapse or the methods that can prevent relapse. Much evidence concerning relapse is based on clinical case histories and concentrates on *failures* to maintain abstinence. Evidence about the factors that precipitate or predict relapse is lacking. A "natural history" of relapse is needed, a study that would include the identification of processes underlying *successful resistance* as well as the analysis of factors involved in relapses or the failure to overcome temptation. This chapter examines theories of relapse and methods that have been developed to prevent its occurrence.

Lapse versus Relapse

Brownell et al. (1986) suggested that there is a need to distinguish between a "lapse," a single episode of a slip from sobriety, and a "relapse," a process entailing a series of lapses. Important questions about the relationship of lapses to relapse and recovery exist. The line between lapse and relapse is vague. Each lapse could be viewed as a step further along the path to the end of a cliff, culminating inevitably with a fall that could be regarded as the relapse. Expectations of failure might occur after a lapse so that an attitude of futility develops. This linear view is the prevalent conception of relapse, but Brownell et al. suggested that lapses could be viewed as a possibly beneficial factor, if the patient could learn or be taught what caused the slip and how it could be prevented.

A somewhat similar model proposed by DiClemente and Prochaska (1982) to deal with self-change in smoking can also be applied to other addictive behaviors such as drinking. They postulate that there is first a *precontemplation* stage when the drinker does not see any problem and feels that everything is under control. However, if problems start to develop, a process of self-change may begin. Hints and negative feedback from others, interpersonal conflict, poor school and work performance, and such may serve to raise consciousness to the possibility that the individual may have a drinking problem. During this *contemplation* stage, the drinker considers cutting back on her or his drinking to see if the situation improves. Next, there must be *commitment* and a decision to take action to reduce drinking. However, addictive habits are difficult to eliminate and considerable vigilance must be employed during *maintenance* to prevent a breakdown or *relapse*. If relapse is seen as failure, the individual may give up, but if it can be seen as a temporary setback and the individual can renew a commitment to overcome the undesired behavior, eventual control may be achieved. Thus, relapse is viewed as a circular rather than a linear process, and the possibility is recognized that lapses can be informative and instructive if they help the individual identify which factors and situations lead to lapses so that successful change can be achieved.

Causes of Relapse

The causes of relapse can be divided into individual or intrapsychic cues versus interpersonal and social-environmental cues. Individuals may differ in the extent to which different cues lead to craving, based on past drinking experience, biological factors, and coping skills. In other words, *reactivity* to cues that affect craving may differ across individuals, with it possibly being stronger for more addicted drinkers.

Retrospective Evidence

Evidence about the causes of relapse has come from both retrospective self-reports and laboratory studies. Negative emotional states have been found to precede relapse in many instances, according to retrospective self-reports from alcoholics (Marlatt, 1985a). Interviews with alcoholics were conducted by Ludwig (1986) to determine the nature of the Pavlovian "bells" that triggered their relapses. Only 11 of the 150 alcoholics interviewed could not identify any "bell," with 71 percent reporting one or two cues. Prominent among the cues were social situations and internal tensions. Also mentioned were external stressors, mealtimes, depression, music, and alcohol advertisements, as well as idiosyncratic cues such as reading in the bathtub or plowing the garden in the spring. It would appear, then, that a wide variety of internal and external cues are believed by alcoholics to trigger their drinking. However, caution is necessary because some of the answers might be excuses offered as attempts to justify their relapse—for example, the stress "made me do it."

Cummings, Gordon, and Marlatt (1980) studied self-reported causes of relapse in more than 300 individuals with a variety of addictions. Negative emotional states such as depression or anger were found in over 30 percent of cases, as shown in Table 13-1 from Marlatt (1985a). This factor accounts for over a third of the relapses not only among alcoholics but for smokers, gamblers, and overeaters as well; the percentage is somewhat lower for heroin addicts. Other major causes were interpersonal conflict and social pressure. An intriguing cause for some relapses was the tendency of a small percentage of abstainers to deliberately place themselves in risky situations in order to test their personal control or their willpower.

Vaillant (1988), in his prospective study of alcohol patients examined over a 12-year span, found that relapse was less likely if there was a substitute dependence, compulsory supervision, new relationships, or inspirational group member-

Table 13-1 Comparison of Relapse Factors for Different Addictive Behaviors

Relapse Situation	Alcoholics (n = 70)	Smokers (n = 64)	Heroin Addicts (n = 129)	Gamblers (n = 19)	Overeaters (n = 29)	Total (n = 311)
Intrapersonal determinants						
Negative emotional states	38%	37%	19%	47%	33%	35%
Negative physical states	3%	2%	9%	—	—	3%
Positive emotional states	—	6%	10%	—	3%	4%
Testing personal control	9%	—	2%	16%	—	5%
Urges and temptations	11%	5%	5%	16%	10%	9%
Total	61%	50%	45%	79%	46%	56%
Interpersonal determinants						
Interpersonal conflict	18%	15%	14%	16%	14%	16%
Social pressure	18%	32%	36%	5%	10%	20%
Positive emotional states	3%	3%	5%	—	28%	8%
Total	39%	50%	55%	21%	52%	44%

Source: from *Relapse Prevention: Maintenance Strategies in the Treatment of Addictive Behaviors* by G. A. Marlatt and J. R. Gordon. Copyright © 1985 by Guilford Press. Reprinted by permission

ship. In addition, the results showed that the individual's level of social competence prior to development of alcoholism, referred to as "premorbid social stability," was a better predictor of relapse than severity of addiction.

Thus, both exteroceptive cues such as physical setting associated with drinking and interoceptive cues such as emotional and physiological signals are implicated as triggers of relapse. The physical setting as well as ingestion, visual, olfactory, and gustatory cues could activate relapse. The physical presence of alcohol itself has also been found to be a cue by Mathew, Claghorn, and Largen (1979). In addition, social influences such as pressure and modeling have also been found to be associated with the urge to drink (Marlatt & Rohsenow, 1980).

Affective reactions may play a role, although different theories disagree as to whether it is the *negative* emotions as suggested by Wikler (1965) or the *positive* appetitional motives proposed by Stewart, deWit, and Eikelboom (1984) that are primarily involved. Positive affective states may activate craving in alcoholics (Marlatt, 1985b) but physiological factors such as the discomfort and pain experienced during withdrawal might also be potent conditions leading to relapse. However, Marlatt and Rohsenow (1980) did not find that the negative physical states experienced during withdrawal increased craving.

A problem with self-report evidence is that it can be biased by attempts to avoid looking bad. That is, someone who has experienced a slip might feel that stress and negative emotions are acceptable extenuating excuses as causes of lapses whereas the claim that the lapse was caused by the discomfort of tremors from not drinking might be seen as a sign of weakness and hence avoided. Furthermore, these states may overlap and be confused with each other by the alcoholic.

Laboratory Studies

Due to the potential self-justification bias and fallibility of memory with retrospective reporting, it is important to obtain direct evidence about the cues that lead to relapse among alcoholics. Researchers have employed controlled experiments to attempt to provide more objective evidence.

The balanced placebo design discussed in Chapter 4 (Marlatt, Demming, & Reid, 1973) has been used to isolate the role of expectancy of drinking alcohol as a factor in the craving to drink. More drinking occurs among alcoholics who are led to believe they have consumed alcohol, regardless of whether they actually did, demonstrating that alcohol consumption per se is not needed to create craving (Laberg, 1986; Stockwell, Hodgson, Rankin, & Taylor, 1982). Thus, psychological factors such as expectancies about beverage content are important factors in relapse.

Responsiveness to alcohol-related cues that trigger drinking may be stronger for alcoholics than for nonalcoholics. Monti et al. (1987) conducted a study in which alcoholics were exposed to alcohol but not allowed to drink. Using salivation as an index of cue reactivity, they presented alcoholics and nonalcoholics with the sight and smell of both their favorite brand of alcoholic beverage and a control beverage. The results showed that alcoholics salivated more to the alcoholic drink whereas there was no difference for the nonalcoholics. Both groups had stronger urges to drink the alcoholic beverage.

Cooney, Gillespie, Baker, and Kaplan (1987) found that alcoholics experienced more physical symptoms, lower confidence about being able to resist temptation, and more guilt than nonalcoholics after being allowed to hold and sniff but not drink their favorite alcoholic beverage. Both groups had an increased desire to drink and expected pleasurable consequences.

In conclusion, it appears that cue reactivity is greater for alcoholics than for controls and may play an important role in relapse following treatment. In the next section, several models are presented that suggest how these cues might trigger relapse.

Models of Relapse

Three models of relapse, the positive appetitional model, the compensatory response model, and the conditioned withdrawal model will be described. They are all based on the associationistic laws of classical conditioning, but differ in their view of what gets associated.

Conditioning Models

According to the classical conditioning paradigm developed by Pavlov (1927), a variety of stimuli that are originally neutral may come to acquire meaning or power to elicit responses that ordinarily occur only to other stimuli. Thus, the well-known experiments of Pavlov with laboratory dogs showed that salivation, which ordinarily occurs to the presentation of food, can become conditioned to occur to stimuli such as a light or tone that were previously neutral with respect to salivation. By pairing these stimuli frequently with the presentation of food, eventually salivation will occur when the previously neutral stimuli occur but in the absence of food.

In the case of alcohol, certain physiological and psychological reactions occur when it is consumed. If other stimuli such as the taste, smell, or visual cues associated with the alcohol occur alone later, there should be some partial activation of the responses that alcohol consumption itself elicits. Thus, these cues act as conditioned stimuli that produce conditioned responses such as craving, physiological arousal, and drug-seeking responses. The strength of the conditioned response is in proportion to factors such as the length of prior drinking, recency of past drinking, and the similarity between past drinking settings and the present one.

The Positive Appetitional Model. Stewart et al. (1984) proposed a model based on classical conditioning that emphasizes the *positive* incentive value of alcohol as a determinant of relapse. This model focuses on events that occur prior to the time when alcohol is consumed. The drinking of alcohol produces a positive affective state, one that is conditioned to other stimuli such as the sight and smell associated with drinking that later have the capacity to trigger subjective desire or craving for alcohol and evoke the motivation to ingest the substance again.

The Compensatory Response Model.   Although derived from the same Pavlovian paradigm, Siegel's (1983) model holds that conditioning involves responses that are *opposite* in direction from the original unconditioned responses, presumably to restore homeostasis. Alcohol intensifies physiological arousal, but this tendency is followed by the attempt of the nervous system to suppress arousal. This process may be one explanation for the phenomenon of *tolerance* discussed in Chapter 3 whereby increasingly larger doses are eventually needed to produce a level of arousal generated earlier by a smaller amount.

In line with the classical conditioning model, these neutralizing reactions may be assumed to occur whenever conditioned stimuli previously paired with the arousing states created by alcohol are encountered. Hence, a relapse into greater drinking may occur since this conditioned response weakens the arousing effects of drinking desired by the alcoholic.

McCusker and Brown (1990) tested the view that contextual cues associated with drinking also become conditioned to the opposite compensatory response activated when consuming alcohol, a response that may be labeled by the drinker as craving, leading to more drinking as tolerance to alcohol develops with repeated drinking in the same context. Four groups of ten male social drinkers were randomly formed. One group received alcohol in a barlike setting and another consumed alcohol in an unexpected place, an officelike setting. A third group was told they were receiving alcohol but received tonic in the bar setting and another control group had juice in the office setting. Impairments to cognitive and motor performance were greatest for the group receiving alcohol in the alcohol-unexpected setting because these cues were not associated with tolerance for alcohol. In contrast, the group receiving alcohol in the bar, an alcohol-expected context, was not impaired in comparison to the two controls, presumably because of tolerance to alcohol acquired from past experiences with alcohol in that type of setting. Similarly, craving, the desire for more drinks, was higher for both the groups with alcohol cues—the group receiving alcohol in the bar and the placebo group that expected to receive alcohol.

The Conditioned Withdrawal Model.   A model developed by Wikler (1973) focused on interoceptive cues such as unpleasant physiological reactions to the absence of alcohol. These cues are conditioned to external cues such as the room or physical setting where excessive drinking previously ended. Later these cues act as conditioned stimuli to activate conditioned withdrawal reactions and experiences of craving. Resumption of drug intake is one means of eliminating these aversive withdrawal responses. The resumption of drinking alleviates this conditioned withdrawal distress, but eventually relapse or loss of control over drinking may ensue.

Although these three different theories based on conditioning differ in many important respects and may seem contradictory, they all emphasize the role of *cue reactivity* as a factor that might lead to relapse following a period of abstinence. All three models focus on the role of classical conditioning but at different temporal points in the development of drinking. The positive appetitional model deals more with the situation prior to the actual consumption of alcohol, especially for relatively inexperienced drinkers, whereas the compensatory response model applies best to the point shortly after drinking has started to have a physiological effect. The conditioned withdrawal model seems to be more appropriate for the period after the alcohol's effect has worn off for individuals with substantial drinking experience who have developed alcohol tolerance and dependence.

The Social Learning Model

In contrast to the classical conditioning models where relapse is analyzed in terms of factors that may operate with low awareness or volition on the part of the drinker, the social learning model proposed by Bandura (1977) and Marlatt and Gordon (1985) places more emphasis on social factors such as the modeling of others and the individual's cognitive appraisal of the factors responsible for his or her drinking. Instead of viewing alcoholism as a disease over which the victim has no control, social learning theory views alcoholism, and other addictions, as a set of strong habits with undesirable consequences that can be offset by the conscious decision to acquire a new set of habits.

Thus, the social learning model is cognitive and focuses on the expectations held about self-efficacy, one's perceived ability to deal effectively with problems. As shown in Figure 13-1, the likelihood of a relapse can be viewed to be related to

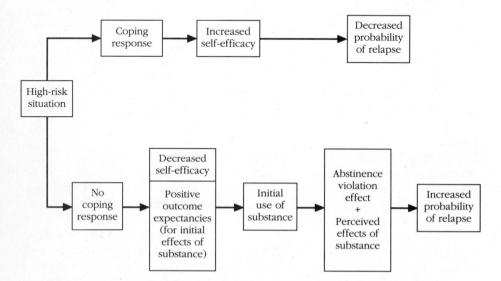

Figure 13-1 A cognitive behavioral model of relapse.
Source: from *Relapse Prevention: Maintenance Strategies in the Treatment of Addictive Behaviors* by G. A. Marlatt and J. R. Gordon. Copyright © 1985 by Guilford Press. Reprinted by permisson

whether or not a coping response enhances or reduces one's feelings of self-efficacy in a situation with high risk for relapse. Strong negative affect might lower personal feelings of self-efficacy in dealing with a problem and lead to the appraisal that alcohol would lower the negative affect. Positive expectations of disinhibition may also stimulate drinking. In theory, a person with adequate coping skills could handle such situations without alcohol even if he or she had previously used it for coping.

Social learning theory predicts that relapse can be minimized by methods that help the alcoholic develop coping skills, both cognitive and behavioral, to aid in resisting temptation. Furthermore, the social support and encouragement of significant others can help prevent relapse.

Marlatt (1978) proposed that a drinker who yields to temptation and returns to the use of alcohol creates an abstinence violation effect (AVE) whereby the realization of the lapse creates cognitive dissonance with the goal of abstinence. The AVE may increase negative affect such as guilt, lower feelings of self-efficacy, and lower attributions of internal control. The magnitude of the AVE is assumed to be a function of factors such as degree of prior commitment to abstinence, duration of the abstinence period, immediate subjective effect of the drug used, and attributions for the lapse.

Attributions are the causal explanations that people generate to account for outcomes (Weiner, 1985). These attributions can vary along several dimensions such as internal-external (self versus other), stable-unstable (constant versus variable), and global-specific (universal versus unique). Following an event such as a lapse where an offered drink is accepted, an alcoholic might try to explain what happened. An example of such an explanation might be: My drinking is due to my own weakness in self-control in refusing the offer (internal), I am always weak when offered a drink (stable), and I am weak in all situations when alcohol is offered (global). Different types of attributions hold different consequences. Internal, stable, and global attributions for an AVE, as in this example, will lead to more negative affect, including conflict and guilt. The larger the AVE, the greater the chances of relapse, if the individual regards alcohol to be an effective method of alleviating these feelings.

Overview of the Relapse Process

Niaura et al. (1988) proposed a model of what happens after a lapse occurs and the likelihood of a relapse that incorporates many of the factors proposed by conditioning as well as social learning models. As diagrammed in Figure 13-2, a complex interplay of cognitive/affective, physiological, and behavioral factors might influence the eventual consequences of a return to drinking by an alcoholic.

First, a combination of contextual or environmental cues in conjunction with affective states, both positive and negative, determine the arousal of urges to drink, physiological activation, and expectations about the effect of a drink. These effects can loop back and alter the initial affective states. Thus, at a party where everyone else is drinking, the craving to drink while thinking about a good time from

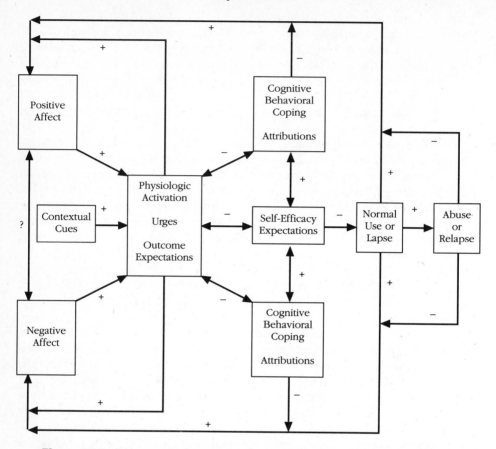

Figure 13-2 Diagram of a dynamic regulatory feedback system linking constructs related to relapse. (Unidirectional arrows indicate direction of influence. Positive/ negative signs indicate whether influence is excitatory or inhibitory. Bidirectional arrows indicate reciprocal interdependence.)

Source: from "Relevance of Cue Reactivity to Understanding Alcohol and Smoking Relapse," by R. S. Niaura, D. J. Rohsenow, J. A. Binkoff, P. M. Monti, M. Pedraza, and D. B. Abrams in the *Journal of Abnormal Psychology,* 1988, *97,* 133–152. Copyright 1988 by the American Psychological Association. Reprinted by permission.

drinking and experiencing physiological arousal might promote positive affective feelings, whereas craving a drink while alone at home and thinking about feeling sick and expecting guilt due to drinking might activate more negative affective states.

At the next stage of the process illustrated in Figure 13-2, feelings of self-efficacy will be activated. Does the person feel that he or she can control the situation or does he or she feel that it is hopeless? Individuals will have different levels or types of cognitive and behavioral coping responses for dealing with such situations. They may also make attributions about the causes of their behavior and urges. These different factors influence each other, as suggested by the bidirectional arrows in the diagram between these components. Thus, urges to drink can lower one's feelings of self-control; conversely, feeling self-control may be associated with a reduction of urges. Similarly, the availability of good coping skills for dealing with a situation where drinking urges are high can reduce those urges and physiological arousal, but the presence of compelling urges might weaken availability or use of these coping skills.

Depending on whether the urges to drink or the inhibitory coping and attributional responses prevail, the outcome will be a lapse, normal use, or nonuse of alcohol. Lapses may, depending on the types of attributions made about the lapse and the effects of the alcohol itself on the affective consequences, eventuate in further lapses and total relapse. If the drinker concludes that the causes of the lapse are internal, stable, and global and/or the alcohol diminishes negative affect, the chances of further deterioration are strong. Conversely, if the lapse is attributed to external, unstable, and specific factors and/or the drink has little influence on the affective state, the lapse may be an isolated event.

Treatment and Prevention of Relapse

Traditionally, as represented by Alcoholics Anonymous, recovery is never assumed to be complete but is a day-to-day lifelong process of abstinence from alcohol. Hence, there is the well-known AA philosophy of "one day at a time." Hospital and clinic treatment programs, partly due to their expense, are considerably shorter in duration than the self-help support of AA but do recognize the need for periodic "booster shots." Indeed, most formal programs operated by professionals add AA as a posttreatment supplement.

Social learning theory, however, holds an opposing view to that of AA about abstinence. AA's requirement of abstinence may increase the sense of failure when a lapse occurs, according to social learning theory, and make relapse more likely to follow lapses. Bandura (1977) emphasized the need for alcoholics to gain a sense of self-efficacy, the feeling that one can control outcomes, in order to deal effectively with the urges to drink. For example, learning how to cope with stress without drinking or learning social skills to know how to refuse a drink could help increase this self-efficacy.

Social learning theorists (Marlatt & Gordon, 1985) believe that AA's view of alcoholics as weak and powerless victims will ironically increase the likelihood of relapse because alcoholics will come to believe that after a single slip, they will suffer a full-blown relapse. Thus, the goal of abstinence offers no margin for error and is equivalent to being "out after only one strike." Such expectations may then become self-fulfilling prophecies for any unfortunate alcoholics who have a slip that will escalate into further drinking.

It would appear that the goal of abstinence, *if successfully achieved,* cannot be faulted, by definition. In that sense, AA is undeniably correct. The problem is what will happen if a lapse or slip occurs. Is the alcoholic more likely to experience a total relapse when moderate drinking or abstinence is the goal? Given that most alcoholics experience some slips during recovery, this issue is important, but thus far the evidence is unclear on this question.

Chapter Thirteen

Motivation and Commitment

Effective relapse prevention strategies might vary with the stage of recovery, according to Brownell et al. (1986). At the outset or first stage, developing motivation and obtaining commitment should be the primary goal. Use of contracts involving contingencies of monetary rewards for sobriety have been tried widely but may work only for a self-selected sample since others may drop out or not even participate.

Screening, a strategy to deliberately choose for admission to treatment those alcoholics who seem more motivated or more likely to succeed, is an approach that might seem to abandon the more difficult cases. While this approach may seem to load the deck in favor of a treatment program, one argument in its behalf is that no one is doing a favor to alcoholics who are highly likely to fail the program by trying to treat them. They may only become further demoralized, even to the point of not accepting other forms of treatment that might prove more palatable and effective for them. Failing patients may also adversely affect other patients who otherwise are more likely to succeed.

Initial Behavior Change

The second stage, where initial changes in behavior occur, has a low likelihood of relapse because the patient is still optimistic and motivated. Brownell et al. (1986) suggested that three important tasks are called for at this stage: decision making, cognitive restructuring, and coping skills. Decision making entails helping the patient identify the immediate as well as long-term positive and negative consequences of either controlled moderate drinking or abstinence versus relapse. Cognitive restructuring involves rational interpretation of attitudes and feelings. For example, instead of blaming a lapse on their own lack of willpower or character, they may be helped to see that the situation they were in involved too much social pressure. They might be taught to think of craving as a normal part of recovery that can be treated rather than as a sign of hopelessness. Marlatt and Gordon (1985) placed importance on the cognitive appraisal of the individual as a factor in whether or not a slip or lapse inevitably leads to relapse. They found more relapse among those persons who attributed their lapses to internal factors than among those who recognized the influence of external factors.

Cue extinction, whereby the environmental stimuli that trigger cravings for alcohol are weakened, may be beneficial at this stage. Extinction deals with the process by which prior conditioned responses are weakened or eliminated. According to this concept based on conditioning models, exposure to alcohol cues *in the absence of actual consumption of alcohol* will eventually weaken drinking urges as the associations lose their strength. This process is known as *covert sensitization*. In addition, since expectancies also have been shown to activate craving, Laberg (1990) suggested that cognitive factors affect reactions to alcohol cues.

Laberg and Ellertson (1987) tested the notion that prolonged exposure to alcohol with prevention of consumption would reduce craving. Sixteen detoxified alcoholics received either a small priming dose of alcohol or a soft drink. The prime was expected to act like a conditioned stimulus. Then they were presented with bottles of either alcohol or a soft drink. A total of six sessions were used. Measures of arousal such as skin conductance and heart rate as well as self-rated arousal were obtained before and after priming. The results showed increased arousal and craving only if subjects had been primed with alcohol before exposure to additional alcohol. Merely being exposed to the sight of alcoholic beverages did not increase arousal. Moreover, these reactions to exposure to alcohol cues decreased over the six successive sessions of cue exposure, indicating that extinction was occurring.

On the other hand, given that the sight and smell of an alcoholic drink are powerful cues that activate craving among alcoholics, there is also the danger that cue exposure to alcohol could backfire and increase the likelihood of relapse. Baker, Cooney, and Pomerleau (1987), cognizant of this danger, pointed out that they take care to explain thoroughly to their patients why they are being exposed to the sight of alcoholic beverages and caution them not to engage in such activities on their own, such as by visiting bars, without supervision. Laberg (1990) also defended the use of cue exposure in treating alcoholics, because it is unrealistic to expect alcoholics to leave the treatment facility and not be exposed to innumerable alcohol cues in their environment, which might induce craving and relapse. By exposing alcoholics to alcohol cues in a treatment setting where they are prevented from consuming the alcohol, alcoholics can be taught coping techniques to deal with such cues when they are discharged. In addition, the cues should become weakened through extinction. Although preliminary studies have shown promising results, Niaura et al. (1988) concluded that more work needs to be conducted on this issue.

Coping skills are needed for dealing with craving in situations where alcoholics are at high risk for relapse. Being able to refuse a drink in a social setting where there is high pressure to be a part of the group, for example, is much more difficult than is implied in the "Just say no" slogan popularized by Nancy Reagan but could be an important social skill for preventing lapses.

Shiffman (1987) argued that such coping is critical for resisting temptation. In his formulation, coping involves doing "something" as opposed to doing "nothing," but it need not involve complex reasoning or problem-solving skills. Cognitive forms of coping could entail distraction, thoughts involving delay, or thinking about the positive benefits of not drinking and the negative consequences of drinking. Behavioral forms of coping include eating, physical activity, escape, delaying action, and relaxation.

Litman, Eiser, Rawson, and Oppenheim (1984) examined coping responses of 256 alcoholics in relation to their relapse at 6 to 12 months following inpatient treatment. Four types of responses were identified; positive thinking, negative thinking, avoidance/distraction, and seeking social supports. Scores on these behaviors did not differentiate eventual relapsers and nonrelapsers at intake. However, at 6 to 12 months after treatment, positive thinking and avoidance/distraction were associated with nonrelapse.

Clinical observations (Ludwig, 1988) concur that alcoholics use a variety of ways of "self-talk" or sobriety scripts to avoid relapse. A few examples from Ludwig will illustrate how alcoholics cope.

The negative-consequences script:

I see my wife and what my drinking did to her. And my son—what it is still doing to him.

Every time I get the urge to drink, I immediately think of being sick, vomiting, shakes, being miserable.

The benefits-of-sobriety script:

I'm a damn fool to take a drink, so I'm not going to take the chance, for the simple reason that I've got too much at stake. I've got a new home now, I've got a wife and family, three partners and a going concern—and one drink stands between me and all that.

The rationality script:

I can stay sober if I want to. It's my decision. A man has a responsibility, and he's got to face it. A man has some kind of control over everything.

The avoid-the-first-drink script:

If I don't drink today, tomorrow will take care of itself. I'm really an alcoholic and I can't handle it. One drink is all it takes.

The prayer script:

Dear God, please don't let me get crazy and continue drinking. The wine on the grocery shelf said, "Man, you want me—you'd better buy me. You can really feel good on me." I prayed, "God, I'm really miserable. You've got to get me through this."

A controlled study by Chaney, O'Leary, and Marlatt (1978) examined the value of a training program designed to provide alcoholics with practice in coping with hypothetical situations assumed to hold high risk for relapse. They assigned 45 middle-aged male alcoholics at random to three different groups—one with skill training aimed at providing alternatives to drinking in situations with high risk for relapse, accompanied by therapist modeling and feedback; a discussion control group, which only talked about the high-risk situations; and a no-training control group, which received the regular hospital treatment program. A year later the skill-training group was superior to the two control groups with respect to number of days drunk, number of drinking days, or amount of alcohol consumed. The two control groups did not differ from each other.

Annis and Davis (1988; 1991) developed a relapse prevention program that focused on creating a sense of self-efficacy in problem drinkers so that they could handle real-life situations where they might be likely to relapse. In treatment, the therapist identifies each client's coping skills and environmental resources for dealing with these problematic situations to help design homework assignments that will serve as the basis for building this self-confidence.

Since problem drinkers differ in the situations where they are more suscepti-ble to drinking, a hierarchy of drinking situations according to the degree of high risk for relapse is first identified for each client. The Inventory of Drinking Situations identifies eight major types of drinking situations: unpleasant emotions, pleasant emotions, physical discomfort, testing personal control, urges/temptations to drink, conflict with others, social pressure to drink, and pleasant times with others.

Annis and Davis had clients do a set of homework exercises starting with situations that had the lowest risk for drinking. As the clients developed a sense of self-efficacy following their success in facing situations lower in the hierarchy they gradually moved up to riskier situations. Homework assignments serve several important goals for clients: increasing awareness of triggering events for drinking, anticipating problem situations so that coping responses can be prepared, planning and rehearsing alternative ways of coping, practicing new behaviors in increasingly more difficult situations, and noticing improved competency.

Studies (Solomon & Annis, 1989) evaluating the relationship between self-efficacy of treatment outcomes have shown that successful abstinence up to 3–6 months after treatment is associated with higher self-efficacy ratings. Rychtarik, Prue, Rapp, and King (1992) measured self-efficacy in male alcoholics at intake for treatment, at discharge, and several times over the next year. Self-efficacy increased over the course of treatment. Those who had lower gains were more likely to relapse during the year after discharge.

It is important not to overlook the role of treatment staff. While it may be obvious that encouragement and support of counselors help recovery, it should also be recognized that anger, hostility, and indifference to clients who have a slip may contribute to relapse (Daley, 1989).

Maintenance

Beyond the initial two stages, sobriety must be maintained on a long-term basis, requiring continued monitoring, social support, and general lifestyle changes. Brownell et al. (1986) recognized their recommendations were limited by the paucity of research on factors affecting successful long-term maintenance. Monitoring can be done by the patient or by professionals, although in the latter instance the line between the end of treatment and the beginning of maintenance becomes blurred.

Social support is helpful for most individuals, although the source of the support may be a critical factor in its effectiveness. Lifestyle changes that allow other forms of gratification to replace the addiction may be helpful. Brownell et al. also suggested alternatives such as exercise, meditation, and relaxation training as aids against relapse.

Easing Reentry

A treated alcoholic moving from a hospital setting back into society might find an easier adjustment and lower likelihood of relapse if the reentry were gradual. Starting in the 1950s, alcoholism halfway houses were introduced as a means of providing a small, homelike environment in which residents could live for about three to six months following hospital treatment while developing self-sufficiency before returning to the community. Halfway house programs generally deal with alcoholics who are chronic abusers and have no homes or jobs to return to, so that conclusions about their value may not apply to all alcoholics.

A controlled study of the effectiveness of such facilities was conducted by Sanchez-Craig and Walker (1982). They compared male and female alcoholics in halfway houses with other groups of alcoholics provided with either covert sensitization or discussion. Although relapse was not the specific focus of the study, the researchers found evidence implying the risk of relapse might be comparable for all groups, because they all scored poorly on a number of drinking and nondrinking outcomes 6, 12, and 18 months following treatment. However, Intaglia (1978) found a better success rate for halfway house programs that involved training in coping skills designed to curtail relapse rates.

Conclusions

The battle for recovery from alcoholism does not end, unfortunately, when a treatment program is concluded with the discharge of the patient. As with other addictive behaviors, relapse occurs all too frequently. Some efforts to reduce relapse involve providing more intense, more complex, or longer treatment programs, as if a higher dose would be more likely to eliminate the problem permanently. However, Brownell et al. (1986) questioned this approach because it assumes erroneously that the cessation of drinking and the maintenance of sobriety are essentially equivalent outcomes. They suggested instead that the processes involved in the two stages may be different, with the long-term maintenance of sobriety requiring additional processes.

Retrospective self-reports have been the primary source of evidence about the factors precipitating relapse, but since relapse may be embarrassing and shameful, alcoholics may rationalize slips. The retrospective reports of many alcoholics that their relapses occurred because of negative emotions such as depression or anxiety may be examples of seeking sympathy or avoiding blame.

Conditioned stimuli for use of alcohol are ubiquitous and unavoidable in daily life; hence, they constitute a powerful force toward relapse. Since these subtle cues are often outside awareness, little direct action can be taken against them. The approach of social learning theory, with its emphasis on cognitive and behavioral coping, offers more hope. If alcoholics can be helped to identify circumstances entailing high risk for lapse, they may be more likely to avoid lapses by staying out of such situations. When they are unavoidably placed in such situations, the existence of coping skills and alternative behaviors may be helpful. In addition to efforts by the individual to avoid temptation to alcohol, it may be desirable to plan social environments that reduce pressures or opportunities to drink. Thus, the host of a party can create an atmosphere that minimizes the expectation or pressure to drink alcohol, such as by providing nonalcoholic alternative beverages to guests. Resistance to temptation may also be strengthened further by the attitudes and behaviors of significant others, who can provide social support and reinforcement to the recovering alcoholic.

References

Annis, H. M., & Davis, C. S. (1988). Assessment of expectancies in alcohol dependent clients. In D. M. Donovan & G. A. Marlatt (Eds.), *Assessment of addictive behaviors* (pp. 84–111). New York: Guilford Press.

Annis, H. M., & Davis, C. S. (1991). Relapse prevention. *Alcohol Health and Research World, 15,* 204–212.

Baker, L. H., Cooney, N. L., & Pomerleau, O. F. (1987). Craving for alcohol: Theoretical processes and treatment procedures. In W. M. Cox (Ed.), *Treatment and prevention of alcohol problems: A resource manual* (pp. 184–202). Orlando, FL: Academic Press.

Bandura, A. (1977). *Social learning theory.* Englewood Cliffs, NJ: Prentice-Hall.

Brownell, K., Marlatt, G. A., Lichenstein, E., & Wilson, G. T. (1986). Understanding and preventing relapse. *American Psychologist, 41,* 765–782.

Chaney, E., O'Leary, M., & Marlatt, G. A. (1978). Skill training with alcoholics. *Journal of Consulting and Clinical Psychology, 46,* 1092–1104.

Cooney, N. L., Gillespie, R. A., Baker, L. H., & Kaplan, R. F. (1987). Cognitive changes after alcohol cue exposure. *Journal of Consulting and Clinical Psychology, 55,* 150–155.

Cummings, C., Gordon, J. R., & Marlatt, G. A. (1980). Relapse: Prevention and prediction. In W. R. Miller (Ed.), *The addictive behaviors* (pp. 291–321). New York: Pergamon Press.

Daley, D. C. (1989). *Relapse prevention: Treatment alternatives and counseling aids.* Blue Ridge Summit, PA: Tab Books, Inc.

DiClemente, C. C., & Prochaska, J. O. (1982). Self-change and therapy change of smoking behavior: A comparison of processes in cessation and maintenance. *Addictive Behaviors, 7,* 133–144.

Hunt, W. A., & Matarazzo, J. E. (1973). Three years later: Recent developments in the experimental modification of smoking behavior. *Journal of Abnormal Psychology, 81,* 107–114.

Intaglia, J. (1978). Increasing the interpersonal problem-solving skills of an alcoholic population. *Journal of Consulting and Clinical Psychology, 46,* 489–498.

Laberg, J. C. (1986). Alcohol and expectancy: Subjective, psychophysiological and behavioral responses to alcohol stimuli in severely, moderately and non-dependent drinkers. *British Journal of Addiction, 81,* 797–808.

Laberg, J. C. (1990). What is presented, and what prevented, in cue exposure and response prevention with alcohol-dependent subjects. *Addictive Behaviors, 15,* 367–386.

Laberg, J. C., & Ellertson, B. (1987). Psychophysiological indicators of craving in alcoholics: Effects of cue exposure. *British Journal of Addiction, 82,* 1341–1348.

Litman, G., Eiser, J. R., Rawson, N.S.B., & Oppenheim, A. N. (1984). The relationship between coping behaviours, their effectiveness and alcoholism relapse and survival. *British Journal of Addiction, 79,* 281–293.

Ludwig, A. M. (1986). Pavlov's "bells" and alcohol craving. *Addictive Behaviors, 11,* 87–91.

Ludwig, A. M. (1988). *Understanding the alcoholic's mind: The nature of craving and how to control it.* New York: Oxford University Press.

Marlatt, G. A. (1978). Craving for alcohol, loss of control, and relapse: A cognitive-behavioral analysis. In P. E. Nathan, G. A. Marlatt, & T. Loberg (Eds.), *Alcoholism: New directions in behavioral research and treatment* (pp. 271–314). New York: Plenum Press.

Marlatt, G. A. (1985a). Relapse prevention: Theoretical rationale and overview of the model. In G. A. Marlatt & J. R. Gordon (Eds.), *Relapse prevention: Maintenance strategies in the treatment of addictive behaviors* (pp. 3–70). New York: Guilford Press.

Marlatt, G. A. (1985b). Cognitive assessment and intervention procedures for relapse preventions. In G. A. Marlatt & J. R. Gordon (Eds.), *Relapse prevention: Maintenance strategies in the treatment of addictive behaviors* (pp. 201–279). New York: Guilford Press.

Marlatt, G. A., Demming, B., & Reid, J. (1973). Loss of control drinking in alcoholics: An experimental analogue. *Journal of Abnormal Psychology, 81,* 233–241.

Marlatt, G. A., & Gordon, J. R. (Eds.). (1985). *Relapse prevention: Maintenance strategies in the treatment of addictive behaviors.* New York: Guilford Press.

Marlatt, G. A., & Rohsenow, D. J. (1980). Cognitive processes in alcohol use: Expectancy and the balanced placebo design. In N. K. Mello (Ed.), *Advances in substance abuse: Behavioral and biological research* (pp. 159–199). Greenwich, CT: JAI Press.

Mathew, R. J., Claghorn, J. L., & Largen, J. (1979). Craving for alcohol in sober alcoholics. *American Journal of Psychiatry, 136,* 603–606.

McCusker, C. G., & Brown, K. (1990). Alcohol-predictive cues enhance tolerance to and precipitate "craving" for alcohol in social drinkers. *Journal of Studies on Alcohol, 51,* 494–499.

Monti, P. M., Binkoff, J. A., Abrams, D. B., Zwick, W. R., Nirenberg, T. D., & Liepman, M., R. (1987). Reactivity of alcoholics and nonalcoholics to drinking cues. *Journal of Abnormal Psychology, 96,* 1–5.

Niaura, R. S., Rohsenow, D. J., Binkoff, J. A., Monti, P. M., Pedraza, M., & Abrams, D. B. (1988). Relevance of cue reactivity to understanding alcohol and smoking relapse. *Journal of Abnormal Psychology, 97,* 133–152.

Pavlov, I. P. (1927). *Conditioned reflexes.* London: Oxford University Press.

Prochaska, J. O., & Clemente, C. C. (1982). Transtheoretical therapy: Toward a more integrative model of change. *Psychotherapy: Theory, Research, and Practice, 19,* 276–288.

Rychtarik, R. G., Prue, D. M., Rapp, S. R., & King, A. C. (1992). Self-efficacy, aftercare and relapse in a treatment program for alcoholics. *Journal of Studies on Alcohol, 53,* 435–440.

Sanchez-Craig, M., & Walker, K. (1982). Teaching coping skills to chronic alcoholics in a coeducational halfway house: I. Assessment of programme effects. *British Journal of Addiction, 77,* 35–50.

Shiffman, S. (1987). Maintenance and relapse: Coping with temptation. In T. D. Nirenberg & S. A. Maisto (Eds.), *Developments in the assessment and treatment of addictive behaviors* (pp. 353–385). Norwood, NJ: Ablex.

Siegel, S. (1983). Classical conditioning, drug tolerance, and drug dependence. In Y. Isreal, F. B. Glaser, H, Kalant, R. E. Popham, W. Schmidt, & R. G. Smart (Eds.), *Research advances in alcohol and drug problems* (pp. 207–246). New York: Plenum Press.

Solomon, K. E., & Annis, H. M. (1989). Development of a scale to measure outcome expectancy in alcoholics. *Cognitive Therapy and Research, 13,* 409–421.

Stewart, J., deWit, H., & Eikelboom, R. (1984). The role of unconditioned and conditioned drug effects in the self-administration of opiates and stimulants. *Psychological Review, 91,* 251–268.

Stockwell, T. R., Hodgson, R. J., Rankin, H. J., & Taylor, C. (1982). Alcohol dependence, beliefs, and the priming effect. *Behavior Research and Therapy, 20,* 513–522.

Vaillant, G. E. (1988). What can long-term follow-up teach us about relapse and prevention of relapse in addiction? *British Journal of Addiction, 83,* 1147–1157.

Weiner, B. (1985). An attributional analysis of achievement motivation and emotion. *Psychological Review, 92,* 548–573.

Wikler, A. (1965). *Conditioning factors in opiate addiction and relapse.* New York: McGraw-Hill.

Wikler, A. (1973). Dynamics of drug dependence. *Archives of General Psychiatry, 28,* 611–616.

FOURTEEN

Alcohol Use and Abuse among Women

Alcoholism research has focused on the male population in the past, perhaps because alcohol use and abuse have traditionally been more prevalent among men. Males drink more and have more alcohol-related symptoms than females (Malin, Croakley, Kaelber, Munch, & Holland, 1982). Moreover, serious social problems with destructive consequences such as aggressive acts and criminal activities are more likely to stem from heavy drinking by men than by women.

Jellinek (1952, 1960) ignored women's drinking in his influential disease formulation of alcoholism (Fillmore, 1986), even though women of his era drank in appreciable numbers, a trend that had steadily increased since the end of Prohibition. By the 1970s social attitudes toward alcoholism had changed. Alcoholism drew public attention as it was portrayed as a great epidemic menacing the public health of the nation. A prime example of this threat was the growth in the number of women drinkers that began with the end of World War II. Currently, of the estimated 15.1 million individuals in the United States in the grip of alcohol dependence or abuse, about one third are female (Williams, Grant, Harford, & Noble, 1989).

This chapter describes the drinking practices of women and examines theories that have been proposed for this behavior. Factors specific to women that may lead to drinking and drinking problems are discussed, followed by an examination of issues related to treatment of alcoholism among women.

The Prevalence of Alcohol Use among Women

In early national surveys of drinking (for example, Cahalan, Cisin, & Crossley, 1969) as well as in other surveys conducted in the 1970s summarized by Wilsnack, Wilsnack, and Klassen (1986) previously discussed in Chapter 2, women have generally reported lower levels of drinking and alcohol-related problems than men. These national surveys also revealed that more women (around 40 percent) than men (about 25 to 30 percent) were abstainers. On the other hand, men (15 to 20 percent) were much more likely than women (3 to 6 percent) to be heavy drinkers. Overall, the evidence led to the conclusion that drinking levels had been stable during this period.

Although these cross-sectional studies can identify age differences at a given point in time, longitudinal designs are needed to reveal how the incidence, duration, and remission of drinking problems vary at different periods of the life span. Therefore, Fillmore (1987) conducted a seven-year longitudinal study of the drinking patterns of 408 women from 1967 to 1974. Their drinking patterns were also compared with those reported by men who participated in the same survey. Incidence rates were measured by the percentage of respondents who engaged in drinking at the first measurement point, and length of duration was defined in terms of the percentage of respondents who were drinking at both the beginning and the end of the seven-year period of observation.

As Figure 14-1 indicates for measures of several different aspects of drinking frequency, quantity, and consequences, the rates for men were higher than for women at all ages, especially in the 20s. While the percentage of men in their 30s

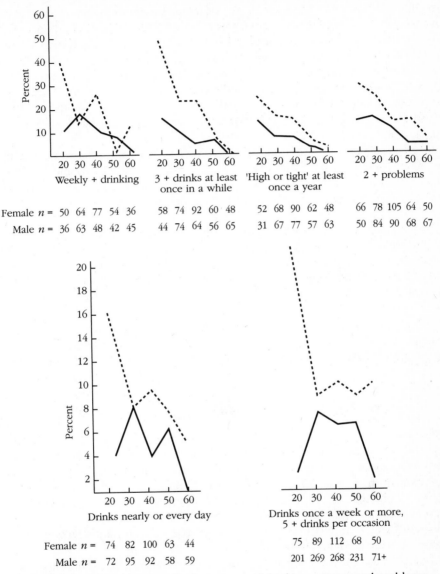

Figure 14-1 Selected longitudinal measures of drinking patterns and problems for women (——) and men (- - - - -) in decades of adult life (age at Time 1): incidence (percentage reporting the behavior at Time 2 of those not reporting the behavior at Time 1). Two longitudinal samples were combined for men for drinking once a week or more, 5+ drinks per occasion.

Source: from "Women's Drinking Across the Adult Life Course as Compared to Men's," by K. M. Fillmore in the *British Journal of Addiction,* 1987, 801–811. Copyright © 1987 by the Society for the Study of Addiction to Alcohol and Drugs.

declined on most drinking indexes, women had their highest rates on many measures of at-risk drinking during this same decade of life. Convergence of rates for men and women was greatest during their 30s. Why does women's drinking peak later in comparison to men? Fillmore argued that since society tries to protect the vulnerable young female from being victimized by drinking, alcohol problems should be delayed among women. Fillmore found that scores on many drinking measures dropped after age 40 for both men and women. The incidence of being "high" dropped sharply after age 50 and many former drinkers over 60 were abstainers.

Drinking over the duration of the seven years, an index of the extent of chronic drinking, occurred for a higher percentage of men in their 40s and 50s but was highest for women during their 30s. Men generally were more likely than women to show chronicity of drinking, but both groups showed declines with increasing age. These differences suggest that at-risk drinking starts later in life and also occupies a smaller temporal space in the lives of women. Finally, Fillmore found that women also showed earlier remission than men across the entire life course.

Fillmore (1987) compared these longitudinal results with cross-sectional findings. Using data from three different national surveys conducted in 1964, 1979, and 1984 by the Alcohol Research Group at the University of California, she found good agreement between longitudinal and cross-sectional results for the rates of abstinence and heavy-frequent drinkers. Abstinence was generally higher for older women and there was a lower percentage of heavy-frequent drinkers for older men and women.

Methodological and Conceptual Issues

Whatever their results, comparisons of drinking levels between males and females can be misleading. Ferrence (1980) noted the possible sex bias involved in determinations of prevalence rates. Due to the greater shame associated with female alcoholism, many women alcoholics are hidden from detection. Lisansky (1957) pointed out that self-reports of men and women may differ in the degree of rationalization. Since alcoholism is more stigmatized for women than for men, women may be more motivated to try to excuse their deviant drinking by calling attention to extenuating stressful events.

Studies of consumption levels often fail to consider sex differences in body weight and composition, leading to underestimates of alcoholism problems among women. Since women weigh less and have a higher proportion of body fat to water, the same dose of alcohol should result in greater impairment for women than for men (Lex, 1991).

Measurement biases also may affect studies of women's drinking (Fillmore, 1984). Schmidt, Klee, and Ames (1990) reviewed research on women's drinking and found that most indicators of alcohol problems that have been used—such as public intoxication, fights, and arrests while intoxicated—may be more applicable to males than to females. The reliance on such measures may have distorted our conceptions of women's alcohol problems.

Even if there were no methodological problems in obtaining comparable indexes, there is the question of sex differences in the meaning or impact of drinking. Does a given level of heavy drinking have the same degree of adverse social and psychological consequences for male and female drinkers?

Drinking styles may differ for men and women. Olenick and Chalmers (1991) examined the role of mood and marital problems in drinking by alcoholic and nonalcoholic women. Among alcoholics, women were more likely than men to drink to alter mood or deal with marital problems. In contrast, nonalcoholic women drank to alter mood more than nonalcoholic men did. Marital problems did not differ in their effect on drinking of nonalcoholic men and women.

Since the context or environment in which men and women typically drink has also been found to differ (Clark, 1981), the type of risk that each experiences could differ even for the same level of drinking. Thus, males often drink in public places such as bars and may be more prone to drive after drinking than females are, exposing themselves (and others) to a higher risk of accidents. On the other hand, women who drink while pregnant risk damage to the fetus, a biologically based hazard that men are spared.

Even though women's drinking problems do not seem as serious as men's, some subgroups are at greater risk than others. Single, part-time employed or unemployed, divorced or separated, and never-married women were noted by Wilsnack et al. (1986) to have a higher chance than other women of having drinking problems.

The Convergence Hypothesis

The view that rapidly changing sex roles in the past quarter century may have led more women to drink in styles similar to those of men suggests that the gender gap should have decreased over this period. Ferrence (1980) examined sex differences on several indexes of alcohol use and alcohol-related consequences and behaviors across many studies and found little evidence for convergence on most measures except for impaired driving. Males had from 3 to 17 times higher rates than females, depending on the particular problem, but these rates did not converge over the 1970s.

The lack of convergence of rates for most indexes of alcohol consumption or alcohol-related problems for men and women was corroborated by Fillmore (1984) and by Temple (1987). However, later research suggests signs that convergence may be occurring, at least for younger drinkers (Helzer & Burnam, 1990). Thus, Mercer and Khavari (1990) compared drinking of 2,746 college students in 1977 and 1985. Their results suggested that convergence was occurring, with increased binge drinking and a drop in abstention among women.

Age differences were also found by Reich, Cloninger, Van Eerdewegh, Rice, and Mullaney (1988), who estimated lifetime prevalence of alcohol abuse for men and women in relation to their date of birth. They found prevalence rates of 12.3 and 4 percent for males and females, respectively, for cohorts born before 1940. In contrast, for individuals born after 1955 the estimated rates were higher but more similar, at 22 and 10 percent for males and females, respectively. Thus, evidence that convergence occurred was found, as men were only twice as likely as women to be alcoholic in the younger cohort whereas they were three times as likely as women in the older cohort.

Theories of Women's Alcohol Use

Most psychological theories about the use of alcohol have been developed from observations of male alcoholics. These explanations have been assumed to be valid for women as well, an assumption that has gone largely untested. Theories that have focused specifically on women have attempted to explain their drinking in terms of their conformance or nonconformance to sex roles. We will look at the usefulness of both psychodynamic and sex-role theories as explanations of women's alcohol use.

Psychodynamic Theories

Early theories about the origins of drinking problems focused on males. Alcohol was seen as a way to deal with dependency conflicts, according to traditional psychoanalytic theories (McCord & McCord, 1960). In contrast, drinking has also been viewed as a means of fulfilling the need for a feeling of power, as proposed by McClelland, Davis, Kalin, and Wanner (1972).

These views may explain some aspects of excessive drinking among women. However, there are numerous reasons to suspect limits to such generalizations since some factors for drinking may be sex specific. Biological differences in metabolism of alcohol and hormones may be one source of sex differences in alcohol use, while sociologically defined sex roles offer more opportunity, encouragement, and approval of drinking, even to excess in some circumstances, for males than for females. In view of these major differences it is important to formulate and test other theories designed specifically to explain alcohol use by women.

Sex-Role Theory

One early explanation for alcoholism among women was that their restrictive traditional sex role centered around hearth and home might create frustration and depression, leading some to turn to alcohol as an escape. However, due to the strong societal restrictions on drinking by women in the past, it was probably likely that they would become hidden or closet drinkers.

A different conception by Wilsnack (1974) proposed that women sought to achieve a sense of "womanliness" from drinking. She studied the fantasies of women before and after they consumed a small amount of alcohol. Using the Thematic Apperception Test, a task that requires the respondent to make up a story that is appropriate to each of a series of ambiguous pictures, she found that after drinking women decreased imagery related to achievement but increased thoughts about traditionally feminine activities. Wilsnack (1976) posited that those women who become alcoholics may feel particularly insecure about their femininity and resort to alcohol as a means of achieving more fantasies that will allow them to feel more womanly.

The change in sex roles over the past generation has altered the picture. On one hand, one might predict that these changes may place the traditionally feminine woman in more conflict, either between her traditional values and her actual nontraditional behavior or between her nontraditional behavior and the traditional expectations of society. Either type of conflict might lead to more alcohol use. Wilsnack (1973) proposed sex-role *conflict* as the underlying factor in problem drinking among women. In other words, it may not be the feminine role or the multiplicity of roles but rather the conflict created by having to choose among roles that is responsible for excessive drinking. In line with this view, Wilsnack (1973) found that alcoholic women had traditionally feminine scores on sex-typed attitudes but masculine tendencies on measures of interpersonal and expressive style. Thus, drinking may be a means to relieve stress and conflict related to sex roles. In line with this view, Johnson (1982) reported that married women working outside the home had higher drinking problem rates than single working women or married women not working outside the home. However, this finding has not been corroborated in other surveys (Parker, Parker, Wolz, & Harford, 1980).

At the other extreme, women who reject values of traditional femininity might experience social ostracism by those expecting them to adhere to feminine values. These women might also experience stress as a result and turn to alcohol to cope with this problem, according to Wilsnack (1976).

Thus, a variety of processes related to sex roles have been proposed as factors that create stress and lead to alcohol problems among women. The risk of alcoholism exists not only for women who accept traditional sex roles but do not feel sufficiently feminine (Wilsnack, 1974) but also for women who reject traditional values of femininity (Wilsnack & Wilsnack, 1978).

Still another factor related to sex role that might be involved in increasing the drinking of women is the stress of the *dual* roles of pursuing a career and being a traditional homemaker. These women might be assumed to suffer more stress and be more likely to develop drinking problems. However, a study by Wilsnack and Cheloha (1987) does not support this view. They found that role *deprivation* rather than multiplicity of roles was more likely to be associated with problem drinking among women at all ages. The youngest women were more likely to drink if they lacked stable marital and work roles; middle-aged women drank more if their marriages dissolved or if they had children growing up and moving out. An additional risk factor for women over 50 was working outside the home.

Wilsnack and Cheloha hypothesized that role deprivation may create alienation and feelings of loneliness that women cope with by drinking. An alternative explanation, however, is that women who drink excessively may contribute to the loss of domestic and job relationships. The researchers rejected this interpretation primarily because most women reported few incidences of problem drinking and the relationship between problem drinking and roles varied for different age groups.

Evidence from several different kinds of studies can be examined to find out whether sex-role theory is supported. Findings from retrospective studies with women who are already encountering drinking problems are difficult to interpret because the drinking could be either a cause or a consequence of sex-role issues, or both. More useful information relevant to this question might come from the prospective study of adolescent girls who have not yet developed strong drinking patterns.

Wilsnack and Wilsnack (1978) conducted a prospective study that involved a national survey of more than 13,000 students. Because heavy drinking is not characteristic of traditional females, they predicted that girls who drank heavily would be those who rejected traditional values of femininity. Measures of the quantity and frequency of drinking, the drinking problems, and symptomatic drinking—for example, gulping, drinking alone, morning drinking—were taken. Feminine values were also assessed on a scale designed to measure traditional femininity. The findings were not conclusive. Orientation toward traditional femininity did *not* predict which adolescent girls were drinking. Among those who did drink, weak relationships with sex-role orientation were found, possibly because of ethnic differences. Thus, drinking and drinking-related problems occurred with rejection of traditional femininity among white, African-American, and Hispanic girls, but not for Native American or Asian-American girls.

Similarly, in a cross-sectional design using a nationwide survey, Rachal et al. (1975) noted that both male and female adolescents who had unfavorable attitudes toward the traditional sex roles expected of them drank more heavily and with more problems than those with favorable attitudes. Girls who drank more often and heavily showed more signs of dependence and trouble than those who did not drink. In contrast, among adult women, Beckman (1978) and Wilsnack (1973) found the opposite pattern, in that those who accepted traditionally feminine roles were more likely to have alcohol problems.

Thus, there is no clear relationship between sex-role attitudes and drinking among women. Other factors such as age may affect the relationship between sex-role orientation and drinking levels. Wilsnack and Wilsnack (1978) suggested that as sex roles continue to change, their relationship to drinking may change also. Thus, if drinking were to become equally acceptable for both sexes, incentives for males to drink to prove their "masculinity" might decrease while socially acceptable opportunities for females to drink might increase. These simultaneous changes would decrease the relationship between sex-role attitudes and drinking. Currently, however, drinking is much more important for males than for females in fulfilling their sex roles. Thus, females are less likely than males to drink due to specific sex-role demands.

Factors in Women's Alcohol Use

A number of factors specific to women may lead to drinking and drinking problems. Biological factors, developmental factors, psychological factors, and generational differences all may have a bearing on women's drinking. We will examine each type of factor in this section.

Biological Factors

Biological factors during adolescence such as the onset of menstruation may affect the onset of drinking. It has been commonly thought that the discomfort during the premenstruum might motivate more drinking, as Beckman (1979) found for a sample of alcoholic women in comparison to controls. Blood alcohol level (BAL) has been found to be highest at the premenstrual point in the menstrual cycle (Jones & Jones, 1976), a factor that might mean that alcohol consumption has a greater effect during this period.

Mello (1980) reviewed research to see if the effects of alcohol varied over different phases of the menstrual cycle. She noted that for an equivalent alcohol dose, women absorbed alcohol faster than men but showed no differences in elimination rate. Blood alcohol levels for women were highest at ovulation and during the premenstruum. Alcohol impairment of some functions such as memory and cognition were unrelated to menstrual phase while impairment of others such as reaction time and sensory acuity were. Brick, Nathan, Westrick, and Frankenstein (1986) tested young women to determine the effects of alcohol on memory, standing steadiness, and a vigilance task. Testing occurred in different sessions corresponding to three different points in the menstrual cycle. Alcohol impaired memory and steadiness, but the deficits were similar at all three measurement points during the menstrual cycle. BAL peaks did not differ across the menstrual cycle either.

Charette, Tate, and Wilson (1990) failed to find that use of alcohol or physical distress was related to menstrual cycle among college women. Mello, Mendelsohn, and Lex (1990) found considerable variations in the drinking-menstrual cycle pattern among a small sample of social drinkers. Those who drank more had more hostility and anger during the premenstrual stage, while those who drank less experienced more physical discomfort. National survey data (Wilsnack, Klassen, & Wilsnack, 1984) showed that heavy drinkers reported more premenstrual discomfort so that drinking may be a means of coping.

The overall evidence shows no consistent relationship between menstrual cycle and alcohol use or consequences. Gomberg and Lisansky (1984) suggested that the expectations and attitudes of women about their menstrual periods must also be considered in accounting for the relationship between menstrual period and drinking levels.

Developmental Factors

Reaching young adulthood leads to more freedom and independence for both sexes, and increased drinking may be an expression of these changes in social status. Sexual involvement and activity also increases for both sexes, but the potential of pregnancy and childbearing for women emphasizes an important biological difference between the sexes that could differentially affect the impact of excess drinking for men and women. Psychological reactions to gynecological problems, conception or infertility, pregnancy and possible complications, all may help lead to drinking as a coping response among some women. It must also be recognized that excessive use of alcohol can be the cause of problems related to sexual and reproductive functioning.

In young adulthood, the entrance into the work force may also be a risk factor for alcohol use for both sexes but possibly in different ways. Men may drink in response to work pressure, but women may often carry the double burden of holding a full-time job as well as being a homemaker. As noted earlier, Johnson (1982) found that married women who worked outside the home had higher rates of alcohol problems than housewives or single working women. In addition, divorced and separated women under the age of 35 also had high problem drinking rates, whereas for women over 35 problem drinking was higher for married women. Whether the marital discord was a cause of the drinking problem or vice versa is not clear.

Parenting is also a major potential stressor that might be related to problem drinking. Cahalan et al. (1969) found that heavy drinking among women peaked at two ages: 21–24 years and 45–49 years. Gomberg and Lisansky (1984) conjectured that the early peak may occur as many women cut back on drinking during childbearing and child-raising years but were unsure as to what creates the peak at middle age.

Psychological Factors

Gomberg and Lisansky (1984) suggested that gender differences may exist in the psychological antecedents of alcohol problems. Although alcoholics as a group report more family disruptions during early years than nonalcoholics do, women alcoholics do so at a higher rate than men alcoholics. Women alcoholics are also able to pinpoint a specific recent life event that apparently triggered their alcoholism. A review by Beckman (1975) suggested that specific stressors such as health problems or a death of a loved one are more instrumental in generating problem drinking for females than for males.

Growing up in an alcoholic home can be a stressful and traumatic experience, not only because of the adverse effect of the alcoholic parent but also because it is often associated with factors such as child neglect and abuse, divorced or absent parents, and financial hardships that may also contribute to future vulnerability. Corrigan (1980) found that women from alcoholic homes recalled their family life as involving deprivation and rejection, and sexual abuse in some cases, more so than those from nonalcoholic homes. However, these studies did not include males so it is not possible to determine if these experiences were more negative for women than for men.

The contribution of factors such as childhood sexual abuse to alcohol problems of women was explored through interviews of 917 adult women from the general population as part of the 1981 National Study of Health and Life Experiences of Women (Wilsnack, Wilsnack, & Klassen, 1984). The rate of reported childhood sexual abuse among problem drinkers was more than double that for nonproblem drinkers. Women who drank at high levels had greater sexual dysfunction (lack of sexual interest, low frequency or lack of orgasm) than light drinkers. Moderate levels of drinking were associated with the lowest frequency of sexual dysfunction.

Blume (1990) and Wilsnack (1984) suggested that childhood sexual abuse contributed to later sexual dysfunction for women. Alcohol abuse may occur, then, as a form of self-medication or disinhibitor for sexual problems, a remedy that ironically often creates further sexual dysfunction by lowering physiological sexual response (Crowe & George, 1989).

A five-year follow-up (Wilsnack, Klassen, Schur, & Wilsnack, 1991) compared subgroups of women who were either problem or nonproblem drinkers at the initial interview. Among problem drinkers, those reporting sexual dysfunction at the initial interview were more likely than those without sexual dysfunction to have more drinking problems at the five-year follow-up. Also, nonproblem drinkers who experienced sexual abuse during the five-year period were more than twice as likely to develop drinking problems as those who did not encounter sexual abuse.

The self-reported motives of men and women for drinking also show differences. Edwards, Hensman, and Peto (1973) found women drank primarily to relieve unpleasant feelings, on one hand, and to participate in celebrations and festive occasions, on the other. Kielholz (1970) found work-related problems were more of a factor for men, while family problems were more strongly related to alcoholism for women. Retrospective accounts of alcoholics showed that women were more likely to resort to alcohol when feeling powerless (Beckman, 1980).

Generational Differences

Due to the radical changes in sex roles in America in this century, it is difficult to interpret age-related differences because they are often intertwined with changing cultural values. An illustration of this problem can be seen in a study of age-related differences in alcohol problems by Gomberg (1984) that examined alcoholic women and age-matched controls in their 20s, 30s, and 40s. Some of the differences found may not be due to age per se but to generational changes. In other words, the era in which each group was in their 20s was not the same, and certain social conditions may have affected drinking behavior of these different groups. Thus, the younger women grew up in an era of greater freedoms for women, with more women working outside the home, more single-parent families, and more couples living together although not married.

A major finding was that the alcoholic women in their 40s did not develop their alcoholism until late in their 30s, whereas the alcoholics who were in their 20s began their alcoholism in their teenage years. Differences in drinking behavior between alcoholic women and the controls were smallest for the women in their 40s. On average, these women were born in 1936, an era of traditional femininity. Gomberg speculated that alcohol was a means of reducing frustration and resentment from lack of fulfillment for some women confined by traditional femininity.

Women in their 20s in this study, born on the average in 1956, showed many problems of impulse control and strained relationships with parents. The women in their 30s were born on the average in 1946 and represented the Baby

Boom generation. This group showed more conflict than the other two age groups, perhaps due to the rapid social transition in sex roles during their adolescence.

The differences among the women of different ages illustrate how the social context may alter the role of alcohol for different generations. Although all of the alcoholic women drank excessively, their drinking may have stemmed from different types of psychological reasons because of the way society's demands and expectations varied for women over this period.

Treatment of Women's Alcoholism

Even if women alcoholics do start drinking later than their male counterparts, they develop problems in a shorter period since, on average, they enter treatment at about the same age as men do (Piazza, Vrbka, & Yeager, 1989). However, Benson and Wilsnack (1983) warned that the *severity* of alcoholism may not be equal for men and women even though they seek help at a comparable age, because women may seek help at an *earlier* stage of their drinking than do men do. Their support system may disintegrate or they may generally seek treatment for problems earlier than men do. In addition, Morrissey and Schuckit (1978) noted the interpretation that women alcoholics drink less and start drinking later than men alcoholics may be confounded by social class since most of the males studied are from lower socioeconomic groups while the females are from middle-class groups.

Treatment Underutilization

Although women appear to have more favorable attitudes than men toward treatment, which might dispose them to seek therapy for alcoholism, they appear to underutilize treatment facilities. Beckman and Amaro (1984) suggested that a number of barriers to treatment exist for women that do not exist for men. On the personal level, women may be slower to detect or admit they have a drinking problem, perhaps due to greater stigma. In addition to having lower self-esteem and feelings of powerlessness, women alcoholics may also experience more depression, which might lower their motivation for treatment. Family responsibilities may prevent women alcoholics from seeking treatment. In addition, other family members may "protect" or hide the woman alcoholic by concealing her problem from outsiders, furthering her own denial of a problem.

Even if these social barriers are overcome, additional barriers may exist in the service delivery component of treatment. Lack of child-care facilities, for example, would make it difficult for the alcoholic mother to receive treatment. In addition, Beckman and Amaro pointed out that treatment staff may be reluctant to either diagnose or treat women alcoholics, because alcoholism may be seen as more congruent with males whereas females may be stereotyped as more likely to suffer from depression. Physicians, for example, tend to be less likely to see symptoms as reflective of physical disease when women are concerned, according to McCranie, Horowitz, and Martin (1978).

Among whites, at least, families and friends of women alcoholics were more prone to oppose their seeking treatment than were families and friends of male alcoholics. In addition, after entering treatment, women alcoholics felt there were a greater number of negative consequences such as negative reactions from family and friends than did men (Beckman & Amaro, 1984).

Treatment Outcomes

Women alcoholics may have more difficulty than men alcoholics benefiting from treatment programs. If true, the poorer prognosis for women might reflect the unsuitability of existing programs that are primarily male-oriented. Alternatively, it could be that by the time women alcoholics overcome the barrier to treatment, they may be "worse cases" than the males.

Vannicelli (1986) reviewed the available research from about 30 years of treatment outcome evaluation for male and female alcoholics. The evidence does not support the popularly held view that women show less improvement from treatment. Annis and Liban (1980) reviewed research on this issue and also rejected that belief. Although the methodology of most studies was weak, often lacking control groups, they found that two thirds of the studies showed no sex differences and about one fifth found more improvement for females.

The types of therapy that might be effective for males might not be as valid for females. Thus, family therapy, group counseling, or separate all-female groups might appear to be more appealing to females, as might the use of female rather than male therapists. Despite these possibilities, Vannicelli (1986) was unable to find a single study evaluating the differential effectiveness of different types of programs for males as opposed to females. No studies comparing the benefits of single- versus mixed-sex treatment groups could be found, either. Most published reports do not bother to mention the sex of the therapist, so they cannot answer the question of whether female alcoholics improve more with male or female therapists.

Conclusions

Although sex roles have undergone substantial changes in our society over the past generation, it is safe to say that men are still allowed or encouraged to drink more often and in greater amounts in a greater variety of contexts than women are. In addition, the motives and meaning of drinking may vary for men and women. Epidemiological studies still show more frequent and larger quantities of alcohol consumption by men in the general population. Men are still more likely than women to be seen in alcoholism treatment facilities, although to some degree the differences reflect biases of access rather than sex differences in prevalence of alcohol problems.

The role of alcohol and its effects on women may be quite different at different ages. During adolescence, drinking may be associated with increased sexual activity, and the patterns of drinking developed at this stage may well serve as "scripts" that influence drinking throughout life. Early drinking may also create conflicts with parents. Adolescents face increasingly greater influence from peers and social norms. Boys traditionally have been encouraged to be more independent and are allowed more deviance from social norms, leading to earlier onset, greater frequency, and greater quantity of alcohol consumption than for girls. Johnston, O'Malley, and Bachman (1991) found that although adolescent males still drink more often and heavily than females do, the gap has been closing.

As a woman marries and begins to have children, there may be pressures that lead to increased drinking, which may impair her relationship with her children and spouse, especially if she neglects, rejects, or abuses them. At middle age, the empty nest syndrome along with the decline of physical health and youthfulness may create stressors that lead to increased alcohol use. Finally, elderly women who become widowed may experience stigma and loneliness. In addition, the physical aches and pains of aging may lead to more alcohol use as a coping response.

Comparison of the effectiveness of treatment for men and for women is complicated by the fact that alcoholism may be defined and reacted to quite differently by society for men and for women. If women do not benefit as much as men from treatment, it is not clear whether it is because a combination of biological and sociological factors make alcoholism more severe for women or if the existing treatments have been biased toward male alcoholics, who in the past constituted the vast majority of treated alcoholics.

In the past, rigid sex roles may have felt imprisoning to some women who used alcohol abuse as one means of escape and placed barriers to their treatment. The recent changes in sex roles, however welcome otherwise, may not reduce the risk of alcohol abuse for women. For some women, the new roles may not be appealing and may create added stress, which may lead to alcohol abuse for them just as the old roles did for other types of women.

References

Annis, H. M., & Liban, C. B. (1980). Alcoholism in women: Treatment modalities and outcomes. In O. J. Kalant (Ed.), *Alcohol and drug problems in women: Recent advances in alcohol and drug problems* (pp. 385–422). New York: Plenum Press.

Beckman, L. (1975). Women alcoholics: A review of social and psychological studies. *Journal of Studies on Alcohol, 36,* 797–824.

Beckman, L. J. (1978). Sex-role conflict in alcoholic women: Myth or reality. *Journal of Abnormal Psychology, 87,* 408–417.

Beckman, L. J. (1979). Reported effects of alcohol on the sexual feelings and behavior of women alcoholics and nonalcoholics. *Journal of Studies on Alcohol, 40,* 272–282.

Beckman, L. J. (1980). Perceived antecedents and effects of alcohol consumption in women. *Journal of Studies on Alcohol, 41,* 518–530.

Beckman, L. J., & Amaro, H. (1984). Patterns of women's use of alcoholism treatment agencies. In S. C. Wilsnack & L. J. Beckman (Eds.), *Alcohol problems in women: Antecedents, consequences, and intervention* (pp. 319–348). New York: Academic Press.

Benson, C. S., & Wilsnack, S. C. (1983). Gender differences in alcoholic personality characteristics and life experience. In W. M. Cox (Ed.), *Identifying and measuring alcoholic personality characteristics* (pp. 53–71). San Francisco: Jossey-Bass.

Blume, S. B. (1990). Alcohol and drug problems in women: Old attitudes, new knowledge.

In H. B. Milkman & L. I. Sederer (Eds.), *Treatment choices for alcoholism and substance abuse* (pp. 185–198). Lexington, MA: Lexington Books.

Brick, J. B., Nathan, P. E., Westrick, E., & Frankenstein, W. (1986). Effect of menstrual cycle phase on behavioral and physiological responses to alcohol. *Journal of Studies on Alcohol, 47,* 472–477.

Cahalan, D., Cisin, I. H., & Crossley, H. M. (1969). *American drinking practices: A national study of drinking behavior.* New Brunswick, NJ: Rutgers Center for Alcohol Studies.

Charette, L., Tate, D. L., & Wilson, A. (1990). Alcohol consumption and menstrual distress in women at higher and lower risk for alcoholism. *Alcoholism: Clinical and Experimental Research, 14,* 152–157.

Clark, W. B. (1981). Public drinking contexts: Bars and taverns. In T. C. Harford & L. S. Gaines (Eds.), *Social drinking contexts* (National Institute on Alcohol Abuse and Alcoholism Research Monograph No. 7, DHHS Pub. No ADM81-1097, pp. 8–33). Washington DC: U.S. Government Printing Office.

Corrigan, E. M. (1980). *Alcoholic women in treatment.* New York: Oxford University Press.

Crowe, L. C., & George, W. H. (1989). Alcohol and human sexuality: Review and integration. *Psychological Bulletin, 105,* 374–386.

Edwards, G., Hensman, C., & Peto. (1973). Drinking in a London suburb: Reinterview of a subsample and assessment of response consistency. *Quarterly Journal of Studies on Alcohol, 34,* 1244–1254.

Ferrence, R. G. (1980). Sex differences in the prevalence of problem drinking. In O. J. Kalant (Ed.), *Alcohol and drug problems in women: Recent advances in alcohol and drug problems* (pp. 69–124). New York: Plenum Press.

Fillmore, K. M. (1984). "When angels fall": Women's drinking as cultural preoccupation and as reality. In S. C. Wilsnack & L. J. Beckman (Eds.), *Alcohol problems in women: Antecedents, consequences, and intervention* (pp. 7–36). New York: Guilford Press.

Fillmore, K. M. (1986). Issues in the changing drinking patterns among women in the last century. In National Institute on Alcohol Abuse and Alcoholism (Ed.), *Women and alcohol: Health-related issues* (Research Monograph No. 16, DHHS Pub. No. ADM86-1139, pp. 69–77). Washington, DC: U.S. Government Printing Office.

Fillmore, K. M. (1987). Women's drinking across the adult life course as compared to men's. *British Journal of Addiction, 82,* 801–811.

Gomberg, E.S.L. (1984). *Femininity issues in women's alcohol use.* Paper presented at the annual meeting of the American Psychological Asociation, Toronto, Ontario.

Gomberg, E.S.L., & Lisansky, J. M. (1984). Antecedents of alcohol problems in women. In S. Wilsnack & L. J. Beckman (Eds.), *Alcohol problems in women* (pp. 233–255). New York: Guilford Press.

Helzer, J. E., & Burnam, M. A. (1990). Alcohol abuse and dependence. In L. N. Robins & D. A. Regnier (Eds.), *Psychiatric disorders in America.* New York: Free Press.

Jellinek, E. M. (1952). Phases of alcohol addiction. *Quarterly Journal of Studies on Alcohol, 13,* 673–684.

Jellinek, E. M. (1960). *The disease conception of alcoholism.* New Brunswick, NJ: Hillhouse Press.

Johnson, P. B. (1982). Sex differences. Women's roles and alcohol use: Preliminary national data. *Journal of Social Issues, 39,* 93–116.

Johnston, L. D., O'Malley, P. M., & Bachman, J. G. (1991). *Drug use among American high school students, college students, and other young adults, 1975–1990. Vol. I. High school seniors* (DHHS Pub. No. ADM91-1813). Rockville, MD: ADHAMA.

Jones, B. M., & Jones, M. (1976). Women and alcohol: Intoxication, metabolism, and the menstrual cycle. In M. Greenblatt & M. A. Schuckit (Eds.), *Alcoholism problems in women and children* (pp. 103–136). New York: Grune & Stratton.

Kielholz, P. (1970). Alcohol and depression. *British Journal of Addiction, 65,* 187–193.

Lex, B. W. (1991). Some gender differences in alcohol and polysubstance users. *Health Psychology, 10,* 121–132.

Lisansky, E. S. (1957). Alcoholism in women: Social and psychological concomitants I. Social history data. *Quarterly Journal of Studies on Alcohol, 18,* 588–623.

Malin, H., Croakley, J., Kaelber, C., Munch, N., & Holland, W. (1982). An epidemiologic perspective on alcohol use and abuse in the United States. In National Institute on Alcohol Abuse and Alcoholism (Ed.), *Alcohol consumption and related problems* (Alcohol and Health Monograph No. ADM82-1190, pp. 99–153). Washington, DC: U.S. Government Printing Office.

McClelland, D. C., Davis, W. N., Kalin, R., & Wanner, E. (1972). *The drinking man.* New York: Free Press.

McCord, W., & McCord, J. (1960). *Origins of alcoholism.* Stanford, CA: Stanford University Press.

McCranie, E. W., Horowitz, A. J., & Martin, R. M. (1978). Alleged sex-role stereotyping in the assessment of women's physical complaints: A study of general practitioners. *Social Science and Medicine, 12,* 111–116.

Mello, N. K. (1980). Some behavioral and biological aspects of alcohol problems in women. In O. J. Kalant (Ed.), *Alcohol and drug problems in women: Recent advances in alcohol and drug problems* (pp. 263–298). New York: Plenum Press.

Mello, N. K., Mendelsohn, J. H., & Lex, B. W. (1990). Alcohol use and premenstrual symptoms in social drinkers. *Psychopharmacology, 101,* 448–455.

Mercer, P. W., & Khavari, K. A. (1990). Are women drinking more like men? An empirical examination of the convergence hypothesis. *Alcoholism: Clinical and Experimental Research, 14,* 461–466.

Morrissey, E. R., & Schuckit, M. A. (1978). Stressful life events and alcohol problems among women seen at a detoxication center. *Journal of Studies on Alcohol, 39,* 1559–1576.

Olenick, N. L., & Chalmers, D. K. (1991). Gender specific drinking styles in alcoholics and nonalcoholics. *Journal of Studies on Alcohol, 52,* 325–330.

Parker, D. A., Parker, E. S., Wolz, M. W., & Harford, T. C. (1980). Sex roles and alcohol consumption: A research note. *Journal of Health and Social Behavior, 21,* 43–48.

Piazza, N. J., Vrbka, J. L., & Yeager, R. D. (1989). Telescoping of alcoholism in women alcoholics. *International Journal of the Addictions, 24,* 19–28.

Rachal, J. V., Williams, J. R., Brehm, M. L., Cavanaugh, B., Moore, R. P., & Bokerman, W. C. (1975). *A national study of adolescent drinking behavior, attitudes, and correlates.* Research Triangle Park, NC: Research Triangle Park Center for the Study of Social Behavior.

Reich, T., Cloninger, C. R., Van Eerdewegh, P., Rice, J. P., & Mullaney, J. (1988). Secular trends in the familial transmission of alcoholism. *Alcoholism: Clinical and Experimental Research, 12,* 458–464.

Schmidt, C., Klee, L., & Ames, G. (1990). Review and analysis of literature on indicators of women's drinking problems. *British Journal of Addiction, 85,* 179–192.

Temple, M. (1987). Alcohol use among male and female college students: Has there been a convergence? *Youth and Society, 19,* 44–72.

Vannicelli, M. (1986). Treatment considerations. In National Institute on Alcohol Abuse and Alcoholism (Ed.), *Women and alcohol: Health-related issues* (Research Monograph No. 16, DHHS Pub. No. ADM86-1139, pp. 130–153). Washington, DC: U.S. Government Printing Office.

Williams, G. D., Grant, B. F., Harford, T. C., & Noble, J. (1989). Population projections using DSM-III criteria: Alcohol abuse and dependence, 1990–2000. *Alcohol Health and Research World, 13,* 366–370.

Wilsnack, R. W., & Cheloha, R. (1987). Women's roles and problem drinking across the lifespan. *Social Problems, 34,* 231–248.

Wilsnack, S. C. (1973). Sex role identity in female alcoholism. *Journal of Abnormal Psychology, 82,* 253–261.

Wilsnack, S. C. (1974). The effects of social drinking on women's fantasy. *Journal of Personality, 42,* 43–61.

Wilsnack, S. C. (1976). The impact of sex roles on women's alcohol use and abuse. In M. Greenblatt & M. A. Schuckit (Eds.), *Alcoholism problems in women and children* (pp. 37–63). New York: Grune & Stratton.

Wilsnack, S. C. (1984). Drinking, sexuality, and sexual dysfunction in women. In S. C. Wilsnack & L. J. Beckman (Eds.), *Alcohol problems in women: Antecedents, consequences, and intervention* (pp. 189–227). New York: Academic Press.

Wilsnack, S. C., Klassen, A. D., Schur, B. E., & Wilsnack, R. W. (1991). Predicting onset and chronicity of women's problem drinking: A five-year longitudinal analysis. *American Journal of Public Health, 81,* 305–318.

Wilsnack, S. C., Klassen, A. D., & Wilsnack, R. W. (1984). Drinking and reproductive dysfunction among women in a 1981 national survey. *Alcoholism: Clinical and Experimental Research, 8,* 451–458.

Wilsnack, S. C., & Wilsnack, R. W. (1978). Sex roles and drinking among adolescent girls. *Journal of Studies on Alcohol, 39,* 1855–1874.

Wilsnack, S. C., Wilsnack, R. W., & Klassen, A. D. (1984). Women's drinking and drinking problems: Patterns from a 1981 national survey. *American Journal of Public Health, 74,* 1231–1238.

Wilsnack, S. C., Wilsnack, R. W., & Klassen, A. D. (1986). Epidemiological research on women's drinking, 1978–1984. In National Institute on Alcohol Abuse and Alcoholism (Ed.), *Women and alcohol: Health-related issues* (Research Monograph No. 16, DHHS Pub. No. ADM86-1139, pp. 1–68). Washington, DC: U.S. Government Printing Office.

FIFTEEN

Age Differences in Alcohol Use and Abuse

Curiosity motivates youth to discover the appeal of alcohol to many adults. Even before they are legally old enough to drink alcoholic beverages, many adolescents experiment with drinking. The processes involved in the initiation into drinking during early adolescence deserve study not only because of the risks that alcohol poses during adolescence but also because of the dangers that may emerge in future years.

Although some parents may even realize that their adolescent sons and daughters engage in underage drinking, they often dismiss the danger because many of them also drank as adolescents and continue to do so. Hence, they may regard alcohol use by their children as a "normal" developmental event. Even when drinking patterns and consequences represent problems for their adolescent offspring, parents may still regard alcohol use as not dangerous, compared to marijuana and cocaine.

At the other age extreme, less awareness of and less concern about alcohol use and abuse by the elderly exists. The adverse consequences of excessive drinking for this group may not be as apparent since economic problems from alcohol abuse due to loss of jobs and poor productivity do not occur to the extent they do for young and middle-aged adults. Older citizens who drink excessively are often tolerated by society with indulgence. If they have retired, their drinking does not jeopardize their work performance. Even boisterous or obnoxious behaviors created by drinking in the elderly are generally viewed as harmless or amusing and not as problems.

Nonetheless, excessive use of alcohol by adolescents or the elderly warrants investigation because it can harm physical, psychological, and social well-being and functioning. It is also important that alcohol use be studied across the life span if we are to understand the impact of drinking on human behavior and experience. The study of drinking behavior during adolescence could help identify and modify the antecedents of adult drinking patterns and problems. In turn, knowledge of adult drinking patterns and effects can help us understand the function of drinking and its influence among the elderly. In the present chapter we will examine findings of research on the causes and effects of alcohol use and abuse at the younger and older ends of the age span.

Adolescent Drinking

Adolescence is a stage of development involving rapid biological, physical, and psychological changes as young people learn the expectations and norms of adult society into which they will be entering. This life stage is characterized by experimentation, a means of learning and discovery about oneself with respect to a variety of concerns such as careers, marriage, and parenthood. Thus, it is acceptable and expected that one dates a variety of persons before considering marriage. Adolescents are counseled to work at a variety of jobs to gain knowledge and experience that will help them make a better choice later. This same attitude of empiricism and experimentation seems to lie behind the approach of many young people to alcohol and other drugs.

Society holds a curious double standard for minors and adults. For individuals over the age of 18 in most states, drinking, often to excess, is acceptable, but the same behavior is prohibited for minors, who are considered "too young" to handle alcohol. However, Newcomb, Maddahian, and Bentler (1986) argued that this question should be examined scientifically and that the harmfulness of alcohol and drug use to adolescents should be tested rather than assumed.

Experimental Use of Alcohol

Shedler and Block (1990) found in a longitudinal study covering from preschool to age 18 that those adolescents who engaged in some experimentation with drugs were best adjusted, whereas those who never experimented were anxious and lacking in social skills. However, those who were frequent users were maladjusted and alienated with emotional distress. They concluded that these differences in drug use were related to differences in parenting; closer ties with parents were found for adolescents who experimented with drugs but did not become heavy users than for either heavy users or nonusers. It was suggested that differences in alcohol and drug use could better be viewed as symptoms rather than causes of these differences.

Heavy Use of Alcohol

Jessor and Jessor (1975) found that young people who were regular users or committed to a lifestyle centered around alcohol and drugs also differed from nonusers or less frequent users along dimensions such as rebellion, lack of conformity to traditional values, and participation in other socially deviant or illegal behaviors. Alienation and distance from family, early sexual activity, and low involvement in school were also associated with the lifestyle of alcohol and drug abusers. Jessor and Jessor (1977) proposed their problem behavior theory to account for the high correlation among a number of socially deviant behaviors as a reflection of a general level of undercontrol by heavy alcohol users.

Donovan and Jessor (1985) regarded problem drinking as a symptom of an undercontrolled behavior style that can lead to a set of other adolescent problem behaviors involving deviance from social norms, one of which is excessive use of alcohol and drugs. Adolescent overinvolvement with drugs may further interfere with the ability of the adolescent to fit into the norms of adult society. Dropping out of school because of drug activity, for example, limits one's opportunities for careers and jobs that are considered successful.

In summary, many young people experiment with alcohol and drugs out of curiosity or due to peer pressure, while others use it to cope with harsh reality. As adolescents mature and assume adult roles with greater responsibility as well as independence, many abandon their youthful alcohol and drug patterns, which may be incompatible with their career and personal objectives. Newcomb et al. (1986) concluded that experimentation with alcohol and other drugs cannot easily be prevented but that if it can be delayed sufficiently there may be adequate time for adolescents to develop better coping skills and higher self-esteem so that when experimentation does occur, it has less chance of becoming a harmful habit.

Understanding the factors that distinguish those adolescents who can drink without developing problems and those who cannot may be helpful when designing alcohol abuse prevention programs. Pentz (1983), for example, found that social skill training for coping with peer pressure can be effective in minimizing adolescent alcohol abuse.

Assessing Adolescent Problem Drinking

It is likely that adolescent problem drinking cannot be assessed accurately with the traditional measures of frequency and quantity of drinking developed for adult samples. The long years of chronic alcohol use by adults associated with the model of alcoholism as a progressive disease may not be applicable to young people for whom physical and medical impairments have not yet surfaced. Adolescents may be more likely than adults to encounter problems from a single drinking episode due to inexperience or lack of knowledge. In addition, some problems associated with drinking are unique to young people, such as troubles with parents or with the law due to underage drinking. In the light of these issues, White and Labouvie (1989) developed a scale, the Rutgers Alcohol Problem Index (RAPI), to assess problems related to adolescent drinking so that it is no longer necessary to rely on measures that may not be valid for this population.

When high correlations are obtained between drinking levels of adolescents and their peers, the usual interpretation is that the peers are the cause of the adolescent's drinking. The converse possibility that the individual influences the drinking of the peers is overlooked. Similarly, a third possibility of a reciprocal relationship between an individual's drinking behavior and peer drinking levels has received less attention.

Surveys of Adolescent Drinking

Invaluable information about the nature of the initial stages of drinking that otherwise would be missed can be gained from the study of drinking by adolescents under the minimum age for drinking. Most national surveys restrict respondents to those over 18 years of age and thereby omit teenage drinkers. Although it is illegal for high school students to drink alcohol in most states, many adolescents do engage in drinking to some extent and have experimented with a variety of licit and illicit drugs before the age of 18. It is conceivable that the consequences of such behaviors may affect the subsequent alcohol and drug attitudes and consumption of young people. One common concern is that early use of legal drugs by adolescents may serve as a stepping stone to hard drugs, crime, and other deviant behaviors.

Rachal, Maisto, Guess, and Hubbard (1982) conducted NIAAA surveys of young adolescents in the 10th–12th grades contacted through a national survey in 1974 and 1978 using probability sampling. They found that about 15 percent of high schoolers (20.9 percent for males versus 8.6 percent for females) reported heavy drinking (five or more drinks per occasion and at least one occasion per week). Not surprisingly, males were always found to drink more frequently and in greater quantity during a given episode than females did. About one third of the sample admitted being drunk at least six times a year, while more than two thirds reported at least one adverse social consequence of their drinking. Problems such as difficulties with friends, drinking and driving, and trouble with teachers were more likely for those who had more frequent episodes of drunkenness.

A major series of annual national surveys, Monitoring the Future, started in the 1970s has documented the extent to which high school seniors use a variety of drugs. Johnston, O'Malley, and Bachman (1986) reported that over 90 percent of the more than 16,000 surveyed high school seniors reported having used alcohol at *some* time in their lives. This high percentage may be misleading, since some of these students may have only used alcohol on a single occasion. These patterns are similar to those found in other surveys between 1970 and 1980 (Zucker & Harford, 1980). More recent use within the past month was acknowledged by about 70–75 percent of males and about 60–65 percent of females, depending on the particular year. Heavy use on three or more occasions (defined as five or more drinks on an occasion) was found with 26 percent of the males and 12 percent of the females.

Despite the disturbingly high rates of use found, Johnston, O'Malley, and Bachman (1989) noted that a reduction had occurred over the period of 1975–88 in use of alcohol by high school seniors within the month prior to being surveyed as well as in the number of occasional heavy drinkers (five or more drinks on an occasion in the past two weeks), as shown in Figure 15-1.

The gender gap has narrowed in more recent surveys of high school seniors (Johnston, O'Malley, & Bachman, 1991), with females increasing while males were decreasing their frequency and quantity of drinking. By any standard, however, the percentage of high school seniors who drink every day or in large quantity (five or more drinks per occasion) is still alarmingly high. Furthermore, since most of these seniors had started drinking at a much earlier age, the implication is that many teenagers below the minimum legal drinking age were already drinking at levels that may be dangerous.

Barnes and Welte (1986a) conducted a study of more than 27,000 New York 7th to 12th graders and found that 71 percent of students drank alcohol, with 13 percent of them drinking at least once a week with typical levels of five or more drinks per occasion. (These rates are not representative of the United States, as drinking levels in the Northeast have been found to exceed those typically found in other regions of the nation.) In addition, these usage levels were associated with delinquency, school failure, and other drug use.

Ethnic differences were reported in this study (Welte & Barnes, 1987), with the minority groups having lower rates of drinking than Caucasians. With the exception of Native Americans, minorities were also less likely to engage in heavy drinking than Caucasians. Barnes and Welte recognized, though, that minority young people who are not enrolled in school probably have higher rates of heavy alcohol use.

Among those abusing alcohol, more than 90 percent also had close friends who drank. They also had more friends who drank weekly, as well as parents who

Age Differences in Alcohol Use and Abuse

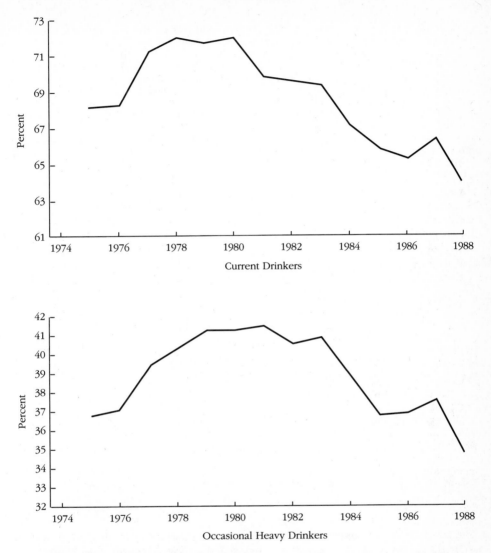

Figure 15-1 Percentage of high school seniors who were current drinkers (used alcohol in the past 30 days) and percentage who were occasional heavy drinkers (took five or more drinks at a sitting during the past two weeks), 1975–1988.

Source: from *Seventh Special Report to U.S. Congress on Alcohol, 1990,* Washington, DC, U.S. Government Printing Office. Based on data from Johnston, O'Malley, and Bachman (1989).

drank. Other behaviors including school misconduct and poor grades were associated with higher alcohol use. The relationship between alcohol abuse and problem behaviors was greater among minority youth (Barnes & Welte, 1986b).

Windle (1991) reported findings of the National Adolescent Student Health Survey conducted in 1987 with more than 11,000 8th- and 10th-grade students in 20 states. Due to the higher dropout rates in the 12th grade, the survey did not include

Table 15-1 Alcohol Consumption among 8th- and 10th-Grade Students

Student Sample	Sample Size	Students Who Had Ever Used Alcohol	Frequency of Alcohol Use during the Past 30 Days (in Percentage)			
			Students Who Abstained	Infrequent Use	Occasional Use	Frequent Use
8th Grade						
Total	5,859	75.9	67.8	20.2	6.9	5.1
Males	2,787	76.8	67.9	19.3	6.7	6.1
White	2,026	79.5	66.8	20.6	6.8	5.8
Black	325	68.3	75.2	12.1	6.7	6.0
Hispanic	218	75.2	58.9	22.3	10.7	8.1
Females	2,875	75.1	67.6	21.1	7.1	4.2
White	2,125	77.6	66.9	21.7	7.5	4.0
Black	300	64.3	75.3	16.1	4.3	4.3
Hispanic	237	75.1	62.6	23.0	9.0	5.4
10th Grade						
Total	5,560	87.3	47.7	25.6	13.6	13.2
Males	2,696	87.3	46.1	24.7	13.9	15.3
White	1.954	90.4	43.2	25.5	14.7	16.6
Black	352	75.9	60.8	22.2	7.9	9.1
Hispanic	235	84.7	45.1	22.8	17.2	14.9
Females	2,687	87.2	49.2	26.5	13.2	11.1
White	1,967	89.9	45.4	27.1	15.0	12.4
Black	365	79.7	65.7	23.8	5.9	4.6
Hispanic	232	81.0	54.8	24.4	10.6	10.1

Note: Numbers in columns may not add up to total or to 100 percent, as not all data for all subgroups are reported.
Source: from "Alcohol Use and Abuse: Some Findings from the National Adolescent Student Health Survey," by M. Windle in *Alcohol Health and Research World,* 1991, *15,* 5–10.

this grade because it might have given a biased picture of developmental trends. The results generally agreed with those from other surveys of adolescent drinking such as the New York State survey (Barnes & Welte, 1986a). As shown in Table 15-1, prevalence of ever having used alcohol was high (75.9 percent for 8th graders and 87.3 percent for 10th graders). Comparable rates were found for boys and girls. African-American students had lower rates than whites or Hispanics.

The frequency of drinking in the past 30 days shows that two thirds of the 8th graders but only half of the 10th graders abstained. The rate of occasional or frequent drinking for the 10th graders was double that for the 8th graders. Heavy drinking, defined as five or more drinks on one occasion in the past two weeks, increased with age, being 23.7 percent for the 8th graders and 36.6 percent for the 10th graders. Sex and ethnic differences were similar to those for lifetime prevalence, with small differences between boys and girls and the least drinking among African Americans. Heavier drinkers of both sexes were found to have started drinking at an earlier age and were more likely to engage in polydrug use.

Most surveys of adolescent drinking have been cross-sectional in design, permitting comparisons of different age groups but not allowing assessment of underlying developmental processes over time. For an understanding of the processes involved in the initiation and development of drinking, longitudinal studies assessing the same individuals before and after drinking begins are needed. Jessor and Jessor (1975) conducted a four-year longitudinal study of male and female junior high school students and examined the contribution of personality variables to the onset of drinking and development of alcohol problems. Age of initiation of drinking was lower for those who placed lower value on achievement, held lower expectations of achievements, and placed a higher value on independence. Early drinkers were also more tolerant of deviance, lower in religiosity, and perceived fewer liabilities of drinking. Problem drinkers and nonproblem drinkers differed in that the former had a greater tolerance for deviance, perceived more positive than negative consequences, and placed lower value on achievement.

Other longitudinal studies have shown similar relationships between general delinquency and problem behaviors and use of alcohol and other drugs. The National Longitudinal Youth Survey conducted by the U.S. Department of Labor demonstrated that the level of antisocial behavior during early adolescence (ages 14–15) was predictive of alcohol and drug use levels four years later (ages 18–19), especially for males (Windle, 1990).

Although the high rates of heavy use by adolescents found in most surveys are disturbing, one encouraging finding is that a high percentage show decreased use of alcohol only a few years later. Donovan, Jessor, and Jessor (1983) found that those adolescents who were not involved with other forms of problem behavior were likely to later lower their drinking levels, suggesting that their earlier use may have been a form of experimentation rather than a precursor of heavier use. More than half of the adolescent problem drinkers who became nonproblem drinkers by young adulthood had married during the period, in contrast to only 20 percent of the adolescent problem drinkers who remained so during young adulthood. Temple and Fillmore (1985) also found that boys who were problem drinkers at age 18 often showed improvement only a few years later.

Similar changes have been found with older adolescents in the transition period from late adolescence to adulthood. Grant, Harford, and Grigson (1988) measured the stability of alcohol consumption patterns among youth aged 17–24 years who were studied in a National Longitudinal Survey of Labor Market Experience in Youth conducted by the U.S. Department of Labor in 1982–83. Grant et al. examined changes in drinking over this two-year period by charting four different groups—new drinkers during the period, drinkers who reverted to nondrinkers during the period, drinkers at both measurement times, and abstainers who did not drink at either measurement time. Most drinkers at the first measurement, 86 percent, were still drinkers at the second measurement, but the percentage of heavy drinkers had declined, especially for women. The prevalence of each consumption category increased between ages 17–22 but then declined for ages 23–24 for both sexes. Grant et al. speculated that this decline in drinking may have occurred at that age because it is a time when many young adults begin to assume more adult responsibilities.

Surveys of College Student Drinking

Although most college students are over 18 years of age, many of them would not be included as part of national probability surveys since they are not living at home. As a whole, they should hold higher values and expectations for achievement than the problem drinkers at the high school level. However, problem drinkers among them might have lower aspirations and achievement relative to nonproblem-drinking college students. Finally, since college students are a group highly selected for intelligence and academic achievement, drinking patterns may be different from their age cohort that is not enrolled in college. Differences in drinking between high school and college students should not be attributed primarily to age differences since the two populations vary in many respects other than age that might affect drinking.

During the period of 1949–52, Straus and Bacon (1953) conducted a survey of drinking of more than 15,000 students at 27 different colleges and universities. Overall, 74 percent reported using alcoholic beverages while 26 percent were abstainers. With each successive college year, the percentage of drinkers increased. Parental drinking levels were related to those of both men and women students. Gender differences were found in the reasons for drinking, with 47 percent of the men and only 17 percent of the women reporting that they drank "to get high." Men, not surprisingly, exceeded women to a greater extent in using alcohol "to get drunk." They drank more frequently and in greater quantity. Negative consequences such as blackouts were reported by 18 percent of the men and 5 percent of the women.

Fillmore and Midanik (1984) and Fillmore (1975) conducted 20- and 25-year follow-ups of the students studied by Straus and Bacon (1953). As Figure 15-2 shows, the college drinking levels of both males and females was closely tied to drinking levels 25 years later for the overall sample. The majority of college nonproblem drinkers remained without problems, with a small percentage becoming either abstainers or problem drinkers. The largest percentage of current abstainers were found among those who had been abstainers in college, although a high percentage of this group had become nonproblem drinkers over the 25 years. Most interesting, perhaps, was that although the highest percentage of problem drinkers 25 years later came from the group who were problem drinkers in college, the majority of college problem drinkers had become nonproblem drinkers and some even abstainers.

Fillmore and Midanik (1984) suggested that many heavy drinkers in college show a reduction or stability in drinking levels only a few years after leaving college, perhaps reflecting a maturing process. The change in drinking may result from the departure from the college environment in which many other students drink frequently and heavily. On the other hand, it should also be noted that some nonproblem college drinkers had developed problem drinking status by middle age.

Wechsler and McFadden (1979) used a mail survey to assess the alcohol drinking patterns, consequences, and correlates of about 7,000 college students at 34 New England colleges and universities, with a return rate ranging from 51 to 87

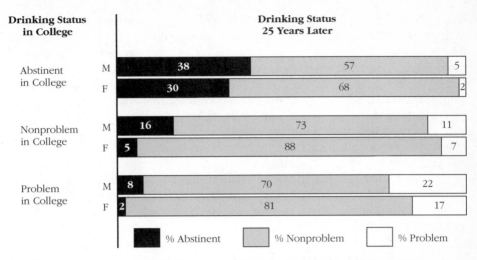

Figure 15-2 Reported drinking status of men and women in college and 25 years later.

Source: from *Alcohol Drinking Behavior and Attitudes Rutgers Panel Study* by K. M. Fillmore, S. Bacon & M. Hyman. NIAAA Contract ADM 281-76-0015. Reprinted by permission of the author.

percent at different schools. Compared with the results found 25 years earlier by Straus and Bacon (1953), they found *increased* drinking among college students. In accord with most other studies of college students since the 1950s, drinking was found to be nearly universal, with fewer than 5 percent abstainers. Men drank more frequently and in larger quantities than women, with a third of men being classified as frequent-heavy drinkers in comparison to a tenth of the women. Parental use of alcohol as well as drinking in high school was found to be related to more college drinking. In agreement with other studies, there was an inverse relationship between academic performance and amount of drinking. Over a third of the men and a sixth of the women were drunk at least once a month. Physical fights and difficulties with authorities due to drinking occurred for a fifth of the men.

A replication of the Wechsler and McFadden survey was conducted by Meilman, Stone, Gaylor, and Turco (1990) at a private rural New England university to optimize comparability. Unlike many surveys that use a convenience sample, Meilman et al. used a random sampling procedure to obtain a sample of 350 mainly white respondents between the ages of 17 and 21, with about 60 percent males and 40 percent females. Their results suggested a lower rate of daily consumption, especially among males, than Wechsler and McFadden had found ten years earlier. In fact, a quarter of the respondents drank less than a drink per week. Nonetheless, alcohol-related problems were still frequent, with more than a quarter of the respondents reporting having had a hangover and 30 percent indicating some disruption of normal functioning due to drinking within the past week.

These findings may not be limited to this type of institution, as O'Hare (1990) obtained comparable results at a large public Eastern university. Overall drinking seems to have declined, because about one fifth of the respondents indicated they were abstainers as compared to only 3.7 percent a decade earlier (Wechsler & McFadden, 1979). However, rates of heavy drinking were still comparable, at about one fifth of the white respondents. Although males drank more than females did, there were comparable levels of alcohol-related problems for both sexes. The combination of small body size for women and the possible differences in social attitudes toward drinking by women might contribute to this discrepancy. Finally, a comparison of drinkers over and under 21 showed that the level of consumption and associated problems were equivalent, implying that legal controls were ineffective as factors affecting drinking by college students.

One must be careful in making comparisons over long time periods, however, as the percentage of the general population that attends college has increased considerably since the early 1950s. Thus, some of the increases in drinking among college students in the 1990s may be due to this broader representation of the general population.

Alcohol and Older Drinkers

"A good drink makes the old young," goes the proverb. As the "graying of America" increases with the Baby Boom generation reaching middle age and later in the 1990s, it becomes even more important to understand the nature of alcohol problems among the elderly. Physiological changes due to normal aging alter the effects of alcohol. The same dose that a younger person can consume has a greater impact on an older person since age changes the body's response to drugs.

As older persons face the psychosocial adjustments of normal aging coupled with physical aches and pains, they may increasingly use drugs and medication, in the form of legal prescription and proprietary over-the-counter drugs. Such drugs may alter the effects of alcohol, often in health-threatening ways. The combination of alcohol with many drugs and medicines taken for old-age-related health problems may produce some dangerous interactions and cross-tolerances.

Psychosocial factors must also be examined as possible determinants of drinking patterns among the older segment of the population. Retirement, declining physical health, death of a spouse and other close friends and relatives, adult children moving out of the home, and the stigma of aging in a youth-oriented society represent major stressors for many elderly.

The Societal Response to the Alcohol Problems of the Elderly

Older persons who are retired may not be regarded by society or their family as requiring treatment for alcohol problems since their jobs are not jeopardized. Even when family members are embarrassed by their excessive drinking, they may find it more convenient to deny or cover up the problem. Thus, the criterion of what constitutes an alcohol problem may vary with age. A retired person may drink to the point of intoxication, but unless he or she becomes aggressive or annoying, it may be tolerated, whereas the same impairment in a younger person would be considered a problem because it would interfere with the ability to hold employment.

Older persons are underrepresented at alcohol abuse treatment centers, suggesting that they may not perceive themselves as having abuse problems. Such perceptions are not entirely independent of societal standards and values. In addition, the elderly may face social and economic barriers to treatment access.

The Prevalence of Alcohol Problems among the Elderly

Surveys of older persons yield a range of estimates about the prevalence of alcohol problems. Community surveys (Atkinson & Schuckit, 1983; Bailey, Haberman, & Alksne, 1965) suggest that from 2 to 10 percent of the elderly suffer from alcohol problems, whereas hospital counts yield higher figures of at least 25 percent due to the high numbers of older psychiatric and medical patients, according to Gomberg (1980).

Surveys of household samples indicate that the rate of alcohol problems among older persons is *lower* than that of other age groups. Several criteria were used in a national survey by Clark and Midanik (1982) to define alcohol problems: alcohol consumption, alcohol dependence symptoms, and adverse social consequences. Defining "heavy drinking" as an average of 60 or more drinks per month for the past year, the survey found that 8 percent of the men between 61 and 70 and 13 percent of the men over 70 were heavy drinkers. Fewer than 1 percent of the women in these two age groups were judged as heavy drinkers. Clark and Midanik (1982) also found that older groups drink *less,* on the average, than younger groups.

In terms of an arbitrary cut off score of symptoms such as loss of control and blackouts, 6 percent of the men aged 61 to 70 and 2 percent of those over 70, but none of the women, were categorized as problem drinkers. Social consequences such as trouble with the law or relationship problems had occurred at least once in the past year for 9 percent of the men in the two age groups but for none of the women.

Overall, this evidence suggests that alcohol use and alcohol-related problems are actually *lower* among older populations than for younger groups. However, this conclusion is qualified by the lack of equivalent criteria to define problem drinking for different age groups. Thus, older drinkers may not have job-related difficulties due to alcohol use simply because many of them have retired.

Assuming the finding of less drinking by older individuals is valid, what factors might be responsible? Due to physiological changes, a level of alcohol use that would not be problematic for a younger person may be disruptive for an older person. Vogel-Sprott and Barrett (1984) found that a given dose of alcohol impaired motor coordination to a greater extent among older than in younger drinkers. A given dose may produce a higher blood alcohol level for older than for younger drinkers.

A major problem in interpreting cross-sectional data is determining whether the age effect reflects the process of aging or instead represents a generational or *cohort effect.* The over-65 group of the present era grew up in a different social climate with different attitudes and patterns of drinking than the younger group with which they are being compared. Many of them grew up when Temperance-era values were still influential. Thus, the over-65 group of 1990 not only is older than the 25-year-old group but also reflects the different attitudes and social values of the 1950s when they were 25. These generational differences, rather than age differences per se, could be responsible for some of the drinking differences.

Furthermore, cross-sectional age comparisons do not reveal the drinking pattern for any one individual growing older. The older group may report drinking levels that are lower relative to that of young people today, but this does not necessarily mean that they are drinking less today than they did when they themselves were younger. On the other hand, there are reasons to assume that most individuals drink less as they get older. In general, older persons have reduced income, lower tolerance for alcohol, and medical problems that may be seriously affected by alcohol use, according to Gomberg (1982).

Other reasons of a methodological nature may explain why older groups have a lower level of alcohol problems. One possible selective process involves the self-limiting nature of alcoholism. Heavy drinking may lead to more accidents, diseases, and other sources of fatality among younger groups, thus leaving the more moderate drinkers as survivors. Another more likely selective process may operate in a longitudinal study: heavier drinkers are less likely to continue through the study. They are more transient and less likely to be married or to have stable employment, and eventually may be lost for inclusion in the study, according to a speculation by Temple and Leino (1989).

Several longitudinal studies of drinking in men have been reported. Glynn, Bouchard, LoCastro, and Laird (1985) compared changes in alcohol use over a period of nine years for a sample of men between 20 and 80 years old. Although different age cohorts varied in their drinking, with the older ones drinking less than the younger ones, the changes *within* a given age cohort were small and essentially stable.

Fillmore (1987) used both longitudinal and cross-sectional designs to examine the relationship of drinking to age for men in the general population during the 1960s and 1970s. The longitudinal studies over periods of five and seven years showed a modest continuity between drinking levels of adolescence and young adulthood. Incidence of heavy drinking and alcohol problems declined with aging among men from 21 to 59, with chronicity or persistence of problems highest in middle age, followed by remission.

Fillmore also made cross-sectional age comparisons for different cohorts studied 15 years apart in 1964 and 1979, containing men who were born from the turn of the century to the 1950s. The era in which the men grew up had little effect on drinking, as the age patterns were similar to those found in the longitudinal comparisons. Helzer and Burnam (1991) also found a decline in drinking after middle age for men in the multisite Epidemiologic Catchment Area study described in Chapter 7.

However, Temple and Leino (1989) failed to find age-related drinking changes in a 20-year follow-up of men from two different general population surveys, one beginning in 1964 with men in their 20s and the other in 1967 with men between ages 21 and 59. It is possible that many men shifted their drinking patterns over the course of 20 years, but for the group as a whole, there was stability. Those individuals who did change tended to decrease rather than increase their drinking as they grew older. The possibility that the sample was biased toward more stable individuals (men who could be located after 20 years) does not account for the findings, because the initial drinking levels of the reinterviewed men and the nonrespondents did not differ.

Social changes regarding alcoholism treatment complicate the interpretation of any changes in alcoholism rates observed over time. If alcoholism treatment quality or availability decreases over the years, we might expect a rise in the number of alcoholics due to that factor alone. But if we assume that alcoholism treatment has improved or become more available over the years and that increased public awareness and more humane attitudes have led to more alcoholics receiving care, we might find that a lower percentage of the older population has drinking problems. Thus, age differences may reflect society's response as well as the biological effects of aging on the individual.

Age of Onset of Problem Drinking

It is important to distinguish between those older alcoholics who developed their problems with alcohol much earlier in life and those whose problems had a later onset. In addition, there may exist a third group of intermittent or episodic problem drinkers whose levels of drinking have fluctuated widely over their lifetimes. The cumulative effects of alcohol should be greater for those who have been drinking longer, all else being equal. Unfortunately, many age comparison studies do not include the distinction based on age of onset of drinking problems.

Early-onset alcoholics will have had many more years of abusive levels of drinking than other older drinkers. According to a model of *accelerated aging* (Ryan & Butters, 1984), early-onset alcoholics might have performance deficits across the life span, as shown in Figure 15-3. An alternative model of *increased vulnerability* mentioned in Chapter 4 holds that the impairment of alcoholics is relatively slight at younger ages and grows with increased age. Thus, we would expect early-onset alcoholics who maintain a lifetime of alcohol abuse to show large performance deficits compared to nonalcoholic elderly cohorts.

Late-onset problem drinkers, or reactive drinkers, are defined as not having problems with alcohol until after about age 40. They may then use alcohol to cope with the medical and physical impairments associated with aging as well as social status changes such as retirement or widowhood. These specific stressors that are not encountered until old age may precipitate the development of drinking problems, according to Bailey et al. (1965). Since their history of excessive drinking would be shorter than that of early-onset alcoholics, one might speculate that alcohol might not be disruptive for them. With the current definition, however, as Gomberg (1990) cautioned, by age 65 many so-called late-onset alcoholics would have had drinking problems for as long as 25 years!

Most of the evidence on the drinking of older individuals comes from clinical observations in hospitals and long-term care facilities, because the sample sizes of

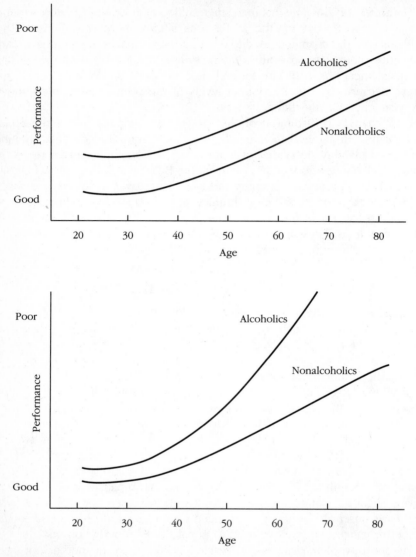

Figure 15-3 *Top:* Expected results from neuropsychological testing if the "accelerated aging" interpretation were correct. At all ages, the performance of alcoholics is poorer than, but parallel to, that of age-matched nonalcoholics. *Bottom:* Expected results if the "increased vulnerability" interpretation were correct. Only after the age of 40 does the performance of alcoholics begin to deviate significantly from that of nonalcoholics.

Source: from "Alcohol Consumption and Premature Aging: A Critical Review," by C. Ryan and N. Butters in *Recent Developments in Alcoholism* by M. Galanter (Ed.). Copyright © 1984 by Plenum Press. Reprinted by permission.

older persons with drinking problems in household survey samples is usually small. Douglass (1984) noted that no definitive epidemiological study exists of the prevalence of elderly problem drinking in the general population. Although clinical samples offer important information, he warned that the generalizability of these self-selected samples to the nonclinical general population is questionable.

A clinical study of 103 alcoholic patients by Rosin and Glatt (1971) identified 37 percent as late-onset and 63 percent as early-onset problem drinkers. Stressful life events such as retirement and loneliness were reported as reasons for drinking for a majority of the late-onset cases but for only 23 percent of the early-onset drinkers.

Finney and Moos (1984), however, cautioned that these findings are based on self-report and are likely to be biased. First, late-onset problem drinking may be more tolerated or excused if the drinker can be seen as using alcohol to cope with overwhelming stressors. Second, due to the longer time involved, early-onset drinkers may not be able to recall specific stressors that may have led to their problem drinking. Thus, it may only *seem* that specific stressors are more often involved in the development of late- as opposed to early-onset problem drinking.

Effects of Retirement on Drinking

Conflicting views about the effects of retirement on drinking exist. Blose (1978) suggested that the boredom and increased leisure time may allow more drinking. On the other hand, Gomberg (1980) argued that retirement may reduce the stresses of work as well as the contact with drinking companions from the workplace that may have contributed to preretirement drinking levels. Ekerdt, Labry, Glynn, and Davis (1989) compared drinking in men over a brief period of two years after retirement with a group of men from the same age cohort who remained employed. Retirees showed more variability in drinking levels during this period but overall were not different from the working group. However, retirees were more likely to report problems caused by their drinking toward the end of the two years. These results suggest that as retirement continues, problems associated with drinking may become more evident.

Finney and Moos (1984) pointed out that many studies of retirement do not control for sex or age. Since a higher percentage of retirees are women and/or are older than the employed comparison group, it is not clear if any of the differences in drinking are due specifically to the adjustment of retirement.

Effects of Drinking for Older Populations

Page and Cleveland (1987) failed to find evidence of greater cognitive impairment due to alcohol among older groups. They studied 322 men divided into nondrinkers, social drinkers, alcoholics (who had abstained for the past 30 days), and abstinent alcoholics (no drinking for the past five years). These men were divided into four age groups—25–34, 35–44, 45–54, 55–65—and tested on eight psychological tests of vocabulary and such.

Both age and alcoholism were associated with generally poorer performance. Older age was associated with poorer performance on all tests except for vocabulary tests. On four of the tests, alcoholics did the poorest, followed by social drinkers and nondrinkers. The age effect was much stronger than the alcoholism effect. However, contrary to the view that aging accelerates the impact of alcohol, the effects of alcoholism were actually smaller, not larger, for the older age groups than for the younger group.

Difficulties in Studying Aging and Alcoholism

Douglass (1984) discussed some of the conceptual and methodological problems of research on alcohol problems of the aged. A lack of consensus exists as to when an adult becomes "elderly"; usually a chronological age is imposed rather than one that is meaningful from a psychosocial or biological standpoint. Many of the measures and criteria that may be appropriate for younger ages may not be valid for older age groups.

Causal interpretation of the relationship of alcohol use to stressful problems such as accidents, health, work performance, relationships with family and friends, and crime is always difficult to make for any age group. The view that major life stressors may increase drinking among the elderly has an intuitive appeal, but Finney and Moos (1984) argued that one must recognize that a large percentage of the older population copes with these stressors without becoming problem drinkers. They also called attention to the number of late-onset drinkers in a study by Rosin and Glatt (1971) who did not appear to be experiencing major life stressors as precipitating factors.

Finney and Moos (1984) suggested the need to include an analysis of sociodemographic and personal factors when analyzing problem drinking among the elderly. Social status and background, as well as level of self-esteem, coping skills, cognitive appraisal, and availability of social resources may alter the impact of stressful events and moderate the need for alcohol abuse as a means of coping.

Social Class Differences. At the lower socioeconomic level, older problem drinkers are more visible because they typically drink publicly in skid row areas (Pittman & Gordon, 1958). Consequently, arrests for public intoxication may be frequent for older alcoholics from this group. In contrast, among middle-class and upper-class background groups, the older problem drinker may be tolerated, hidden, and even encouraged to drink if the drinking makes him or her more manageable.

Gender Differences. Research into the effects of alcohol on the elderly has largely ignored the female drinker. Inasmuch as gender is an important variable in drinking patterns and consequences (Wilsnack, Wilsnack, & Klassen, 1986), it is important to examine these effects for women as well as for men.

Although increased use of medication occurs for both men and women as they age, there is a higher use of tranquilizers, sedatives, and stimulant drugs by women, according to Mellinger, Balter, and Manheimer (1971). Since alcohol may have dangerous side effects and cross-tolerances with many of these drugs, alcohol use may be particularly disruptive for older women.

Conclusions

Most of us have some initial experience with drinking before we are legally eligible to drink alcohol. We enter these encounters with expectations and beliefs about the effect of alcohol based on a lifetime of vicarious learning from others and from observation of models in life and fictional accounts. By the time we have the first opportunity to drink, the event has been eagerly anticipated. One's first drink is a rite of passage from adolescence into adulthood.

Early-onset drinkers who are the most precocious with respect to alcohol use differ from later-onset drinkers or abstainers even before the first drink. They are often more rebellious, undercontrolled, impulsive, and poorer in academic achievement. Because underage drinking itself is a mild form of social deviance, it is not surprising that many early-onset drinkers also engage in a number of other behaviors that violate social norms such as use of other drugs, sexual activity, delinquency, and even criminal activities.

Attempts by adults to restrict or prohibit underage drinking may backfire by providing the added challenge to some adolescents of defying parental controls. Continually surrounded by attractive and sophisticated images of the pleasures of alcohol, adolescents are strongly motivated to at least experiment with alcohol. Those adolescents who have important activities and goals that would be jeopardized by excessive use of alcohol seem best able to avoid alcohol-related problems. In contrast, those adolescents with low self-esteem and little hope of being able to achieve success may be more likely to find excessive use of alcohol a convenient means for coping with their frustrations and failures.

College students living away from home for the first time may be exposed to more peer pressure and opportunities for drinking than they might have if they had lived at home. The academic pressures are greater than those in high school, which may also contribute to some alcohol abuse as either a cause or an effect of poor academic performance. Some of the increases in drinking found in college students may simply reflect the influence of age rather than of the college environment. No comparison is typically made of the drinking of college students with an age-matched control group of noncollege students.

Any type of environment provides its own norms and opportunities regarding alcohol use that affect the individual's drinking behavior. When students leave college, many return to a setting where alcohol use is not expected and drinking levels may decline. Many students who engage in heavy drinking due to participation in fraternities, for example, may revert to lighter drinking after graduation because they are in new environments that are not conducive to excessive drinking.

At the other end of the age distribution, one might expect the transition from full-time work to retirement to affect drinking opportunities. But while the demands of employment might keep drinking in control for most people, the freedom of retirement may be boring and allow more drinking to occur without adverse work consequences. These drinking opportunities may be even more dangerous for early-onset drinkers who have been drinking regularly or excessively for many years. By the time they reach old age, physiological changes, organic damage to the liver and other organs from excessive alcohol use, and interactions with medicines may mean that alcohol use produces more detrimental effects for older populations.

Comparisons of age effects are complicated by the fact that most studies involve cross-sectional comparisons of groups that also differ in the era during which they grew up. Since our attitudes and behaviors related to alcohol are formed by the norms that prevailed during our formative years, differences in these norms rather than physiological differences may account for the results of comparisons of the drinking of persons who differ in age.

The majority of the findings, however, do suggest that alcohol-related problems decline with age. Some of the decrease may reflect the medical complications created by drinking, Thus, if alcohol is recognized as a threat to health, older samples may voluntarily cut down consumption or may be advised by physicians to do so. In addition, if alcoholism is a self-limiting disease so that the worst cases die at an earlier age, part of the decline could be due to this elimination process. Finally, lower estimates of alcohol problems for older citizens may be partly illusory if society ignores or tolerates alcohol abuse in the elderly that it would not accept among the younger population.

References

Atkinson, J. H., Jr., & Schuckit, M. A. (1983). Geriatric alcohol and drug abuse. In N. K. Mello (Ed.) *Advances in substance abuse* (pp. 195–237). Greenwich, CT: JAI Press.

Bailey, M. B., Haberman, P. W., & Alksne, H. (1965). The epidemiology of alcoholism in an urban residential area. *Quarterly Journal of Studies on Alcohol, 26,* 19–40.

Barnes, G. M., & Welte, J. (1986a). Patterns and predictors of alcohol use among 7–12th grade students in New York State. *Journal of Studies on Alcohol, 47,* 53–62.

Barnes, G. M., & Welte, J. W. (1986b). Adolescent alcohol abuse: Subgroup differences and relationships to other problem behaviors. *Journal of Adolescent Research, 1,* 79–94.

Blose, I. L. (1978). The relationship of alcohol to aging and the elderly. *Alcoholism: Clinical and Experimental Research, 2,* 17–21.

Clark, W. B., & Midanik, L. (1982). Alcohol use and alcohol problems among U.S. adults: Results of the 1979 national survey. In National Institute on Alcohol Abuse and Alcoholism (Ed.), *Alcohol consumption and related problems* (Monograph No. 1, pp. 3–52). Washington, DC: U.S. Government Printing Office.

Donovan, J., & Jessor, R. (1985). Structure of problem behavior in adolescence and young adulthood. *Journal of Clinical and Consulting Psychology, 53,* 890–894.

Donovan, J., Jessor, R., & Jessor, L. (1983). Problem drinking in adolescence and young adulthood: A follow-up study. *Journal of Studies on Alcohol, 44,* 109–137.

Douglass, R. L. (1984). Aging and alcohol problems: Opportunities for socioepidemiological research. In M. Galanter (Ed.), *Recent developments in alcoholism* Vol. 2 (pp. 251–266). New York: Plenum Press.

Ekerdt, D. J., Labry, L. O., Glynn, R. J., & Davis, R. W. (1989). Change in drinking behaviors with retirement: Findings from the Normative Aging Study. *Journal of Studies on Alcohol, 50,* 347–353.

Fillmore, K. M. (1975). Relationships between specific drinking patterns in early adulthood and middle age: An exploratory 20-year follow-up study. *Journal of Studies on Alcohol, 36,* 882–907.

Fillmore, K. M. (1987). Prevalence, incidence and chronicity of drinking patterns and problems among men as a function of age: A longitudinal and cohort analysis. *British Journal of Addiction, 82,* 77–83.

Fillmore, K. M., & Midanik, L. (1984). Chronicity of drinking problems among men: A longitudinal study. *Journal of Studies on Alcohol, 45,* 228–236.

Finney, J. W., & Moos, R. H. (1984). Life stressors and problem drinking among older adults. In M. Galanter (Ed.), *Recent developments in alcoholism* (pp. 267–288). New York: Plenum Press.

Glynn, R. J., Bouchard, G. R., LoCastro, J. S., & Laird, N. M. (1985). Aging and generational effects on drinking behaviors in men: Results from the Normative Aging Study. *American Journal of Public Health, 75,* 1413–1419.

Gomberg, E. S. (1980). Drinking and problem drinking among the elderly. *Alcohol, drugs, and aging* (Usage and Problems Series, No. 1). Ann Arbor, MI: University of Michigan, Institute of Gerontology.

Gomberg, E. S. (1982). Alcohol use and problems among the elderly. In National Institute on Alcohol Abuse and Alcoholism (Ed.), *Alcohol and health monograph no. 4: Special population issues* (pp. 263–292). Washington, DC: U.S. Government Printing Office.

Gomberg, E.S.L. (1990). Drugs, alcohol, and aging. In L. Kozlowski, H. M. Annis, H. D. Cappell, F. B. Glaser, M. S. Goodstadt, Y. Isreal, H. Kalant, E. M. Sellers, & E. R. Vingilis (Eds.), *Recent advances in alcohol and drug problems* (Vol. 10, pp. 171–213). New York: Plenum Press.

Grant, B. F., Harford, T. C., & Grigson, M. B. (1988). Stability of alcohol consumption among youth: A national longitudinal survey. *Journal of Studies on Alcohol, 49,* 253–260.

Helzer, J. E., & Burnam, M. A. (1991). Epidemiology of alcohol addiction: United States. In N. S. Miller (Ed.), *Comprehensive handbook of drug and alcohol addiction* (pp. 9–38). New York: Marcel Dekker.

Jessor, R., & Jessor, S. (1975). Adolescent development and the onset of drinking: A longitudinal study. *Journal of Studies on Alcohol, 36,* 27–51.

Jessor, R., & Jessor, S. (1977). *Problem behavior and psychosocial development: A longitudinal study.* New York: Academic Press.

Johnston, L. D., O'Malley, P. M., & Bachman, J. G. (1986). *Drug use among American high school, college students, and young adults: National trends through 1985.* (DHHS Pub. No. ADM86-1450). Rockville, MD: ADHAMA.

Johnston, L. D., O'Malley, P. M., & Bachman, J. G. (1989). *Drug use, drinking, and smoking: National survey results from high school, college, and young adult populations, 1975–88* (DHHS Pub. No. ADM89-1638). Rockville, MD: ADHAMA.

Johnston, L. D., O'Malley, P. M., & Bachman, J. G. (1991). *Drug use among American high school students, college students, and other young adults, 1975–1990. Vol 1. High school seniors* (DHHS Pub. No. ADM91-1813). Rockville, MD: ADHAMA.

Meilman, P. W., Stone, J. E., Gaylor, M. S., & Turco, J. H. (1990). Alcohol consumption by college undergraduates: Current use and 10-year trends. *Journal of Studies on Alcohol, 51,* 389–395.

Mellinger, G. D., Balter, M. B., & Manheimer, D. I. (1971). Patterns of psychotherapeutic drug use among adults in San Francisco. *Archives of General Psychiatry, 25,* 385–394.

Newcomb, M. D., Maddahian, E., & Bentler, P. M. (1986). Risk factors for drug use among adolescents: Concurrent and longitudinal analyses. *American Journal of Public Health, 76,* 525–531.

O'Hare, T. M. (1990). Drinking in college: Consumption patterns, problems, sex differences and legal drinking age. *Journal of Studies on Alcohol, 51,* 536–541.

Page, R. D., & Cleveland, M. F. (1987). Cognitive dysfunction and aging among male alcoholics and social drinkers. *Alcoholism: Clinical and Experimental Research, 11,* 376–384.

Pentz, M. (1983). Prevention of adolescent substance use through social skill development. In T. J. Glynn, C. G. Leukefeld, & J. P. Ludford (Eds.), *Preventing adolescent drug use* (pp. 195–225). Rockville, MD: National Institute of Drug Abuse.

Pittman, D. J., & Gordon, C. W. (1958). *Revolving door: A study of the chronic police case inebriate.* Glencoe, IL: Free Press.

Rachal, J. V., Maisto, S. A., Guess, L. L., & Hubbard, R. L. (1982). Alcohol use among adolescents. In National Institute on Alcohol Abuse and Alcoholism (Ed.), *Alcohol consumption and related problems.* (Alcohol and Health Monograph No. 1, pp. 525–531). Washington, DC: U.S. Government Printing Office.

Rosin, A. J., & Glatt, M. M. (1971). Alcohol excess in the elderly. *Quarterly Journal of Studies on Alcohol, 32,* 53–59.

Ryan, C., & Butters, N. (1984). Alcohol consumption and premature aging: A critical review. In M. Galanter (Ed.), *Recent developments in alcoholism Vol. 2* (pp. 223–250). New York: Plenum Press.

Shedler, J., & Block, J. (1990). Adolescent drug use and psychological health. *American Psychologist, 45,* 612–630.

Straus, A., & Bacon, S. (1953). *Drinking in college.* New Haven CT: Yale University Press.

Temple, M., & Fillmore, K. M. (1985). The variability of drinking patterns and problems among young men, age 16–31: A longitudinal study. *International Journal of Addictions, 20,* 1595–1620.

Temple, M. T., & Leino, V. (1989). Long-term outcomes of drinking: A 20-year longitudinal study of men. *British Journal of Addiction, 84,* 889–900.

Vogel-Sprott, M., & Barrett, B. (1984). Age, drinking habits and the effects of alcohol. *Journal of Studies on Alcohol, 45,* 517–521.

Wechsler, H., & McFadden, M. (1979). Drinking among college students in New England. *Journal of Studies on Alcohol, 40,* 969–996.

Welte, J. W., & Barnes, G. M. (1987). Alcohol use among adolescent minority groups. *Journal of Studies on Alcohol, 48,* 329–336.

White, H. R., & Labouvie, E. W. (1989). Toward the assessment of adolescent problem drinking. *Journal of Studies on Alcohol, 50,* 30–37.

Wilsnack, S. C., Wilsnack, R. W., & Klassen, A. D. (1986). Epidemiological research on women's drinking, 1978–1984. In National Institute on Alcohol Abuse and Alcoholism (Ed.), *Women and alcohol: Health-related issues* (Research Monograph No. 16, DHHS Pub. No. ADM86-1139, pp. 1–68). Washington, DC: U.S. Government Printing Office.

Windle, M. (1990). A longitudinal study of antisocial behaviors in early adolescence as predictors of late adolescent substance use: Gender and ethnic group differences. *Journal of Abnormal Psychology, 99,* 86–91.

Windle, M. (1991). Alcohol use and abuse: Some findings from the National Adolescent Student Health Survey. *Alcohol Health and Research World, 15*(1), 5–10.

Zucker, R. A., & Harford, T. C. (1980). National study of the demography of adolescent drinking practices in 1980. *Journal of Studies on Alcohol, 44,* 974–985.

SIXTEEN

Ethnic Differences in Drinking Patterns and Consequences

Alcohol is consumed in virtually all cultures, although the traditions and customs governing its use vary widely. Similarly, the extent to which problems arise with the use of alcohol appears to depend on societal values and responses to alcohol consumption. Therefore, it is important to examine the role of the broad context of sociocultural factors in alcohol use to fully comprehend drinking behavior and consequences. A complete understanding of the nature of alcohol problems cannot be achieved by studying biopsychological variables and processes exclusively. This chapter looks at sociocultural differences in drinking patterns and drinking problems with an emphasis on ethnic minority groups in the United States.

Cross-Cultural Comparisons of Drinking

Although alcohol consumption is a widespread activity, the social and cultural factors that affect drinking vary widely across cultures, according to ethnographers such as Horton (1943) and MacAndrew and Edgerton (1969).

Using data on drinking in 77 different primitive societies from the Yale University Cross-Cultural Survey, Horton (1943) found that alcohol consumption was higher in those societies with more primitive food-gathering techniques. He hypothesized that because subsistence anxiety would be greater in these societies, greater use of alcohol would occur to lower this anxiety.

Bales (1946) proposed that alcohol consumption meets four different kinds of needs: religious, ceremonial, hedonistic (pleasure), and utilitarian (tension reduction). The first two needs are social whereas the latter two are individual. Societies differ in the extent to which these needs are emphasized. The Jewish, for example, place an emphasis on the ritual aspects of alcohol consumption but are less likely to use alcohol to meet hedonistic needs.

The temporal pattern of drinking also differs for various cultures. Whereas citizens of wine-drinking countries such as France may consume alcohol frequently throughout the day and week, the pattern in the United States is markedly different. Drinking may be light during the work week, especially during working hours, but become heavier during cocktail and "happy hours" and especially on weekends.

Furthermore, the incidence of problems associated with drinking varies across nations. In comparison to other major nations, the United States does not have the highest level of liver cirrhosis mortality, but falls near the top of the distribution even though its per capita consumption is closer to the middle of the range. Figure 16-1 presents information about the level of per capita alcohol consumption and the incidence of liver cirrhosis, a widely used index of alcoholism, and shows the close correspondence between the two measures across a number of nations. Alcoholism is higher in countries such as France where wine consumption is a daily practice for many. On the other hand, rates of alcoholism lower than those found in the United States can be found in many Asian countries and among the Jews.

Ethnic Differences in Drinking Patterns and Consequences

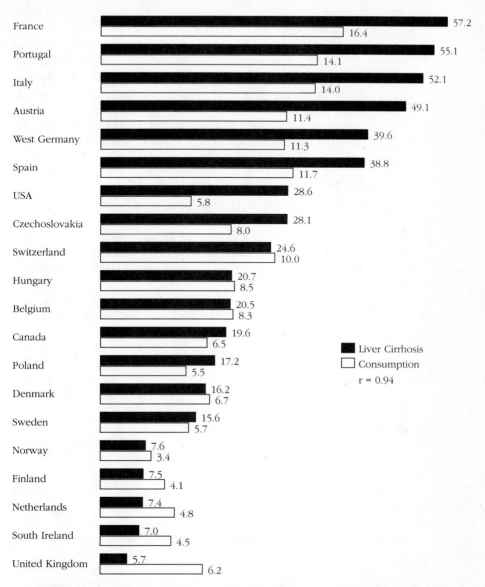

Figure 16-1 Cirrhosis mortality per 100,000 population 25 years of age and older and alcohol consumption per capita. (Death rates for the United States and Belgium are for 1971; all other death rates are for 1972. Consumption figures are the 1968–70 averages.)

Source: from "Cirrhosis and Alcohol Consumption: An Epidemiological Perspective" by W. Schmidt in G. Edwards and M. Grants (Eds.), *Alcoholism: New Knowledge and New Responses.* Copyright © 1977 by Croom Helm. Reprinted by permission.

Explanations of Cross-Cultural Differences

Both heredity and environment create variance in alcoholism rates across different nations. Citizens of different nations not only have different genetic and physiological factors but also vary with respect to cultural norms and values. The extent to which social institutions such as religion control behavior varies. Economic and political conditions are not the same across nations or even within the same country over different years. All of these factors may combine to determine the nature of drinking patterns and the consequences of such behavior.

Italian, Irish, and Jewish Drinking

A brief examination of the sociocultural contexts for three different ethnic groups illustrates the diversity of influences environmental context can exert on drinking. Italian society involves widespread consumption of alcohol, especially wine, but does not have extreme levels of alcoholism. In contrast, Irish society has suffered excessively from high rates of alcohol problems, while Jewish society is noted for its low alcoholism rates.

In Italian society, wine plays an integral role, being a part of daily life and mealtime activities. The symbolic association between wine and the blood of Christ leads to the belief that wine may have beneficial effects on health. Accordingly, wine is consumed daily, usually with meals, and in the home with family members. It also has a significant role in religious experience since the Catholic faith uses wine to represent the blood of Christ during the sacrament of Communion. Wine is highly regarded as a health-promoting substance, to be preferred to the unpalatable and often unsafe drinking water.

In this cultural context, it should not be surprising that Lolli, Serianni, Golder, and Luzzatto-Fegiz (1958) found that a large proportion of the Italian population could drink regularly and in large amounts without suffering immediate alcohol-related social problems such as drunkenness or public intoxication, although delayed physical damage such as cirrhosis might occur at a high rate. Simboli (1985) reported that Italian Americans continued these practices with similar consequences. However, it appears that succeeding generations of Italian Americans that are more acculturated to American drinking styles have increasing problems associated with drinking.

In contrast, alcohol problems have historically been high among the Irish (Bales, 1946). It should be noted that the Catholic church in Ireland places a strong emphasis on maintaining chastity while delaying marriage. Hard pub drinking serves as a rite of passage for the high percentage of bachelors, even though the Catholic church regards drunkenness as a mortal sin. Hard drinking is expected and valued among males, who often drink in groups of bachelors as part of the communal conviviality, although drunkenness is not condoned. In addition, this nation had been devastated for years by poor economic conditions, a factor that may be conducive to drinking as a form of escape.

The large numbers of Irish who immigrated to the United States in the late 1900s also faced economic hardship and obstacles to marriage (Stivers, 1985). Their tendency to settle in large urban areas ensured the creation of ethnic slums where saloon life and drinking played a central role. The establishment of street gangs as well as political machines also promoted drinking among males. Stivers (1985) noted that drink eventually acquired a sacredness, as if it were a core part of Irish lifestyle and community. To be Irish obligated one to engage in hard drinking as a key aspect of personal identity. Irish Americans became stereotyped as drunkards, which in turn served to further promote an ethic of hard drinking among them.

Finally, the example of Jewish drinking values reveals the influence of culture as a factor that can actively work to minimize excessive drinking and its adverse consequences. Snyder (1958) suggested that the religious traditions of Orthodox Judaism fostered ceremonial use of alcohol and taught drinking norms that prevented excessive use. Although surveys by Cahalan, Cisin, and Crossley (1969) found that a large percentage of American Jews drink, their alcoholism rates are actually low, according to Greeley, McCready, and Theisen (1980).

Glassner and Berg (1980) interviewed a cross section of New York Jews about their drinking attitudes and practices. Alcohol problems were perceived to be non-Jewish, or something that happened in non-Jewish cultures. To the extent that one was strongly Jewish, one confined most of one's social contacts to other Jews; thus, peers protected each other from undue influence of non-Jewish drinking patterns. Glassner and Berg (1980) observed that some Jews devised avoidance repertoires or strategies to resist the pressure from Gentiles to engage in non-Jewish drinking styles. One respondent noted that "my not drinking tends to make more people uncomfortable than their drinking makes me." Consequently, at parties one couple worked out a scheme whereby the wife would reprimand the husband for drinking too much, when actually he was still nursing his first or second drink. In short, unlike the alcoholic who is searching for excuses to drink, many Jewish respondents sought rationalizations for *not* drinking.

Drinking of Ethnic Minorities in the United States

A different comparison of ethnicity as a determinant of alcohol use can be obtained by looking at subcultural differences among ethnic minority groups within the same country, rather than across different societies. Interpretations must be cautious, however, since some of the observed differences can be attributed to social class and religious differences rather than to ethnicity per se.

A number of national surveys (Caetano, 1988; Clark & Midanik, 1982; Herd, 1988a) have shown that the patterns and consequences of drinking differ widely across ethnic minority groups in America. Moreover, a parallel exists between the drinking levels of these minority groups and the patterns shown in their countries of origin, according to Bales (1946) and Blane (1977).

One important additional factor is the minority status held by subgroups in the host culture. Minority group members in the United States are often the targets of racial prejudice and discrimination. Lack of education and unfamiliarity with the English language, especially for recent immigrants, are additional burdens relegating these groups to lower incomes. Thus, minority group members differ from majority group members not only in culture and heredity but also in social status, making explanations of drinking differences among subgroups more difficult.

In the following discussion of alcohol use and abuse among American minority groups, it must be emphasized at the outset that each of the minority groups to be examined—African Americans, Hispanic Americans, Native Americans, and Asian Americans—are not homogenous groups, as often implied, and that much subgroup variation in ethnic styles exists. Lex (1987) warned that caution must be used in interpreting minority-majority group differences, because other factors such as socioeconomic level, health status, and education level may also differ among the various groups. Moreover, generalizations about each group are often based on observations of a limited subset of drinkers, mainly those who are male, unemployed, or with low incomes. The focus on problems created by drinking for these groups should not allow us to ignore comparisons of problems among groups such as women, the employed, and the affluent.

Methodological Issues

Lex (1987) described two approaches, which differ widely in methodology, used to provide evidence about the drinking behavior of ethnic minorities. The *community* or *population survey* uses standard and objective methods to obtain self-reports from a representative sample of the total population, including, of course, members of all minority groups. In contrast, *ethnography* uses the methods of field researchers such as anthropologists and makes field observations and inferences about the meaning or role of drinking in the context of an ethnic group's values and traditions rather than focusing narrowly on quantitative descriptions of the quantity and the frequency of consumption of various types of alcoholic beverages. Ethnographers typically have used nonrandom samples, relied on indigenous reports about drinking, and reported modal patterns. Despite these important differences, Lex felt that each approach is useful and that together the data can be meaningfully combined to further understanding of drinking behaviors.

African Americans

African Americans, representing 12 percent of the population in 1990 (Bureau of the Census, 1992), are the largest minority group in the United States. This group has suffered heavily from the adverse effects of alcohol, according to Harper (1976). Economic factors may be related to heavy drinking among African Americans as both contributing factors and consequences. Living in poverty without hope of improvement might lead to more drinking. At the level of individual behavior, drinking by African Americans has been viewed as a reaction to stress or a form of escape to deal with poverty and racism (Harper, 1976; Stern, 1967). However, heavy drinking can also reduce one's economic condition by jeopardizing the ability to gain or hold employment.

Alcohol Consumption. In general population surveys, measures of drinking patterns are often based on combinations of two aspects of consumption, the frequency and the amount, instead of the total volume of alcohol. Measures of drinking patterns allow identification of different drinking styles that involve the same total volume of alcohol, but which can produce marked differences in consequences. Thus, a daily frequency of consuming one drink each day is less likely to create problems compared to a once-a-week consumption of six drinks each time, even though the total consumption over a whole month would be similar.

"Frequent" drinking is arbitrarily defined in these surveys as consumption of alcohol one or more times per week while "less frequent" drinking involves drinking less than once a week. An infrequent drinker consumes alcohol less than once a month. "Heavy" drinking is defined arbitrarily as always drinking more than five drinks per sitting. Maximum refers to the largest number of drinks per sitting, with a "low max" referring to never drinking five or more drinks at a sitting and a "high max" involving occasionally drinking more than five drinks at a sitting.

The earlier population surveys by Cahalan et al. (1969) found a comparable percentage (21 percent) of heavy drinking among African-American and white men, but a percentage three times higher for African-American women (11 percent) as for white women (4 percent). Later national surveys by Clark and Midanik (1982) showed heavier drinking for white than for African-American males but the reverse among females.

Herd (1990) found that the age distributions for drinking differed for African-American and white men, with the levels increasing over age 30 for African Americans, but declining after 30 for whites, as shown in Table 16-1. She also found (not shown) that whites drank more if they had higher income and lived in "wet" regions, while the opposite pattern existed for African-American men. Abstention rates were higher for African-American men than for white men.

Alcohol Problems. As noted earlier, white and African-American males report similar drinking patterns in surveys taken by Cahalan et al. (1969), yet African Americans develop higher rates of physial health problems as a result, according to Herd (1987). She attributed this disparity to factors such as racial prejudice, unemployment, poor health, and poor living conditions. Among the physical health hazards increased by heavy drinking among African Americans, was higher liver cirrhosis mortality in several urban areas for African-American men (Malin, Croakley, Kaelber, Munch, & Holland, 1982). Rimmer, Pitts, Reich, and Winokur (1971) found substantially more African-Amercan than white alcoholics with medical complications in psychiatric hospitals even though lifetime prevalence rates of alcoholism were comparable at around 14 percent for African-American and white males, as defined by DSM-III criteria (Robins, Helzer, Weissman, Orvascel, Gruenberg, Burker, & Regier, 1984).

The utilization of alcoholism treatment facilities is one index of the extent of drinking problems. However, ethnic comparisons can be misleading because economic and social factors may bias access to treatment. The 1989 National Drug and Alcoholism Treatment Unit Survey (NDATUS) report (National Institute of Drug Abuse/National Institute on Alcohol Abuse and Alcoholism, 1990) on alcoholism treatment in the United States showed that 15 percent of the total alcoholism clients were African American. Since African Americans constitute only about 12 percent of the population, they are overrepresented in alcoholism treatment.

Table 16-1 A Comparison of African-American and White Drinking Levels as a Function of Age

Drinking Category	18–29		30–39		40–49		50–59		60+	
	Blacks n = (208)	*Whites* n = (201)	*Blacks* n = (169)	*Whites* n = (167)	*Blacks* n = (115)	*Whites* n = (97)	*Blacks* n = (77)	*Whites* n = (90)	*Blacks* n = (145)	*Whites* n = (187)
Abstainers	23%	17%	15%	13%	37%	21%	29%	30%	60%	41%
Infrequent	10	8	6	10	8	16	23	7	14	12
Less frequent, low maximum	10	11	8	8	9	14	4	6	6	9
Less frequent, high maximum	13	10	7	9	3	2	3	8	1	0
Frequent, low maximum	10	4	15	12	13	10	14	13	7	24
Frequent, high maximum	17	20	33	26	17	17	7	19	6	10
Frequent, heavier	16	31	17	21	14	19	20	17	5	4

Source: Reprinted with permission from *Journal of Studies on Alcohol,* vol. 51, pp. 221–232, 1990. Copyright by Alcohol Research Documentation, Inc., Rutgers Center of Alcohol Studies, New Brunswick, NJ 08903.

Cultural Factors. It is difficult to define a single African-American "drinking style" in that both heavy drinking and abstinence orientations can be found, according to Herd (1985). The strong influence of fundamentalist Protestant beliefs among many African Americans may contribute to the high level of abstinence, while the need for a coping response to deal with prejudice and poverty might contribute to the high level of problem drinking.

Herd maintained that an ethnohistorical understanding is needed to explain African-American alcohol use. In the early days of slavery, alcohol was valued and was a part of an African-American tradition that was not accompanied by high rates of disorderly drunkenness. Then came a shift toward temperance in the United States, partly in concert with the move toward abolition of slavery. African Americans assumed a strong attitude of abstinence, as alcohol was viewed as a symbol of white oppression. The African-American church emerged as a powerful advocate for temperance. When Prohibition came, along with white supremacist and segregationist views, African-American views of alcohol as a form of oppression were strengthened. Later, mass migration from the rural South to the industrial cities of the North served to loosen African Americans from social forces such as their church, which discouraged excess drinking. Surrounded by the urban environment with its night life and tavern drinking, alcohol again shifted in its significance toward a symbol of urbanity and freedom. Even today, alcohol represents sophistication, prestige, and affluence for many urban African Americans.

Studies that fail to recognize the historical context tend to focus on deviant drinking by African Americans, particularly by youth who are assumed to engage in alcohol abuse due to alienation from society. In part, this misrepresentation stems from the use of small and usually unrepresentative samples.

The primary measures of alcohol consumption in most studies are the quantity and the frequency of use, but Gaines (1985) argued that for African Americans it is especially important to consider the *quality* of the beverage and the *place of consumption*. A concern with quality can be seen in the focus on brand-name liquors as the only suitable beverages. Drinking in public places is disfavored since drinking is regarded as more appropriate at private social gatherings to enhance conviviality. Whether or not drinking is viewed as a problem is not a simple matter of the amount consumed but rather is decided more based on type and context of drinking and its impact on family relationships and job performance.

Analysis of data from a 1984 national probability survey by Herd (1988b) showed evidence suggesting some major changes in African-American drinking behavior. Unlike in the past, in the 1980s African-American men reared in dry areas such as the rural South were drinking more than those who grew up in the urban North. No such pattern reversal was found for whites, who drank more heavily if they came from traditionally "wet" areas. Arrests for public drunkenness and driving while intoxicated were more comparable for African Americans and whites than in the past, when African Americans showed a higher incidence. Herd also found that heavier drinking for African-American males did not cluster around the same social factors found for whites (for example, Catholics, high income, residents of urban North).

Herd (1987) argued that contrary to past beliefs that African-American drinking was due to psychopathology, the rapid changes in African-American drinking behavior suggest that such behavior may be highly responsive to social conditions and changes. Analysis of the social meaning of drinking may be needed to understand these patterns as well as to plan effective interventions. She speculated that the past emphasis on family environment as a determinant of African-American drinking may be less salient than legal, political, and economic factors.

Treatment for African-American alcoholism has not considered the definition of alcoholism as viewed in African-American communities, and more culturally sensitive approaches are advocated by Brisbane and Wells (1989). They point out the strong influence of church and family on a view prevalent among African Americans that the alcoholic person, not the alcohol, is responsible for the problems and could, if he or she wished, control his or her behavior. The AA conception of alcoholism as a disease is not consistent with a common view in African-American communities of alcoholism as immoral or sinful behavior.

Hispanic Americans

Hispanic Americans comprise a heterogenous population of more than 22 million persons primarily with Mexican, Cuban, Puerto Rican, or Central and South American heritage, being the second largest ethnic minority in the United States (Bureau of the Census, 1992). With the rapid growth over the past decade, it represented about 9 percent of the population in 1990.

Caetano (1990) pointed out the lack of comparability across different studies— most previous national surveys on drinking focused on the general population (for example, Cahalan et al., 1969) and did not adequately measure Hispanic drinking. Anthropological and sociological studies, primarily limited to the Southwest, did focus on Hispanics but dealt mostly with deviant drinking. Finally, Caetano noted that the research with larger samples that are more representative of Hispanics has been primarily with Mexican Americans, who represent only about 60 percent of Hispanics.

Analysis of survey data collected in the 1984 National Alcohol Survey by Caetano (1988) showed that Mexican Americans have a more serious problem with alcohol than the other Hispanic groups such as those with Central and South American backgrounds. Mexican Americans have a higher incidence of alcohol-related problems such as accidents, homicides, and arrests than the general U.S. population.

Alcohol Consumption. One of the first general population surveys (Cahalan et al., 1969) found that about 30 percent of all Hispanic Americans who drank were in the heavy drinker category, as compared to only about 17 percent of all whites who drank. Later studies (Alcocer, 1982; Caetano, 1984) comparing drinking of Hispanic groups and the general population with comparable indexes of quantity and frequency of drinking found smaller differences. As with population surveys of

African Americans described earlier, drinking patterns were based on an index that combined measures of frequency and quantity of consumption.

Findings from several different studies, summarized by Gilbert and Cervantes (1987) in Table 16-2, show that Mexican-American males in California samples, in comparison with national samples, have higher percentages of drinkers in frequent drinking categories. Regional factors were also important, as Mexican-American males in urban areas (Hisp1) were less likely to abstain and more likely to be frequent drinkers than those in barrio and rural areas (Hisp2). Caetano (1984) also found (not shown) that Mexican-American males are much more often intoxicated than white males.

Differences in consumption level were found between California samples of Mexican-American and white women in the United States. Mexican-American women in urban areas (Hisp1) had a lower pecentage of abstainers and infrequent drinkers than whites while Mexican-American women in barrio and in rural areas (Hisp2) had a greater percentage of abstainers and infrequent drinkers than whites. In urban areas (Hisp1) the percentages of Mexican-American women were comparable to those for U.S. white women for most of the frequent drinker categories and both were higher than the level found for barrio and rural areas (Hisp2).

Age seems to be another important factor. In national samples studied by Caetano (1988), drinking levels appeared to peak before age 30 and then decline. However, Caetano found that the peak was at a later age, 30–39, for Mexican-American males. Unfortunately, these data on age differences were based only on cross-sectional studies of Hispanics and do not permit the inference that the patterns of young drinkers will decline as they grow older. Roizen (1983) found, to the contrary, that alcohol use tends to increase or stay high for older men in Mexico. Socioeconomic factors are also related to Hispanic drinking levels. Caetano (1990) noted that the 1984 National Survey showed that Hispanic male drinking was higher among those with higher education and higher income, contrary to expectations based on views that Hispanic drinking might be due to social deprivation.

Alcohol Problems.   High rates of DSM-III alcohol abuse or dependence were reported by Burnham (1985) for Hispanics in the Los Angeles Epidemiologic Catchment Area study in 1982–83. Rates of alcohol abuse or dependence in the past six months for those under age 40 were higher for Hispanic than for white males (11.2 percent versus 7.7 percent), but the opposite held for females (2.0 percent versus 4.5 percent). Similar patterns were found for those 40 and older. Lifetime prevalence rates confirmed the ethnic and gender differences found for the six-month diagnoses.

According to the 1989 NDATUS report (NIDA/NIAAA, 1990) on alcoholism treatment in the United States, 10 percent of clients were of Hispanic heritage. These statistics indicate Hispanic Americans are slightly overrepresented among clients in relation to their percentage of the national population, 9 percent. Such overutilization has been consistently reported over the past decade (Gilbert & Cervantes, 1988). Gilbert and Cervantes concluded that the estimated magnitude of Hispanic use of treatment is probably lower than the actual extent, because the

Table 16-2 Comparison of California Hispanic Alcohol Consumption Levels with U.S. General Population

	Males				Females			
	U.S. n = (1053)	CA. n = (1047)	Hisp1 n = (279)	Hisp2 n = (242)	U.S. n = (1067)	CA. n = (1280)	Hisp1 n = (355)	Hisp2 n = (366)
Abstainers	30%	11%	14%	27%	44%	29%	32%	55%
Occasional	8	9	6	8	18	19	20	18
Infrequent	14	13	17	16	18	23	24	14
Freq Lo Max	14	20	16	6	12	14	14	4
Freq Hi Max	23	26	21	22	10	9	7	6
Freq Heavy	12	21	26	21	3	6	3	3

Source: from *Mexican Americans and Alcohol* by M. J. Gilbert and R. C. Cervantes. Copyrighted © by Regents of the University of California. Reprinted by permission.

percentage of the Hispanic population that is under 20 years of age is greater than in the total population and the treatment data do not include many clients under that age. Hence, the adult Hispanic Americans receiving treatment actually represent a much larger percentage of the much smaller adult segments among Hispanic populations.

Frequent drinking at levels involving intoxication was related to higher levels of liver cirrhosis mortality found in major cities for Hispanics (Alcocer, 1982). A study in California found that Hispanic men also account for a high percentage of the arrests for driving under the influence of alcohol and for public drunkenness (Department of Alcohol and Drug Programs, 1982).

Cervantes, Gilbert, de Snyder, & Padilla (1990–91) compared drinking among U.S.-born Mexican Americans and a mixture of immigrants from Mexico and Central America enrolled in community adult schools in Los Angeles. High levels of depression were found; they were predictive of drinking levels among the men but not the women. Cervantes et al. also found higher positive expectations about the effects of alcohol among men and such expectations were directly related to greater alcohol consumption, a factor that they feel may have contributed to greater use of alcohol by men to cope with depression.

Cultural Factors. Alcocer (1982) suggested that the norm of machismo makes alcohol consumption an integral component of Mexican-American male behavior patterns while stigmatizing it for females. Machismo is a cultural value that emphasizes strength, personal autonomy, and honor but also connotes masculine virility, an aspect that might be seen as promoting heavy drinking. This is a speculation since no studies have clearly defined machismo or measured how it changes over the lifetime in conjunction with alcohol usage.

Caetano (1990) argued that cultural explanations for male Hispanic drinking using vaguely defined constructs such as "exaggerated machismo" are simplistic. The item on the 1984 National Alcohol Survey that comes closest to embodying this idea ("a real man can hold his liquor") was endorsed by only 16 percent of Hispanic males and 15 percent of Hispanic females and by lower percentages of more acculturated Hispanics.

Native Americans

The minority group most afflicted with alcohol abuse is the Native American, as exemplified by the widely held stereotype of the "drunken Indian." Weibel-Orlando (1985) pointed out the wide diversity of drinking attitudes and patterns among various American Indian tribes, as documented by ethnographic or field observations. If there are high rates of heavy drinking among Indians, there are also high rates of abstinence. It is also important to consider urban-rural differences since Indians in cities have been found to drink at a higher level than those in rural settings.

Alcohol Consumption. A larger percentage of Native American (from 56 to 89 percent) than white (from 53 to 73 percent) adolescents consume alcohol at levels that create problems (May, 1982). Among adults, however, there is more variation across different tribes than commonly assumed. May (1982) pointed out that past studies found heavy drinking occurs in some tribes such as the Sioux at levels similar to the U.S. male norms of 18 percent (Cahalan et al., 1969) whereas others such as the Utes (26 percent) and the Ojibwa (42 percent) have a much higher level.

Current use of alcohol among the Navajo is at a much lower level, 30 percent, than the U.S. norm of 67 percent (Cahalan et al., 1969). The rate of drinking among the Sioux is comparable to the national percentage while the Ute (80 percent) and Ojibwa rates (84 percent) are higher. In summary, Indian drinking levels vary widely across different tribes.

Alcohol Problems. One index of the severity of alcoholism problems for Indians is their disproportionate representation in treatment programs. Although representing less than 1 percent of the total population, they comprised about 6 percent of the outpatients treated in federal treatment facilities (National Institute on Alcohol Abuse and Alcoholism, 1981). Another index of the extent of alcoholism among Native Americans is the high liver cirrhosis mortality rate, which is 3.5 times the national rate (Indian Health Service, 1982). Other health problems related to alcohol abuse such as pancreatitis, malnutrition, fetal alcohol syndrome, and heart disease were also prevalent (Indian Health Service, 1988). Suicide rates (Heath, 1988), as well as homicide rates (Lex, 1985), are about twice as high for Native Americans as they are for the general population, reflecting the association between alcohol and violent death (Murdoch, Pihl, & Ross, 1990).

Cultural Factors. One sociological theory to explain this situation is that alcohol was new to the American Indian in colonial times, and their culture had no traditions for regulating its use. Another explanation is that the loss of their land and hunting prey as the white settlers expanded westward produced a frustration that was assuaged by excessive use of alcohol. Lack of traditional social roles and loss of autonomy due to the cultural losses might have exposed some Indian tribes such as the Plains tribes to more risk of alcohol problems than others such as the Pueblos (May, 1982).

Although Indians are viewed by outsiders as a homogenous ethnic group and their drinking is assumed to have common features, Weibel-Orlando (1985) noted important variations in their attitudes related to alcohol. Thus, some tribes adhere to the myth of the Noble Savage, that Indians were unspoiled before the European settlers arrived on this continent with their corruptive influence. In relation to this myth, alcohol is seen as the prime example of the profane influence of the white man, and thus is regarded as something to be scrupulously avoided, especially at any sacred ceremony.

Some Native Americans adopt a second stance in relation to alcohol, one of profane separation or deviant solidarity, in which there is a collective and public display of flagrant abuse of alcohol. This attitude apparently derives from a rebellion against paternalistic prohibitionist policies that once restricted Indian access to alcohol long after it was allowed to every other group. Violating laws and wreaking social havoc, these Indians present a unified reaction to discriminatory policies of the government.

Finally, "maintaining" or controlling one's liquor consumption is a third possible response to alcohol. In the past, the powwow, an Indian ceremonial event of tribal music and dance, often involved heavy drinking and antisocial behaviors. However, a change toward better monitoring and control of drinking has been observed at powwows by means such as greater physical separation of space allocated for the sacred and the profane activities, according to Weibel and Weisner (1980).

There is not, as popularly thought, a single drinking style among Indians. For example, Ferguson (1968) distinguished between recreational and anxiety drinkers among the Navajo. In the former style, males drink in groups on weekends and special occasions in large quantities for long periods and with the intent to become intoxicated. In contrast, anxiety drinking is typified by the solitary and regular use of alcohol by socially marginal individuals, akin to skid-row alcoholics, who have been rejected by their tribes. Among the Chippewa, Westermeyer (1972) noted that both unrestrained "Indian" and restrained "white" styles of drinking exist, even in the same individuals, depending on the time and place. Indian drinking styles vary by time and location. One recreational style is accompanied by loud talking, warm interpersonal relationships, and hilarity, and may continue until all financial resources are depleted. This style is generally reserved for drinking with other Indians.

This information about drinking styles has implications for the types of treatments that might be successful for Indians with drinking problems. First, it should be noted that the label "alcoholic" is not used by most Indians, although they recognize that some people "drink too much." Typically, an Indian in an alcoholism treatment facility is there not because he or she has come to recognize himself or herself as an alcoholic with a treatable disease, but because the alternative, usually jail, is worse.

An unfortunate example of this failure of recognition comes from Popham (1979), who provided a verbatim transcript of an interview between a social worker and a young Algonkian Indian mother, Miss Lucie, whose child had been taken from her and placed in court custody because of her drinking excesses. The caseworker kept trying to describe the various aspects of treatment programs, hoping to motivate Miss Lucie to consent to participate. Throughout the interview Miss Lucie expressed little active interest but was agreeable toward any suggestions offered to her, prompting the social worker to finally observe, "You seem to want to agree with just about everything I say," which elicited a response of laughter from Miss Lucie. It seems evident that Miss Lucie's real concern was to do whatever was required to get her child back, and that she had little concern about her drinking. Throughout the interview she showed a superficial amiability and air of indifference, a reaction to stressful situations typically noted in Indians by other observers.

Due to the lack of correspondence between the Indian's view of the drinking and that of the treatment facility, the high failure rate is not surprising. Weibel-Orlando (1985) noted that differences of philosophy exist in various facilities, many of which are culturally sensitive but still short of meeting the typical Indian client's needs. It must be kept in mind that some forms of intoxication have traditionally been an integral part of Indian sacred ceremonies. In contrast, today alcohol is associated with secular or nonreligious activities to a greater extent. Successful treatment programs for Indians seem to be those that combine spiritual elements and activities with their treatment procedures.

Asian Americans

Asian Americans represent a wide variety of cultures, but the total population is quite small compared to other ethnic minority groups despite rapid growth in the past decade. Combined, all Asian Americans still comprise less than 3 percent of the U.S. population in 1990 (Bureau of the Census, 1992). As a whole, Asian Americans come from cultures that have traditionally emphasized Confucian ideals of moderation. Consistent with these views, moderate use of alcohol for males and little or no alcohol consumption for females has been the norm. Public drunkenness is highly frowned upon as disgraceful and unacceptable conduct. In view of these cultural roots, one would expect that these groups would have low-to-moderate use of alcohol and be relatively free from alcohol problems.

Alcohol Consumption. Surveys of Asian Americans reveals some diversity of drinking levels by these groups. Kitano and Chi (1986–87) surveyed over 1,100 respondents from four different Asian subcultures in Los Angeles: Chinese, Filipino, Korean, and Japanese. Among males, the lowest rates of drinking and the highest rates of abstainers were found for Chinese Americans, who used alcohol in smaller quantities than the general U.S. population, with a higher percentage of abstainers as well, agreeing with the findings of earlier studies by Wilson, McClearn, and Johnson (1978) and by Sue, Kitano, Hatanaka, and Yeung (1985). Indirect evidence of low alcoholism rates was found in the low rates of admission for alcoholism treatment for Chinese, although this might partly reflect a cultural bias in seeking treatment rather than an absence of problems.

Heavy drinking for males was highest among Japanese Americans (Kitano & Chi, 1986–87) in agreement with results of a survey from random households in Los Angeles by Kitano, Hatanaka, Yeung, and Sue (1985) that found more Japanese-American males in both the abstainer and heavy-drinker categories than for other Asian-American groups. However, drinking was not closely related to problem behavior.

Kitano and Chi (1986–87) found that Filipino-American males also had high drinking rates. Lubben, Chi, and Kitano (1988) also found a high percentage of Filipino males, over 29 percent, to be heavy drinkers, a rate that is higher than for the general population.

Korean-American males showed a bimodal distribution, with many heavy drinkers as well as many abstainers (Kitano & Chi, 1986–87). Similarly, Lubben, Chi, and Kitano (1988b) found a sizeable percentage of heavy drinkers among Korean-American males, with over 25 percent. However, almost 45 percent of Korean-American males were abstainers.

Drinking among Asian-American females was generally low but there were differences among subgroups (Kitano & Chi, 1986–87). The highest percentage of heavy drinkers (11.7) was with Japanese Americans, followed by Filipino Americans (3.4) but this category was virtually nonexistent for the Chinese and Korean groups. Only one fourth of the Japanese Americans abstained, compared to half of the Chinese Americans and three-fourths of the Korean Americans.

Chi, Lubben, and Kitano (1989) compared drinking among Asian-American groups from Chinese, Japanese, and Korean backgrounds. Their findings, shown in Table 16-3, confirmed the findings of earlier studies in the Los Angeles area. Overall, the drinking rates are low in comparison with national norms, but variation exists among different Asian-American cultures and they cannot be viewed as a homogenous group.

Physiological Factors. The lower use of alcohol by Asian Americans has been attributed to a greater physiological reactivity to alcohol among Asian peoples, as reflected by facial flushing, which occurs in substantially more Asian than Caucasian adults (Wolff, 1972) and infants (Zeiner & Paredes, 1978). The facial flushing created by vasodilation due to alcohol is one indication that alcohol has a stronger or quicker effect on peoples of Asian descent.

It is interesting to note that although the evidence is mixed (Bennion & Li, 1976), it is suspected that American Indians, like Asians, metabolize alcohol differently (at a slower rate, so that they have an adverse physiological reaction) from other ethnic groups. If this biological factor serves to prevent persons of Asian descent from having serious drinking problems, why then do American Indians, who apparently have similar biological reactions to alcohol, have such serious problems with heavy drinking and alcoholism? One explanation is that Asians place a premium on maintaining "face" so that the threat of losing control of one's behavior due to alcohol reduces the risk of drinking problems. In contrast, it has been argued that Indians use alcohol to enhance visionary experiences so that intoxication is congruent with such goals despite the adverse biological reactions.

Cultural Factors. Asian cultures strongly discourage public intoxication and ostracize the alcohol abuser. The family traditionally plays a strong role in Asian cultures, influenced by Confucian ideals, and discourages public drunkenness in favor of moderation. Integration of drinking with meals has also been suggested by Lin (1982) as a factor minimizing alcohol problems. Although most Asian cultures have low alcoholism rates, there is still some variability among them. For example, men in Japan seem to drink at higher levels than in the United States, but the opposite is true for women (Kitano, Chi, Rhee, Law, & Lubben, 1992). Differences in cultural values, norms, and institutions regulating alcohol use exist among Asian cultures.

Akutsu, Sue, Zane, and Nakamura (1989) examined both physiological differences and cultural differences between Asians and Caucasians in the United States to compare their relative effects on drinking. They found that physiological reactivity and attitudes toward drinking were the best predictors of ethnic differences in drinking.

Table 16-3 Alcohol Consumption of Asian Americans by Ethnicity and Gender

	Males[a]				Females[b]			
	Total (n = 608)	Japanese (n = 235)	Chinese (n = 218)	Korean (n = 155)	Total (n = 265)	Japanese (n = 60)	Chinese (n = 80)	Korean (n = 125)
Heavy drinkers	22.9%	28.9%	14.2%	25.8%	3.0%	11.7%	0.0%	0.8%
Moderate drinkers	14.0	13.6	17.9	9.0	7.2	13.3	10.0	2.4
Light drinkers	27.6	24.7	36.7	19.4	23.0	41.7	21.3	15.2
Infrequent drinkers	10.0	16.2	9.6	1.3	9.8	6.7	17.5	6.4
Abstainers	25.5	16.6	21.6	44.5	57.0	26.7	51.3	75.2

[a]$p < .001$.
[b]$p < .001$ (heavy and moderate drinking categories were merged to calculate χ^2 due to small cell sizes).

Source: Reprinted with permission from Journal of Studies on Alcohol, vol. 50, pp. 15–23, 1989. Copyright by Alcohol Research Documentation, Inc., Rutgers Center for Alcohol Studies, New Brunswick, NJ 08903.

The Influence of Acculturation

Some stability in drinking patterns over successive generations was found for most ethnic groups studied by Greeley et al. (1980), but Blane (1977) found that the influence of acculturation is also evident as the drinking patterns seem to move away from those in the country of origin toward those found for the U.S. general population. Thus, Irish Americans drink less than the Irish in Ireland, whereas the Jews in America drink more than those in Israel. Similarly, Kitano et al. (1992) found that the drinking attitudes and alcohol use of Japanese Americans in California and Hawaii were more similar to those of white Americans than to those of the Japanese in Japan.

Caetano and Mora (1988) studied the acculturation process by which Mexican immigrants develop changes in drinking patterns after they move to the United States. They compared responses to a drinking questionnaire completed by Mexican Americans as part of a national probability sample and by men living in the surroundings of Morelia, Mexico. While Mexican-American men drank more frequently than the Mexicans, they typically drank smaller amounts, suggesting a shift toward U.S. drinking norms. Less difference was found among women, but Mexican-American women did tend to drink more often and in larger quantities than Mexican women. Caetano (1990) suggested that acculturation involves a greater change for Mexican women, hence a greater increase in drinking occurs among them than for men.

Interestingly, despite lower amounts of drinking by Mexicans, they reported experiencing more problems related to alcohol than did Mexican Americans. This discrepancy shows that the values and reactions of the society must also be considered in determining the impact of drinking.

Caetano (1990) noted that acculturation was related to Hispanic drinking but the relationship was not always the same—acculturation was associated with either abstention or more frequent drinking, depending on national origin (Puerto Rico, Mexico, Cuba) and place of relocation. Heavier drinking was found for Hispanics in California than in Texas, reflecting the drinking norms of these locales, with more drunkenness and alcohol-related problems in California than in Texas.

A simple acculturation model may not provide a complete explanation of the drinking of minorities. A study by Neff, Hoppe, and Perea (1987) compared drinking of Mexican-American and white men across a wide age range controlled for social class. Mexican Americans were found to drink less frequently but in higher quantity than whites but to have comparable levels of problems. Quantity was higher for the *less* acculturated men, suggesting that the stress of marginality led to higher drinking.

Conclusions

Although alcohol is consumed almost universally, consumption patterns and problems related to its use vary widely across different cultures. Within U.S. society, ethnic minority groups differ among themselves and from the white norms of drinking. In addition to the biological and psychosocial factors that might influence the drinking patterns of any ethnic group, the stress of marginality, poverty, and racial prejudice may also serve as motivating factors for drinking and determinants of drinking outcomes.

Comparisons of drinking levels and alcohol-related problems between minority groups and whites can be highly misleading if socioeconomic level is not first equated. As is true for whites, social class differences among minority groups also influence drinking styles and consequences.

As among whites, women drink much less than men among the ethnic minorities examined. Whereas males in some ethnic minorities match or exceed the drinking levels of white males, the female minorities typically drink less than white females.

Another commonality among most ethnic minorities is a distribution of drinking that appears more bimodal, with more abstainers as well as more heavy drinkers, than for whites. Also, the age at which drinking seems to reach its peak is generally later for ethnic minorities than for whites.

To understand the nature of drinking among minorities, it is important to consider the historical background of alcohol within specific ethnic groups. The factors that lead to alcohol use and the role it plays are not the same for each minority group. As immigrant groups become acculturated to America, their drinking patterns begin to resemble more closely those of the host culture than the country of origin.

References

Akutsu, P. D., Sue, S., Zane, N.W.S., and Nakamura, C. Y. (1989). Ethnic differences in alcohol consumption among Asians and Caucasians in the United States: An investigation of cultural and physiological factors. *Journal of Studies on Alcohol, 50,* 261–267.

Alcocer, A. (1982). Alcohol use and abuse among the Hispanic American population. In National Institute on Alcohol Abuse and Alcoholism (Ed.), *Alcohol and Health Monograph No. 4: Special population issues* (pp. 361–382). Rockville, MD: National Institute on Alcohol Abuse and Alcoholism.

Bales, R. F. (1946). Cultural differences in rates of alcoholism. *Quarterly Journal of Studies on Alcohol, 6,* 480–499.

Bennion, L. J., & Li, T. K. (1976). Alcohol metabolism in American Indians and whites. Lack of racial differences in metabolic rate and liver alcohol dehydrogenase. *New England Journal of Medicine, 294,* 9–13.

Blane, H. T. (1977). Acculturation and drinking in an Italian American community. *Journal of Studies on Alcohol, 38,* 1324–1346.

Brisbane, F. L., & Wells, R. C. (1989). Treatment and prevention of alcoholism among Blacks. In T. D. Watts & J. R. Wright (Eds.), *Alcoholism in minority populations* (pp. 33–52). Springfield, IL: Charles C Thomas.

Burnham A. (1985). *Prevalence of alcohol abuse and dependence among Mexican Americans and nonHispanic whites in the community.* Paper presented at the NIAAA Conference on the Epidemiology of Alcohol Use and Abuse among U.S. Ethnic Minorities, Bethesda, MD.

Caetano, R. (1984). Ethnicity and drinking in Northern California: A comparison among whites, blacks, and Hispanics. *Alcohol and Alcoholism, 18,* 1–14.

Caetano, R. (1988). Drinking patterns and alcohol problems in a national sample of U.S.

Hispanics. In National Institute of Alcohol Abuse and Alcoholism (Ed.), *Alcohol use among U.S. ethnic minorities*. Washington, DC: U.S. Government Printing Office.

Caetano, R. (1990). Hispanic drinking in the U.S.: Thinking in new directions. *British Journal of Addiction, 85,* 1231–1235.

Caetano, R., & Mora, M. E. (1988). Acculturation and drinking among people of Mexican descent in Mexico and the United States. *Journal of Studies on Alcohol, 49,* 462–471.

Cahalan, D., Cisin, I. H., & Crossley, H. M. (1969). *American drinking practices: A national study of drinking behavior*. New Brunswick, NJ: Rutgers Center for Alcohol Studies.

Cervantes, R. C., Gilbert, M. J., de Snyder, N. S., & Padilla, A. M. (1990–91). Psychosocial and cognitive correlates of alcohol use in younger adult immigrant and U.S.-born Hispanics. *International Journal of the Addictions, 25,* 687–708.

Chi, I., Lubben, J., & Kitano, H.H.L. (1989). Differences in drinking behavior among three Asian-American groups. *Journal of Studies on Alcohol, 50,* 15–23.

Clark, W. B., & Midanik, L. (1982). Alcohol use and alcohol problems among U.S. adults: Results of the 1979 national survey. In National Institute on Alcohol Abuse and Alcoholism (Ed.), *Alcohol consumption and related problems* (Monograph No. 1, pp. 3–52). Washington, DC: U.S. Government Printing Office.

Department of Alcohol and Drug Programs. (1982). *The Black population and indicators of alcohol use/misuse*. Sacramento, CA: Author.

Ferguson, F. N. (1968). Navajo drinking: Some tentative hypotheses. *Human Organizations, 27,* 159–167.

Fillmore, K. M., & Kelso, D. (1987). Coercion into alcoholism treatment: Meanings for the disease concept of alcoholism. *Journal of Drug Issues, 17,* 301–319.

Gaines, A. D. (1985). Cultural conceptions and social behavior among urban Blacks. In L. A. Bennett & G. M. Ames (Eds.), *The American experience with alcohol: Contrasting cultural perspectives* (pp. 171–197). New York: Plenum Press.

Gilbert, M. J., & Cervantes, R. C. (1987). *Mexican Americans and alcohol*. Los Angeles: University of California Press.

Gilbert, M. J., & Cervantes, R. C. (1988). Alcohol treatment for Mexican Americans: A review of utilization patterns and therapeutic approaches. In M. J. Gilbert (Ed.), *Alcohol consumption among Mexicans and Mexican Americans: A binational perspective*. Los Angeles: UCLA Spanish-Speaking Mental Health Research Center.

Glassner, B., & Berg, B. (1980). How Jews avoid alcohol problems. *American Sociological Review, 45,* 647–667.

Greeley, A., McCready, W. C., & Theisen, G. (1980). *Ethnic drinking subcultures*. New York: Praeger.

Harper, F. (1976). *Alcohol abuse and black America*. Alexandria, VA: Douglass.

Heath, D. B. (1988). American Indians and alcohol: Epidemiological and sociocultural relevance. In National Institute on Alcohol and Alcoholism (Ed.), *Alcohol use among U.S. ethnic minorities*. Washington, DC: U.S. Government Printing Office.

Herd, D. (1985). Ambiguity in Black drinking norms. In L. A. Bennett & G. M. Ames (Eds.), *The American experience with alcohol: Contrasting cultural perspectives* (pp. 149–170). New York: Plenum Press.

Herd, D. (1987). Rethinking Black drinking. *British Journal of Addiction, 82,* 219–223.

Herd, D. (1988a). A review of drinking patterns and alcohol problems among U.S. Blacks. In National Institute on Alcohol Abuse and Alcoholism (Ed.), *Alcohol use among U.S. ethnic minorities*. Washington, DC: U.S. Government Printing Office.

Herd, D. (1988b). Migration, urbanization and black drinking patterns: Results from the 1984 national survey. In L. Towle, T. Harford, & D. Spiegler (Eds.), *Influences of acculturation and migration on drinking patterns*. Washington, DC: U.S. Government Printing Office.

Herd, D. (1990). Subgroup differences in drinking patterns among Black and white men: Results from a national survey. *Journal of Studies on Alcohol, 31,* 221–232.

Horton, D. J. (1943). The functions of alcohol in primitive societies: A cross-cultural study. *Quarterly Journal of Studies on Alcohol, 4,* 199–320.

Indian Health Service. (1982). *Analysis of fiscal year 1981 Indian Health Service and U.S. hospital discharge rates by age and primary diagnosis.* Rockville, MD: Author.

Indian Health Service. (1988). *Indian Health Service chart series book.* DHHS Pub. No. 1988 0-218-547: QL 3. Washington, DC: U.S. Government Printing Office.

Johnson, C. A., Pentz, M. A., Weber, M. D., Dwyer, J. H., Baer, N., MacKinnon, D. P., & Hansen, W. B. (1990). Relative effectiveness of comprehensive community programming for drug abuse prevention with high-risk and low-risk adolescents. *Journal of Consulting and Clinical Psychology, 58,* 447–456.

Kitano, H., & Chi, I. (1986–87). Asian Americans and alcohol use. *Alcohol Health and Research World, 11,* 42–46.

Kitano, H., Chi, I., Rhee, S., Law, C. K., & Lubben, J. E. (1992). Norms and alcohol consumption: Japanese in Japan, Hawaii, and California. *Journal of Studies on Alcohol, 53,* 33–39.

Kitano, H.H.L., Hatanaka, H., Yeung, W., & Sue, S. (1985). Japanese-American drinking patterns. In L. A. Bennett & G. M. Ames (Eds.), *The American experience with alcohol: Contrasting cultural perspectives* (pp. 335–357). New York: Plenum Press.

Lex, B. W. (1987). Review of alcohol problems in ethnic minority groups. *Journal of Consulting and Clinical Psychology, 55,* 293–300.

Lin, T. Y. (1982). Alcoholism among the Chinese: Further observations of a low-risk population. *Culture, Medicine, and Psychiatry, 6,* 109–116.

Lolli, G., Serianni, E., Golder, G. M., & Luzzatto-Fegiz, P. (1958). *Alcohol in Italian culture.* Glencoe, IL: Free Press.

Lubben, J., Chi, I., & Kitano, H. L. (1988a). Exploring Filipino-American drinking behavior. *Journal of Studies on Alcohol, 49,* 26–29.

Lubben, J., Chi, I., & Kitano, H. L. (1988b). The relative influence of selected social factors on Korean drinking behavior in Los Angeles. *Advances in Alcohol and Substance Abuse, 8,* 1–17.

MacAndrew, C., & Edgerton, R. B. (1969). *Drunken comportment: A social explanation.* Chicago: Aldine.

Malin, H., Croakley, J., Kaelber, C., Munch, N., & Holland, W. (1982). An epidemiologic perspective on alcohol use and abuse in the United States. In National Institute on Alcohol Abuse and Alcoholism (Ed.), *Alcohol consumption and related problems.* (Alcohol and Health Monograph No. ADM82-1190, pp. 99–153). Washington, DC: U.S. Government Printing Office.

May, P. A. (1982). Substance abuse and American Indians: Prevalence and susceptibility. *International Journal of the Addictions, 17,* 1185–1209.

Murdoch, D., Pihl, R. O., & Ross, D. (1990). Alcohol and crimes of violence: Present issues. *International Journal of the Addictions, 25,* 1065–1081.

National Institute on Alcohol Abuse and Alcoholism. (1981). *Indian clients treated in NIAAA-funded programs.* Rockville, MD: Author.

National Institute on Drug Abuse/National Institute on Alcoholism and Alcohol Abuse (NIDA/NIAAA). (1990). *National Drug and Alcoholism Treatment Unit Survey (NDATUS) 1989: Main findings report.* Rockville, MD: Author.

Neff, J. A., Hoppe, S. K., & Perea, P. (1987). Acculturation and alcohol use: Drinking patterns and problems among Anglo and Mexican American male drinkers. *Hispanic Journal of Behavioral Sciences, 9,* 151–181.

Popham, R. E. (1979). Psychocultural barriers to successful alcoholism therapy in an American Indian patient. *Journal of Studies on Alcohol, 40,* 656–676.

Rachal, J. V., Williams, J. R., Brehm, M. L., Cavanaugh, B., Moore, R. P., & Bokerman, W. C. (1975). *A national study of adolescent drinking behavior, attitudes, and correlates.* Research Triangle Park, NC: Research Triangle Park Center for the Study of Social Behavior.

Rimmer, J., Pitts, F. N., Reich, T., & Winokur, G. (1971). Alcoholism: II. Sex, socioeconomic status, and race in two hospitalized samples. *Quarterly Journal of Studies on Alcohol, 32,* 942–952.

Robins, L. N., Helzer, J. E., Weissman, M. M., Orvascel, H., Gruenberg, E., Burker, J. D., Jr.,

& Regier, D. A. (1984). Lifetime prevalence of specific psychiatric disorders in three sites. *Archives of General Psychiatry, 41,* 949–958.

Roizen, R. (1983). *Alcohol dependence symptoms in cross-cultural perspective: A report of findings from the World Health Organization study of community response to alcoholism.* Berkeley, CA: Alcohol Research Group.

Simboli, B. J. (1985). Acculturated Italian-American drinking behavior. In L. A. Bennett & G. M. Ames (Eds.), *The American experience with alcohol: Contrasting cultural perspectives* (pp. 61–76). New York: Plenum Press.

Snyder, D. (1958). *Alcohol and the Jews.* New Haven, CT: Yale University Press.

Stern, M. (1967). Drinking patterns and alcoholism among American Negroes. In D. Pittman (Ed.), *Alcoholism.* New York: Harper & Row.

Stivers, R. (1985). Historical meanings of Irish-American drinking. In L. A. Bennett & G. M. Ames (Eds.), *The American experience with alcohol: Contrasting cultural perspectives* (pp. 109–129). New York: Plenum Press.

Sue, S., Kitano, H.H.L., Hatanaka, H., & Yeung, W. (1985). Alcohol consumption among Chinese in the United States. In L. A. Bennett & G. M. Ames (Eds.), *The American experience with alcohol: Contrasting cultural perspectives* (pp. 359–371). New York: Plenum Press.

U.S. Bureau of the Census. (1992). Census of Population and Housing (CPH-1). Washington, DC: U.S. Department of Commerce.

Weibel, J., & Weisner, T. (1980). *An ethnography of urban Indian drinking patterns in California.* Report presented to the California State Department of Alcohol and Drug Problems.

Weibel-Orlando, J. (1985). Indians, ethnicity, and alcohol: Contrasting perceptions of the ethnic self and alcohol use. In L. A. Bennett & G. M. Ames (Eds.), *The American experience with alcohol: Contrasting cultural perspectives* (pp. 201–226). New York: Plenum Press.

Westermeyer, J. (1972). Chippewa and majority alcoholism in the Twin Cities: A comparison. *Journal of Nervous and Mental Disorders, 155,* 322–327.

Wilson, J. R., McClearn, G. E., & Johnson, R. C. (1978). Ethnic variation in use and effects of alcohol. *Drug and Alcohol Dependence, 2,* 147–151.

Wolff, P. (1972). Ethnic differences in alcohol sensitivity. *Science, 125,* 449–451.

Zeiner, A., & Paredes, A. (1978). Differential biological sensitivity to ethanol as a predictor of alcohol abuse. In D. Smith (Ed.), *Multicultural view of drug abuse* (pp. 591–599). Cambridge, MA: Schenkman.

SEVENTEEN

Prevention of Alcoholism and Alcohol-Related Problems

A Systems Approach: The Public Health Model
Primary Prevention
The Influence of Mass Media
The Impact of Advertising
Control of the Availability of Alcohol
Economic Controls
Educational Controls
Legal Controls
Reducing the Minimum Legal Drinking Age
Raising the Minimum Legal Drinking Age
Prevention for Specific At-Risk Groups
Adolescents
Women
The Elderly
Minorities
Secondary Prevention
The Example of Drinking Drivers
Early-Stage Problem Drinkers
Heavily Drinking College Students
Workplace Intervention
Future Directions
Conclusions
References

A tremendous amount of suffering and pain is inflicted on large numbers of people by the misuse of alcohol. Alcohol dependency devastates the lives of many drinkers. Serious adverse consequences are experienced by their friends and family members, who must deal with emotional, financial, and social damage. In addition, even casual drinkers can cause serious physical harm from accidents due to a single episode of drinking. It is fitting that the concern of this final chapter is the prevention of alcoholism and alcohol-related problems.

Prevention is a difficult task, given the strong desires of many to consume alcohol and given the powerful traditions of drinking in America. Society has generally failed to deal with the roots of the problem and has resigned itself to treating victims of alcoholism on the one hand and punishing alcohol abusers who create social problems such as drunk driving, violence, and crime on the other hand. But in the 1980s a growing awareness of and concern about the dangers of nonmedical aspects of alcohol problems and drunken driving developed. Attempts to bring about wide, sweeping social changes in the forms of increased alcohol taxes, zoning regulations for alcohol outlets, a higher legal minimum drinking age, control of advertising, and stiffer penalties for drunken driving were part of this effort. This decade also saw the development of a more health-conscious nation and the acceptance of the belief that individuals can and should be more responsible for their health through their lifestyle. Education about the role of proper diet and exercise increased, resulting in major shifts in eating habits and patterns of exercise. Similarly, shifts occurred in the preferred types of beverages from mixed alcoholic drinks and distilled spirits to less potent alcoholic beverages as well as to nonalcoholic beverages.

Alcohol availability is affected by policies set by a variety of federal agencies. The Bureau of Alcohol, Tobacco, and Firearms deals with alcohol excise and import taxes. Numerous other federal agencies concerned with safety such as the National Highway Safety Administration, the Environmental Protection Agency, the National Transportation Safety Board, the Consumer Product Safety Commission, and the Food and Drug Administration also affect alcohol use in the United States. The federal government can play a greater role in confronting and solving this problem that afflicts the whole nation. Although the federal government funded about 64 percent of prevention activities in 1982, only about 4 percent of federal expenditures for alcohol-related programs were allocated to prevention (Nathan, 1983).

The types of problems associated with alcohol consumption differ in the extent to which alcohol actually creates the problem. Thus, as Moskowitz (1989) noted, consumption of alcohol is directly tied to drunk driving, but for many other problems such as aggression or depression alcohol may only be a secondary factor. Whether drinking leads to a "social problem" also depends on social norms and definitions; for instance, public drunkenness may be viewed as a problem by some but not all societies. It may be necessary to develop different strategies for dealing with each different type of problem.

A Systems Approach: The Public Health Model

A systems approach to the analysis of public health problems examines the interactions of the agent, the host, and the environment, as shown in Figure 17-1. The

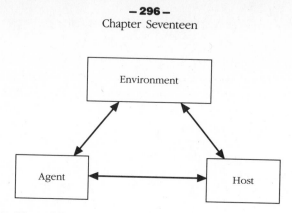

Figure 17-1 The public health model of prevention of alcohol problems recognizes three components: the agent, the host, and the environment, each of which influences the others. Prevention strategies vary according to which component is the focus.

agent is the "germ" or causal substance. In the case of alcoholism it is obviously alcohol. Prevention efforts directed toward the agent might focus on restricting its availability through pricing, limiting the hours when it can be sold or served publicly, and establishing minimum drinking age laws. Such approaches emphasize external factors that might affect the level of drinking and associated problems.

The *host* represents the victims afflicted by the health hazard. Prevention efforts in this area might attempt to reduce the public's incentive to drink through means such as education. In other words, although alcohol might be available in the environment, it may be possible to reduce the drinkers' desire or need to use it so that it does not become a problem.

Finally, the *environment* includes both the physical and social context in which the agent and host reside. A prevention focus on the environment might include the shaping of social attitudes and norms or the regulation of the physical environment in which alcohol might be consumed. For example, the promotion of "happy hours" by commercial bars suggests that one must drink to be "happy." Marketing ploys such as "2 for 1" specials on drinks might be discouraged. Similarly, attempts to prevent drinking and driving problems must begin by instilling societal values that strongly discourage such dangerous behavior. The alcoholic beverage industries, through their advertising, are influential in shaping public attitudes and behavior toward alcohol. Although their self-interest is in encouraging drinking, if they are to continue to prosper financially, they must also recognize their social responsibility.

Successful prevention strategies may need to consider all of these components of the system of interrelated factors rather than focusing on only one. Individuals who, in the absence of external cues, can ordinarily control their drinking may weaken their restraint when placed in heavy-drinking environments. The "Just say no" solution offered by Nancy Reagan may sound reasonable in theory but in practice may be more difficult. In a society inundated with advertisements promoting the attractiveness of drinking and where situations encouraging drinking abound, saying no is virtually impossible.

Instead of placing the burden of responsibility entirely on the individual, the drinking environment can be restructured to help individuals control their drinking. For example, in many major league baseball stadiums, beer cannot be purchased after the seventh inning. Such policies aim at reducing the levels of intoxication among the fans at the end of the game when they all exit the parking lots and drive on public thoroughfares.

The multiplicity of social and environmental forces, often beyond the control of individuals, that affect drinking must be recognized. As Figure 17-2 illustrates,

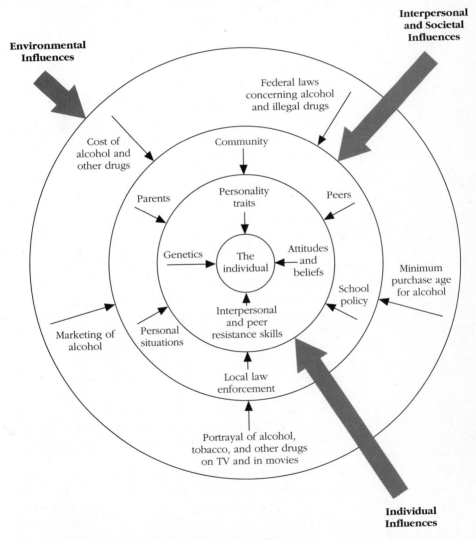

Figure 17-2 Factors that influence alcohol use.

Source: from *Prevention Plus II: Tools for Creating and Sustaining Drug-Free Communities* from the Office for Substance Abuse Prevention: National Clearinghouse for Alcohol Information, Rockville, MD 1989.

laws and their enforcement, marketing and pricing, and media depictions are just some of the contextual factors that must be considered in addition to any individual genetic or psychological factors when designing prevention strategies. We will take a closer look at these contextual factors in the following pages.

Primary Prevention

Primary prevention has traditionally focused on school education and public information programs in the hope that knowledge could prevent the occurrence of drinking problems. This goal has often received a lower priority than *secondary prevention* (the early identification of potential drinking problems) or *tertiary prevention* (the treatment of persons already suffering from alcohol problems). Although the immediate plight of those already afflicted with alcoholism seems more pressing than the development of programs presumed to prevent or intercept future alcohol problems, these goals need not compete against each other for funding as is often the case. As Wallack (1984) noted, treated alcoholics would be better served if they could return to a society that promoted alcohol consumption less than it currently does.

The Influence of Mass Media

The images of alcohol use and its effects portrayed in mass media entertainment programming are potentially a major environmental influence on the drinking attitudes and behavior of viewers. Breed, Defoe, and Wallack (1984) examined the content of television programs to determine how many acts of drinking of alcoholic beverages are portrayed per hour. They found an increase from the 1976–77 season to the 1981–82 season from about five to more than eight acts per hour. By 1987 (Wallack, Breed, & Cruz, 1987), the number had risen to more than ten acts per hour. It is difficult to evaluate the effects of such programming since the types of individuals who view different types and amounts of programs vary. Whether exposure to such content actually has a causal influence on the level of alcohol use is conjectural. An alternative view is that media presentations reflect societal norms.

In addition to having an influence on the context for drinking through entertainment programming, mass media have been widely used for promoting alcohol awareness and factual knowledge in the community. Wallack (1981) argued persuasively against the likelihood that such programs can produce much change. The indirect nature of mass media, as compared to the personal touch of in-person communication, may limit their impact. The advantage of mass media is that in theory they can reach large numbers of people rapidly; but in practice, people may not attend to, remember, or even correctly interpret many messages in the presentations. Even if they learn the information, they may not modify their drinking behavior, because many other factors help maintain its level.

Moreover, there is the possibility of reactance created by strong messages that backfire by increasing motivation to drink. Bensley and Wu (1991) demonstrated this effect by presenting college students with either a high- or low-threat message against drinking. Later the subjects participated in a beer taste-rating task designed to unobtrusively measure consumption. Subjects who had received the high-threat message, especially among male heavy drinkers, consumed more beer than those who had had the low-threat message.

The Impact of Advertising

Alcoholic beverage advertising, in contrast to mass media public information health messages about alcohol, often involves distorted and misleading depictions of the effects of alcohol. The goal is to market alcoholic products through the creation of images and fantasies associated with drinking rather than to impart factual information. Not surprisingly, marketers of alcoholic beverages may sacrifice humane considerations for profit goals. Examples of new products proposed in 1991–92 created with images that appeal to specific targets include a malt liquor (PowerMaster) targeted at African Americans, a malt liquor (Crazy Horse) aimed at Native Americans, and a vodka (Black Death) geared toward young macho males. The creation of such brand names for alcoholic products, especially malt liquors that have high alcohol content, to generate sales to groups already afflicted with serious alcohol problems are of questionable propriety and have stirred strong public outcry ("It's a Two-Way Street," 1992).

Huge sums of money, over $1 billion each year since 1984, have been spent to advertise alcoholic beverages in the United States. After reaching a peak in 1986 of about $1.4 billion, the amount has since declined gradually (National Institute on Alcohol Abuse and Alcoholism, 1992). One might assume that advertising is highly effective in encouraging alcohol consumption to justify such expenditures. However, a review by Frankena et al. (1985) assessing the effects of brand-specific advertising found no strong effects on overall consumption levels.

Atkin, Neuendorf, and McDermott (1983) conducted a national survey of 1,200 adolescents between 12 and 21 and found a moderate correlation between exposure to ads for alcoholic beverages and higher alcohol consumption. But it is difficult to interpret such results due to the possibility that those who already favor a position may be more likely to attend to those messages. Thus, those who drink more often and more heavily may notice or recall alcohol advertising precisely because they are already more interested in drinking than those who pay less attention to such messages. Strickland's (1983) evaluation of the effect of alcohol advertising on television on teenager drinking concluded that its impact was not alarming.

Another strategy for assessing the effects of advertising is to examine what happens when advertising is withdrawn or banned. Smart and Cutler (1976) and Ogbourne and Smart (1980) had opportunities to measure this effect in the 1970s in Canada when British Columbia banned all alcohol advertising and Manitoba banned beer advertising. In comparison to a province where no ban was in effect, the levels of consumption were comparable, suggesting that overall consumption is unaffected by advertising. However, the fact that the sales of alcohol had already had a long history relative to the brief duration of the experimental ban limits the interpretation.

Smart (1988) noted that bans on alcohol advertising do not reduce sales nor were total advertising expenditures reliably related to increased sales. Correlational studies to examine the relationship between the amount of consumption and exposure to alcohol advertising have yielded mixed findings, and the direction of causality is not clear with this type of evidence. People who like to drink also may enjoy watching advertisements for alcoholic beverages more than lighter drinkers or nondrinkers.

Makowsky and Whitehead (1991) reported on the opposite situation when a 58-year ban on advertising of alcoholic beverages was lifted in Saskatchewan in 1983. A time series analysis covering 1981 to 1987 indicated that beer sales rose but distilled spirits sales declined after the reintroduction of advertising in 1983, with no effect on the total sales of alcohol.

Correlational and survey research evidence does not examine the immediate impact of alcohol advertising on alcohol consumption. Kohn and Smart (1984) used a controlled laboratory experiment to directly assess the effect of exposure to no, four, or nine beer commercials during videotapes of sporting events on either an immediate or a 30-minute-delayed opportunity to drink. The subjects, all of whom were male, were led to believe that the purpose of the videotape viewing was to compare the appeal of a new televised sport, indoor soccer, with an established TV sport (professional football). They were told that to make conditions realistic, they would be allowed to have as many as four beers during the study, which lasted about two hours.

Moderate exposure to alcohol ads increased consumption, but only briefly, in comparison to the control group (no beer commercial). Overall, the amount of exposure to alcohol ads had no significant effect on drinking for either immediate or 30-minute-delayed access to alcohol. However, because laboratory studies involve artificial conditions dissimilar to real-life drinking contexts and last for very short durations, they may not be generalizable to drinking in naturalistic contexts (Smart, 1988).

Control of the Availability of Alcohol

Obviously, alcohol must be available before it can cause problems. On the basis of this premise, prevention attempts have often used economic and legal methods to limit the availability of alcohol (the agent) instead of trying to work directly on influencing the drinker (the host). It is assumed that if alcohol is less readily available in the environment, it will be consumed to a lesser extent and with fewer related problems.

The *single distribution of consumption model* (Ledermann, 1956) provides a theoretical basis for this reasoning. In comparisons of alcohol consumption made in many nations, Ledermann found a correlation between per capita consumption of alcohol and rates of heavy drinking, as inferred from deaths due to liver cirrhosis. The frequency distribution of drinking quantity was not a normal or symmetrical curve but rather one where the majority of citizens drank at moderate or low levels, with a small percentage consuming alcohol at the high end of the

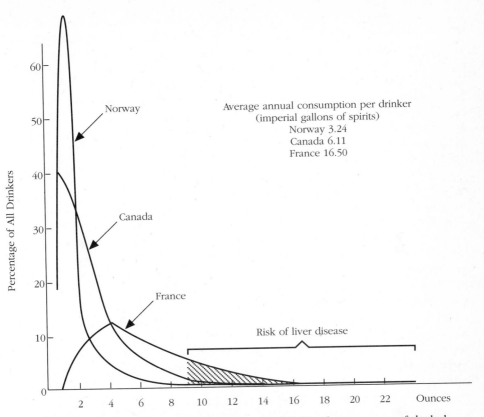

Figure 17-3 The Ledermann Consumption Model: Distribution curves of alcohol use in Norway, Canada, and France in 1968 by average daily consumption. The higher the average per capita intake, the more the distribution curve shifts toward the high-intake end of the scale. The hatched area indicates the levels of intake associated with a proven risk of liver disease.

Source: from *Drugs, Society, and Personal Choice* by H. Kalant and O. J. Kalant. Copyright © 1968 by Alcohol Research Foundation. Reprinted by permission.

continuum as depicted in Figure 17-3. Parker and Harmon (1978) pointed out some limitations of the model's assumptions and some weaknesses of the supporting evidence but acknowledged the impact the model has had on the study of patterns of alcohol use in populations. The major implication drawn by policymakers from the model is that if availability of alcohol in the society as a whole is reduced, the level of alcoholism also should decrease.

Most research to test this assumption has involved quasi-experimental and correlational studies based on indirect measures of drinking such as admission rate of hospitalized alcoholics, alcohol sales revenues, or alcohol-related accidents rather than direct measures of actual drinking.

Prohibition is the most extreme example of government policy directed at reducing alcohol availability. Although it did not prove viable because it created other problems, it was effective in its goals when tried in the United States between

1919 and 1932, according to Warburton (1932). A more frequently used method has been to increase taxes to raise the price of alcohol. This economic approach is assumed to reduce drinking by making it more costly for the drinker. As noted before, Cook (1981) showed that increased liquor taxes between 1960 and 1975 in many states was associated with a decline in alcohol consumption. However, differences in the effectiveness of pricing may exist for different beverage types. Ornstein and Levy (1983) found that consumption of beer is price-inelastic—that is, its consumption level has not varied with the price, whereas consumption of distilled spirits, and to some extent wine, is price-elastic and has been reduced by higher prices.

Alcohol availability is a function of the number of retail establishments in a community. A larger number of outlets should be directly correlated with the amount of alcohol sales, and presumably, consumption of alcohol. MacDonald and Whitehead (1983) conducted a review of studies and concluded that a larger number of retail outlets involving *off-premises* consumption in a community was associated with increased consumption, but this relationship was not found for *on-premises* drinking outlets.

This difference may be due to the fact that servers can restrict or limit the sale of alcohol to intoxicated patrons on-premises, whereas the purchaser alone has control over the off-premises use of alcohol. Thus, if a drinker continues to drink beyond a safe level, servers can intervene and stop serving. The recognition that servers in commercial establishments can help keep alcohol consumption at socially and legally acceptable levels for patrons has led to the development of programs to teach servers how to help maintain safe drinking environments for their customers (Saltz, 1986; Vegega, 1986).

One type of retail outlet of social concern is the convenience store that sells gasoline as well as alcoholic beverages. Such a practice might increase the risk of drinking and driving together. Ryan and Segars (1987) found that whereas alcohol sold in supermarkets was more likely intended for at-home use, alcoholic beverages purchased at liquor stores and mini-marts were more likely to be consumed in cars.

Economic Controls

Is it possible to reduce consumption by increasing the price of alcoholic beverages? The assumption is that higher costs might lead to reduced consumption because the drinker will be able to buy less with the same amount of disposable income. Popham, Schmidt, and de Lint (1975) noted a lowered per capita consumption in countries with higher relative price and concluded that price can affect consumption. While this reasoning might apply to many light drinkers, it is less likely to apply to the highly addicted drinker who will forego other needs to spend economic resources on alcohol. Aggregate comparisons do not allow us to identify *which* persons are drinking less. As price goes up, does drinking decline evenly across the whole population or more so for some groups than for others? If social policy leads to increased prices that affect only lighter drinkers, it will not reduce the alcohol-related problems of heavier drinkers.

State and federal alcohol taxes have been relatively stable or had small increases since the 1950s (Coate & Grossman, 1987). When adjusted for inflation, the real price of alcoholic beverages actually declined between 1960 and 1980 (Cook, 1981). Grossman, Coate, and Arluck (1987) estimated that small price increases would lead to moderate reductions in alcohol consumption by young people, which in turn might reduce their involvement in automobile accidents and fatalities involving alcohol.

A study with a before-after design by Cook (1981) examined the effects of increased state alcohol taxes on alcohol consumption. Between 1960 and 1975 liquor taxes increased in 39 states and in 30 of them alcohol consumption declined, as inferred by liquor tax revenues.

Educational Controls

School-based alcohol education programs aim at the general population under 18 as well as special at-risk populations to modify their alcohol knowledge, attitudes, and consumption (Hewitt & Blane, 1984). While it appears that some gains in knowledge occur, corresponding changes in attitudes about alcohol and reductions in actual drinking behavior have not generally accompanied the gains in factual knowledge (Wittman, 1982).

A pioneering large-scale education program known as the Cambridge and Somerville Program for Alcohol Rehabilitation was introduced in the curriculum of grades 3–12 in Boston public schools (Carifio, Biron, & Sullivan, 1978). Specially trained teachers as well as peer leaders serving as role models were used to present the alcohol curriculum. The model assumed that a student-centered curriculum focusing on knowledge and attitude about alcohol could help promote responsible use of alcohol. A rigorous set of evaluations assessed the changes over time in self-reported knowledge and use of alcohol among the participants as well as for two control groups, one of nonparticipants from the same school system and one of students from schools in a neighboring community. Students who received the full curriculum showed more gains in knowledge, and to some degree, in attitude change than the control groups. Among the teachers who participated, there were gains in knowledge and a positive change in opinions about the possibility that adolescents could benefit from the curriculum and achieve responsible drinking. However, there were no significant changes in alcohol use.

Goodstadt, Shepard, and Chan (1982) observed increased knowledge gained through alcohol education in seventh to tenth graders was associated with less drinking as compared to controls who did not receive this curriculum. However, alcohol attitudes were not strongly affected by the program; in fact, drinking boys in ninth and tenth grades held more positive attitudes about drinking than the controls after the program.

Schlegal, Manske, and Page (1984) employed a pretest-posttest design using a curriculum focused on facts and found lower alcohol consumption after the completion of the curriculum, even at a six-month follow-up. A second focus of the curriculum was to improve self-esteem and decision-making skills with affective education. Thus, values clarification and decision-making components were provided in addition to the education component in another treatment. However, contrary to prediction, this group drank at a higher posttest level than the group given only facts.

Hopkins, Mauss, Kearney, and Weisheit (1988) conducted an evaluation of a kindergarten through 12th grade curriculum designed to provide alcohol knowledge, shape positive alcohol attitudes, and build self-esteem. This large-scale study used a curriculum—"Here's Looking at You!"—that involved 15 different sessions over the year. The study involved 6,808 students, 75 percent white, from a number of different school districts. A two- and three-year follow-up showed minimal benefits of these programs to the students in comparison to students in control schools that did not participate. Although experimental and control schools were selected to be as comparable as possible, random assignment of treatments was not possible due to the need to respect the wishes of different school administrators.

A further analysis of this curriculum by Mauss, Hopkins, Weisheit, and Kearney (1988) found demographic variables such as religion and relationships with parents and peers to be stronger predictors of drinking than the curricular content of school-based alcohol and drug prevention programs. They hypothesized that school-based curricula have weak effects because experiences outside and occurring prior to schooling may have already shaped tendencies to use alcohol.

An emphasis of some later programs has been the development of resistance skills and social competence (Botvin, Baker, Botvin, Filazzola, & Millman, 1984). These models assume that resistance can be developed with experience just as inoculation can improve immunity to diseases. Ninth graders who participated in such a social influences curriculum aimed at building resistance to peer pressure (Duryea, Mohr, Newman, Martin, & Egwaoje, 1984) had more knowledge about alcohol and were less likely to be influenced by peers regarding alcohol use on tests after two weeks and six months. However, Duryea and Okwumabua (1988) found that these differences had disappeared at a three-year follow-up.

One attempt (Johnson, Pentz, Weber, Dwyer, Baer, MacKinnon, & Flay, 1990) to go beyond the school-based curricula to include efforts to improve community attitudes about alcohol involved a large-scale three-year longitudinal study with sixth and seventh graders in 42 schools in the Kansas City metropolitan area. Using a school-based curriculum as well as a mass media community campaign, these researchers randomly assigned classes of students to several different experimental treatment groups and one control group (mass media and community organization). Johnson et al. found little effect of the program on the use of alcohol although it did reduce use of cigarettes and marijuana.

Variability in the quality of program delivery is another reason why school-based programs have not generally shown much influence on drinking. Hansen, Graham, Wolkenstein, and Rohrbach (1991) presented two types of programs, one involving resistance training and one focusing on the influence of social norms. Four conditions—normative education curriculum only, resistance training curriculum only, both curricula, and neither curricula—were compared among about 3,600 fifth graders in 128 different classes in 45 different schools. The results showed that the quality of program delivery, enthusiasm of the teachers, receptiveness of the students, and proper delivery of the program components, as judged by trainers, observers, and program specialists, was a determinant of the success of the students in acquiring resistance skills and perceived self-efficacy.

Receptiveness of students to programs can depend on whether peers or teachers deliver the program. Peers may establish better rapport and/or credibility with students than adults can. Perry and Grant (1988) reported on an alcohol education program conducted in four different countries that generally found that peer-led groups had lower alcohol use after one month than teacher-led groups. A meta-analysis of school-based substance abuse programs by Bangert-Drowns (1988) supported these findings on the effectiveness of peer-led groups.

At the higher-education level, Kraft (1984) implemented a large-scale program at the University of Massachusetts. Mills, McCarthy, Ward, Minuto, and Patzynski (1983) successfully replicated and expanded it at the University of North Carolina. These programs altered the campus environment by changing regulations regarding alcohol use. Rather than focusing on individuals, the strategy was to alter the attitudes and awareness of the total campus environment including campus residences and pubs with a campaign involving mass media messages, campus newspaper articles, posters, public displays, pamphlets, workshops, lectures, and academic courses. Peer educators were trained to provide workshops, lectures, and other programs. Working with administrators, they tried to alter institutional policies and practices regarding intervention, counseling, and treatment.

The program evaluation involved annual mail surveys of a random sample of students to assess attitudes and drinking behavior. Other indexes were less direct, including data on alcohol-related arrests and incidents, alcohol sales on campus, health center cases of alcohol-related problems, and alcohol-related property damage on campus. Although evidence of gains in awareness, knowledge, and positive attitudes occurred over a three-year period of evaluation, there was little behavioral change or reduction in problems related to alcohol. Furthermore, the lack of a control group not exposed to the program made the findings ambiguous.

Legal Controls

Laws are often stronger methods than education or economics for altering alcohol-related behaviors. For example, a major societal problem is driving after drinking. Education has not been adequate to alter this behavior, so in recent years more states have passed more stringent laws, imposed heavier sanctions, and applied stronger enforcement in dealing with this dangerous behavior (Farrell, 1989). Ross (1984) noted that when stronger laws were instituted in several countries, they had immediate benefits, but the gains were often short-lived after the initial publicity (Epperlein, 1987).

The results of surveys by Snortum and Berger (1989) suggest that these laws are having an effect, even if subtle, in lowering drinking. It is not clear whether declines in consumption in a group as a whole reflect reduced drinking by most individuals or whether they reflect some strategy among groups in which one member reduces drinking and is designated as the driver for other group members who continue to drink at levels too high to drive safely.

Snortum and Berger found that reduced consumption occurred despite a decline in the perceived chances of apprehension and arrest of a drinking driver. However, at the same time, the perceived severity of the punishment, if arrested, increased. Most important, there was increased credibility of laws—that is, the belief that if apprehended, one not only would be arrested but also would receive the full penalty. They concluded that the law itself, a simple deterrent, is ineffective. However, if it is accompanied by a moral commitment among citizens to enforce the laws aimed at drinking drivers, a greater shift toward compliance with the laws will occur. Increased enforcement of laws will lead to public perceptions that penalties will occur for violations and thereby improve compliance (Ross, 1984). In short, the social environment must reinforce and support laws for them to be effective.

Reducing the Minimum Legal Drinking Age. One of the best-known legal controls on drinking is the minimum drinking age law. These laws assume that youth should be protected (or prevented) from alcohol consumption until they reach adult status. In the 1960s, as part of the movement toward greater individual rights and other forms of civil activism, there was a widespread acceptance of a lower minimum drinking age. The logic was that if 18-year-olds were old enough to risk dying for their country in the Vietnam War, they were old enough to drink alcohol legally. Accordingly, many states lowered their minimum drinking age to 18 or 19.

Leaving the political issues aside, the question of the impact of this legal change on adverse consequences such as highway accidents due to earlier drinking by youth was raised. Studies in several states comparing the fatality rates on highways before and after the legal change suggested that the lower age was related to higher traffic fatality rates.

A statistical method called a *time series* in which comparisons are made at a series of points in time was employed in many locations including Massachusetts, Michigan, Texas, and some Canadian provinces, using as controls, states and provinces without minimum age changes that were matched in size, population, and geographical region. Rates of accidents before and after the minimum age laws were lowered were compared to allow inferences about the effects of these changes. In most instances, traffic fatalities increased substantially following the lowering of the minimum age for drinking, as compared to changes in comparable states without changes in the minimum age (Wagenaar, 1983).

Wagenaar (1982) found that the reduction in the minimum drinking age from 21 to 18 by Michigan in 1972 also was related to increased consumption, but only for draft beer sales. Smart (1977) compared per capita consumption over three years in 25 states that lowered the minimum age with neighboring states that did not. Overall, there was an increase in beer and liquor sales for the states lowering the minimum drinking age.

Raising the Minimum Legal Drinking Age. The trend of the 1960s toward lowering the minimum drinking age to 18 was reversed in the 1980s due to increased evidence and concern that young persons are at higher risk for accidents when they drink and drive. The assumption was that raising the minimum drinking age back to 21 would reduce the fatal accident rate for young drivers. Wagenaar

(1982) found a 30-percent reduction in fatal accidents for 18-to-20-year-olds after the change in the minimum drinking age back to 21. A review of the research evaluating the effects of raising the minimum drinking age (O'Malley & Wagenaar, 1991) confirmed the reduction of alcohol use and traffic accidents involving alcohol use after the change.

Fell and Nash (1989) reported a general decline in fatal automobile crashes involving intoxicated drivers from 30 to 25 percent between 1982 and 1987. The improvement was even greater for teenage drivers, dropping from 29 to 19 percent. In addition to the influence of raising the minimum drinking age, Fell and Nash noted that other factors could be responsible for the improvement such as the general decline of alcohol consumption in the 1980s, increased public awareness and concern about the problem, intervention and prevention programs, and a smaller proportion of young drivers aged 16–24, a group that accounts for a disproportionately high percentage of fatal crashes (Fell, 1987).

Raising the minimum drinking age should also affect behaviors other than drinking and driving. Wagenaar (1982) also found a decline in liquor and beer sales when the minimum age was increased in Michigan.

Prevention for Specific At-Risk Groups

Prevention programs designed primarily for the white middle-class population may not be suitable for other groups of individuals. Nathan (1983) criticized the failure to develop prevention programs that might be more appropriate and effective for specific at-risk groups. The following sections examine the special needs of these at-risk groups: adolescents, women, the elderly, and minorities.

Adolescents

Although considerable study of youthful drinking has been done, most programs for prevention of adolescent alcohol problems are based on the classic disease model involving physical dependence, which usually develops only after many years of heavy drinking. Heavily drinking adolescents do not generally have these characteristics, so that this model may be invalid for this population. Early intervention with adolescents also risks the danger of labeling heavily drinking youth as "alcoholic," even though many of them may only be going through a stage of growth and development into adulthood. Nontraditional approaches (Institute of Medicine, 1990) that stress outreach and a wide range of activities including recreational, vocational, and educational programs with the use of peer counselors may be more appropriate prevention strategies.

Women

As noted in earlier chapters, women traditionally have consumed alcohol less often and less heavily than men, but they are at greater risk for many alcohol-related disorders such as drinking-related cancers, cardiovascular diseases, and brain damage, as well as suicide, accidental deaths, and cirrhosis of the liver. And, of course, the unique risk to pregnant women of alcohol-related birth defects such as the fetal alcohol syndrome described in Chapter 3 is of great concern, as evidenced in numerous campaigns to publicize this danger (Waterson & Murray-Lyon, 1990). One evaluation of such a campaign over six years (Little, Grathwohl, Streissguth, & McIntyre, 1981) suggested a positive impact in that public awareness of the dangers of drinking during pregnancy was widespread. Unfortunately, misconceptions still existed since many who knew about the risk still mistakenly thought that "safe drinking" for pregnant women allowed as many as three drinks daily. However, changing social norms toward lighter drinking may have accounted for some of the decline attributed to prevention campaigns (Waterson & Murray-Lyon, 1990). Despite some progress in the development of prevention programs directed toward women, the available evidence is not yet clear about their effectiveness in reducing alcohol problems among women.

Many reasons can be found to suggest that the types of prevention programs that would be most effective for women should differ from those that are effective for men (Ferrence, 1984). In addition to the obvious biological differences, the patterns and drinking contexts differ for men and women. Furthermore, women are more likely than men to seek help in general, even regarding nonhealth issues. Ferrence noted that in the 1980s greater attention was given to development of programs aimed at specific target populations such as women.

The Elderly

Elderly populations show a decline in the percentage of drinkers after age 50. Nonetheless, those with alcohol problems face serious hazards when the effects of alcohol combine with those from physical aging processes. Furthermore, some who were not problem drinkers before age 50 develop drinking problems in response to depression, loneliness, and boredom in their later years. Nathan (1983) suggested that the negative attitudes and lack of awareness of some mental health workers about the seriousness of alcohol problems for this population heightens their plight.

Minorities

As noted in Chapter 16, most minority groups face serious levels of alcoholism and alcohol-related problems, especially among males. However, there have been few attempts to develop prevention programs targeted at these populations, and where such programs have existed, minorities have not been motivated to participate at effective levels. For example, Gilbert and Cervantes (1988) noted the cultural barriers created by differences in alcohol beliefs and attitudes of Mexican-American immigrants and those held at treatment facilities. Recognition of the faith of many immigrants in folk medicine is also important when dealing with their alcohol problems. Culturally sensitive programs directed toward minorities, especially the youth, need more development (Dawkins, 1988; Edwards & Edwards, 1988; Galan, 1988).

Secondary Prevention

If we cannot prevent alcohol problems from occurring due to the many factors in the environment that make the use of alcohol attractive and easily accessible to those who expect alcohol to provide pleasure and relief from pain, we can and must still develop countermeasures for the reduction and minimization of existing problems stemming from excessive alcohol use. This type of secondary prevention can be illustrated with several examples: drinking drivers, early-stage problem drinkers, heavily drinking college students, and employees with drinking problems.

The Example of Drinking Drivers

Given the nature of our highly mobile society in which public transportation is inadequate or less attractive to most people than their private automobiles and given the widespread availability and popularity of alcoholic beverages in public and private situations outside the home, it is almost impossible to prevent many from driving vehicles while under the influence of alcohol. People want to socialize, dine in restaurants, and engage in other activities that often involve consumption of alcoholic beverages. Lacking other attractive means of transportation to get home, many people end up driving under varying degrees of intoxication.

It is impossible for law enforcement personnel to apprehend every person driving under the influence of alcohol, and people realize that they may have a good chance of not being detected. If, of course, they have a traffic accident, they are likely to face stiff penalties and possibly injuries, assuming they are not killed outright. Nonetheless, these fears are usually minimized or rationalized since the driver who has been drinking needs to get home and knows that every drinking driver on the road cannot be detected or apprehended.

Secondary prevention deals with preventing recurrences of this type of behavior among those who are apprehended for driving while intoxicated (DWI) or driving under the influence (DUI), as jurisdictions variously call it. The federally sponsored Alcohol Safety Action Project (ASAPs) in local communities focus on such secondary prevention for drinking drivers. One form of countermeasure involves education coupled with small group interactions to increase awareness. Another focus on deterrence uses the threat of punishment such as loss of license and driving privileges as well as a fine. Deterrence programs attempt to reduce the likelihood of future drinking and driving behavior of those apprehended for this offense as well as those who have not yet either committed or been detected for such practices. Participants must perceive that the probability of their being apprehended for violations is high in order for these programs to be effective.

ASAPs vary in structure, ranging from education courses of two to six weeks to therapy for more than a year. Although some reviews (Nichols, Weinstein, Ellingstad, & Struckman-Johnson, 1978) have shown that ASAPs lead to a decrease in arrests and repeat offenses among social drinkers, no reduction for heavy drinkers has been found. Success of these programs has been high for first-time offenders but there is no evidence that these programs help heavier drinkers.

ASAPs also refer many DWIs to alcoholism treatment facilities. The assumption has been that for many DWIs, the primary problem is alcohol abuse, rather than drunk driving per se, which is only a consequence, albeit serious, of the basic problem. For this group, the way to reduce their DWI behavior is to correct their drinking problem. It should be noted, however, as Klajner, Sobell, and Sobell (1984) argued, that the main goal of the treatment center is to correct the alcohol problem, not the DWI problem. While many DWIs appear to have alcohol problems, it is dangerous to overgeneralize. Armor, Polich, and Stambul (1978) suggested that the tendency to treat all DWIs as if they were alcohol abusers and refer them to treatment programs, psychotherapy, or AA may be unnecessarily costly, ineffective, and unwarranted for nonabusers of alcohol.

In support of the view that DWIs are likely to need alcoholism treatment, Wilson and Jonah (1985) found that drinkers who admitted driving under the influence of alcohol reported more prior accidents and convictions, drank more alcohol, used seatbelts less, and reported being less likely to cut down on drinking at a party before driving than drinkers who did not report drinking and driving. Jonah and Dawson (1987) proposed a risk behavior syndrome that involved risky driving behaviors including the use of alcohol. They found some support of the model, but mainly for young drivers.

Donovan, Umlauf, and Salzberg (1991) compared high-risk bad drivers (those with many traffic arrests and violations) prospectively over a three-year period. This group was similar at the outset of the study in demographics, personality, and risk-enhancing driver attitudes. At the three-year follow-up, they were more likely to have been arrested for DWI (11.4 versus 2.0 percent) than the general driving population. And the subgroup of bad drivers who were cited for DWI drank more often than the other high-risk drivers. The implication of these results is that high-risk drivers are a target group for early intervention for alcohol problems.

Donovan and Marlatt (1982) went beyond a simple dichotomy of problem and nonproblem DWIs, identifying several subtypes of DWI offenders in terms of personality traits and accident-related driving attitudes. The most common subtype involved individuals with infrequent and light drinking, a good driving record, good emotional adjustment, and the least driving-related aggression. A less frequent subtype showed depression, resentment, and low assertiveness. Using this taxonomy as the basis, they proposed different secondary prevention approaches for each subtype. For the first type, they recommended a controlled drinking emphasis to help these offenders identify situations with high risk for DWI and how to cope with them. For the second type they endorsed a program focusing on self-management training on the assumption that it could help them improve their feelings of control and efficacy.

Evaluation of the effectiveness of ASAP diversionary programs, however, needs improvement. Seldom are offenders randomly assigned to different treatments so that researchers can adequately evaluate their effectiveness by controlling other factors. Available studies have not shown ASAPs to be effective in reducing repeat offenses. One large evaluation by Ellingstad and Struckman-Johnson (1978) was able to compare program sites where offenders were randomly assigned to treatment and control conditions, where treatment involved a mixture of group and individual therapy plus DWI school. The results were not encouraging since none of the treatment combinations had any better impact than the control treatment on drunk driving, drinking, or social adjustment.

One reason (Nichols, 1990) why programs may not be more effective is that when repeat DWI offenders have their licenses suspended, they do not always have to prove that they have gained control of their drinking problem for their licenses to be reinstated. Also, many jurisdictions have diversionary programs that allow first-time DWIs to attend "traffic school" (education/treatment programs) to avoid having their arrests appear on their records or getting their licenses suspended (National Transportation Safety Board, 1987).

Whether this option is justifiable depends on numerous factors such as its impact on subsequent traffic violations involving alcohol. Perrine and Sadler (1987) compared California DWI offenders given license actions (suspensions, fines) versus referral to rehabilitation programs. They found fewer crashes subsequently by those who received traffic citations, suggesting that the harsher policy may be more effective.

The option of traffic school and alcoholism counseling to avoid traffic citations for DWI, which may allow alcohol-dependent drivers to avoid receiving needed treatment, declined in the 1980s because of disapproval by the Presidential Commission on Drunk Driving (1983), but it still occurs in many locales.

Early-Stage Problem Drinkers

AA and most treatment programs that are based on the disease conception of alcoholism are designed to deal with those chronic alcoholics who have reached "rock bottom" and are generally ready to accept help. In contrast, as Sanchez-Craig, Wilkinson, and Walker (1987) noted, there are many problem drinkers who do not consider themselves alcohol-dependent and will not seek or accept any intervention. The all-or-none conception of alcoholism represented by the disease model, according to Sanchez-Craig et al., acts to prevent the early-stage problem drinker from recognizing that he or she has any drinking problem.

Sanchez-Craig et al. interviewed 52 male and 18 female early-stage problem drinkers to assess their perceptions of the causes and effects of specific drinking incidents that they could recall. Overall, their responses resembled those of chronic alcoholics with two notable differences. First, they also recalled heavy drinking motivated by pleasure and social activities. Second, drinking episodes often involved a deliberate and conscious decision to drink.

In view of such differences, Sanchez-Craig et al. felt that the methods for helping these early-stage problem drinkers before they develop further problems should not be the same as those used to treat alcoholics. They viewed early-stage problem drinking as an inappropriate coping method for dealing with negative situations and feelings that can be replaced with more suitable cognitive and behavioral coping responses. Due to the more stable social status of early-stage problem drinkers, they also hypothesized that a goal of controlled or moderate drinking, rather than abstinence, was feasible for them.

Evaluation of their program to provide coping skills to early-stage problem drinkers showed that both a controlled-drinking and an abstinence group reduced their drinking, but the group given a moderation goal drank less than the group told to abstain. At follow-up, the differences had disappeared, but both groups were able to drink at a moderate level that was an improvement from the pretreatment levels.

Sanchez-Craig et al. viewed their program as a form of secondary prevention. They developed an intervention that could be used to prevent problem drinking from worsening. By way of such early intervention programs, they believe that more effective and lower cost treatment can be provided to deal with alcohol problems.

Heavily Drinking College Students

Similarly, Kivlahan, Marlatt, Fromme, Coppel, and Williams (1990) recognized that while many college students drink heavily, most do not seek treatment because they do not consider themselves to be alcoholics. These researchers proposed that a secondary prevention program teaching coping skills and emphasizing more moderate drinking might be more effective with this population in arresting the alcohol abuse than trying to refer them for alcoholism treatment.

They recruited 43 students who drank heavily and frequently, with at least one negative consequence of heavy frequent drinking, for an eight-week training program. Based on random assignment, one group received the traditional information lecture program based on the disease model of alcoholism that stressed negative effects of alcohol abuse. A second group received a cognitive-behavioral coping skills training course that included drinking moderation skills, relaxation training, blood alcohol level estimation, and recognition of situations with high risk for alcohol abuse. A control group completed daily records of alcohol consumption. The researchers screened out heavily dependent drinkers by referring them to an alcoholism treatment program emphasizing abstinence.

The results of several follow-ups over a one-year period suggested that significant reductions in self-reported drinking occurred, with the most improvement shown by the skills training group, followed by the information-only group, and least for the control group. Unfortunately, about half the students still reported drinking occasionally at levels exceeding a BAL of .10 mg. % during follow-ups. Kivlahan et al. were cautiously optimistic that their approach would prove more successful in the future.

Workplace Intervention

The adverse effects of alcohol abuse and dependence often extend beyond the drinker's personal activities, impairing performance and productivity in the workplace as well. Prior to the temperance movements of the 19th century, alcohol use on the job was not always regarded as undesirable but was commonly accepted. As the hazards of drinking at work became recognized, management's "solution" was typically to discharge such personnel. In the 1940s, a move arose to provide employee assistance programs (EAPs) in which supervisors were taught to see poor or deteriorating work performance as a sign of possible alcohol problems. Then attempts to counsel and refer the employee to alcoholism treatment would be made. The idea of EAPs was more humane than firing employees, but it was also hoped that the programs would be cost effective by avoiding the expense of retraining, new hiring, worksite accidents, and poor productivity. However, EAPs were often difficult to implement due to resistance from both employers and employees.

It was not until the late 1980s that EAPs finally became widely accepted (Nathan, 1984; Roman, 1987; Trice & Beyer, 1984). Although not legally required to have EAPs, companies concerned about possible legal actions of discrimination if they fired alcoholics on grounds other than poor work performance began to recognize the value of EAPs. A national survey of health promotion activities on worksites conducted by the Office of Disease Prevention and Health Promotion (1987) reported that 24 percent of worksites with 50 or more workers and more than half of those with 750 or more employees had EAPs. At the same time that EAPs have become more commonplace, they have also adopted a more "broad brush" approach extending beyond intervention for alcohol problems to include referral and treatment for illegal drug abuse as well as other psychological problems that might hamper work performance. The goal of EAPs is to improve work performance, reduce turnover, and cut absenteeism. The potential of EAPs to motivate alcoholics to seek treatment rests in the fact that employers have one type of leverage with alcohol-dependent employees that family members and friends lack—control over the drinker's job. However, threats of dismissals and penalties are less effective than "constructive confrontation" (Trice & Sonnenstuhl, 1988) and peer referral in motivating help seeking.

In theory, EAPs promised a means of early intervention for alcoholism, but in practice a number of problems exist in implementing them such as risks of loss of confidentiality, coerced treatment, and invasion of privacy. While employers have a right to expect work performance to meet certain criteria, it is only when alcohol abuse interferes with these goals that employers can legitimately urge employees to accept alcoholism treatment. However, overzealous employers may sometimes exceed these limits and try to monitor and control employee behaviors that employers and supervisors find unacceptable but that do not interfere with work performance (Fillmore & Kelso, 1987). In addition to these political concerns is the concern that the effectiveness of EAPs in modifying drinking problems has not been adequately evaluated (Babor, Ritson, & Hodgson, 1986). Such evaluation is difficult because cooperation of companies and employees is not easy to obtain, and there is typically an absence of control groups.

Future Directions

Beauchamp (1980) called for more leadership from the federal government in shaping attitudes, laws, and policies related to alcohol. In response to the growing awareness and concern about alcohol and drug abuse problems in local communities across the nation, Congress appropriated $52.5 million in 1986 to create the

Office for Substance Abuse Prevention (OSAP). The mission of OSAP is to provide support and guidance to efforts at the local and state level addressing the issues of community-based prevention. However, Beauchamp also insisted that local community leaders must do their share in supporting healthier and safer use of alcohol by citizens. The church, he suggested, has steered clear of alcohol issues, perhaps due to unpleasant memories of Prohibition, but could be an influential force today.

Grassroots organizations such as Mothers Against Drunk Driving (MADD), Students Against Drunk Driving (SADD), and Remove Intoxicated Drivers (RID) have drawn national attention to a major social problem as well as to the fact that citizens can and should mobilize to deal with the societal reluctance to confront the dangers created by drunk driving. These forces helped pressure the federal government to create the Presidential Commission on Drunk Driving in 1982, which has helped states and local communities take a tougher stance to enforce laws pertaining to drinking and driving. The withholding of federal highway funds from uncooperative states has also served to motivate compliance.

Similarly, increased publicity, education, and awareness about the risks of fetal alcohol syndrome and other birth defects created by drinking among pregnant women illustrate changing public attitudes and concern about the health-related dangers of drinking. In some states, laws require establishments serving alcohol to post prominent signs warning patrons of the health risks of alcohol. Warning labels on alcoholic beverage containers have also been proposed by the Department of Health and Human Services (1987) and by activist organizations such as the nonprofit Center for Science in the Public Interest as an effective method of reducing alcohol consumption. However, as noted many years ago (Haggard, 1945) when Massachusetts considered a warning label requirement, one problem is that those who need to heed the warning the most are the ones who are least likely to read such labels.

Langton (1991) pointed out that during the eras of Temperance and Prohibition, prevention strategies centered on controlling the agent, alcohol. Then, the focus shifted to the host, or individual drinkers, during the alcoholism movement of the 1970s. The concept of *responsible drinking,* initially promoted but later abandoned in 1977 by the National Institute on Alcohol Abuse and Alcoholism in favor of a psychosocial perspective, illustrates this approach.

In the 1990s the emphasis in prevention strategies seems to have moved more toward creating an environment with reduced alcohol and drug problems by decreasing the availability of alcohol in society as a whole and modifying social attitudes through education. For example, instead of looking for causes of alcohol problems in the worker, many work organizations recognize the impact of the work environment in creating these problems. Historically, employers resisted the view that the workplace environment could be a factor affecting alcohol problems among employees (Ames, 1989). If workers could be blamed for their drinking excesses, employers could dismiss them or impose sanctions, but the recognition that the physical, social, or ideological working conditions contribute to alcohol problems calls for changes in the work environment as well as early intervention to motivate the alcohol-dependent workers to seek treatment.

In a somewhat similar manner, the diversion programs for DWI offenders represent an early intervention to pressure individuals into alcoholism counseling and treatment sooner than they would otherwise seek it. As with EAPs, the positive aspect of ASAP diversion programs is the possible prevention of more serious drinking problems. However, the negative feature is the coercive nature of the interventions, which threatens civil rights. Furthermore, Weisner (1990) noted that it is difficult to prove that individuals who are coerced into treatment do benefit, because it is rarely possible to include control groups of either alcohol-dependent workers or DWI offenders who do not receive treatment.

Coerced treatment is problematic not only for those given the "choice" between treatment and going to jail (for DWI) or being fired (for alcohol-related work impairment), but also for the climate in alcoholism treatment and recovery facilities. For example, AA participants traditionally were individuals who had reached "rock bottom" and were ready to admit they were powerless. However, with the large influx of coerced participants in AA and in public treatment facilities, many of whom are hostile and uncooperative, the situation is drastically altered in ways that may impair the effectiveness of these programs for voluntary participants (Weisner, 1987).

A public health model for prevention that reflects a new temperance movement (Beauchamp, 1980, 1988; Heath, 1989) has arisen over the past decade. It stresses the primary prevention of alcohol-related problems through social policies that modify the availability of alcohol, rather than the treatment of alcohol-dependent individuals. If the costs of alcohol-related problems to society are to be minimized, prevention can no longer be a responsibility left entirely to each individual, but becomes a challenge to be confronted by the whole society and all its institutions.

The battle will not be easy. As Mosher and Jernigan (1989) pointed out, the alcohol industry is a formidable opponent to changes in social policies affecting alcohol availability. Alcoholic beverage producers have skillfully influenced legislators through financial donations and lobbyists, derogated alcohol industry critics, formed powerful alliances with other groups that also face the threat of increased excise taxes, and provided research funds for scientific investigators. They have also improved public relations by funding public service campaigns such as warnings against drinking and driving and sponsoring sporting activities and cultural events.

Public recognition or opposition to the alcohol industry has been blunted by the prevailing tendency to regard alcohol problems as the fault of the individual while overlooking the sophisticated marketing practices of the alcohol industry that create an environment that promotes and encourages drinking. However, Mosher and Jernigan suggested that public health proponents can form coalitions at the state and federal level to affect legislation and also organize local constituencies to combat alcohol problems. Efforts to pass legislation for warning labels, increase excise taxes, and obtain equal broadcast media time for counteradvertising are examples of recent campaigns involving the joint efforts and support of health, consumer advocate, educational, religious, and alcohol treatment groups.

Chapter Seventeen

Conclusions

The public health model illustrates the complex interplay between several components—host, agent, and environment—that must be examined when planning prevention programs. Prohibition of alcohol in the United States proved unworkable because it was too unpopular and impossible to enforce. Education has been inadequate and often irrelevant to prevention because mere ignorance does not fully account for alcohol abuse.

Because most drinkers seem to enjoy the benefits of drinking without suffering any apparent harm, society appears willing to tolerate the price of having a certain number of alcohol-dependent individuals. As long as they are viewed as not harming anyone but themselves, the public seems willing to allow them to pay the price for their excesses. But, as evidenced by the increased public reaction against drinking drivers, the line is drawn when the alcohol abuser begins to victimize the innocent. More awareness and concern about fetal alcohol syndrome may similarly focus public attention on the dangers that a drinking mother may create for her unborn fetus. The message may be that instead of trying to motivate the drinker to control his or her drinking, we may be more successful in preventing problems if we can increase the awareness of everyone of the dangers that alcoholics and alcohol abusers create for the "rest of us." Once alerted to the dangers, nonalcoholics will be motivated to look out for themselves and indirectly for alcoholics.

A clash between individual rights and the well-being and safety of the public occurs in many situations when government attempts to act in the public behalf. There is often resistance when the perception exists that the government is meddling with individual freedoms and attempting to control the personal lives of its citizens. Therefore, laws and social policies that restrict access to alcohol or minimize the threat to others from excessive drinkers are often opposed vigorously by those who want to preserve their rights to drink when, where, and in as large a quantity as they wish.

The difficulty of proving that prevention is effective is in part due to the lengthy interval needed before an intervention takes hold. And where preventive measures are successful, it is not so readily acknowledged because nothing dreadful happened to alarm us. We do not realize that we have been saved because we did not observe the danger firsthand. Whereas one can clearly see dramatic tangible benefits when alcoholics are successfully rehabilitated, one can only speculate on how terrible the situation would have been if preventive measures had not existed.

As Cahalan (1987, p. 124) concluded in his perceptive analysis of alcohol problems in the United States, "It is easy to count the numbers we have pulled out of the stream, but it is hard to count the numbers who would have fallen in if more effective control programs had not been adopted." Unfortunately, most people are galvanized to take action only after serious damage has occurred. An ounce of prevention may be worth the proverbial pound of cure, but most people apparently would rather not spend the ounce, on the chance that no treatment will ever be required.

References

Ames, G. M. (1989). Alcohol-related movements and their effects on drinking policies in the American workplace: An historical review. *Journal of Drug Issues, 19,* 489–510.

Armor, D. J., Polich, J. M., & Stambul, H. B. (1978). *Alcoholism and treatment.* New York: Wiley.

Atkin, C., Neuendorf, K., & McDermott, S. (1983). The role of alcohol advertising in excessive and hazardous drinking. *Journal of Drug Education, 13,* 313–326.

Babor, T. F., Ritson, E. B., & Hodgson, R. J. (1986). Alcohol-related problems in the primary health care setting: A review of early intervention strategies. *British Journal of Addiction, 81,* 23–46.

Bangert-Drowns, R. L. (1988). The effects of school-based substance abuse programs: A meta-analysis. *Journal of Drug Education, 18,* 243–264.

Beauchamp, D. (1980). *Beyond alcoholism.* Philadelphia: PA: Temple University Press.

Beauchamp, D. (1988). *The health of the Republic: Epidemics, medicine, and moralism as challenges to democracy.* Philadelphia, PA: Temple University Press.

Bensley, L. S., & Wu, R. (1991). The role of psychological reactance in drinking following alcohol prevention messages. *Journal of Applied Social Psychology, 21,* 1111–1124.

Botvin, G. J., Baker, E., Botvin, E. M., Filazzola, A. D., & Millman, R. B. (1984). Alcohol abuse prevention through the development of personal and social competence: A pilot study. *Journal of Studies on Alcohol, 45,* 550–552.

Breed, W., Defoe, J. R., & Wallack, L. (1984). Drinking in the mass media: A nine-year project. *Journal of Drug Issues, 14,* 655–664.

Cahalan, D. (1987). *Understanding America's drinking problem: How to combat the hazards of alcohol.* San Francisco, CA: Jossey-Bass.

Carifio, J., Biron, R. M., & Sullivan, D. (1978). *Selected findings on the impact of the CASPAR alcohol education program on teacher training and curriculum implementation* (Evaluation Report No. 8). Somerville, MA: CASPAR, Inc.

Coate, D., & Grossman, M. (1987). Change in alcoholic beverage prices and legal drinking ages: Effects on youth alcohol use and motor vehicle mortality. *Alcohol Health and Research World, 12,* 22–26.

Cook, P. J. (1981). The effects of liquor taxes on drinking, cirrhosis and auto accidents. In M. H. Moore & D. R. Gerstein (Eds.), *Alcohol and alcohol policy: Beyond the shadow of Prohibition* (pp. 255–285). Washington, DC: National Academy Press.

Dawkins, M. P. (1988). Alcoholism prevention and Black youth. Special issue: Alcohol problems and minority youth. *Journal of Drug Issues, 18,* 15–20.

Department of Health and Human Services. (1987). *Review of the research literature on the effects of health warning labels: A report to the U.S. Congress.* Rockville, MD: National Institute on Alcohol Abuse and Alcoholism.

Donovan, D. M., & Marlatt, G. A. (1982). Reasons for drinking among DWI arrestees. *Addictive Behaviors, 7,* 423–426.

Donovan, D. M., Umlauf, R. L., & Salzberg, P. M. (1991). Bad drivers: Identification of a target group for alcohol-related prevention and early intervention. *Journal of Studies on Alcohol, 51,* 136–141.

Duryea, E., Mohr, P., Newman, I. M., Martin, G. L., & Egwaoje, E. (1984). Six-month follow-up results of a preventive alcohol education intervention. *Journal of Drug Education, 14,* 97–104.

Duryea, E. J., & Okwumabua, J. O. (1988). Effects of a preventive alcohol education program after three years. *Journal of Drug Education, 18,* 23–31.

Edwards, E. D., & Edwards, M. E. (1988). Alcoholism prevention/treatment and Native American youth: A community approach. Special issue: Alcohol problems and minority youth. *Journal of Drug Issues, 18,* 103–114.

Ellingstad, V. S., & Struckman-Johnson, D. L. (1978). *Programme level evaluation of ASAP diagnosis, referral and rehabilitation efforts. Vol 3: Analysis of rehabilitation coun-*

termeasures effectiveness. Prepared for the Department of Transportation, National Highway Traffic Safety Administration (Report No. 802-044). Springfield, VA: National Technical Information Source.

Epperlein, T. (1987). Initial effects of the crackdown on drinking drivers in the state of Arizona. *Accident Analysis and Prevention, 19,* 285–303.

Farrell, S. (1989). Policy alternatives for alcohol-impaired driving. *Health Education Quarterly, 16,* 413–427.

Fell, J. C. (1987). Alcohol involvement in fatal crashes. A focus on young drivers and female drivers. *31st annual proceedings of the American Association for Automotive Medicine* (pp. 1–30). New Orleans, LA: NHTSA Report DOT HS 807 104).

Fell, J. C., & Nash, C. E. (1989). The nature of the alcohol problem in U.S. fatal crashes. Special issue: Drinking, driving, and health promotion. *Health Education Quarterly, 16,* 335–343.

Ferrence, R. G. (1984). Prevention of alcohol problems in women. In S. C. Wilsnack & L. J. Beckman (Eds.), *Alcohol problems in women: Antecedents, consequences, and intervention* (pp. 413–442). New York: Academic Press.

Filkins, L. D., Clark, C. D., Rosenblatt, C. A., Carlson, W. L., Kerlan, M. W., & Manson, H. (1970). *Alcohol abuse and traffic safety: A study of fatalities, DWI offenders, alcoholics, and court-related treatment approches.* Final report to the U.S. Department of Transportation. Ann Arbor: Highway Safety Research Institute, University of Michigan.

Fillmore, K. M., & Kelso, D. (1987). Coercion into alcoholism treatment: Meanings for the disease concept of alcoholism. *Journal of Drug Issues, 17,* 301–319.

Frankena, M., Cohen, M., Daniel, T., Ehrlich, L., Greenspun, N., & Kelman, D. (1985). Alcohol advertising, consumption and abuse. In *Recommendations of the staff of the Federal Trade Commission: Omnibus petition for regulation of unfair and deceptive alcoholic beverage marketing practices* (Docket No. 209-46). Washington, DC: Federal Trade Commission.

Galan, F. J. (1988). Alcoholism prevention and Hispanic youth. Special issue: Alcohol problems and minority youth. *Journal of Drug Issues, 18,* 49–58.

Gilbert, M. J., & Cervantes, R. C. (1988). Alcohol treatment for Mexican Americans: A review of utilization patterns and therapeutic approaches. In M. J. Gilbert (Ed.), *Alcohol consumption among Mexicans and Mexican Americans: A binational perspective.* Los Angeles: UCLA Spanish-Speaking Mental Health Research Center.

Goodstadt, M. S., Shepard, M. A., & Chan, G. C. (1982). An evaluation of two school-based alcohol education programs. *Journal of Studies on Alcohol, 43,* 352–369.

Grossman, M., Coate, D., & Arluck, G. M. (1987). Price sensitivity of alcoholic beverages in the United States: Youth alcohol consumption. In H. D. Holder (Ed.), *Control issues in alcohol abuse prevention: Strategies for states and communities* (pp. 169–198). Greenwich, CT: JAI Press.

Haggard, H. W. (1945). The proposed Massachusetts "label" and its place in education against inebriety. *Quarterly Journal of Studies on Alcohol, 6,* 1–3.

Hansen, W. B., Graham, J. W., Wolkenstein, B. H., & Rohrbach, L. A. (1991). Program integrity as a moderator of prevention program effectiveness: Results for fifth-grade students in the Adolescent Alcohol Prevention Trial. *Journal of Studies on Alcohol, 52,* 568–579.

Heath, D. W. (1989). The new temperance movement: Through the looking-glass. *Drugs and Society, 3,* 143–168.

Hewitt, L. E., & Blane, H. T. (1984). Prevention through mass media communication. In P. M. Miller & T. D. Nirenberg (Eds.), *Prevention of alcohol abuse* (pp. 281–323). New York: Plenum Press.

Hopkins, R. H., Mauss, A. L., Kearney, K. A., & Weisheit, R. A. (1988). Comprehensive evaluation of a model alcohol education curriculum. *Journal of Studies on Alcohol, 49,* 38–50.

Institute of Medicine. (1990). *Broadening the base of treatment for alcohol problems.* Washington, DC: National Academy Press.

It's a two-way street: If drinkers must act responsibly, so must beverage makers. (1992, July 23). *Los Angeles Times,* p. B10.

Johnson, C. A. Pentz, M. A., Weber, M. D., Dwyer, J. H., Baer, N., MacKinnon, D. P., Hansen, W. B., and Flay, W. B. (1990). Relative effectiveness of comprehensive community programming for drug abuse prevention with high-risk and low-risk adolescents. *Journal of Consulting and Clinical Psychology, 58,* 447–456.

Jonah, B. A., & Dawson, N. E. (1987). Youth and risk: Age differences in risky driving, risk perception, and risk utility. *Alcohol, Drugs, and Driving, 3,* 13–29.

Kivlahan, D. R., Marlatt, G. A., Fromme, K., Coppel, D. B., & Williams, E. (1990). Secondary prevention with college drinkers: Evaluation of an alcohol skills training program. *Journal of Consulting and Clinical Psychology, 58,* 805–810.

Klajner, F., Sobell, L. C., & Sobell, M. B. (1984). Prevention of drunk driving. In P. M. Miller & T. D. Nirenberg (Eds.), *Prevention of alcohol abuse* (pp. 441–468). New York: Plenum Press.

Kohn, P. M., & Smart, R. G. (1984). The impact of television advertising on alcohol consumption. *Journal of Studies on Alcohol, 45,* 295–301.

Kraft, D. (1984). A comprehensive prevention program for college students. In P. M. Miller & T. D. Nirenberg (Eds.), *Prevention of alcohol abuse* (pp. 327–369). New York: Plenum Press.

Langton, P. A. (1991). *Drug use and the alcohol dilemma.* Needham Heights, MA: Allyn & Bacon.

Ledermann, S. (1956). *Alcool, alcoolisme, alcoolisation: Donnes scientifiques de caractere physiologique, economique, et social.* Cahier No. 29. Paris: Presses Universitaires de France.

Little, R. E., Grathwohl, H. L., Streissguth, A. P., & McIntyre, C. (1981). Public awareness and knowledge about the risks of drinking during pregnancy in Multinomah County. *American Journal of Public Health, 71,* 312–314.

MacDonald, S., & Whitehead, P. (1983). Availability of outlets and consumption of alcoholic beverages. *Journal of Drug Issues, 13,* 477–486.

Makowsky, C. R., & Whitehead, P. C. (1991). Advertising and alcohol sales: A legal impact study. *Journal of Studies on Alcohol, 52,* 555–567.

Mauss, A. L., Hopkins, R. H., Weisheit, R. A., & Kearney, K. A. (1988). The problematic prospects for prevention in the classroom: Should alcohol education programs be expected to reduce drinking by youth? *Journal of Studies on Alcohol, 49,* 51–61.

Mills, K. C., McCarthy, D., Ward, J., Minuto, L., & Patzynski, J. (1983). A residence hall tavern as a collegiate alcohol abuse prevention activity. *Addictive Behaviors, 8,* 105–108.

Mosher, J. F., & Jernigan, D. H. (1989). New directions in alcohol policy. In L. Breslow, J. E. Fielding, & L. B. Lave (Eds.), *Annual review of public health* (pp. 245–279). Palo Alto, CA: Annual Reviews, Inc.

Moskowitz, J. M. (1989). The primary prevention of alcohol problems: A critical review of the research literature. *Journal of Studies on Alcohol, 50,* 54–88.

Nathan, P. E. (1983). Failures in prevention: Why we can't prevent the devastating effect of alcoholism and drug abuse. *American Psychologist, 38,* 459–467.

Nathan, P. E. (1984). Alcohol prevention in the workplace. In P. M. Miller & T. D. Nirenberg (Eds.), *Prevention of alcohol abuse* (pp. 387–406). New York: Plenum Press.

National Institute on Alcoholism and Alcohol Abuse. (1992, Feb./Mar.) *Epidemiologic report.* Rockville, MD: Author.

National Transportation Safety Board. (1987). Deficiencies in enforcement, judicial, and treatment programs related to repeat offender drunk drivers. *Alcohol, Drugs and Driving, 3,* 31–42.

Nichols, J. L. (1990). Treatment versus deterrence. *Alcohol and Health Research World, 14,* 44–51.

Nichols, J. L., Weinstein, E. B., Ellingstad, V. S., & Struckman-Johnson, D. L. (1978). The specific deterrent effect of ASAP education and rehabilitation programs. *Journal of Safety Research, 10,* 177–187.

Office of Disease Prevention and Health Promotion. (1987). *National survey of worksite health promotion activities: A summary.* Monograph series. Silver Springs, MD: ODPHP National Health Information Center.

Ogbourne, A. C., & Smart, R. G. (1980). Will restrictions on alcohol advertising reduce alcohol consumption? *British Journal of Addiction, 75,* 293–296.

O'Malley, P. M., & Wagenaar, A. C. (1991). Effects of minimum drinking age laws on alcohol use, related behaviors and traffic crash involvement among American youth: 1976–1987. *Journal of Studies on Alcohol, 52,* 478–491.

Ornstein, S., & Levy, D. (1983). Price and income elasticities of demand for alcoholic beverages. In M. Galanter (Ed.), *Recent developments in alcoholism Vol. 1* (pp. 303–345). New York: Plenum Press.

Parker, D. A., & Harmon, M. S. (1978). Distribution of consumption model of prevention of alcohol problems. *Journal of Studies on Alcohol, 39,* 377–399.

Perrine, M. W., & Sadler, D. D. (1987). Alcohol treatment program versus license suspension for drunken drivers: The four-year traffic safety impact. In P. C. Noordzij & R. Roszbach (Eds.), *Alcohol, drugs, and traffic safety.* New York: Elsevier.

Perry, C. L., & Grant, M. (1988). Comparing peer-led to teacher-led youth alcohol education in four countries. *Alcohol Health and Research World, 12,* 322–326.

Popham, R., Schmidt, W., & de Lint, J. (1975). The prevention of alcoholism: Epidemiological studies of the effects of government control measures. *British Journal of Addiction, 70,* 125–144.

Presidential Commission on Drunk Driving. (1983). *Final report.* Washington, DC: U.S. Government Printing Office.

Roman, P. M. (1987). Growth and transformation in workplace alcoholism programming. In M. Galanter (Ed.), *Recent developments in alcoholism* (pp. 131–158). New York: Plenum Press.

Ross, H. L. (1984). *Deterring the drinking driver: Legal policy and social control.* Lexington, MA: D. C. Heath.

Ryan, B. E., & Segars, L. (1987). Mini-marts and maxi-problems: The relationship between purchase and consumption location. *Alcohol Health and Research World, 12,* 322–326.

Saltz, R. (1986). Server intervention. Will it work? *Alcohol Health and Research World, 10,* 12–19, 35.

Sanchez-Craig, M., Wilkinson, D. A., & Walker, K. (1987). Theory and methods for secondary prevention of alcohol problems: A cognitively based approach. In W. M. Cox (Ed.), *Treatment and prevention of alcohol problems: A resource manual* (pp. 287–331). Orlando, FL: Academic Press.

Schlegal, R., Manske, S., & Page, A. (1984). A guided decision making program for elementary school students: A field experiment in alcohol education. In P. Miller & T. Nirenberg (Eds.), *Prevention of alcohol abuse* (pp. 407–439). New York: Plenum Press.

Smart, R. G. (1977). Changes in alcoholic beverage sales after reductions in the legal drinking age. *American Journal of Drug and Alcohol Abuse, 4,* 101–108.

Smart, R. G. (1988). Does alcohol advertising affect overall consumption? A review of empirical studies. *Journal of Studies on Alcohol, 49,* 314–323.

Smart, R. G., & Cutler, R. E. (1976). The alcohol advertising ban in British Columbia: Problems and effects on beverage consumption. *British Journal of Addiction, 71,* 13–21.

Snortum, J. R., & Berger, D. E. (1989). Drinking-driving compliance in the United States: Perceptions and behavior in 1983 and 1986. *Journal of Studies on Alcohol, 50,* 306–319.

Strickland, D. E. (1983). Advertising exposure, alcohol consumption and misuse of alcohol. In M. Grant, M. Plant, & A. Williams (Eds.), *Economics and alcohol: Consumption and controls* (pp. 201–222). London: Croom Helm.

Trice, H. M., & Beyer, J. M. (1984). Work-related outcomes of the constructive confrontation strategy in a job-based alcoholism program. *Journal of Studies on Alcoholism, 45,* 393–404.

Trice, H., & Sonnenstuhl, W. (1988). Constructive confrontation and other referral processes.

In M. Galanter (Ed.), *Recent developments in alcoholism* (pp. 159–170). New York: Plenum Press.

Vegega, M. E. (1986). NHTSA responsible beverage service research and evaluation project. *Alcohol Health and Research World, 10,* 20–23.

Wagenaar, A. C. (1982). Aggregate beer and wine consumption: Effects of changes in the minimum legal drinking age and a mandatory beverage container deposit law in Michigan. *Journal of Studies on Alcohol, 43,* 469–488.

Wagenaar, A. C. (1983). *Alcohol, young drivers, and traffic accidents: Effects of minimum-age laws.* Lexington, MA: D. C. Heath.

Wallack, L. (1981). Mass media campaigns: The odds against finding behavior change. *Health Education Quarterly, 8,* 209–260.

Wallack, L. (1984). Practical issues, ethical concerns and future directions in the prevention of alcohol-related problems. *Journal of Primary Prevention, 4,* 199–224.

Wallack, L., Breed, W., & Cruz, J. (1987). Alcohol on prime-time television. *Journal of Studies of Alcohol, 48,* 33–38.

Warburton, C. (1932). *The economic results of Prohibition,* Studies in History, Economics and Public Law, No. 379. New York: Columbia University Press.

Waterson, E. J., & Murray-Lyon, I. M. (1990). Preventing alcohol-related birth damage: A review. *Social Science and Medicine, 30,* 349–364.

Weisner, C. (1987). The social ecology of alcohol treatment in the U.S. In M. Galanter (Ed.), *Recent developments in alcoholism* (pp. 203–243). New York: Plenum Press.

Weisner, C. M. (1990). Coercion in alcohol treatment. In Institute of Medicine (Ed.), *Broadening the base of treatment for alcohol problems* (pp. 579–609). Washington, DC: National Academy Press.

Wilson, R. J., & Jonah, B. A. (1985). Identifying impaired drivers among the general driving population. *Journal of Studies on Alcohol, 46,* 531–537.

Wittman, F. D. (1982). Current status of research demonstration programs in the primary prevention of alcohol problems. In National Institute on Alcohol Abuse and Alcoholism (Ed.), *Prevention, intervention and treatment: Concerns and models* (Alcohol and Health Monograph No. 3, DHHS Publication No. ADM82-1192, pp. 3–57). Washington, DC: U.S. Government Printing Office.

—NAME INDEX—

TO THE OWNER OF THIS BOOK:

I hope that you have found *Under the Influence: Alcohol and Human Behavior* useful. So that this book can be improved in a future edition, would you take the time to complete this sheet and return it? Thank you.

School and address: _____

Department: _____

Instructor's name: _____

1. What I like most about this book is: _____

_____

2. What I like least about this book is: _____

_____

3. My general reaction to this book is: _____

_____

4. The name of the course in which I used this book is: _____

_____

5. Were all of the chapters of the book assigned for you to read? _____

   If not, which ones weren't? _____

_____

6. In the space below, or on a separate sheet of paper, please write specific suggestions for improving this book and anything else you'd care to share about your experience in using the book.

_____

_____

_____

_____

_____

_____

Optional:

Your name: _____ Date: _____

May Brooks/Cole quote you either in promotion for *Under the Influence: Alcohol and Human Behavior* or in future publishing ventures?

Yes: _____ No: _____

Sincerely,

John Jung